D1823163

New Directions in Latino American Cultures

A series edited by Licia Fiol-Matta and José Quiroga

New Concepts in Latino American Cultures

A series edited by Licia Fiol-Matta and José Quiroga

Sports and Nationalism in Latin/o America

Edited by

*Héctor Fernández L'Hoeste, Robert McKee Irwin,
and Juan Poblete*

SPORTS AND NATIONALISM IN LATIN/O AMERICA

Copyright © Héctor Fernández L'Hoeste, Robert McKee Irwin, and Juan Poblete, 2015.

All rights reserved.

First published in 2015 by
PALGRAVE MACMILLAN®
in the United States—a division of St. Martin's Press LLC,
175 Fifth Avenue, New York, NY 10010.

Where this book is distributed in the UK, Europe and the rest of the world, this is by Palgrave Macmillan, a division of Macmillan Publishers Limited, registered in England, company number 785998, of Houndmills, Basingstoke, Hampshire RG21 6XS.

Palgrave Macmillan is the global academic imprint of the above companies and has companies and representatives throughout the world.

Palgrave® and Macmillan® are registered trademarks in the United States, the United Kingdom, Europe and other countries.

ISBN: 978–1–137–48718–6

Library of Congress Cataloging-in-Publication Data

Sports and nationalism in Latin/o America / edited by Héctor Fernández L'Hoeste, Robert McKee Irwin, Juan Poblete.
pages cm.—(New directions in Latino American culture)
Includes bibliographical references and index.
ISBN 978–1–137–48718–6 (hardback)
1. Sports—Latin America—History. 2. Nationalism and sports—Latin America—History. 3. Sports—Social aspects—Latin America.
I. Fernández l'Hoeste, Héctor D., 1962– II. Irwin, Robert McKee, 1962– III. Poblete, Juan.

GV586.S57 2015
796.098—dc23   2014043779

A catalogue record of the book is available from the British Library.

Design by Newgen Knowledge Works (P) Ltd., Chennai, India.

First edition: May 2015

10 9 8 7 6 5 4 3 2 1

This book is dedicated to:

the loving memory of Héctor's father, Héctor Fernández Angulo, who shared his love for the Yankees

Robert's late parents, Kathryn and Robert Irwin

and Juan's father, Juan Poblete Merino, who never practiced sports, but embodies the best of their spirit

Contents

Part III   Sports and Alterity

Part IV   Sports as Transnational Mediation

TABLES

Acknowledgments

This project got off the ground thanks to funding from the College of Arts and Sciences and Center for Latin American and Latino/a Studies at Georgia State University. We are also deeply grateful for the support of Robyn Curtis, Farideh Koohi-Kamali, Mark Rinaldi, and Sara Doskow at Palgrave Macmillan, and most especially of Licia Fiol-Matta and José Quiroga for their enthusiastic encouragement.

Cassandra White, Wendy Gosselin, Luis Lorenzo Esparza Serra, and Katherine Clarkson made an invaluable contribution in carrying out conscientiously prepared translations of articles by Latin American scholars originally written in Spanish or Portuguese. Juan Miranda offered important assistance in helping edit translations.

Finally, the editors wish to thank the authors for their patience and cooperation in working with us throughout the long process of drafting, revising, and editing their scholarship. We'd also most especially like to thank each other for the years of collaboration and friendship that made this lengthy process a pleasure.

Introduction

Héctor Fernández L'Hoeste, Robert McKee Irwin,
and Juan Poblete

Sports and nationalism are two forms of imagining and actively constructing the connections that justify and explain our belonging to a community. In fact, sports could be said to be one of the key modern terrains for the habitualization of nationalism, for they are practiced, lived experience as opposed to nationalism's ideologically explicit inculcations in more formal settings such as the school system. Indeed, there are few aspects of everyday life that more passionately invoke patriotic sentiments than international sports competitions such as the World Cup or the Olympic Games.

The formation of a national habitus—that is, of a physically entrenched and fully absorbed, and thus naturalized, set of dispositions and performative orientations—is, for instance, regularly practiced and developed when, at the start of any major sports event in the United States or any international competition, the national anthem is respectfully sung (Billings et al.). But, as this example implies, sports are also a space for international and intranational contestation and even exclusion, as seen here in essays by Nadel, Rutter-Jensen, and Moreno on challenges to national models through the practice of sports by women and the "disabled."

As both community—to which we feel we belong naturally and voluntarily as we enjoy sports, whether as players or fans—and social spaces—within which we can experience conflict with and our distinctiveness from others—sports are often seen and lived, contradictorily, as both the opposite of the political and one of its most powerful manifestations in everyday life. Thus, beyond whatever defines our personal experience of them, sports have been more often than not a key arena for official forms of nationalism aimed at integrating a given society in the face of internal differences or for schemes aimed at taking advantage of sports' deep popularity to obtain political gains and legitimation (as explored here by multiple contributors, including Irwin and Fernández L'Hoeste).

More recently, sports have also turned out to be an arena for an expansion of the concept and feeling of the nation, as a veritable diaspora of global south players moves and succeeds abroad to the enjoyment of their national audiences back home via global media networks. This is different from the more conventional occasion for a feeling of nationalism when the national team in a given sport plays in another country and more of a manifestation of the migratory processes that have come, paradoxically, to redefine the nation and even nationalism under globalization. Latin American dailies, for example, often feature, in their web-based or app version, news that systematically covers the performance of expatriate athletes or sports personalities (such as club managers). Every little comment or reference made by a foreign media source on how well or badly a certain soccer player (Falcao, Messi, Neymar, Sánchez, Suárez, etc.) played in a European game is carefully scrutinized as is any reference to the corresponding career of team managers working abroad (Bielsa, Fossati, Pellegrini, Pinto, Sampaoli, etc.). Nationalist pride or anger in the global context is thus experienced vicariously through the performance or criticism of these transnational agents. A different but connected issue is that of massive international migrations of populations who, as either practitioners or spectators, create the basis for alternative versions of the nation, whether the host or the sending nation (as explored here by Rodríguez and Poblete).

In addition to this transnational dimension, sports are often closely associated with particular styles of the nation or even broader stereotypes constructed around notions of civilization. Thus it is still common to hear of: a European style of soccer playing (based on strategic and collective planning and thorough physical conditioning) often contrasted to its Latin American or African counterparts (based on exceptional individual skills); a Chinese type of gymnastics grounded in sheer mechanical repetition; or an African American style of basketball (see Colás in this volume). Certain sports are indelibly and popularly associated with specific nations: US American football and basketball, Chinese table tennis, Japanese sumo, Korean taekwondo, and so on. Others have a broader association with "civilizing" or other imperialistic influences, as seen in the introduction of British soccer and US baseball to Latin America, explored later in this chapter.

Sports are also, finally, not just an arena for professional teams and performance spectacles, but also the preferred recreational practice of many nonprofessional athletes and a huge market of goods and services. In addition to consuming the media coverage of their sport and favorite teams or players, millions of citizens practice, at different levels of competiveness, a sport. Their practices create a demand for, on the one hand, multiple products and services in highly competitive national markets and, on the other, state resources and policies fostering, making possible, and regulating such practices (as shown here by Casaqui, Toledo and Bega, and Hough-Snee).

The remainder of this introduction is divided into four sections: the first explores the intersection of nationalisms and British and US imperialism within the history of sports in the Western hemisphere; the second surveys the fields of Latin America-related sports studies; the third further develops the connection between sports and nationalisms; and the fourth summarizes the chapters featured in this volume.

BRITISH AND US IMPERIALISM AND LATIN AMERICAN SPORTS HISTORY

In *Under Fire* (1983), a film by Canadian director Roger Spottiswoode, Nick Nolte is baffled when he meets a Nicaraguan baseball player who, amid the context of the Sandinista Revolution, given his ability to pitch and throw well, has become a menace for Somoza's National Guard: with astonishing accuracy, he's able to throw explosives against the enemy. It is ironic that it is by way of a US sports practice that the character manages to stick it to the armed forces of the man whose progenitor Franklin Delano Roosevelt so proudly designated "our SOB." In *Golpe de estadio* (1998), the film by Colombian director Sergio Cabrera, guerrillas and police in the town of New Texas establish a truce to watch a soccer game against Argentina, which ends with an historic 5–0 score in favor of Colombia. In the film, soccer not only stands as the cultural practice before which all political differences are set aside—for a moment, guerrillas and police sit amicably side by side—it also contributes to the creation of an other (Argentina, a Latin American country theoretically bereft of ethnic mixture) for Colombia (a Latin American country allegedly brimming with ethnic mixture). Thus, just as in the case of the baseball player in Spottiswoode's film, a nationally embraced sport signifies a key practice in the definition of national identity. Within this scheme, it is crucial to consider both the origin of and the geopolitical context to and from which cultural practices, such as sports, are imported.

The geocultural influence of empire is keenly evident in the history of sports in Latin America. The two sports previously mentioned, association football (soccer) and baseball, illustrate how the diffusion of sports serves as evidence of soft power (Nye). Through the dissemination of a sport, a polity is able to reaffirm its political tenets and cultural prestige and circulate its interpretation of mores and fairness in following the rules of a game. Emerging from the two great Western powers of the nineteenth and twentieth century, respectively, the histories of the British sport of soccer and the United States' game of baseball in the

Americas clarify how sports can operate as means of transculturation once they've been embraced and appropriated by young nations in other latitudes. Together, association football and baseball reveal key elements in the configuration of new constructs of nation and their appeal hints at particular characteristics of national identity.

In the case of soccer, the sport emerged from the academic environment of the British Empire. In fact, the first set of rules for the game was known as the Cambridge Rules (1848), emanating from the Cantabrigian college scene. By 1867, less than twenty years later, the first recorded association football match in South America was played by British railway workers at the Buenos Aires Cricket Club Ground (AFA; Archetti, *Masculinities*). The fact that Argentina was a young nation under heavy British influence undoubtedly played a role in the early arrival of the sport. Within the same year, the Buenos Aires Football Club was created. In 1891, nearly a quarter century later, the first league of the Americas was born: the Association of Argentine Football, which, though lasting only a year, became the oldest league outside the United Kingdom. Its successor, the Argentine Football Association, founded two years later, remains active to this day. In Chile, football arrived with British immigrants to various seaports, including Valparaíso, during the 1880s. The birth of Chilean football serves as example of the rivalry between railroad workers and sailors as primary sponsors of the sport in this part of the Americas. They point clearly toward the way in which British cultural capital came by the hand of economic intervention. By 1895, the Football Association of Chile, the second oldest one in the Americas, was born (ANFP; Marín).

As in Argentina, railway workers in São Paulo contributed to the dissemination of the sport in Brazil. In 1888, the first association football club, the São Paulo Athletic Club, was founded (Clube SP; Witter). Locals who had been educated in the United Kingdom were among its players, contributing largely to the rapid popularization of the sport through recurrent contests with British teams (e.g., Corinthians F.C.). English immigrants also introduced soccer in Uruguay where the Albion Football Club was founded in 1891 (Albion F.C.; Luzuriaga). By the turn of the century, the sport had established itself as a South American staple, principally around the Southern Cone. The Uruguayan Football Association and the Brazilian Football Confederation were born in 1900 and 1914, respectively (AUF; Luzuriaga).

In Colombia, British railroad engineers introduced football in 1903. By 1908, scions of the local elite, including recent arrivals from the United Kingdom, promoted the sport actively, eventually forming the first football team in Colombia: the Barranquilla Fútbol Club. Also, British sailors involved in the banana trade contributed to the popularization of the sport along Colombia's Caribbean coast. Nonetheless, in comparison with the Southern Cone, the birth of the Federación Colombiana de Fútbol in 1924 was rather delayed (FCF; Ramírez). In Venezuela, though football isn't as popular as in Colombia, the game dates as far back as 1876, with documented records of exhibitions by British workers from the mining and rubber industry. The Federación Venezolana de Fútbol, however, was established only in 1926 (Federación Venezolana de Fútbol; Laya). The arrival of associated football in Costa Rica (see Villena here) wasn't much different: chiefly, by way of British expats and scions of the local upper class educated in the United Kingdom playing as early as 1876. Just like in Venezuela's case, however, it took decades, till 1921, for the Federación Costarricense de Fútbol to be born (FEDEFUTBOLCR; Urbina Gaitán). In Mexico, British subjects introduced association football in the late nineteenth century. The first Mexican football club was founded in 1898, but its soccer practice only started in 1901. The Federación Mexicana de Fútbol was only established decades later, in 1927 (FEMEXFUT; Ramírez).

Overall, what appears clear is that association football arrived in the Americas via various means of cultural and economic penetration—whether through the railways, the mining industry, the exploitation of rubber, the banana trade, or the academy—of the British Empire. Given the sport's background—its roots in the British collegiate environment—as a game of "gentlemen," the rules and organization of its practice must have served to introduce and popularize what the Brits contemplated as a sense of "fair play" in sports, endorsing a way to entertain youth in a healthy setting and thus condoning hegemonic privilege in the definition of a "civilized" sports practice. The harshness of the tropics or the year-round benevolent weather in some corners of the Americas must have influenced the game's potential, style, and popularity along the way. In addition, the fact that the game could be enjoyed with a minimal set of equipment served as incentive across classes. Even the field's rectangular shape, easy to improvise in any setting, added to its appeal. While the salaried class (railroad engineers, businessmen, in many cases) contributed to its popularization, a working-class component (sailors, miners, etc.) also influenced the game. Thus, soccer served to transgress as well as to fortify class barriers, therefore justifying its popularity in thoroughly class-oriented societies across the Americas.

In contrast, baseball arrived and gained popularity mostly around the Caribbean, a by-product of the US presence in the region. To this day, baseball remains the most popular game in Cuba, the Dominican Republic, Puerto Rico, Nicaragua, Panama, and Venezuela, though soccer is making inroads in many of these nations. In the case of some, like Colombia or Mexico, baseball remains common in parts of the country, despite soccer's overall superior popularity. However, unlike soccer, the fact that baseball demands more equipment (a bat and a ball, at the very least; gloves, helmets, and gear, at best) and a field with a more irregular shape, has hindered its wider dissemination. Also, more so than soccer, baseball tends to emphasize attention to sheer statistical data.

In Cuba, the country that has served as champion for the diffusion of baseball in the Americas, the sport arrived by way of Cuban students from the United States and US sailors in the port of Havana in the 1860s (Seymour; Pérez). The Havana Baseball Club was formed in 1868. By late 1878, three teams—Almendares, Havana, and Matanzas—made up the Cuban Baseball League. In turn, Cuban sugar planters contributed to the arrival of baseball in the Dominican Republic in the 1870s (Oleksak and Oleksak). The first professional contest was played in 1890 between teams Ozama and Nuevo Club. By the early twentieth century, a few professional teams had been established. However, in both cases, US military campaigns—the Spanish American War in Cuba's case, the US occupation from 1916 to 1924 in the Dominican Republic's—played a key role in the grounding of the sport at the local level (LIDOM; Ruck). In Puerto Rico, the case was similar: baseball arrived by the hand of Cuban refugees and Puerto Ricans who had studied in the United States (Oleksak and Oleksak). Baseball was embraced earnestly as a national pastime, but it was only in 1938–1939 that the first Liga de Béisbol Profesional was formed, with the participation of six teams (Liga PR; Van Hyning).

In the case of Venezuela, baseball arrived in 1894, when some scions of the upper class returned from the United States with bats, gloves, and balls (Oleksak and Oleksak). The construction of the railroad, which brought along a team of players, established the sport even further. In July 1895, the first Venezuelan team, Caracas, was created. By 1927, when many more teams had been founded, the Federación Venezolana de Béisbol was born. In 1931, Gonzalo Gómez, the son of dictator Vicente Gómez, even imported Cuban players, adding to the sport's popularity and solidifying official support. This same decade witnessed the appearance of Vidal López, an Afro-Venezuelan who eventually played in Mexico and Puerto Rico and is considered Venezuela's best player ever. In 1946, thanks to the great effervescence generated by Venezuela's triumph over Cuba in the World Amateur Championship of 1941, the Liga Venezolana de Béisbol Profesional was formed (LVBP; González).

Given Mexico's constant contact with the United States, it's hard to point out the actual moment of baseball's arrival, but it is safe to say it occurred between 1870 and 1890 (FEMEBE; Hernández and Hernández). Without a doubt, contact with Cubans and US armed forces played a role in the dissemination of baseball. On July 4, 1889, Coronel Joseph Robertson allowed railroad workers to celebrate independence by playing baseball. By 1925, Mexican baseball leagues were already in place, with Mexico City and Monterrey as main locations.

There are various versions on the origin of Panamanian baseball (Oleksak and Oleksak), which arrived in the 1880s, when the region was still a part of Colombia. In some cases, it is assigned to US railroad workers, laboring on the Trans-isthmus Railroad (construction began in 1850); in others, to US sailors crossing the isthmus. However, it was only in 1945 that the Liga de Béisbol Profesional de Panamá was born (FeDeBeis; Pérez Medina). In Nicaragua, Americans introduced baseball in 1888. The US consul in Nicaragua, Carter Donaldson, founded the first continuous team in 1904. Even US marines stationed in the country contributed to the sport's popularization. On the Pacific side of Nicaragua, on the other hand, baseball arrived by way of scions of the upper class, returning from their studies in the United States. As in previous cases, the creation of the Liga Nicaragüense de Béisbol Profesional occurred at a much later date: 1956 (LBPN; Arellano).

Aside from these nations, baseball is played in a number of other countries in the Americas including: Guatemala, Colombia, Ecuador, Chile, Argentina, and Brazil. In these nations, however, baseball doesn't carry the high profile of other, more popular sports. At worst, it is viewed as a tangential practice, fruit of some dated encounter with another culture or the sheer willingness of locals to embrace an amusing curiosity; at best, it's identified with the cultural idiosyncrasy of a peripheral region. What remains clear is that baseball is part of the US footprint on the Americas, a remnant of the Monroe doctrine, indicating clearly where the country has treaded and influenced disproportionately the development of events in regional history. It is no coincidence that many Latinos whose backgrounds trace back to these countries have played in the Major Leagues.

Unlike association football, which requires a steady physical demand and the ability to anticipate immediate action, baseball runs on attentiveness, patience, and statistical prowess. In each game, there is the possibility to recognize traits valued highly by the cultures of nations at the height of their power. British imperial domination was based on discipline and collective responsibility (the duty to serve the British Empire in the administration of colonies). In no other way is it possible to imagine that, at its height (1922), a population of 45 million was responsible for the administration of almost a quarter of the Earth's total land area. US hegemony, on the other hand, was based on economic domination through soft power, mostly backing away from direct involvement in nation building (until recently). Thus, baseball came across more as a cultural interest, appealing to locals willing to emulate Americana, rather than as a way to advocate empire structurally. While football denotes the British capability for organization, establishing clear rules for a game founded on intercollegiate participation, baseball emerged from rounders and other similar games, gradually evolving in a US setting. Its distinctive nature is more linked with a subset of Americana (traditional cultural references such as hot dogs and apple pie) than football is related with contemporary British culture. A baseball cap is no-nonsense headgear alluding to a specific location (the Big Leagues, a US context), whereas a football jersey is a contemporary fashion statement shared by cultures throughout the world. Thus, as a symbol of political hegemony, baseball is more culturally determined than soccer, which has emerged as the global game, sanctioning the British way of being universal. Rather than cosmopolitanism, the United States argued for exceptionality, deferring management of its economic "colonies" to locals (as long as, financially, US interests were protected). Turning outward, as an island, the British Empire sought to reproduce its order across the globe, imposing UK standards. The dynamics run in opposite directions. In this sense, each sport exemplifies how US and British identity have influenced the evolution of nationality in the Americas. In imagining the nation through baseball or soccer, each community prioritizes different imperatives.

LATIN AMERICAN SPORTS STUDIES

The mythical birth of the field of sports studies has been identified with the publication of *Soziologie des Sports* by Heinz Risse, a student of Theodor Adorno, in 1921. In 1969 Bero Rigauer, who has been referenced as "the first scholar to develop a consistently Marxist approach to sport" (Dunning 106) published *Sport und Arbeit* (Sport and work). The book, a major work of "'critical theory' dealing with sport" (Coakley and Dunning xxii), introduced a "radical critique of sport" in an era in which "sports activism" took on meaning in alignment with both revolutionary social movements (as seen in John Carlos and Tommie Smith's controversial black power salute at the Mexico City Olympics) and new popularly oriented studies such as Harry Edwards's *The Revolt of the Black Athlete* (1969) and Jack Scott's *The Athletic Revolution* (1971) (Carrington and McDonald 2).

At the same time, the field of sociology had begun to take seriously the study of sport, giving rise to what soon became known as the sociology of sport. Indeed the *International Review for the Sociology of Sport* was founded several years prior to the publication of the works mentioned earlier, although the foundational publications for the field, including Loy and Kenyon's edited volume *Sport, Culture and Society* (1969) and Harry Edwards's *The Sociology of Sport* (1973), would not follow until a few years later. While scholarly activity grew rapidly among sociologists, spreading to fields such as anthropology, history, geography, and economics, it remains a relatively small (if lively) subfield, even within sociology (Coakley and Dunning xxiv–xxv).

The growth of the field coincided with the rapid mediatization of sports in countries such as the United States. As both professional sports and nationalist oriented amateur sports (notably the Olympic Games) became increasingly massive and politically charged media spectacles, especially in the 1960s, 1970s, and 1980s, critical studies of sports increasingly took seriously the ideologically oriented critiques of the sports activists mentioned earlier. As the field of cultural studies, also founded in the 1960s upon a reoriented Marxism (via Gramsci) that took seriously the role of culture in both political formations and everyday life, began itself by the 1980s to assume international prominence, it too turned its critical eye to sports (Rowe 5; Carrington and McDonald 3). The field's foundational and emblematic program, the Center for Contemporary Cultural Studies at the University of Birmingham, itself sponsored several projects on such themes as football hooliganism, sports and media, and sports and gender (Hargreaves and McDonald 51), leading to the publication of key volumes such as Jennifer Hargreaves's edited collection *Sport, Culture and Ideology* (1982), Richard Gruneau's *Class, Sports, and Social Development* (1983), and Garry Whannel's *Blowing the Whistle: The Politics of Sport* (1983). Cultural studies, an emerging field that had begun to gain international attention for its elaborate critiques of both popular and mass culture, both from the perspectives of production (e.g., culture industries) and consumption (e.g., fan subcultures), gave special impetus to the rapid rise in the late 1980s and 1990s of sports media studies (Rowe 8), represented by key works including Jay Goldlust's *Playing for Keeps: Sports, the Media and Society* and Lawrence Wenner's edited volume *Media, Sports, and Society* (1989).

In the context of Latin America, while a few interesting but isolated early studies exist, including, notably, Mario Rodrigues Filho's *O negro no futebol brasileiro*, originally published in 1947, and Argentine Julio Mafud's *Sociología del fútbol* (1967), the field of critical sports studies began to emerge in the 1980s, in two main contexts: (1) that of soccer studies, focused principally on Latin America's two greatest historical soccer powers, Brazil and Argentina; and, beginning a few years later, (2) a competing line of baseball studies, carried out mainly from the United States and focusing on countries of the Caribbean, especially the Dominican Republic and Cuba. Key foundational texts include Roberto da Matta et al.'s collection of essays *Universo do futebol: esporte e sociedade brasileira* (1982), Argentine Juan José Sebreli's *Fútbol y masas* (1981), US-based Janet Lever's *Soccer Madness: Brazil's Passion for the World's Most Popular Sport* (1983), and Gare Joyce's *The Only Ticket Off the Island* (1990) along with Alan Klein's *Sugarball: The American Game, the Dominican Dream* (1991).

A key figure on promoting this field of inquiry in the United States has been historian Joseph Arbena, whose works include the early edited volume *Sport and Society in Latin America* of 1988 and his 2002 collection, edited in collaboration with David LaFrance, *Sport in Latin America and the Caribbean*. This latter volume expands significantly on the first by covering a wider range of sports (including soccer and baseball, of course, as well as basketball, volleyball, cricket, and equestrian sports) in multiple national contexts (Mexico, Peru, Brazil, Argentina, Costa Rica, Nicaragua, Cuba, Dominican Republic), indicating the significant growth in the field in the United States in the fields of history, sociology, anthropology, and literature, among others. British scholars have also made important contributions, among the most significant: Tony Mason's critical history *Passion of the People?: Football in Latin America* (1995) and the anthology *Football in the Americas: Fútbol, Futebol, Soccer* (2007), edited by Rory Miller and Liz Crolley.

By the 1990s, in Latin America, critical studies of soccer were taking on an even greater significance. A few popular texts, including José Ramón Fernández's *El fútbol mexicano: ¿un juego sucio?* (1994), Uruguayan Eduardo Galeano's *El fútbol a sol y sombra*, and Fernando Araújo Vélez's *Pena máxima: juicio al fútbol colombiano* (both 1995), created momentum that set the stage for the establishment of an emergent academic movement by the early 2000s. Eduardo Archetti, author of the mostly overlooked *Fútbol y ethos* (1984), published his seminal study *Masculinities: Football, Polo and the Tango in Argentina* in 1999, while another Argentine, Pablo Alabarces, coauthor with María Graciela Rodríguez of an earlier provocation, *Cuestión de pelotas* (1996), formed the transnational working group "Deporte y Sociedad" through the Consejo Latinoamericano de Ciencias Sociales (CLACSO), which was active from 1999 through 2003. The various CLACSO-sponsored edited volumes produced by this collective, including *Peligro de gol: estudios sobre deporte y sociedad en América Latina* (2000) and *Futbologías: fútbol, identidad y violencia en América Latina* (2003), as well as Costa Rican-based Bolivian Sergio Villena Fiengo's *Golbalización: siete ensayos heréticos sobre fútbol, identidad y cultura* (2006) and Alabarces's own influential *Fútbol y patria: el fútbol y las narrativas de la nación en Argentina* (2002), firmly established critical studies of soccer as an important rubric for critical debate throughout Latin America. Alabarces and Archetti brought the theme to the forefront of Latin American critical dialogue through critical approaches deeply influenced by the emerging field of cultural studies. Some other key texts for the field include Ruben Oliven and Arlei Damo's *Fútbol y cultura*, published in Colombia (2001); Edison Gastaldo and Simino Lahud Guedes's Brazilian edited volume *Nações de campo: copa do mundo e identidade nacional* (2006); Mexican Arturo Santamaría Gómez's *Fútbol, emigrantes y neonacionalismo* (2010) and *Offside/Fuera de lugar: fútbol y migraciones en el mundo contemporáneo* (2012), a collection of essays coordinated by Mexicans Guillermo Alonso Meneses and Luis Escala Rabadán.

While Latin America has seen a boom in cultural studies of soccer, much of the critical inquiry regarding baseball in Latin America has been realized from the United States, where the great popularity of the sport and the prominence of Latin American recruits in professional leagues have led to an interest among Anglophone social scientists—and sports fans. Examples include Alan Klein's *Baseball on the Border: A Tale of Two Laredos* (1999), Roberto González Echevarría's *The Pride of Havana: A History of Cuban Baseball* (2001), Thomas Zeiler's *Ambassadors in Pinstripes: The Spalding World Baseball Tour and the Birth of American Empire* (2006), and Robert Elias's *The Empire Strokes Out: How Baseball Sold US Foreign Policy and Promoted the American Way Abroad* (2010). As is clear from their titles, some of these books are clearly transnationally oriented studies formulated in terms that reflect rubrics of US history and culture, rather than in Latin America's own terms. With González Echevarría as a significant exception, the vast majority of these scholars are not specialists in Latin American history, society, or culture, nor do they publish in the Spanish language or in Latin American venues.

In general, these trends are noteworthy for two reasons: (1) their limited focus: aside from studies on soccer and baseball, there is very little critical work on sports in Latin America, even with regard to highly popular sports such as boxing, or on those in which Latin Americans have excelled in international arenas (track and field, tennis, diving, field hockey, basketball, etc.); and (2) the very limited role of US-based scholars, excepting their English language publications on baseball.

While the former issue will likely work itself out gradually as the work of Latin America-based scholars of the cultural studies of sports, sports media studies, or the sociology of sports continues to advance, the latter trend is more troubling as the majority of US-based sports studies scholars, including those of transnational baseball studies, are not Latin Americanists, and US Latin Americanist scholars have been slow to fill the void. The issue perhaps lies in the differences in how cultural studies get configured in each context. For example, in many Latin American countries, cultural studies has affiliated more closely with social science than with humanities fields (Trigo 30). While this tendency has not been uniform across national boundaries, nor absolute, it contrasts significantly with the United States, where cultural studies, particularly in the context of research on Latin America, has taken root much more deeply in the humanities, most especially in Spanish departments.

Critical studies of sports, although often interdisciplinary in nature, have their deepest historic links with the fields of sociology and history.

Scholars with degrees in literary criticism, who with the arrival of cultural studies have frequently crossed over into film or media studies, have been hesitant to move from studying the texts of narrative fiction or poetry to the realm of sports studies. For this reason, the critical studies of sports that currently flourish in Latin America, whether in Buenos Aires, Bogotá, Rio de Janeiro, Mexico City, San José, Santiago, Lima, San Juan, or Montevideo, guided by a social science oriented cultural studies, have not seen the same boom in the United States where cultural studies has remained more firmly seated in the humanities. Indeed, one of the goals of this volume is to bring cultural studies of sports into the forefront of contemporary US-based research on Latin American culture, while ensuring that the latter is informed by critical debates on sports (mostly soccer) in Latin America.

Its three editors all have backgrounds in literary criticism and primary appointments in US departments of languages or literature, but have been protagonists in pushing the limits of the field of Spanish by bringing the theoretical, methodological, and pedagogical tools of cultural studies into humanities-oriented research on such areas of cultural production as film, popular music, and comics, and including a transnational perspective that includes both Latin American proper and the Latino United States (e.g., Pacini Hernández, Fernández L'Hoeste, and Zolov; Fernández L'Hoeste and Poblete; Poblete; Irwin and Szurmuk; Irwin and Castro Ricalde). We believe that the questions raised by this volume's focus on sports and nationalism are best addressed through cultural studies oriented paradigms of interrogation and that humanists as well as social scientists have something to add to the discussion. We furthermore insist that as the United States has one of the largest Spanish speaking populations in the world, it is imperative that the US academy participate actively in these Latin America-based studies, and not limit inquiry to transnational (but always ultimately US-oriented) studies on a single sport (baseball).

Sports and Nationalisms

More than 30 years ago, in his classic book *Imagined Communities*, Benedict Anderson posited the crucial role the reading of newspapers and novels, as forms of imagining the social collective, had in the emergence of modern nationalisms. Since then, both the concept of the social imaginary and the attribution to written literature and its reading of a key function in the task of constructing—in the context of everyday life and within the subjectivities of the citizens—that form of belonging and mooring we call nationality, have had an important critical trajectory and a clear impact on the study of culture in Latin America and elsewhere.

Without fully revisiting Benedict Anderson's well-known argument, it is useful to highlight for our purposes here how, in Anderson's thesis, print-capitalism and its two main nineteenth-century forms, the novel and the newspaper, created an important part of the cultural basis on which a political entity such as the nation-state could be both defined and practiced by the active imagining of common literate people. The claim about these two forms of print culture in Anderson is that they made possible what could be expressed as the emergence of the nation as a categorical form for the imagination of the social (as both a link and a space) and for its practice in everyday life. This meant an expansion of the space of politics now based on the circulation of ideas and narratives, images and behaviors that allowed the active imagination of a common frame of reference in a cultural imaginary whose forms of legitimation and meaning were self-generating. This new form of modern temporality, connectivity, and meaningfulness afforded the nation by reading practices was, however, paradoxical. Existing as individual agents who in a daily ceremony of cultural communion imagine themselves as belonging to and pertinent in a community, national citizens remained mostly anonymous and unknown to each other. Citizen-readers actively imagined the nation in absentia or, mostly, as a virtual presence.

But there were surely other ceremonies of co-presence in which this collective imagination of the national took place. Explaining the history of nationalism, Ernst Gellner has placed emphasis on those practices promoted by state agents (school system, efficient bureaucracy, and communications systems) and the cultural literacy needs of an expanding industrial capitalism. They respond as daily practices to a much more intentional design reflected in cultural and social policies. Likewise, as Stuart Hall has argued, mass communications media, much more than literature, have assumed an ever greater role in "providing the images, representations and ideas around which the social totality [...] can be coherently grasped as a 'whole'" (340). In Latin America, in particular, where substantial sectors of the population until relatively recently received little schooling and read little, if at all, the rise of the culture industries were key in consolidating national cultures that until several decades into the twentieth century had effectively excluded large swaths of its citizens (Monsiváis). The practice of sports within a country and the consumption by many national citizens of these sports as a spectacle are two modern forms of active imagination of the nation both in physical co-presence and as mass-mediated spectacles. They combine the active imagination in the practice of daily-life emphasis of Anderson's theory of nationalism within print-capitalism with Gellner's stress on the modern nation-state/industrial capitalism nexus and the need for a homogenized and shared national culture and language as basic conditions for production and consumption. They occur at the point at which structure and agency, the macro-social and the micro-social, meet.

As part of the social history of modernity, sports and the nation share other distinctive features: they are historically male-centered both as practice and spectacle; they are as much about the production of unity and identity as they are of distinction, separation, and exclusion. In other words, they are as often the glue holding communities together as they are the way in which those communities distinguish themselves from others or imagine themselves as unique, self-sustaining, and closed off to others. In this regard, sports and nationalism share traits of both the ethnic concept of community (distinctive and exclusive) and the civic concept of community (changing and inclusive). The dynamics, however, are not just of internal cohesion and external distinction. As Alan Bairner usefully reminds us, the topic of sporting nationalism should always include a consideration not just of the ways in which national sports and international competition allow an experience of the national as unity, but also of the forms of intraethnic contestation and subnational regional or local identification through which sports can challenge official nationalisms (18).

In fact, in one of the best-known theories of sports in modernity, Norbert Elias sees sports, as part of a civilizing process that involves the capacity of a community to organize itself at the micro- and macrosociological levels, on one hand, controlling "bodily functions, eating practices, sexual habits, and violence" (Giulianotti 149), and on the other, through political and economic disputes, by way of civilizing practices of self-restraint and mutually agreed upon rules. According to Elias, "both sports and parliamentary contests involve non-violent battles between competing groups according to rules or procedures" (Giulianotti 150). But in allowing modern nation-states to come into being, both sports and liberal democracy also involved the common global spread of Western material culture and political imperialism. Moreover, Elias's central point is that this civilizing process is a complex game of separation and amalgamation. In it, first, the upper classes of the British Empire distinguish themselves from its internal and external others by their exclusive civilized habitus (including the practice of sports) and then, second, they forcefully invite those others to become civilized by embracing those habits. As a civilizing and colonial tool of the British Empire, the practice of sports nationally and internationally became associated as much with a Christian control of the self and the body as with broader, collective "civilized behavior regarding rule-following, team-work, obeying one's captain and accepting the adjudication of an 'impartial' sovereign figure (the empire)" (Giulianotti 152). For Elias, then, the practice of sports is both a microcosm of politically civilized behavior and an emotional outlet or escape from those norms and even their intensifier within a controlled setting. It is also clear that those frequently masculine energies are as often contained within the game as spilled outside of the stadium.

The national history of sports in Latin America shares a number of the traits highlighted so far in our discussion of nationalism and sports. In this region, sports have been historically connected to the late-nineteenth and early-twentieth-century presence of British businessmen (Archetti, *Masculinities*) and the US military (Elias); they have also been as much about national integration as regional or intraurban segmentation. They have been centrally masculine affairs as practices and spectacles until relatively recently, producing shared ceremonies of communion and violent disputes and rancor. An interesting early example of the faith different kinds of intellectuals place on the power of soccer to unite national communities, help heal national divisions, and channel youth energies is provided by Mario Rodrigues Filho's *O Negro no futebol brasileiro* (1947, second expanded edition in 1964). According to Antonio J. Soares, Filho's book has crucially influenced all subsequent reflection on soccer in Brazil by proposing that there are three clear and distinctive moments in the history connecting blacks and the national sport in Brazil. First, blacks are altogether excluded from its practice. In a second moment, they engage in struggles for inclusion while actively resisting their exclusion. Finally, in the truly national moment, blacks and the country succeed as the former are fully accepted and celebrated in a game which, like the nation within which it's played, declares itself fully democratized (Soares 113). Filho's ideas are an extension of the efforts of Gilberto Freyre to promote his theory of *mulatismo* or racial and cultural hybridization of the three races (whites, blacks, and indigenous peoples) defining Brazilian society. As such, Brazilian soccer provided for Freyre a perfect example of the traits defining mulatismo: *malandragem* and *jogo de cintura*. Both refer to a certain popular *savoir faire* or creative style to negotiate one's place in social relations. In soccer they would manifest as a Brazilian style of playing defined, in counterdistinction to the English who invented the game, by its almost dance-like quality of improvisation and agility (traits that it shared, according to Freyre, with the other two defining Brazilian practices: carnival and capoeira). In fact, in the prologue to Filho's book Freyre would extend his thesis to include what can be called a general civilizing effect of soccer on the rest of Brazilian society and culture as it provided a channel for otherwise overabundant and dangerous male social energies. In Freyre and Filho, Brazilian soccer had found two intellectuals willing to make it one of the clearest examples of the overcoming of racial discrimination and the harmonizing of races supposedly defining modern Brazil (Mendes Capraro; Soares).

While the national (and nationalistic) history of sports in Latin America is already long, the academic field studying it in Latin America is fairly new and, as mentioned earlier, it is often almost exclusively focused on soccer (with Latin America-focused baseball studies limited mostly to the US academy). A brief review of some key texts in soccer studies will highlight some historical trends. Surveying the field, Pablo Alabarces ("Entre la banalidad"), focusing on soccer, proposes two actors and two discourses that have prevented its full development until recently. On the one hand, journalists who often reproduce a romantic common sense about the sport (its struggles, heroes, beauty) claim that intellectuals know nothing about *fútbol*, while on the other, traditional intellectuals have too often limited their interventions to denouncing the sport as the opium of the people, a distraction from real political and economic struggles. Roberto da Matta's 1982 collection, *Universo do futebol: esporte e sociedade brasileira*, changed this situation by using the category of ritual, its symbolic dimensions and their "problematic articulation with the political" (Alabarces, "Entre la banalidad" 75), to better understand the central role of sports, soccer in particular, in the production of national, and more generally, social narratives.

Ruben Oliven and Arlei Damo, in *Fútbol y cultura*, suggest that soccer and the nation as social discourses often enter into three types of relations: metaphoric (territory must be defended from the enemy, counterattacks must be mounted until the other is defeated), analogic (as when soccer fans of a given club identify themselves as a nation), and complementary (when, for instance, soccer functions as a diplomatic tool) (21). Thus when the Brazilian national team loses a crucial World Cup game, it is often argued that it was because improvisation and lack of concentration (i.e., underdevelopment) characterized the training process leading to the event. Whereas when the team did prepare itself properly and still lost, the failure is attributed to the betrayal of the true nature of Brazilian soccer, including its creativity, spontaneity, and improvisation (24). Nation and soccer, both based on deeply felt belonging and unquestioned, life-long loyalty (92–93), clearly reflect each other.

As a strategic game that has afforded venues of upward mobility for countless working-class popular heroes, soccer is also often connected not just to civilizing processes or, on the contrary, outright violence, but to magic and subversion of dominant culture. Eduardo Archetti has pointed out that in addition to being crucial sites for the production of national masculinity (identity), sports are also spaces for the manifestation of freedom and cultural creativity, for hybridity and liminal contact with otherness (i.e., a "threat to official ideologies") (*Masculinities* 18). If their history and the media and state deployments of sports directly link soccer to modernity, Oliven and Damo want to also rescue the magical residue of the game. The magic, unexpected moment of scoring and/ or celebrating a goal is made possible by the recuperation of the lower hemisphere of the body in both the game itself (the hands, the architects of civilization, are here forbidden) and in its jocular and carnivalesque celebrations (65–69).

Pablo Alabarces has provided what is undoubtedly one of the most sustained and sophisticated efforts at mapping the connection between sports and the nation in Latin America. In his *Fútbol y patria: el fútbol y las narrativas de la nación en la Argentina*, he posits soccer as one of the main "cultural machines" (this concept is Beatriz Sarlo's) for the production of national identities that are historically masculine and oscillate between tribal or fragmented and all-encompassingly national (19). In this scheme, soccer as a para-state apparatus both complements and closely follows the more formal efforts of the state to generate national narratives capable of producing hegemonic forms of identification. Among those state narratives are those of upward mobility and inclusion. The history of soccer in Argentina has been closely associated with its capacity to provide examples of both narratives or, when they enter into crisis at the turn of the twentieth century and exclusion and disintegration become the key words, to offer an easily accessible alternative primary identity. Thus, in collaboration with the media machine, soccer came to be a powerful alternative interpellation and a form of consolation citizenship for millions of Argentines at a time of crisis. If assimilating state narratives had provided the background and the lead for the mass-mediatic operators of national narratives associated with sports, including, in historical order of predominance: photographic, written, filmic, and televisual forms, when the unifying welfare state entered into systemic crisis, the cultural industry seemingly became "the only operator of identity" (Alabarces, *Fútbol* 205). Instead of actually integrating the nation as a society, the cultural industry conceives of it as a tribe of consumers and a segmented market. The nation here becomes an empty signifier used by the technical operations of a highly effective marketing discourse. Soccer itself is no longer the cultural machine, just one of its most successful genres and products (208).

But the new outsized role of the media and the emergence of supranational interpellations in the production of national identities are not just a result of social and economic crisis in a given country. They are also two of the defining aspects of life in times of globalization. In *Globalization and Sport*, Richard Giulianotti and Roland Robertson present the case of soccer to exemplify the defining dual properties of glocalization, which registers "the societal *co-presence* of sameness and difference, and the intensified *interpenetration* of the local and the global, the universal and the particular, and homogeneity and heterogeneity" (60; emphases in the original). Using supporter subcultures (fans), they highlight the existence of transnational affiliations manifesting two kinds of cosmopolitanism: banal (when the existence of others, equal-but-different, is simply recognized) or thick (when transnational fan communities establish networks of cooperation based on diasporic or media-enabled associations). In this context, the media operators of Alabarces's analysis have become transnationally oriented national journalists who follow, for instance, the global market of emigrant players, their stories of success, or their lack of adaptation to new environments. Thus the explosion of global media coverage of multiple national and international soccer leagues around the world produces and is sustained by a thin spreading cosmopolitanism of audiences that can sometimes thicken into more purposeful forms. Moreover, such transnational orientation coexists with similarly media-enhanced and heightened sports nationalism at the level of clubs or national teams participating in international contests.

AN OUTLINE OF THIS VOLUME

In addition to this introduction, the volume has four sections: the first focuses on sports and national imaginaries; the second deals with the links between sports and state policies; the third covers non-dominant or non-normative practices and subjects; and the final section is dedicated to the relationship between sports and alterity.

In the first section, specific sports act as mediators between the idea of nation fostered by the state and the idea of nation shared by the general population of a country. Subsequently, the object of these first four essays is to clarify the standing of sports as cultural practices that bring visibility and acceptance to some sectors of the nation ignored or neglected by the state. Crucial here, however, is to understand how soccer, as a sport that is essential to national identity, has been embraced to support consecrated official narratives and to validate particular social and political orders.

In the initial chapter of this volume, Pablo Alabarces chronicles his research on the role of association football in Argentina. From the beginning of his career as a scholar, Alabarces has been attentive to the relationship between the sport and nationalism, particularly early on in his career, when the state had ceased being the single unifying voice behind a nationalist discourse in Argentine reality. Seeking new approaches to the subject, he now contemplates gender as an additional complicating factor, further entangling the way in which his fellow nationals participate. The constants from the past—exceptional players and the state—remain, but they seem to have now acquired new airs of complexity, given the travails of the country, with an economic meltdown in the early 2000s. In the end, almost expressing disappointment, Alabarces concludes that under current global conditions, sport heroes no longer hold on dearly to a fixed relationship with a state or territory, answering instead to a transnational mercantile logic.

In this sense, Joshua Nadel's chapter on women's soccer at a continental level strikes a contrasting note. Nadel establishes a dual chronology—pre- and post-1991, the year of the first Women's World Cup—in his quest to understand how it was that women were written out of the dominant narrative of the sport, being effectively excluded from a prevailing construct of the nation. Nadel's main argument is that this operation took place because female soccer players were perceived as antinational and consequently represented a threat to the nation. His detailed analysis shows how sports can be appropriated in the pursuit of exclusionary interests.

Sergio Villena Fiengo adopts the outlook of the outsider to examine how nationalist narratives reacted to shortcomings in the established discourse, embracing soccer as an opportunity to redefine nationality. Villena Fiengo examines the arrival of soccer in Costa Rica, its first international victory and the ensuing profound nationalization of the sport, its first and most successful participation in the World Cup, and finally, the qualification of the national squad for a second time in a more recent version of the event. His contention is straightforward: each of these moments—which he describes as "liminal"—plays an important part in the transformation of the sport into a "patriotic game."

Next, Héctor Fernández L'Hoeste traces an evolution in the development of a cohesive national discourse based on sports in Colombia, a country fragmented by inner strife, social disparity, and regional differences. In Colombia, as in Brazil, race played a key role in the relationship between sports and nationalism. The chapter chronicles the evolution of a nationalist discourse pertinent to sports, shifting along the lines of regional allegiances to specific sports, correspondingly coded along racial constructs, only to arrive eventually at a negotiated balance: a practice that could include all ethnicities while preserving the hegemonic interest of the central government. Passing through boxing and cycling, sports that served initially as improvised champions of nationalism, Fernández L'Hoeste demonstrates how soccer's ultimate success as a vehicle for a nationalist discourse resulted from its greater capability to embody representation from all corners of Colombia's geography, effectively replicating demographic diversity, contributing to the greater visibility of many peripheral regions, and furthering identification with a weak state, incapable of mustering the strength necessary for a solid presence across national territory.

The second set of essays in this anthology discusses how the state and the private sector manage to incorporate sports into national narratives through the implementation of concrete measures and policies related to these very sports, hoping to attain legitimacy from the masses, avid followers of these cultural practices.

Vander Casaqui's chapter explains how, operating in sync with a renowned brand of beer, the media embraced the members of the Brazilian national soccer squad participating in the 2010 South African World Cup to advance a series of national allegories: mainly, portraying Brazil as a fighting nation, a country that, through much effort and hard work, was able to emerge finally as the top contender for the title of South American champion of the world economy (Brazil was ultimately eliminated in the quarterfinals). By way of a critique of the identity mechanisms of capitalism—advertising and marketing—Casaqui's chapter describes how the national team became the means for an image of the country designed for consumption.

Along the same lines, albeit with a different object in mind, Renata Toledo and Maria Silva Bega explore the conflict resulting from the symbolic connection between sport and nationalism and the principle of democratization of sports practices granted by Brazil's current constitutional order. Given a historic imperative for a cultural association with elite sports and the sense of political legitimacy that these very sports may provide the government, Toledo and Bega claim that the symbolic connection continues to hinder the effective implementation of more democratic policies in sports. That is to say, despite the use of mechanisms to broaden access to sports, the idea of sports as a national symbol, though of a nonstate nature, orients sports politics in such a way that prioritizes high-performance sports and the political legitimacy this form of sports generates for the government, which serves to marginalize the democratization of sports in the process of formulating and implementing public policies for them.

In his chapter on baseball and documentaries in Cuba, Juan Carlos Rodríguez discusses the evolution in the role of documentary films in representing baseball's contribution to the understanding of the Cuban nation. While early documentaries toe the official line, embracing baseball as a sort of choreographic rendition of Cuba, with all the implications the many tropes commonly employed in the sport might suggest, more recent ones speak of a more extended, transnational nation, in which dialogue with exiles or other blemished figures becomes a must. Stories of baseball players from the US Major Leagues returning to Cuba and truncated careers resulting from stringent economic policies suggest the need for a reexamination of the Cuban construct of nation.

The third section of the book introduces three essays engaging in themes that are new to Latin American sports studies, moving far from the well-trodden terrain of soccer and baseball to look at sporting contexts embedded in questions of sex, race, and ability that raise a range of interesting issues and significantly enrich the field.

Chloe Rutter-Jensen brings disability studies theory to bear on issues of sports and nationalism, showing how the triumphs of Colombia's Paralympic teams inspire media coverage that symbolically expands the purview of the nation to incorporate diversity and difference, while masking material inequities that continue to exclude the disabled, particularly those of lesser economic means or otherwise marginalized groups. Rutter-Jensen's interviews with members of Colombia's Paralympic swim team support her call for a reassessment of national culture that aims for full accessibility.

Hortensia Moreno's ethnographic research on the increasingly popular phenomenon of female boxing in Mexico shows that as boxing, a "combat sport," has traditionally served to affirm a hyper-masculine national identity, women's participation in the sport presents major challenges to Mexico's masculinist national project, and consequently evokes a good deal of hostility from both within the sports establishment and among fans, although the latter have increasingly begun to embrace these challenges and celebrate the triumphs of Mexico's most successful *boxeadoras.*

The third study in this group, that of Dexter Hough-Snee, reflects on the rise of surfing as a major national sport of Peru. Recent triumphs of Peruvian surfers in international competitions have led to the formulation of a decolonial rhetoric that aims to disassociate surfing from California, often assumed to be the sports epicenter and origin, by articulating a revised history of the sport as innately Peruvian, with indigenous origins that go back centuries before its earliest practice in California.

The book's final section leaves the realm of hegemonic nationalism, shifting its focus to the transnational context of the United States and its bearings on Latin American nationalisms.

Yago Colás looks at how basketball signifies racial difference in the United States. His detailed formalist analysis of Argentine Manu Ginobili's style of play and media image in the United States, where he plays professionally, brings to light the racially charged and US-centric ideologies underlying the meanings produced about him. The introduction of Latin American players such as Ginobili to a professional sport imagined through the black-white lens that determined US racial politics for many years necessarily complicates stereotypes and calls attention to the racially infused power dynamics through which US professional basketball continues to play out.

Juan Poblete reads the US soccer field as a "border zone" in which Latino immigrant recreational soccer players engage with the mainstream of US culture in a variety of different ways. Their presence on the field concretely represents many of the often contradictory dynamics that transpire with and around Spanish speaking immigrants and other Latinos in the contemporary United States. Latino soccer players represent both the growing contribution of Latinos to the US culture and economy and their threat to white Anglo-American cultural dominance. Within this context, the racial politics that ensue are highly indicative of the sort of frictions that continue to surface as Latinos gradually gain a demographic majority in the United States. On the other hand, the soccer field can serve as a more egalitarian space of interaction with both white Americans and other immigrant groups, a space from which to build a potentially empowering cultural citizenship and an opportunity for the negotiation of differences and the efficacious resolution of ethnic conflict.

Robert McKee Irwin's study of Argentine tennis player Guillermo Vilas's image in the US press during the years of his greatest success on the international tennis tour, a period that coincided roughly with the Argentine military dictatorship of the late 1970s and early 1980s, shows how the US sports media's particular set of national biases puts it at odds with foreign nationalisms. In the case of Vilas, he argues that the US sports press ignored both Argentina's reputation as a site of major human rights abuses and its government's attempts to project a new image of a disciplined but just nation, instead recalling a well-known archetype from Hollywood film, the Latin lover, casting Vilas in a way that produces a national image of Argentina in the terms most palatable and marketable to US sports fans.

Bibliography

Alabarces, Pablo. "Entre la banalidad y la crítica: Perspectivas de las ciencias sociales sobre el deporte." *Fútbol-espectáculo, Cultura y Sociedad*. Edited by Samuel Martínez. Mexico City: Afínita Editorial, 2010. 69–101.

———. *Fútbol y patria. El fútbol y las narrativas de la nación en la Argentina*. Buenos Aires: Prometeo Libros, 2002.

———, comp. *Peligro de gol*. Buenos Aires: Consejo Latinoamericano de Ciencias Sociales, 2000.

Alabarces, Pablo, and Carlos Alberto Máximo Pimenta, eds. *Futbologías: fútbol, identidad y violencia en América Latina*. Buenos Aires: Consejo Latinoamericano de Ciencias Sociales, 2003.

Alabarces, Pablo, and María Graciela Rodríguez. *Cuestión de pelotas: fútbol, deporte, sociedad, cultura*. Buenos Aires: Atuel, 1996.

Albion Football Club. Web. December 8, 2012. Available at http://www.albion.com.uy/.

Alonso Meneses, Guillermo, and Luis Escala Rabadán, coords. *Offside/Fuera de lugar: fútbol y migraciones en el mundo contemporáneo*. Tijuana/Mexico City: Colegio de la Frontera Norte/CLAVE, 2012.

Anderson, Benedict. *Imagined Communities. Reflections on the Origins and Spread of Nationalism*, 2nd ed. London: Verso, 1991 [1983].

Araújo Vélez, Fernando. *Pena máxima: juicio al fútbol colombiano*. Bogotá: Planeta, 1995.

Arbena, Joseph, ed. *Sport and Society in Latin America: Diffusion, Dependency, and the Rise of Mass Culture.* New York: Greenwood Press, 1988.

Arbena, Joseph, and David LaFrance, eds. *Sport in Latin American and the Caribbean.* Wilmington, DE: Scholarly Resources, 2002.

Archetti, Eduardo P. *Fútbol y ethos.* Buenos Aires: Facultad Latino americana de Ciencias Sociales, 1984.

———. *Masculinities. Football, Polo and the Tango in Argentina.* Oxford: Berg, 1999.

Arellano, Jorge Eduardo. *El béisbol en Nicaragua: (rescate histórico y cultural, 1889–1948).* Managua: Academia de Geografía e Historia de Nicaragua, 2007.

Argentine Football Association (AFA). Web. October 23, 2013. Available at http://www.afa.org.ar/.

Asociación Nacional de Fútbol Profesional (ANFP). Web. October 23, 2013. Available at http://www.anfp.cl/.

Asociación Uruguaya de Fútbol (AUF). Web. October 23, 2013. Available at http://www.auf.org.uy/.

Bairner, Alan. *Sport, Nationalism, and Globalization: European and North American Perspectives.* Albany: State University of New York Press, 2001.

Billings, Andrew, Michael L. Butterworth, and Paul D. Turman. *Communication and Sport: Surveying the Field.* London: Sage, 2011.

Carrington, Ben, and Ian McDonald. "Marxism, Cultural Studies and Sport: Mapping the Field." *Marxism, Cultural Studies and Sport.* Edited by Ben Carrington and Ian McDonald. London: Routledge, 2009. 1–12.

Clube Atlético São Paulo (Clube SP). Web. October 23, 2013. Available at http://clubespac.wordpress.com/.

Coakley, Jay, and Eric Dunning. "General Introduction." *Handbook of Sports Studies.* Edited by Jay Coakley and Eric Dunning. London: Sage, 2010 [2000]. xxi–xxxviii.

Dunning, Eric. *Sport Matters: Sociological Studies of Sport, Violence and Civilisation.* London: Routledge, 1999.

Edwards, Harry. *The Revolt of the Black Athlete.* New York: The Free Press, 1969.

———. *Sociology of Sport.* Homewood, IL: Dorsey Press, 1973.

Elias, Robert. *The Empire Strikes Out: How Baseball Sold U.S. Foreign Policy and Promoted the American Way Abroad.* New York: The New Press, 2010.

Federación Colombiana de Fútbol (FCF). Web. October 23, 2013. Available at http://www.federacionvenezolanadefutbol.org/.

Federación Costarricense de Fútbol. Web. October 23, 2013. Available at http://fedefutbolcr.com/.

Federación Mexicana de Béisbol (FEMEBE). Web. October 17, 2013. Available at http://www.femebe.net/.

Federación Mexicana de Fútbol Asociación, A.C. Web. October 23, 2013. Available at http://www.femexfut.org.mx/.

Federación Panameña de Béisbol (FeDeBeis). Web. October 17, 2013. Available at http://fedebeis.com.pa/.

Federación Venezolana de Fútbol. Web. October 23, 2013. Available at http://www.federacionvenezolanadefutbol.org/.

Fernández, José Ramón. *El fútbol mexicano: ¿un juego sucio?* Mexico City: Grijalbo, 1994.

Fernández L'Hoeste, Héctor, and Juan Poblete, eds. *Redrawing the Nation: National Identity in Latin/o American Comics*. New York: Palgrave Macmillan, 2009.

Freyre, Gilberto. "Prefácio." *O negro no futebol brasileiro*. Mário Rodrigues Filho. Rio de Janeiro: Pongetti, 1947.

Galeano, Eduardo. *Soccer in Sun and Shadow*. Translated by Mark Fried. London: Verso, 1998 [1997] (Translation of *Fútbol a sol y sombra*. Madrid: Siglo XXI, 1995).

Galvis Ramírez, Alberto. *100 años de fútbol en Colombia*. Bogotá: Planeta, 2008.

Gastaldo, Edison Luis, and Simoni Lahud Guedes, eds. *Nações em Campo: Copa do Mundo e identidade nacional*. Niterói, Brazil: Intertexto, 2006.

Gellner, Ernst. *Nations and Nationalism*. Ithaca, NY: Cornell University Press, 1983.

Giulianotti, Richard. "Civilizing Games: Norbert Elias and the Sociology of Sports." *Sports and Modern Social Theorists*. Edited by Richard Giulianotti. New York: Palgrave Macmillan, 2004. 145–160.

Giulianotti, Richard, and Roland Robertson. "Recovering the Social: Globalization, Football and Transnationalism." *Globalization and Sport*. Edited by Richard Giulanotti and Ronald Robertson. Malden, MA: Blackwell, 2007. 58–78.

Goldlust, John. *Playing for Keeps: Sport, the Media and Society*. Melbourne: Longman Cheshire, 1987.

Golpe de estadio. Dir. Sergio Cabrera. Perf. Emma Suárez, Nicolás Montero, and César Mora. Caracol Televisión, 1998. Film.

Gónzález, Javier. *El béisbol en Venezuela: un siglo de pasión*. Caracas: Biblioteca Nacional, 1996.

González Echevarria, Roberto. *The Pride of Havana: A History of Cuban Baseball*. New York: Oxford University Press, 1999.

Gruneau, Richard. *Class, Sports, and Social Development*. Amherst: University of Massachusetts Press, 1983.

Hall, Stuart. "Culture, the Media and the 'Ideological Effect.'" *Mass Communication and Society*. Edited by James Curran, Michael Gurevitch, and Janet Woollacott. London: Edward Arnold, 1977. 315–348.

Hargreaves, Jennifer, ed. *Sport, Culture and Ideology*. London: Routledge a Kegan Paul, 1982.

Hargreaves, Jennifer, and Ian McDonald. "Cultural Studies and the Sociology of Sport." *Handbook of Sports Studies*. Edited by Jay Coakley and Eric Dunning. London: Sage, 2010 [2000]. 48–60.

Hernández, Ramón, and Jorge Hernández. *El brillo del diamante: historia del béisbol mexicano*. Xalapa, Mexico: Universidad Veracruzana, 2004.

Irwin, Robert McKee, and Maricruz Castro Ricalde. *Global Mexican Cinema: Its Golden Age*. London: British Film Institute/Palgrave Macmillan, 2013.

Irwin, Robert McKee, and Mónica Szurmuk, eds. *Dictionary of Latin American Cultural Studies*. Gainesville: University Press of Florida, 2012.

Joyce, Gare. *The Only Ticket Off the Island*. Toronto: Lester & Orpen Dennys, 1990.

Klein, Alan M. *Baseball on the Border: A Tale of Two Laredos.* Princeton, NJ: Princeton University Press, 1997.

———. "Culture, Politics, and Baseball in the Dominican Republic." *Latin American Perspectives* 22:3 (1995): 111–130.

———. *Sugarball: The American Game, the Dominican Dream.* New Haven, CT: Yale University Press, 1991.

Laya, Luis. *El fútbol en Venezuela.* Caracas: Fundación Bigott, 2004.

Lever, Janet. *Soccer Madness : Brazil's Passion for the World's Most Popular Sport.* Chicago, IL: University of Chicago Press, 1983.

Liga de Béisbol Profesional de la República Dominicana (LIDOM). Web. October 17, 2013. Available at http://www.ligapr.com/.

Liga de Béisbol Profesional Nacional (LBPN). Web. October 17, 2013. Available at http://www.lbpn.com.ni/.

Liga Béisbol Profesional Roberto Clemente (Liga PR). Web. October 17, 2013. Available at http://www.ligapr.com/.

Liga Metropolitana de Béisbol (Béisbol Metro). Web. October 17, 2013. Available at http://www.beisbolmetro.com.ar/.

Liga Venezolana de Béisbol Profesional (LVBP). Web. October 17, 2013. Available at http://www.lvbp.com/index.asp.

Loy, John and Gerald Kenyon. *Sport, Culture and Society.* New York: Macmillan, 1982.

Luzuriaga, Juan Carlos. *El football de novecientos: orígenes y desarrollo del fútbol en el Uruguay (1875–1915).* Montevideo: Fundación Itaú, 2009.

Mafud, Julio. *Sociología del fútbol.* Buenos Aires: Editorial Éméricalee, 1967.

Marín, Edgardo. *Centenario historia total del fútbol chileno, 1895–1995.* Santiago: Editores y Consultores REI Ltda., 1995.

Mason, Tony. *Passion of the People?: Football in South America.* London: Verso, 1995.

Matta, Roberto da, Luiz Felipe Baêta Neves, Arno Vogel, and Simoni Lahud. *Universo do futebol: esporte e sociedade brasileira.* Rio de Janeiro: Edições Pinakotheke, 1982.

Mendes Capraro, André. "O Futebol na obra de um ensaísta: Gilberto Freyre e o ideal da integração social." *Maringá: Revista da Educação Física* 22:1 (2011): 139–149.

Miller, Rory, and Liz Crolley. *Football in the Americas: Fútbol, Futebol, Soccer.* London: Institute for the Study of the Americas, 2007.

Monsiváis, Carlos. "Notas sobre la cultura mexicana en el siglo XX." *Historia General de Mexico* 4. Mexico City: Colegio de México, 1976. 303–476.

Nye, Joseph, Jr. *Bound to Lead: The Changing Nature of American Power.* New York: Basic Books, 1991.

Oleksak, Michael, and Mary Adams Oleksak. *Béisbol: Latin Americans and the Grand Old Game.* Dallas, TX: Masters Press, 1991.

Oliven, Rubén, and Arlei Damo. *Fútbol y cultura.* Buenos Aires/Bogotá: Editorial Norma, 2001.

Pacini Hernández, Deborah, Eric Zolov, and Héctor Fernández L'Hoeste, eds. *Rockin' the Americas: The Global Politics of Rock in Latin/o America.* Pittsburgh, PA: University of Pittsburgh Press, 2004.

Pérez, Louis A. "Between Baseball and Bullfighting: The Quest for Nationality in Cuba, 1868–1898." *The Journal of American History* 81:2 (1994): 493–517.

Pérez Medina, Ramón G. *Historia del baseball panameño.* Panama City: Dutigrafia, 1992.

Poblete, Juan. *Critical Latin American and Latino Studies.* Minneapolis: University of Minnesota Press, 2003.

Ramírez, Carlos F. *¿Cuál es la historia, al día, del fútbol mexicano?* Mexico City: Editorial Novaro, 1960.

Rigauer, Bero. *Sport and Work.* New York: Columbia University Press, 1981 (Translation of *Sport und Arbeit.* Frankfurt: Suhukamp Verlag, 1969).

Risse, Heinz. *Soziologie des Sports.* Berlin: A. Reher, 1921.

Rodrigues Filho, Mario. *O negro no futebol brasileiro,* 2nd ed. Rio de Janeiro: Editôra Civilização Brasileira, 1964 [1947].

Rowe, David. "Introduction: Mapping the Media Sports Cultural Complex." *Critical Readings: Sports, Culture and the Media.* Edited by David Rowe. Berkshire, UK: Open University Press, 2009 [2004] 1–22.

Ruck, Rob. *The Tropic of Baseball: Baseball in the Dominican Republic.* Westport, CT: Meckler, 1990.

Santamaría Gómez, Arturo. *Fútbol, emigrantes y neonacionalismo.* Culiacán, Mexico: Universidad Autónoma de Sinaloa, 2010.

Scott, Jack. *The Athletic Revolution.* New York: The Free Press, 1971.

Sebreli, Juan José. *Fútbol y masas.* Buenos Aires: Editorial Galerna, 1981.

Seymour, Harold. *Baseball: The People's Game.* New York: Oxford University Press, 1990.

Soares, Antonio J. "História e a invenção de tradições no futebol brasileiro." Alabarces (comp.) 2000.

Trigo, Abril. *Crisis y transfiguración de los estudios culturales latinoamericanos.* Santiago: Cuarto Propio, 2012.

Under Fire. Dir. Roger Spottiswoode. Perf. Nick Nolte, Ed Harris, Gene Hackman, and Joanna Cassidy. Lion's Gate Films, 1983. Film.

Urbina Gaitán, Chester. *Costa Rica y el deporte (1873–1921). Un estudio acerca del origen del fútbol y la construcción de un deporte nacional.* Heredia, Costa Rica: EUNA, 2001.

Van Hyning, Thomas E. *Puerto Rico's Winter League: A History of Major League Baseball's Launching Pad.* Jefferson, NC: McFarland & Company, 1995.

Villena Fiengo, Sergio. *Golbalización: siete ensayos heréticos sobre fútbol, identidad y cultura.* San José, Costa Rica: Norma, 2006.

Wenner, Lawrence, ed. *Media, Sports, and Society.* Newbury Park, CA: Sage, 1989.

Whannel, Garry. *Blowing the Whistle: The Politics of Sport.* London: Pluto Press, 1983.

Witter, J. S. *Breve História do Futebol Brasileiro.* São Paulo: FTD, 1996.

Zeiler, Thomas. *Ambassadors in Pinstripes: The Spalding World Baseball Tour and the Birth of the American Empire.* Lanham, MD: Rowman & Littlefield, 2006.

Sports and the Construction of Nationalism

CHAPTER 1

Football and *Patria*, Ten Years Later: Sports Nationalism as a Commodity

Pablo Alabarces

Translated by Wendy Gosselin

Fútbol y Patria was my PhD thesis at the University of Brighton. I finished it in December of 2001, in the middle of the Argentine crisis of that year. The dating is literal: I was in the protests in Plaza de Mayo on the night of December 19 with 300 pages under my arm. I presented my thesis on December 21 and it was approved on February 8 of 2002. When my editor proposed its publication as a book, I reviewed the last chapter in order to supplement the analysis of the Korea-Japan World Cup held during the crisis: with that addition, the thesis was published in December of 2002.

I attempted to analyze the relationship between national narratives and soccer during the Argentine twentieth century—that is, during the entire Argentine history of soccer—with different focal points, organized by a complex periodization that combined elements of key sporting events—for example, the World Cups or the appearances of the figure of Diego Maradona—crossed with political history—Peronism or the military dictatorships. I combined methodologies—the analysis of audiovisual texts, historical documentation, journalistic clippings, ethnographic interviews—and disciplines; the book is inscribed within the sociology of culture and of sports, cultural studies, and history. I basically wanted to analyze the relationship between sports, politics, national identity narratives, and mass culture.

The book aimed to discuss various theoretical matters simultaneously. The most immediate one might seem to be the relationship between nationalism and sports, since there were no published texts in

Latin America about this topic besides the ones produced by the founders of anthropological studies of soccer such as Roberto Da Matta and Eduardo Archetti, Brazilian and Argentine respectively. In those first years of the new century, I had coordinated a working group called Sport and Society, sponsored by the Latin American Social Science Council (CLACSO), that allowed me to launch a discussion on the subject with colleagues from different countries of the continent, including: Sergio Villena Fiengo, a Bolivian researcher working in Costa Rica; Andrés Dávila, Colombian; Luis Antezana, Bolivian; Fernando Carrión and Jacques Ramírez, Ecuadorians; and Eduardo Santa Cruz, Chilean. This network kept me up to date on the state of sports studies in their countries and allowed us to begin, together, a comparative discussion.[1] One of the first things we learned was that there would be a huge difficulty in establishing a general theory. We carried out a second comparison, in this case with European studies that we knew bibliographically; again it seemed hard to go beyond the obvious statement that sports and national narratives were related. However, the ways in which this relationship varied, according to each specific case, demanded the consideration of multiple variables, among them, the degree of international success, the role of certain exceptional subjects, sports heroes, government involvement in sports, along with the production of national or nationalist narratives, and, finally, the role of mass culture, of course, the great narrator of Latin American sports during the twentieth and twenty-first centuries.

Actually, my real preoccupation was not sports nationalism, but the general theories of nationalism. The starting point was that the invention of "nation"—a concept established by Hobsbawm (1990), one of the few historians of nationalism who paid attention to sports at the time, and further developed in the context of Argentine sports by Archetti (1999)—was produced in multiple spaces: the central, visible, and legitimate ones (the state, the university, and politics), but also those of the peripheries: mass culture, popular practices and consumptions, food, dance, and sports—what Archetti called "the free zones of culture." Sport constituted, at the same time, a fundamental repertoire of what Michel Billig (1995) called *banal nationalism*, which proposes that the objects and spaces of our everyday lives are the ones in which nationalism becomes, precisely, quotidian and banal.

In the debate around nationalisms at the time, both culture and economy assumed important roles on the global stage, producing significant consequences for real states and nations—the supposed loss of economic and political sovereignty, of particularisms, and even of the category of *national culture* itself—as well as for the theory on states and nations. It seemed very difficult to produce new reflections on nationalism in the midst of varied and contradictory phenomena of globalization and tribalization, the deterritorialization of some identity narratives and the microterritorialization of others, migrations and diasporas, the ethnification of some national narrations, and the permeability of some borders and the closure of others (sometimes of the same ones simultaneously). In the Argentine case, there was another Latin American particularity: the country was experiencing, at the beginning of the twenty-first century, the consequences of a decade of neoconservatism with the consequent inheritance of its internal fragmentation, the crisis of the unifying narratives, and the central position of the market as a provider of identity narratives. Those were the times of *consumers as citizens*, paraphrasing the title of García Canclini's (1994) book. Citizenship—hence, nationality— seemed to be more a consequence of certain symbolic consumptions than of state narratives and political affirmations.[2]

In the context briefly outlined here, my work found that national narratives had always been, historically, very dependent of the actions of the state. In contrast to other countries of the continent, early Argentine modernity and the weight of its public school system had subordinated mass culture as the great provider of those narratives; furthermore, beginning in the 1950s, the role of Peronism as the provider of the national-popular narrative of the state had been decisive in adding sport as a support of that narration. That is why the important place of sports, particularly soccer, in national narratives had been dependent of those produced by the state until the last two decades of the twentieth century. In those years, three particular circumstances made the Argentine case very special: first, the dictatorships, especially the last one (1976–1983), which had even organized the 1978 World Cup won by the Argentine team; second, the appearance of the exceptional figure of Diego Maradona, who occupied the center of any discussion about soccer and nation from 1977 to 1994; and finally, as I have already mentioned, the neoconservative decade and the withdrawal of the state from everyday life, with the simultaneous social, economic, political, and *identitary* fragmentation and impoverishment of Argentine society. Therefore, I concluded that the unifying discourse of the nation seemed to be vanishing with its great narrator, the Argentine state, which, at the same time, could not be replaced by a weakened civil society. Upon his retirement, soccer was deprived of its last hero, Maradona, which, had he kept on playing, would have meant the continuity of the great plebeian, national, and popular narration of the nation established by Peronism; Maradona's absence meant the impossibility for soccer to propose an alternative national narrative, and its tribalization and fragmentation: clubs, micro-territories, local fan organizations. The narrative remained, then, in the hands of the market: commercial advertising of products directly or indirectly related to soccer proliferated in mass culture each time an international event (World Cup, Americas Cup, Olympic Games, etc.) was at hand. Those advertisements insisted, on the contrary, on the permanence of a nationalist narrative that could not be verified as socially effective. The advertisements recuperated the weight of a national-popular tradition and its permanence in the imaginary, transforming it into a desire and a commodity. Media cannot replace the nation nor propose a democratic narrative because they cannot narrate the ruptures and conflicts that a truly democratic society builds. On the contrary, they sustain the absence of conflict as an imaginary horizon that conceals the domination that exists in every class-based society. Thus the market took charge of the boundaries of the nation by replacing existing national-popular discourse with commodities (beer, mobile phones) that could "unite the homeland" behind an epic narrative that was not political but built around sports.

Following Beatriz Sarlo's (1998) metaphor, my work consisted of postulating soccer as a postmodern cultural machine, that is, as a producer of national narratives. But my conclusion was that the machine was television, not soccer, and that sport was only one of its many shows.

FIVE AND TEN YEARS LATER: NEW FOCAL POINTS

In 2006, the success of *Fútbol y Patria* led my editor to propose a new revised edition. My initial idea was to do it before the World Cup in Germany, during that same year; I finally postponed the project one more year so it might not seem opportunistic. I extended my analysis of Maradona, who had been twice near death due to his excesses and had transformed himself into a television host. I prophesized, as a joke, not imagining that my prophesy might come true, that in a future edition of the book Maradona would be the coach of the national team and lead it to win a Cup. I also added the analysis of the World Cup in Germany, especially of the advertisements: if in 2002 all of them had to take note of the huge economic, political, and social crisis, four years later they could forget about it, as Argentina had seemingly come out of the crisis, and they could simply keep on projecting a banal, success-oriented, and narcissistic nationalism.

The year 2006 marked Lionel Messi's first World Cup competition, at only 20 years of age; he was becoming a star in Barcelona and globally, he had won a gold medal in the Olympic Games in Beijing, and his possibilities of becoming Maradona's "heir" grew rapidly. That is why my conclusions that in 2002 were titled "To Die for Batistuta?" had to be changed to "To Die for Messi?" Two years later, the German edition bore that title: *To Die for Messi?* (*Für Messi sterben?*) (Alabarces, 2010).

Since then, I have tried to avoid the subject. I oriented my research towards other matters: fundamentally, the paths of popular culture in neopopulist times. Nevertheless, the 2010 World Cup found me attentive: on one side, the confluence of Maradona's reappearance and Messi's stardom and, on the other, the way in which the Argentine state, in its *Kirchnerite* cycle, claimed new relationships with both soccer and national narratives.

I want, then, to return to the topic, limiting my analysis to textual genres: journalistic articles, advertising, and, once again, audiovisual materials. The continuity of my debate and exchange with Latin American colleagues led me to attempt to enrich my analysis from five and ten years ago by incorporating new data and a new reading approach. I propose to analyze three problematical knots. One of them is new or had been displaced in my original work: gender. The others were already present in *Fútbol y patria*, but the events of the last two years demand new readings on them: the matter of exceptional subjects and sport heroes (both Messi and Maradona) and the role of the state in the production of new national narratives, with a focus on the relationship between the World Cup and the creation of a new state program, *Fútbol para todos* (Soccer for Everyone), nationalizating the broadcasting of local soccer.

THE *CHICAS* AND THE *MACHOS*

In *Fútbol y patria* I emphasized a *masculine* narrative of the nation that was produced, reproduced, conducted, and administered by men, as is the case with most nationalist narratives, especially Argentina's.

Nevertheless, the analysis cannot avoid the fact that Argentina's most successful sport in the international context is not a men's sport: it's women's field hockey. Data is pretty clear on this. Argentine soccer obtained two Olympic golden medals, in 2004 and 2008, but, as is well known, Olympic soccer is a second class competition, with age restrictions (23 years old being the maximum possible age) for players. The national team obtained three under-20 cups, once again, a second class tournament limited to juvenile players. Since 1993's Americas Cup, the men's national soccer team has not won a major tournament. Meanwhile, women's field hockey obtained Olympic silver medals in 2000 and 2012 (a year in which the men's soccer team did not even qualify to compete) and bronze medals in 2004 and 2008, and won two World Cups in 2002 and 2010, earning a third place finish in 2006. They have also won the gold medal in four of the last ten Champions Trophies, a sort of a mini World Cup played every year.

Other men's sports that are both popular and successful have not attained the same level of success: the men's rugby team dominated the American competition but has only obtained a bronze medal in the 2007 World Cup, which was celebrated as if it had been gold. Basketball, a sport with great Latin American rivalries (Brazil, Puerto Rico, and Venezuela), exploded in the same decade, and the men's team won second place in the

2002 World Cup, defeating the North American dream team and obtaining a gold medal in the Olympic Games of Athens 2004 and bronze in Beijing 2008. Those international successes are also bigger than soccer's: but, once again, they cannot match those of the women's field hockey team, "las chicas" (the girls).

The Argentine use of the word *chicas* is not usually meant to be insulting, implying not smallness but youth. The coach of the successful Argentine teams, Sergio Cachito Vigil, frequently used the term. In 2000, during the Sydney Olympics, the players decided to rename the team *Las Leonas* (the lionesses). The choice, despite its inventors' claim that it was based on the characteristics of strength and courage, echoed the denomination of the national rugby team, *Los Pumas*.

Despite all their successes, no national narrative could be or has been constructed around the chicas of Argentine hockey. Las Leonas, despite being the Argentine team with the greatest international success, have not been fodder for nationalist arguments. There were some operations of *soccerization*—for example, in the chants of the followers or in the presence of the players in media—but Las Leonas have not become the objects of a fundamental metonymy in relation to the nation. Their presence in advertising is significant: it is more graphic than televisual because of the fragmentary audiences—both female and from upper middle classes. Even though they share sponsors with soccer, basketball, and rugby, such as Adidas or Visa, there are no televised advertisements referring to the typical nationalist narration of soccer. There is a limited but meaningful exception and it is focused on the best player in history, Luciana Aymar, who has been chosen as the best hockey player in the world in seven of the last ten years by the IHF, a continuity and a consensus that only Lionel Messi could emulate. In a Gatorade ad, a magnificent goal made by Aymar is narrated by the voice of Víctor Hugo Morales (the most important soccer narrator in the country) but describing Maradona's goal against England in 1986 (his most famous and intense narration). The end of the advertisement claims "Thanks *Lucha* [the familiar nickname for Luciana] for making us feel like this." Not enough to position Aymar in the place of the national sport hero who can build national meanings.[3]

The impossibility of building a national hero of her is not related to class. Female hockey is a sport played and consumed by the upper middle classes; nevertheless, in a mass culture in which sport became a transclass commodity, this limitation is not an obstacle in constructing sports heroes. This is confirmed by the comparative example of another Argentine sport strictly restricted to the upper middle classes: rugby. Besides its class restriction, and despite the fact that international successes are limited to a continental domain, Los Pumas and rugby have in fact been objects of nationalist operations. Even more: precisely because of its class location, rugby allows the construction of a radically antiplebeian nationalist narra-tive. Those narratives circulate in two zones: journalistic reports and, once again, advertisements. The former were especially abundant in the 2007 World Cup held in France. There, Los Pumas surprisingly defeated the local team in the opening match, to continue with a brilliant campaign that crashed with the South African Springboks—the champions of that Cup—in the semifinals, but ended with a victory over France to achieve the bronze medal. That world-level campaign was surprising and led to the multi-plication of texts that proposed Los Pumas as a national example: hard working but respectful of fair play, tough but gentle, successful but especially noble in defeat. They were presented as "gentlemen," that is, male and antiplebeian. The advertisements, at the same time, insisted on those meanings using two clearly nationalist arguments: first, the construction of a national *todos* [everyone]—Los Pumas belong to everyone and, therefore, could operate as a metonymy of the homeland. Second, a recurring image was that of the team singing the national anthem before their matches, embracing each other with tears in their eyes—a clearly nationalist image that was replicated by the *chicas* of field hockey.

The dependence of the nationalist narrative on sporting success is strong. In this way, rugby cannot build a narration with the same strength as soccer, notwithstanding its possibilities. Class is not the obstacle, suc-cess is. Class works, on the contrary, as a possibility: the one of building a national narrative focusing on the middle classes. The other possibility is gender: Los Pumas are, above all, machos, virile, brave, undiminished by pain or even defeat. Las chicas cannot build those meanings. They must win, they must continue to be women, being the chicas, they must continue imitating men and limit themselves to that. They must never even dream of becoming the heroes of the nation.

The Exceptionality of the Hero

The centrality of the sports hero is, in soccer, decisive. But we can find some tensions this have led to the transformation of its role. In *Fútbol y patria* I extensively analyzed the epic struggles of Maradona, the main character of the patriotic narration in Argentine soccer for two decades. I pointed out two decisive features: his condition of being an articulation of the old national-popular and plebeian discourse, contemporary to the political decline of that discourse, on the one hand; and on the other, that his departure from the sports scene drastically altered the possibility of the narration of the national-popular hero because of the impossibility of recreating him—in sport through an exceptional player and in the cultural and political context that had been produced around him. Maradona, I concluded, was an index of the past, limited only to the memory of the myth and the search for an impossible successor.

The 2006 World Cup introduced new tensions around two new figures. One of them was, obviously, Messi: besides the fact that he played only as an occasional substitute, Messi was already presenting some anomalous features: basically, his middle-class origin and his formation as a European player in Barcelona from the age of 14. The other figure was Carlos Tévez, from a class extraction close to Maradona's, the popular classes of greater Buenos Aires, marked by some physical features (scars as a result of a domestic accident). His nickname, the *Apache*, related to his neighborhood *Fuerte Apache*, known as one of the most dangerous and violent areas of greater Buenos Aires. Nevertheless, the great *popularity* of Tévez contrasted with his refusal to play on the Argentine youth teams, instead preferring his local team, Boca Juniors. Maradona, on the contrary, had begun his epic trajectory by winning the first under-20 World Cup in 1979. Any further claims that either was heir to Maradona's charismatic exceptionality between 1982 and 1994 were quickly dismissed upon the elimination of Argentina in the quarterfinals and because neither was a protagonist on the team.

In 2010, things changed—not only because of Messi and Tévez's presence as starting players, but because they had become international superstars and had generated great expectations around their performances (despite the fact that the team had had a lousy campaign in the qualifying rounds). The main change was Maradona's reappearance, as a coach, a role he took on beginning in 2009. This implied a new mise en scène of the magnificent concentration of meanings that he provoked even though he was no longer a sports hero; he became now a hero of speech. In other words: Maradona's acting was purely discursive, both as a coach and in his statements to journalists. What remained closed was the possibility of corporeal performance: Maradona's epic had been built mainly around his athletic performances. That is the exceptionality of the sports hero: it is not only about discourses, but also about an embodied performance, impossible to fake, related to its narration, but not mere fiction or discursive production. A constellation of discourses had been articulated around Maradona—basically the national-popular plebeian narrative—but that articulation was possible because of the uncontestable fact, mainly corporal, of his famous goal against England in 1986, among many others. This kind of corporeal performance was no longer possible.

Maradona's acting proved to be very productive. He filled the media space with both words and images, tending to displace the contemporary heroes (Messi and Tévez) favoring the narration about his own role as a national hero of the past. I suspect that it was a motivational endeavor: Maradona concentrated both the pressure and the expectations on himself thereby liberating his own players from them. Meanwhile, his tactical weaknesses as a coach—nobody knew how his teams played and his changes in strategies were infinite, even in the same match— were offset by his incomparable quality as a speaker: technical conversations were replaced by invocations of memory, tradition, glory, or the social commitment of the players (he was known to have presented, before matches, dramatic videos in which the exhibition of the poverty in Argentina was thought to be a motivation for his players). Maradona was the perfect coach for the *passionate* stage of Argentine soccer: its soccer culture seemed to be, and still is, reduced to the exhibition of courage and effort by the players and *aguante* (tenacity) by the supporters.

Moreover, intertwined with Maradona's acting, many discourses appeared vindicating his role as a national-popular myth. If in 2002 Maradona was identified as a sort of postmodern Perón—the continuity of Peronism by other means—his reappearance in new Peronist times necessarily evoked that role. Presidents Néstor and then Cristina Kirchner, in office since 2003, had reinstalled into public debate the old topics of traditional Peronism. In a movement that transformed those discourses into both hegemonic and state rhetoric, the classic national-popular and plebeian figure of Maradona was perfect to be articulated in the sports scene. Different texts from officialist journalists glorified the plebeian continuity of Maradona, destined to lead his players to the popular victory in the World Cup. But, consequently, in the dialectics of political debate, that succession of laudatory discourses implied the reappearance of counterdiscourses that, far from reproducing adoration of the old hero, condemned him for his neo-*officialism*.

What none of the actors of this mini-debate seemed to discern were the transformations that were happening in both Argentine society and in Maradona himself; there was need for a good theoretical reflection that could explain them, beyond the superficiality of the politicians that read the evidence as "mirrors" of the social and cultural context. Argentina was not the same country as when Maradona began to play and he could not be the same man, not only because he was now an overweight former soccer player but also because his national-popular plebianism had lost all the potential irreverence it had represented in neoconservative times: he was now part of the hegemonic discourses of neopopulist times. An incident prior to the World Cup confirms this change. The night in which Argentina qualified for the World Cup, October 14, 2009, after a dramatic victory against Uruguay in Montevideo, Maradona, out of control, began to insult the journalists

who had criticized him. At the press conference, he answered one of
their questions as follows:

> —Diego, to whom do you dedicate this qualification? [...] To those who
> did not believe in you in its moment ... the family, friends?
> —You are among them ... I have a good memory, bro. To those who didn't
> believe ... Pardon me, ladies, suck it and suck it again.[4]

The homophobic and rude remarks made by Maradona generated a small
scandal and even a mild sanction from FIFA. The condemnations, which
came from both journalists and conservative and opposition politicians,
focused on the negative image of Argentina in the international scene
and on Maradona's intolerance of criticism that matched a similar characterization of Kirchnerism. Maradona insulted the journalists because
he was an *officialist*, they concluded, and because he showed his deep-
seated lack of culture, an argument that some expressed in class oriented
racist terms.[5] His supporters emphasized all the common places of populism: Maradona was once again the reincarnation of the infuriated masses
of October 17, 1945, when Peronism was born, and his insults were the
proof of his irreverence toward those in power—even though the insults
were not directed at the Pope or the Argentine military, but to modest
and irrelevant sport journalists.

What nobody could read was that his plebeianism had become a show
that no longer held any irreverence. His language was limited to contributing to the macho code of the aguante, the dominant logic of soccer
culture according to which the condition of being a macho is tested in violent confrontation and superiority expressed through tropes of anal penetration or oral sex. The fact is that Maradona did not question power: he
simply reproduced it, duplicating the dominant language of the macho.
Maradona's transgressive potential had been annulled: his only choices
seemed to be to complain or to live in exile. Consequently, he lived in the
United Arab Emirates until his new sacking in July 2012.

The Comeback of the State Machine

The most important transformation had occurred far from soccer. In
May of 2010, barely a month before the beginning of the World Cup,
Argentina was celebrating the Bicentennial of its independence. The
national government, led by Cristina Fernández de Kirchner, celebrated
it with major street parades that lasted many days and included popular
music concerts attended by millions. The parades ended with allegoric
chariots that proposed a version of Argentine history according to the
national-popular progressive perspective with a massive attendance that

was fascinated by the show. The success of the celebrations was over-whelming—even the most critical of the current government were silent in front of millions of spectators and participants of the celebrations—and many analysts agree that the event was the beginning of the growth of the positive image of the government that lead, more than a year later, to the reelection of the president with 54 percent of the votes.

I am not interested in the political analysis of the event or in its aesthetic details. I find the event to be decisive to understand the reappearance of the state as a great narrator of the patria. If in *Fútbol y Patria* I insisted that the relationship between soccer and national narratives at the end of the twentieth century was marked by the retirement of the great narrator of the century—and that Maradona had increased his patriotic representation during its absence—this new presence of the state as a producer of discourses about nationality changed the whole picture. I think that a part of this affected the possibility of Maradona returning to the patriotic center in 2010; if his image had grown massively in conservative times, it was displaced (because of its redundancy?) during the reappearance of the populist narration.

The Bicentenary celebrations meant a kind of coronation, a massive mise en scène, of a tendency that was being consolidated in the previous seven years. Kirchnerism had proposed a new legitimacy for the traditional discourses of Peronism: the old national-popular narrative, with a certain adequacy to the new times that included the condemnation to the neoconservative decade—even though it had also been a Peronist one. That new legitimacy meant the explicit affirmation of the comeback of the state as a main actor in both social and economic life. Even though it cannot be completely verified—the economic organization continued to be centralized in the hands of private corporations—the affirmation was strong: the state had come back to fulfill the functions it should have never lost. Among them, even if it wasn't explicitly said, were its narrative functions.

In that context, soccer could not propose alternative discourses because it had never done so, not even in conservative times. When Maradona's figure had allowed an autonomous narration, it had consisted in showing the continuity of the old national-popular narration of Peronism. With its comeback, and once again proposed by the state, as in the old missed times of Peronism—that continue to work as a sort of Golden Age of modern Argentina—soccer could not incarnate any efficient national narration. It could barely propose its survival as a commodity proposed by the market, with advertising as the most important supporter of its texts. As the meanings of the patria were being rediscussed in political spaces, soccer was powerful only in the empty rhetorics of the sponsors that continued to be full of the commonplace patriotic statements. A maximum example of this was the advertisement of Quilmes beer for the 2002 and 2006 World Cups that I analyzed at length in both editions of my book. The 2010 ad showed images of the everyday lives of Argentine audiences in the streets, stopping traffic and their activities in order to listen to the voice of... God, who claimed he was an Argentine supporter and had good predictions for the World Cup to come. Narcissistic Argentine fandom had deepened to the level of becoming psychotic.[6]

This description has another twist. In August 20, 2009, facing the claims of the AFA for more money from the owner of the transmission rights for local soccer, the multimedia Group Clarín, the state offered the demanded sum and, in a few days, the AFA unilaterally terminated the contract and signed a new one with the government. Henceforth, the state program *Fútbol para todos* managed the televised transmissions, especially using public television. Until then, local soccer was transmitted through cable or pay-per-view; since then, the transmissions have been free and financed by state advertisements promoting the actions of the government and some campaigns of public interest—for example, the needed precautions against dengue fever and the flu. This tight relationship between the government and local soccer is also verified by the fact that, after Néstor Kirchner's death, the following tournament was named "Torneo Néstor Kirchner." The last one, in the first semester of 2012, was called "Torneo Crucero General Belgrano," as a commemoration of the ship sunk during the Malvinas war.

Nevertheless, this process that I analyze elsewhere (Alabarces and Duek, 2012) is only marginally related to sport nationalism. It marks an orientation of the state communication policies linked to hegemonic populism: soccer was transformed into a popular right that should be distributed "to everyone." At the beginning of 2011, the Federal Authority of Audiovisual Communication Services (AFSCA), created by a new law of communication to both organize and regulate media transformations, took a new step towards televised transmissions of sporting events. According to what was established by law, AFSCA regulated what it called "the universal access to the informative content of relevant interest," in this case limited to sport events. A list of both national and international sports events was established and their transmission should be universally accessible: that is, through open television, forcing the owners of the rights to transfer—voluntarily or not—the broadcasting to open networks and forbidding the transmissions through cable or pay-per-view systems.

The list includes local and international events of multiple sports: soccer, hockey, basketball, rugby, or volleyball. However, it was limited to sports with mass audiences, leaving aside other practices such as athletics, cyclism, or handball, sports that, even with a good number of players in Argentina, do not have important audiences in their transmissions. This points out a radical new fact: the democratization of television access to certain cultural goods—sport practices—continues to be subject to the logics of supply and demand of the cultural industry. The politics of patrimonialization of the symbolic is presented—to consider certain intangible goods as public patrimony—as being designed out of a radically democratic policy but ends up being organized by the same logics it is trying to change. The political-cultural decisions appear to be dominated by the logics of the market, even though in this case it is only about the income of the audiences and the political revenue of the government.

The Argentine state had produced, then, a legal instrument that finally related sport and patria, as patrimony of the national-popular culture: a kind of definitive affirmation of the nationalist possibilities of sport. Nevertheless, it was limited to produce it—it could only produce it—as a cultural commodity: a kind of reaffirmation that, besides the democratic temptations, the dominant logics are the ones of the cultural industry. That is, definitely not patria, but another commodity.

The gesture can (only) be read as the apparent combination of two logics that, until now, were described as both irreducible and in conflict: on one side, the national-popular logic that understands the state as a machine that produces democratic meanings and, on the other, the neoliberal one that trusts the market—which it calls *civil society*—as the only enunciator and narrator. Actually, what I intend to describe here is what Beasley-Murray (2010) proposes as contact points between populism and neoliberalism: populism is limited to adding passion, affectivity, and massiveness to what neoliberalism has transformed into television merchandise. In addition, even with the novelty of the appropriation cultural patrimony of broadcast sports by television—radically original in the Latin American context where no state has dared to interfere in the giant business of big networks—these processes could be described as a new crease: the conciliation of logics, both political and narrative, becomes a neoliberal progressive neopopulism, the new horizon of expectations of Peronism—and not only of Peronism, continentally speaking.

A False Conclusion (Because It Is Not a Conclusion but a Redundancy)

More than ten years ago I said, in an article for an academic journal, that Maradona was one of the most famous people on earth. An anonymous North American referee said that he did not know him.

In an episode of the last season of the television series *A gifted man*, produced by Jonathan Demme for CBS, a Latino patient of Dr. Holt

(Patrick Wilson) is afraid before a major surgery. Dr. Holt tries to calm him down:

—Who is your favorite sport player?
—Messi
—Ok, then, this doctor is the Messi of surgeons.

Like Dr. Holt, my referee could not say that he did not know who Messi was. In contrast with Maradona—or Pelé, Eusebio, Garrincha, or even Johan Cruyff, the soccer heroes of modernity—contemporary sport heroes can be heroes, but not national ones. Deprived of epic narrations, they are magnificent figures of show-business, so they become necessarily global, deterritorialized or with a reterritorialization marked by their team, inevitably a European one, even though in the future they could also be part of a Chinese team.

In consequence, contemporary soccer heroes, key figures of the nationalist narrations, cannot be patrimonialized by a national state because they are subject to the mercantile logic of global shows and of the cultural industry that the national state cannot, nor does it wish, to transform. While TV transmissions of sport can only be captured by the state as a commodity, and owned by the state, not as a democratic patrimony of the citizens, the new heroes are immune to nationalization— there is no state that could pay for it nor any club that could use it.

The figure of Messi must be analyzed in this frame. He plays simultaneously in two narratives: the patriotic one, the renewed possibility of becoming a national hero; and the global one, the spectacular star. *Time* magazine, in its issue of January 2012, presented this simultaneity on its cover: "King Leo: Lionel Messi is the best football player in the world, possibly of all time. So why won't his countrymen love him?"[7] Any answer should imply the recognition of their assumption as a valid one, a validity that should be discussed. First, because of gender: we do not know if Argentine women already love him. Second, because the recent appearances of Messi in the matches played in different localities in Argentina reveal that his figure is growing among the supporters of the provinces: *countrymen* refers here to the *porteño* supporters (the inhabitants of the City of Buenos Aires). In Rosario, for example, the fans decided to privilege Messi's condition as native to that city above any moral or soccer consideration. What Messi cannot be, is, nevertheless, the repetition of Maradona, and that is the immediate frame of interpretation. What the Argentine heroic sport narration expects from him is that repetition: the national-popular plebeian hero that leads the patria to the victory.

As I have already said, that repetition is impossible for several reasons: first, social class reasons, as Messi is not and cannot pretend to be a plebeian subject—there is neither poverty nor hunger in his story. Second, historical reasons: even though he plays against England and scored 43 goals, the context would not happen again four years after a war. Third, political reasons: a national-popular construction (that Messi turns into an impossible one besides any fabricated fiction) would not occur in front of an absent narration, but precisely at its height—as we have already mentioned, the national-popular kirchnerite narration. Fourth, sport reasons: if his soccer quality is exceptional, his formation is organized around the famous treatment of body growth that he received in Barcelona since he was 14 that subtracts him from the epics of the *potrero* and the football school—the classic spaces of football formation of Argentine players, the *pibe* that Archetti (1999) describes—to impregnate him with the logic of the European factory's—the *Masía*, the Catalalonian school—pure control and discipline, so that possible narration is closed. And finally, moral reasons: Messi is not charismatic, he limits his exhibit to the script that global show business claims—an abundant script, by the way, but predictable and previewed—he barely speaks: and when he does, he speaks with his body, strictly in the matches.

In sum: of all the mythogenic conditions (Burke, 1997) that Maradona presented, Messi has only one: the exceptional condition of his game that is more than enough to talk about soccer, but pretty insufficient to talk about nationalist myths and patriotic narratives. Messi, lacking the tears and the conflicts—and the radically popular plebeian condition of Maradona—cannot articulate the sports narration of the homeland. Even though he could win a World Cup, he will never be more than a good guy, never a *pibe*.

NOTES

1. These debates led to two collective books whose arguments can be found in Alabarces 2000 and 2004.
2. I dedicated a great part of the conclusions of *Fútbol y Patria* to the discussion of the Canclinean analysis; although it was useless, it is still stubbornly hegemonic in Latin American academia.
3. The spot can be seen in: http://www.youtube.com/watch?v=RwPthQ2G_a0 (accessed 07/07/12).
4. The video can be seen in http://www.youtube.com/watch?v=BZky5flA8BI (accessed 8/7/12).
5. Maradona has always been, for the conservative groups, barely a *negrito*.
6. The spot can be seen in http://www.youtube.com/watch?v=72TO8fIAePw (accessed 8/7/12).
7. The cover can be seen, for example, in the coverage that local media made: http://canchallena.lanacion.com.ar/1443562-time-pone-a-messi-en-su-tapa-y-se-pregunta-por-que-no-lo-aman-en-la-argentina (accessed 09/10/12).

BIBLIOGRAPHY

Alabarces, Pablo, *Für Messi sterben? Der Fußball und die Erfindung der argentinischen Nation.* Berlin: Suhrkamp Verlag, 2010.

———. *Fútbol y Patria. El fútbol y las narrativas nacionales en la Argentina.* Buenos Aires: Prometeo Libros, 2002.

———, ed. *Futbologías.* Buenos Aires: CLACSO-ASDI, 2004.

——— ed. *Peligro de gol. Estudios sobre deporte y sociedad en América Latina.* Buenos Aires: CLACSO-ASDI, 2000.

———. *Peronistas, populistas y plebeyos.* Buenos Aires: Prometeo Libros, 2011.

Alabarces, Pablo, and Duek C. "2012 Football for Everyone: Soccer, TV and Politics in Argentina." *Sport, Public Broadcasting, and Cultural Citizenship.* Edited by J. Scherer and D. Rowe. London: Sage, forthcoming.

Archetti, Eduardo. *Masculinities: Football, Polo and the Tango in Argentina.* London: Berg, 1999.

Beasley-Murray, John. *Poshegemonía. Teoría política y América Latina.* Buenos Aires: Paidós, 2010.

Billig, Michael. *Banal Nationalism.* London: Sage, 1995.

Burke, Peter. *Varieties of Cultural History.* Cambridge: Polity Press, 1997.

García Canclini, Néstor. *Consumidores y ciudadanos.* Mexico: Grijalbo, 1994.

Garriga, Zuca. *Nosotros nos peleamos. Violencia e identidad de una hinchada de fútbol.* Buenos Aires: Prometeo Libros, 2011.

Hobsbawm, Eric. *Nations and Nationalism since 1780: Programme, Myth, Reality.* Cambridge: Cambridge University Press, 1990.

Sarlo, Beatriz. *La máquina cultural. Maestras, traductores y vanguardistas.* Buenos Aires: Ariel, 1998.

CHAPTER 2

The Antinational Game? An Exploration of Women's Soccer in Latin America

Joshua Nadel

"Women's football," wrote FIFA president Sepp Blatter 2007, "has been part and parcel of the sports arena for over thirty years...[but] has come on in leaps and bounds since FIFA staged the first women's world championship in...1991." There is more than a little truth to this statement. Women's soccer *has* grown astronomically since Blatter publicly declared in 1995 that the future of soccer was "feminine." As of 2011, 29 million girls and women played soccer around the world, compared with 20 million a decade earlier (*FIFA Health and Fitness* 5; and Fahmy). Blatter's comments, however, elide an inconvenient truth: women have been playing organized soccer for much more than 30 years. Almost since the creation of modern soccer in the mid-1800s, women and girls took to the game. The first women's world championship, much as FIFA still refuses to acknowledge it, occurred not in 1991 but in 1970. And significantly, Blatter ignored the obstacles that women and girls have had to overcome and continue to struggle against in order to play the game that they love.

Perhaps nowhere have women fought for their right to play soccer as hard for as long as in Latin America. Women have played in the region for over 100 years despite legal bans and social scorn. Playing soccer was considered unfeminine or masculinizing, as soccer reputedly gave women strong legs and caused permanent scars. Public health experts expressed concerns over the effects of soccer on women's reproductive capacities, while other critics questioned women players' sexuality, suggesting that women who played soccer were homosexual and that soccer served as a "recruiting ground" for lesbians. These attitudes served—and at some level continue to serve—to marginalize both women's soccer and women and girls who played the game.

Women's soccer has deep roots in the region. Histories of the sport in Latin America suggest that women's interest in soccer for much of the twentieth century was limited to cheering on and admiring the bodies of their husbands, friends, and objects of attraction. Women, according to this version, had no desire to play. Yet, throughout the region, from soccer powers like Brazil to nations like Panama, Cuba, and Costa Rica, women began playing in the early twentieth century. For the most part, however, this history has been written out of the dominant narrative of the sport. Given the importance of soccer in the region, this is no minor elision: in Latin America soccer is essential to national identity, so excluding the women's game means excluding women from a crucial construct of the nation. Indeed, it is not just that women's soccer has been ignored by history until recently. Rather, national leaders sought to bury it. With the support of public health "experts" who claimed that soccer damaged women's reproductive capacities, sport authorities systematically closed down options for women to play the game. Why? Quite simply, girls who played soccer were perceived as antinational. They were threats to the nation.

This contribution has two interrelated goals. The first is to sketch the contours of the women's game in Latin America from its beginnings in the early 1900s until the present. This is by no means a conclusive chronology. Records of women's soccer appear only sporadically in printed sources, and much remains to be uncovered about the history of women's soccer in the region. Nevertheless, I suggest a trajectory that appears at least plausible. In essence I suggest two eras: pre-1991, when the game existed on the margins and generally in the face of national scorn; and post-1991, when FIFA support—limited as it remains—began to change the landscape for women's soccer. While FIFA's eventual support has been crucial to its development, women's soccer survived due to the players and coaches who risked reputations and faced criticism in order to create a field for women. Increased financial and institutional backing from the world governing body has done little to alter attitudes about the sport in the region. The second goal is to explore these attitudes about women's soccer to suggest why it was seen as a threat to the nation. Indeed, the enduring difficulties for women's soccer have little to do with the game itself and more to do with the meaning of soccer for Latin American nations.

ARCHAEOLOGY (WOMEN'S SOCCER BEFORE 1991)

Viewed by the outside observer, women's soccer in Latin America would seem to be a relatively new phenomenon, begun in the late 1980s or early

1990s. At this time, the different national governing bodies of soccer in the region began to pay nominal attention to the sport. FIFA started to organize women's competitions in 1988 with the FIFA Women's Invitational in China, which was followed three years later with the first Women's World Cup. But there is more to the history than that. Soccer arrived in Latin America as a part of the massive wave of migrants and expatriates that began in the late 1800s and continued until around 1930. These imports disseminated the rules of Association Football—known around the world today as football or soccer, codified in England in 1863—and established the first matches. Names like Hogg, Miller, Hutton, and Poole germinated the sport in the region. These hybrid elites saw the sport as a part of the modern lifestyles that emanated from Europe at the time. At first played in elite athletic clubs, within a generation more plebian soccer teams developed. They challenged the upper-class nature of the sport and diffused the game outward.

Women quickly became involved in the sport as avid fans and began playing the game recreationally. Magazines that promoted modern lifestyles presented Latin Americans with images of sportswomen and articles detailing their exploits. In 1920, the Argentine sports magazine *El Gráfico*, perhaps the most important sports-only publication in the region in the 1920s, ran a series of pictures highlighting Club Atlético Harrods in Rivadavia, Argentina. Along with images of women playing tennis and croquet, the magazine showed three young "enthusiastic soccer players": Erminda Uzdi, María Hansen Magoll, and María Bocio (*El Gráfico*, January 31, 1920). Though published in Argentina, *El Gráfico* was one of the most important sports magazines in the region during the era, circulating in Chile, Ecuador, Peru, and Colombia, and as far as Costa Rica and Mexico (Archetti, *Masculinities* 57). The June 13, 1925, cover of the same magazine showed the kickoff of a woman's football match in England. Placing women soccer players on the cover of the magazine implied the acceptability of the sport in the most modern of nations.

A more common vision of women and soccer comes from match reports that discussed the men and women who attended matches to cheer on this or that side, who fawned over this or that player, who dressed in the latest style for a quintessentially *social* event. The cream of the social elite attended matches in both Brazil and Argentina. Reporting on a match in 1908, *Gazeta de Notícias* noted the "select and numerous [...] gentle ladies," who "flocked" to the field to cheer on their team (quoted in Lessa de Moura 19). According to Priscila Campos, women's presence at early soccer matches was an "incentive" to clubs and players, a type of adornment to the game. Other Brazilian historians and social scientists have pointed to the "demure ladies" who helped make soccer matches into "gala events" (Ferreira Campos 26); or the "elegant young women" who filled the stands (de Souza Junior et al.). Path breaking soccer historian Mario Filho described what he called a typical scene at a Brazilian match during the 1920s. According to Filho, girls sat with their mothers and fathers "in the bleachers [...] opening and closing fans, serious, smiling, quiet, nervous, as they were on display." At halftime, "the field and the bleachers became one," as players "appeared in the stands, sweaty and tired, to compliment the girls" (Filho 23). In other words, women's presence at soccer matches was not only common, it was both socially acceptable and desired.

So too in Argentina and Uruguay, women regularly attended soccer matches. On May 1, 1920, *El Gráfico* reported on a match between Gimnasia y Esgrima, from Rosario, and Club Atlético River Plate, from Buenos Aires. Along with the match report, the magazine published a series of photos. In one, women wearing bonnets and stylish dresses can be seen in the River Plate cheering section (*El Gráfico*, May 1, 1920, 5). Most clubs had auxiliary committees comprised of young women, who organized social events around club matches. These took the form of tea parties, postgame dances, and other events that were of "capital importance" to soccer in the region (*El Gráfico*, April 11, 1925, 23). Just as the sport spread from the elite to the popular classes, fandom among women did as well. A 1926 article in *El Gráfico* noted that women at interclub matches "clearly pertained almost exclusively to the popular classes." These fans, observed the author, acted much as the rest of those in attendance, shouting profanities at the referees, and insulting opposing players (*El Gráfico*, September 25, 1926, 41). Yet even as nonelite women attended games more frequently than their upper-class compatriots, articles still noted the special seating sections for women and published photographs of well-dressed women in the stands (*El Gráfico*, February 8, 1930).

Women did not participate solely as fans, however. According to Paraguayan soccer historian Miguel Angel Bestard, a woman player suited up for the club team Nacional in 1911 (41), and reports of women playing in Chile date to 1880s. Brazil, however, may have had the earliest organized women's soccer in the region (Marín Méndez 72). The first recorded women's *match* in Brazil occurred in 1921. That year, two women's teams from the São Paulo suburbs of Trembembé and Cantareira played what many consider the first organized women's soccer game in Brazil. By the early 1930s, a number of Brazilian women and girls took to the game. According to the *Jornal dos Sports*, women's soccer provided an "attractive festival," that was "watched with great satisfaction" by those in attendance (quoted in Mourão and Morel 76). *O Imparcial* noted the "intuition" with which women "thrilled" the audience (Lessa de Moura 33). By the 1940s women played soccer in the

Brazilian states São Paulo, Rio, Belo Horizonte, and Rio Grande do Sul, and likely elsewhere in the country as well. More, the sport received support from local and regional federations such as the Suburban Federation of Football in São Paulo state. Official support for women's soccer was short-lived, however. In 1941, Brazilian president Getúlio Vargas passed Decree Law 3199, banning women from participating in certain sports, including soccer.

While the ban on women's soccer effectively closed off the chance that the sport would grow, some clubs continued to support the women's game. For example, in Pelotas, a small city in Rio Grande do Sul province, two clubs had women's teams in the 1950s. Vila Hilda and Corinthians Futebol Club (not to be mistaken for the São Paulo-based Corinthians Sport Club) both formed teams in April 1950. Photos of a match between the two clubs in July of that year show packed stands, signaling—at the very least—curiosity about women's soccer. Indeed, according to Luiz Carlos Rigo, the sport retained popularity. The two Pelotas clubs played exhibition matches throughout Rio Grande do Sul state in 1950, and by November at least five women's teams played soccer in the province (Rigo et al. 173–188). Nevertheless, the ban on women's soccer made it difficult to develop the sport in any coherent manner.

While Brazil suppressed women's soccer, it began to grow in other parts of the region. In Central America and the Caribbean, for example, active teams formed throughout the first half of the twentieth century. The sport's popularity and importance should not be overstated, but it is clear that women's soccer appeared throughout the isthmus. In Panama a short-lived girls league called the Liga Católica organized tournaments from 1939 to 1942, and games continued—apparently sporadically—from the 1950s until the 1970s, when women's teams from around the country competed for the Air Force Cup. During the 1980s, the sport seems to have receded, resurfacing permanently in the 1990s (Ballesteros and Schoggl; Martínez Vega; pandeportes.gob.pa/index.html#). In Cuba, women's teams played in Havana from the 1930s to the 1950s, while in Honduras and Guatemala women's teams formed in the 1950s as well (Lotina and Hernández Luján; Zeledon Cartín 98–100).

Costa Rica also developed women's soccer in this era, with *Tica* teams acting as missionaries for the sport. In 1949 Deportivo Femenino de Costa Rica formed, debuting with an exhibition match at the National Stadium in March 1950 before embarking on extended tours of Central America and the Caribbean. In August and September, the team traveled to Curação for ten days, where thousands of spectators watched a series of exhibition matches. In April 1951 Deportivo Femenino toured Honduras, Guatemala, Cuba, and Colombia, playing exhibition matches against each other and local teams. Meanwhile, back in Costa Rica, five other teams formed by 1952. Femenino La Libertad, América, Evita Perón, ODECA, and Independiente played each other throughout the 1950s in and around San José (Zeledon Cartín 128; Rojas 14; "Aqui es el reto," 33; and Méndez). And while the sport's popularity in Costa Rica occasioned congressional hearings on its safety and morality, no measures were put in place to slow the growth of women's soccer.

The impact of the Costa Rican women's teams extended beyond national boundaries. Perhaps inspired by the Costa Rican tour in 1951 and a 1960 tour of two British teams to raise money for the Colombian Red Cross, women's soccer became a regular fixture in Bogotá in the late 1960s (*El Tiempo* September 1, 1969, 10). Many of the women who played in the Bogotá mini-league had ties to professional soccer in the country: husbands, brothers, sons who played on or directed club teams supported their female relatives' desire to play (Ocampo 8). Interest was enough to send a women's national team to Venezuela in 1966, where the Colombians defeated their hosts, 2–1. Venezuelan women themselves may have been inspired by a tournament hosted at the University of Caracas in May 1960, that pit two teams from Costa Rica against two from England (Pérez).

In the Rio de la Plata women played soccer as well. Women's soccer in Uruguay experienced a minor flowering in the early 1970s with the development of the Amateur Association of Women's Football (AAFF). The league formed in 1971 and had disbanded by 1976, but over the course of its six-year existence, eighteen teams played at one point or another ("Nacional conoce a sus rivales"). By 1971 women's soccer was popular in the provinces as well: six women's teams from in and around the city of Paysandú organized a league that, famously, sent one of its players—Claudina Vidal—to a local men's team. Though she never played an official match with the team, Vidal became a minor international sensation when the British Broadcasting Corporation aired a 12-minute television story on her. Play continued around the country after the league disbanded, with women's clubs playing "friendly" matches against one another ("El operativo Claudina). In Argentina reports of women's soccer matches appeared in the newspaper *Clarín* as early as 1964. An Argentine national team traveled to Peru to play an international match in 1970, hosted by the Mexican national team, and finished third at the Women's World Championship held in Mexico in 1971 (*Mundo Deportivo*; "Mundial").

Mexico, in fact, likely had the most fully developed women's soccer in the region. There, as elsewhere, women's soccer developed in waves beginning in the 1950s. According to scattered reports in the magazines

Afición and *Esto* from Mexico City, women played soccer as early as the 1950s in the Distrito Federal. By 1969 Liga América held Mexico's first women's championship, boasting 17 teams in and around Mexico City. The liga played 60-minute games on a dirt field. In 1970 the Mexican Association of Women's Football was created to oversee the sport, a second league formed, and the Mexican women's national team finished third at the first Women's World Championship in Italy. By 1971 *fútbol femenil* reached its peak, as more than 1,000 women's soccer teams played throughout the country, and Mexico hosted the second Women's World Championship in 1971 (Carreño Martinez 105). Nearly 110,000 people packed into the Estadio Azteca in Mexico City to watch Mexico and Denmark contest the finals, which Denmark won 3–0.

Top three finishes in 1970 and 1971 brought spectators, press, and notoriety to women's soccer in Mexico, but did not bring stability. After 1971, women's soccer receded to the margins, with no support from the Mexican Federation. While girls and women continued to play, many observers saw the women's games as spectacles rather than sporting events. The women's league that survived—the "liga de la Cabeza de Juárez"—played on a "dirt and rock filled field" and relied on volunteer support and word of mouth until official support began in the 1980s. The same was true throughout Latin America: while women and girls played soccer, the sport's presence was either ignored or actively suppressed.

1991–Present

In the aftermath of the second Women's World Cup in 1995, FIFA declared that the future of soccer was feminine. Though it took a number of years for the organization to begin developing the women's game in a systematic way, there can be little doubt that FIFA has succeeded in raising the profile of women's soccer over the past 15 years. In that time, FIFA has supported women's football in a variety of ways: it has sponsored training seminars for coaches and referees; helped establish women's sections in member associations; and opened up greater opportunities for women and girls to play. While the number of women players prior to the turn of the twenty-first century is difficult to ascertain, the sport has grown substantially since 2000. Just within the five years from 2006 to 2011, the number of female soccer players has increased rapidly, from 26 million to more than 29 million, and the growth rate of women's soccer has outstripped that of men's over the past decade (Fahmy).

Latin America represents a substantial part of that growth. In 2006, FIFA reported that 10 percent of all players in the world were female, but in much of Latin America the percentage of woman players exceeded the world average: 15 percent of players in Mexico, 14 percent in Honduras,

11 percent in Brazil, and nearly 17 percent in Ecuador. These numbers compared favorably to most other countries in the world: only in Scandinavian countries and the United States did women and girls play at a higher rate. But growing numbers of female players has not translated into institutional support uniformly across the region: in 2010, 15 percent of all soccer players in Paraguay were female yet FIFA noted that the women's section of the Paraguayan Federation was inactive (FIFA, *Big Count*). Indeed, in much of Latin America, even with FIFA's prodding the women's game receives scarce resources and falls prey to lack of interest.

Nevertheless, national associations are now required to fund women's soccer out of the development money provided by FIFA. Since 2004, a percentage of the money that FIFA provides to member associations as part of its Financial Assistance Program (FAP) has been earmarked for women's soccer (FIFA Circular 1246). This amounts to FIFA setting aside approximately 10 million dollars per year for the development of women's soccer.

The strength of FIFA's commitment, however, can be questioned. First, FIFA has no way of enforcing the FAP requirement. Though its regulations state that if associations fail to meet a 15 percent threshold for women's soccer in a given year, they need to spend 30 percent on women's soccer the following year, there is neither an enforcement protocol nor a threat of FAP funds being withheld for failure to fund women's soccer. Of greater concern, however, may be FIFA's own inconsistent use of minimum expenditures on women's soccer. Twice after the 2010 World Cup in South Africa—on July 9, 2010, and January 21, 2011—FIFA provided additional "one-off FAP bonus" payments. Over this 18-month period FIFA agreed to pay out an extra $550,000 per association in Financial Assistance Program money. However, while most FAP regulations applied to these bonuses, the requirement to spend 15 percent on women's soccer did not. In other words, FIFA could have required an extra $21.7 million to be spent worldwide on women's soccer, but opted not to (FIFA Circulars 1232 and 1254). Nevertheless, if FIFA's support for the women's game has been less than complete, it has helped create new levels of institutionalization.

In Mexico, for example, FIFA support has led to substantial growth of the sport at the local level and of the women's national team—*el Tri Femenil*. In 1990, and again in 1994, the FMF decided to "throw a national team together" for the World Cup Qualifiers, both times finishing behind the United States and Canada. By 1997, the Mexican federation decided to develop an administrative structure for the women's game. Instead of placing the women's team under the umbrella of all the other national teams (Men's, Under-17, and Under-20), however, the

FMF relegated women's soccer to the Amateur Division. This meant that women's soccer received fewer resources than any of the men's national teams and often less than amateur leagues. Even when the Mexican women's national team qualified for World Cup 1999 in the United States, the Director of National Teams said "the Women's National Team is the last priority when it comes to national teams." Indeed, to prepare for the World Cup that year, the women's team received $70,000 (Rodebaugh).

As with administrative support, so too with financial backing and facilities. For years, instead of training at the Centro de Alto Rendimiento, where the other Mexican national teams (including the Under-17 boys) trained, the Mexican women's team trained at a rudimentary facility based high in the mountains outside of Mexico City. The women's facility had one shower and poor fields. The team borrowed practice uniforms from the men's team, which were ill-fitting, and used the previous year's men's uniforms in the run to the Women's World Cup in 1999. The jerseys still had the names of the old wearer still visible on the back. The FMF had few expectations for the women's team, had no oversight over the way that funds were administered, and never evaluated the team's performance. Unlike men's teams, which had intensive training camps leading up to tournaments and debriefing afterward, the women had little pre-tournament preparation and no follow-up afterward (Rodebaugh).

Recently, however, the situation has changed. In 2009 the Mexican Soccer Federation reorganized and the Mexican Women's team came under the control of the National Team director. This has meant a lot: regular uniforms sized for women, training kits, a monthly stipend for some—though not all—of the players, and a per diem during tournaments. Training is now held at the national training center, and the women's national team budget is around $1 million annually. This top-down interest has trickled through the system. Age-range teams for girls now go from Under-17 to Under-20, and FMF has hired a full-time coordinator for women's football. In fact, women's soccer in Mexico is much stronger than it has been, with the possibility of women and girls playing in recreational/amateur leagues around Mexico City 5–6 times per week (Rodebaugh). Results have showed on the field as well. In 2011 Mexico qualified for the Women's World Cup for the first time since 1999, beating the United States in a crucial match, and its Under-17 and Under-20 teams have also qualified for major tournaments.

Mexico is not the only Latin American team that has shown marked development since the infusion of FIFA support. The Colombian women's team has become something of a regular in world tournaments, qualifying for the 2008 and 2012 installments of the Under-17 World Cup, as well as the 2010 Under 20 and 2011 Women's World Cup in

Germany. Costa Rica and Chile have supported their women's teams more systematically, and Argentina too has begun to invest in women's soccer, visible in its qualification for multiple Under-17 and Under-20 finals. But nowhere in Latin America is women's soccer as successful as in Brazil.

Once the sport became legal again in Brazil in 1975, leagues began developing. By 1987 over 2,000 teams with 40,000 women played the sport (Moreira). Since the Brazilian Football Confederation had no women's division, it sent the best team from the women's leagues, Radar, to represent Brazil at FIFA's 1988 Women's Invitational. Radar would again make up the majority of the national team at the inaugural Women's World Cup in 1991. Between 1999 and 2003 the national soccer federation provided a minimum of support to the Brazilian women's team. As in Mexico the team was formed just prior to tournaments, with little planning and no real institutionalization of the sport. Training facilities, stipends, and coaching for the women's team did not receive high priority. This situation began to change in 2004. According to the then-captain of the Brazilian women's team Juliana Cabral, the naming of Rene Simões as coach had a major impact on changing perceptions of women's soccer. As a former player and successful men's coach—he led Jamaica to its only World Cup berth in 1998—Simões, Cabral claims, brought a new attitude to the federation. Among other things, he demanded that the national federation treat the women's team seriously (Cabral). This is not to diminish the importance of the women players, who had committed years of their lives to the sport they loved. However—and this remains the case today—men continue to dominate national soccer institutions. Unfortunate though it may be, only after a successful men's coach took the women's game seriously did attitudes begin to change at the sport's upper echelons in Brazil. After 2004 the Brazilian Soccer Confederation (CBF) took over control of women's leagues around the country in order to further develop the game and held regular training camps for the women's team for the first time. In part as a result of better training and conditioning, Brazil won silver medals in both the 2007 World Cup and the 2008 Olympics. In recent years, however, there appears to have been a reversion to form: while the Brazilian national team continues to dominate in South America, the CBF has cut back on training and resources for the women's team. In 2011 the team held few practices prior to the World Cup, were among the last teams to arrive in Germany, and their lack of fitness showed throughout the tournament as they lost in the quarterfinals. Again in the 2012 London Olympics, an underprepared Brazil—wearing men's national team jerseys—exited at the quarterfinal stage.

What should be clear through this brief archaeology of women's soccer is that women have been involved in the game from the early twentieth century. FIFA, in short, did not create women's soccer overnight in Latin America (or anywhere else in the world). That women's soccer existed in any form in the late twentieth century speaks to the tenacity of women who played the sport in the early and mid-1900s. These women, often against the wishes of family and friends, and almost always contravening attempts by national associations, governments, public health experts, and the international governing body itself, fought to create space to play the game that they loved—the national game. The barriers placed in front of women's soccer all related, in one way or another, to the idea that women who played soccer transgressed national gender norms, and thus presented a threat to the nation.

Destructive Nuclei of the Nation?

Almost from the moment that women began playing soccer in Latin America, three interrelated perceptions about both the sport and women have generated opposition to the game: soccer was an inherently masculine sport; women who played became more muscular and aggressive (more "masculine"); and the sport could damage women's fertility and morality. Underlying these concerns was the often—but not always— unstated premise that soccer defined both masculinity and nations. As such, opposition to women's soccer related not only to the sport itself, but to the meaning of the sport and its role in constructing both nations and masculinity.

Soccer arrived in Latin America in the context of rapid changes that swept the region in the late nineteenth century. As states consolidated and economies modernized, regional leaders turned to Europe for political, economic, financial, and social models. In these models, attitudes about gender were of critical importance. According to George Mosse, discourses of masculinity played a "determining role" in the construction of new nations in the late nineteenth and early twentieth centuries. Nationalist thinkers "adopted the masculine stereotype as one of the means of national representation" (Mosse 7–9). In other words, the nation itself was defined along masculine lines. At the same time, however, the construction of new nations heralded changes in social structures as well, including those related to gender. Michael Messner termed the era from 1870 to 1920 as one of "crisis" for masculinity, marked by "drastic changes in work and family" (199). Throughout Latin America in the early twentieth century, women agitated for increased rights both inside and outside the home. From expanding educational opportunities to changing divorce laws and efforts to attain suffrage, women actively sought new roles in society. In short, at the same time that soccer arrived in the region, debates flared about the proper place of men and women in society.

Amidst these discussions, sports became a prominent way to define both masculinity and the nation. For Eric Hobsbawm, the two reinforced each other. As modern states developed, the abstract notion of the nation crystallized on the field: "the imagined community of millions," he wrote, "appears more real as eleven players." As the sporting expression of the nation, soccer was "uniquely effective" at stimulating nationalist sentiment "among males" (Hobsbawm 143). Eduardo Archetti argued that as Argentina industrialized and incorporated massive waves of new immigrants, finding new forms of national cohesion became paramount. Soccer, according to Archetti, became "a powerful, masculine expression of national capabilities and potentialities." Soccer games served as sites where "'national masculine' identity" could be displayed (*Masculinities* 15 and 42). Moreover, the sport served to "delimit fields [...] of social organization" (Archetti, *Fútbol y ethos* 5). In Brazil, Marcos Alves da Souza argued that soccer is not only a game but in fact a "confrontation between two communities *represented by men*" (47; emphasis mine).

But soccer did not only represent the male nation, it also played a major role in teaching boys to be men. Quoting Umberto Eco, da Souza argues that "soccer is for men what playing mother is for girls: a pedagogical game that teaches one's appropriate place" (47). Soccer is, in other words, a rite of initiation into masculinity. In Argentina in the early twentieth century, soccer's "practice, discourse [...] and representation was constituted as a masculine world," according to Gabriela Binello and her colleagues (34). So too in Chile, where Brenda Elsey highlighted the belief that soccer helped develop "masculine traits including independence, initiative, and vigor," all of which Chileans saw as "essential qualities for the ideal citizen" (94). The values expressed by the game were "in principle, values of a masculine world," and so playing soccer imparted important lessons about gender (Vogel 98). Because soccer served as both a representation of the masculine nation and a training ground for young men and boys, the women's game, by its very existence, threatened the foundation of the sport, the nation, and gender norms.

Starting in the early 1900s, interest in sports for men and women grew the world over as the belief that a healthy body led to a healthy mind, good citizenship, higher moral values, and greater intelligence came into vogue. Doctors, journalists, eugenicists, and progressive moralizers lobbied governments to include physical education in primary and secondary school. There was little agreement, however, as to whether and how girls should participate in sports and games. For some, strenuous activities and competitive games like soccer, basketball, cricket, or volleyball could be beneficial to young girls' development. For others, even mild competition and physical stress could damage girls' "fragile" constitution. Soccer, as a "rough" sport, represented a danger to women's health—and by extension national health. Indeed, it was seen by some as a threat to the construction of a healthy nation.

In Brazil, concerns over public health reached a fevered pitch in the 1940s as a result of the short-lived Paulista women's league. On April 25, 1940, José Fuzeira wrote to Brazilian president Getúlio Vargas about a "calamity" threatening the nation: girls and young women playing soccer. The danger, according to Fuzeira, stemmed from the inherent violence in the game that could "seriously damage the physiological equilibrium" of women's "organic functions." Soccer, in other words, endangered girls' and women's reproductive capabilities. More, the girls would become "prisoners of a depressive mentality" leading to "rude and extravagant exhibitionism." With over 10 teams in Rio, and others in Belo Horizonte and São Paulo, Fuzeira worried that within a year over 200 teams would form "destructive nuclei for [...] future mothers" (quoted in Franzini 319–320). Fuzeira's logic paralleled that of experts throughout the country. Doctor Leite de Castro, for example, argued in *A Gazeta Esportiva* that soccer brought with it "defects and vices," including "general alterations to women's delicate physiology" that could "seriously compromise" their reproductive capacity (quoted in Franzini 321). Dr. Humberto Ballariny, a specialist in physical education, concurred. He suggested that soccer would cause "pelvic damage [...] harmful to the female organs." In other words, under no situations should girls and women be allowed to play soccer, as they risked their potential as mothers (Ballariny 36).

Vargas's reaction was swift. In May he charged his minister of health with protecting women from football. "There exists an interminable bibliography," noted a memo from the subdivision on specialized medicine, suggesting that soccer "caused trauma that can affect particularly important and delicate female organs" (quoted in Franzini 320). Within a year, women's soccer was banned throughout the nation. Decree Law 3199, passed on April 14, 1941, limited women in the sports that they could play. Soccer headed the list of the sports, which included judo and rugby, considered incompatible with the nature of women. After the ban passed, *A Gazeta Esportiva* printed an article in support of the decision, suggesting that women's soccer "could seriously compromise the reproductive organs" ("Uma opinião autorizada, 10). The ban would last 35 years.[1] Similar concerns in Costa Rica led to a senate hearing on the sport, which ultimately deemed women's soccer to be safe (Zeledon Cartín 34).

While childbearing likely caused the most official concern, women's soccer faced opposition for other reasons as well. Many would have agreed with the Costa Rican commentator who wrote that soccer was of "masculine ink." The sport, reputedly, would masculinize women by giving them overly muscled legs and an aggressive demeanor. Since

the sport was based on vigor and action, and women's nature was supposedly "harmonious" and soft, the sport went against biology and
nature. "When a woman attempts to invade a male field," wrote one
Argentine commentator, "it is an irregularity, it is not natural and it is
shocking." Women who played soccer, he continued, "appear [...] to
be neither male nor female" ("Notas de la semana"). For Brazilian public health experts, the sport was "anti-aesthetic" for girls and women.
It purportedly caused women to become overly muscular, develop
"deformed knees," and occasioned a loss of feminine "harmony." So
too women's soccer brought about a certain aggressiveness that, in
the mind of many, was "incompatible" with the "female character"
(Ballariny 36 and 52).

Concern about women's soccer centered around more than biology
and appearance. For some, women's soccer represented a potential risk to
national morals. The Colombian government, for example, stopped the
Costa Rican team Deportivo Femenino upon entry in 1951, causing the
team to cancel exhibition games. The reason: the team's uniforms revealed
too much of the young women's legs and thus violated Colombia's morality laws (*Radar Deportivo*, October 6, 1951; *El Espectador*, September 29,
1951; Zeledon Cartín 100–103). So too in Brazil, according to Silvana
Vilodre Goellner, the elite feared that the "exhibition and spectacularization" of girls' and young women's bodies would "undermine feminine
morals" ("Mulheres" 145).

Continuing Challenges

FIFA's support for the women's game has had complex and sometimes
contradictory outcomes. It cannot be denied, as mentioned earlier, that
official support for women's soccer has led to increased avenues for women
to play the game. Yet, FIFA backing women's soccer has not diminished
the cultural barriers to girls playing the game. Indeed, women's soccer
remains marginalized and stigmatized despite its growth in the last two
decades. And, to a certain extent, FIFA itself is responsible, given the way
that it markets the women's game. Women soccer players must constantly
defend not only their right to play, but continue to face prejudices based
around the same issues that justified the suppression of the sport in earlier eras. From the moment that women began playing soccer, they had
to contend with the idea that playing the game would somehow make
them more masculine.

Concerns over the "masculinizing" effects of the game retain their
grip on many in the region. Players still face the assumption that they
will get "strong legs," and begin to "develop into a male." In Mexico,
according to former Under-20 Women's National Team coach Andrea

Rodebaugh, "women are supposed to be feminine, soft, sweet […] look pretty and sexy," all traits that—according to opponents of the sport— soccer players lack (Rodebaugh). Since the early twentieth century women have contended with societal norms that dictate delicacy and fragility as ideals for feminine beauty. These attitudes have led parents to punish their daughters for playing the game. So it is that Maribel Dominguez, one of Mexico's foremost women players, began her soccer life as Mario Dominguez, cutting her hair short so that she would be able to pass as a boy. Her mother feared that her daughter would be "masculinized" and so would hide her soccer shoes to make it more difficult for her to play ("Estoy casada con el balón"). So too in Brazil, girls continue to struggle to play soccer. One informant recounted to Brazilian psychologist Jorge Knijnik that she regularly fought with her brothers and father over her desire to play soccer. Others reported to Knijnik that they faced a good deal of opposition from their families, even if they did not admit to facing physical abuse. "Dulce" noted that her mother begged her to find another sport. So too Prentinha, who played in four World Cups and four Olympic Games for Brazil, was beaten by both her mother and brothers for playing soccer (Knijnik 148 and 113).

Alongside the fear that women will become more masculine through playing soccer runs the fear that women who play will become lesbian. "You can't talk about women's soccer," according to one former player, "without this [the issue of sexuality] coming up." Women who play soccer, she says, are considered "male-like, tomboys, dykes, lesbians, it is inevitable. It always comes up!" (Rodebaugh). This attitude has existed in the region at least since 1970, when the official position of the Paraguayan government, in its representation to FIFA, held that "women who enjoyed playing soccer […] went against nature" ("Deportes de aquí y de allá"). The idea that homosexuality is common in women's soccer continues to inhibit the growth of women's soccer in the region. While this stereotype likely exists throughout the world, in Latin America it remains strong enough to dissuade girls from playing the game. In discussing her own history in soccer, one former Mexican women's player noted that she faced the same attitudes in Mexico in the 1990s that she had faced growing up playing soccer in the 1970s in the United States: women who played were "either tomboys or lesbians." So too Ana, a 23-year-old Brazilian soccer player, recalled facing prejudice because people believed that "in football there are many lesbians, so they think that if you play you are one of them" (Knijnik 451).

The resilience of stereotypes about soccer, sexuality, and beauty has meant that girls still face resistance when trying to play the game, both personally and societally. And increased FIFA support has done little to help overcome these barriers. In fact, since FIFA began to support women's soccer, there have been many efforts—perhaps misguided—to shed the masculine image of women's soccer, in Latin America and around the world. While men players are judged solely on their skill, women players cannot only play well: they must also "look pretty" (Rodebaugh). In 2001, for example, the São Paulo Football Federation and Pelé Sports and Marketing decided to market the Paulista women's championship by highlighting the "beauty and sensuality of the women players to attract a male public." This meant, among other things, that the uniforms included short shorts. In 2004, Sepp Blatter suggested that women's soccer would be more popular if the players wore "more feminine clothes" such as "tighter shorts." Since women players were "pretty," he argued, a "more female aesthetic" would benefit the sport (Christenson and Kelso). For Blatter, in other words, sexualizing female athletes promised to bring more fans to the sport.

Though public outcry forced Blatter to backtrack, FIFA continues to promote women's soccer based partly on image. A 2010 article about women's soccer on FIFA's website emphasized the glamour, sex, and femininity of the players. The article highlighted semi-nude photo shoots, women players' fetish for shoes and clothes, and the use of nail polish to draw attention to themselves. These images all conform to dominant male ideas about women and women's sexuality, which tend to objectify women. According to FIFA, for example, Chinese national team player Han Duan spends "a large portion of her income on beauty care." This would no doubt please the Chinese Federation, whose vice-president suggested that women players "draw attention to themselves through their beauty" ("Eye-Catching Girls Enhance Allure"). In other words, FIFA contends that reinforcing dominant social stereotypes about "proper womanhood" is an important way to popularize the women's sport.

FIFA continues to sexualize female soccer players despite research that suggests that "a major consequence of the media's tendency to sexualize" women athletes is to "suppress interest in, not to mention respect for, women's sports" (Kane). Indeed, in a 2011 study, Mary Jo Kane and Heather D. Maxwell set out to "empirically address [...] the [...] assumption that 'sex sells'" and found conclusively that it does not. Instead, they found that women's sports—and women athletes—are taken more seriously when they are portrayed as athletes rather than either "wholesome 'girls next door' or 'sexy babes.'" The authors argue that sexualizing female athletes "trivializes their efforts and [...] suppresses interest" in women's sports (Kane and Maxwell 205 and 214). So too Daniels and Wartena found that "sexualized images of female athletes [...] may contribute to the devaluation of female athleticism" (Daniels and Wartena

576), while Knight and Giuliano show that sports coverage that focuses on attractiveness trivializes athletic prowess (Knight and Giuliano 227). In other words, FIFA's efforts to "promote" women's soccer may in fact be undercutting it as a sport to be taken seriously.

Conclusion

Throughout Latin America, from soccer powers like Brazil to nations like Costa Rica, women's involvement in soccer dates almost to its introduction to the region. While women's soccer experienced a brief period of semi-respectability, for much of the last century women's soccer survived on the margins, played on makeshift fields in the face of national scorn. But the grassroots nature of the sport helped it to keep going until it received recognition from the sport's governing bodies. In the past 20 years, top-down support has brought with it greater stability and respectability for women players. So too attitudes about women and girls who play soccer have evolved slightly since the early days, when the sport was considered antipatriotic and threatening to the future of the nation. No longer do Latin Americans see soccer as risking potential motherhood or causing cancer. However, dominant patriarchal ideas about gender and "appropriate" womanhood persist. In much of the region teenage girls still face the stigma that playing soccer will "masculinize" them. So too the perception remains that women's soccer—more than basketball or volleyball, also popular sports for girls—is a fertile "recruiting ground" for lesbians.

The resilience of these ideas has made it hard for women's soccer to gain ground in Latin America and highlight the challenges faced by the sport. While FIFA has attempted to rectify this by funneling money and training to regional and national governing bodies, this support—while welcome—nevertheless has done little to change entrenched attitudes. Indeed, some of the tactics used by FIFA and others to promote the sport do more to marginalize the game. By promoting dominant images of beauty and womanhood, which effectively sexualize the sport, soccer's governing body denigrates female athletes and the sport that they play. Until the stereotypes about women's soccer, both official and unofficial, are erased, women's soccer will continue to be a sideline—a spectacle of sorts—within the soccer world of Latin America.

Note

1. There is some debate about when the ban ended. Ludmila Mourão and Marcia Morel say 1976 while an earlier article by Mourão and Sebastião Votre says 1979.

BIBLIOGRAPHY

CORRESPONDENCE

Pérez, Eliezer. Personal Correspondence. July 25, 2010.
Rodebaugh, Andrea. Personal Correspondence. March 11, 2010.

PERIODICALS

El Espectador. September 29, 1951. Print.
El Gráfico. 1920–1930. Print.
El Mundo Deportivo. September 18, 1971, 4. Print.
"Aquí está el reto." *La Nación.* July 29, 1959. Print.
"Ayer Tarde Llegaron a Bogotá los Equipos Ingleses de Fútbol Femenino." *El Tiempo.* June 23, 1960. Print.
"Deportes de aquí y de allá." *La Nación.* October 4, 1970. Print.
"El operativo Claudina: La historia de una jugadora de fútbol." *MDZ Online.* March 11, 2008. Web. May 10, 2012.
"Estoy casada con el balón." *BBCMundo.com.* September 9, 2005. Web. April 3, 2010.
"Eye-Catching Girls Enhance Allure." *FIFA.com.* April 14, 2010. Web. May 4, 2011.
"Mundial (Women), 1971." *RSSSF.com.* Web.
"Nacional conoce a sus rivales." *Deportes24.com.* Web. November 1, 2011.
"Notas de la semana." *El Grafico.* July 2, 1921. Print.
"Report of the Joint Committee on the Physical Education of Girls." *The Lancet.* August 12, 1922. Print.
"Uma opinião autorizada: não é no futebol que a juventude feminina se aperfeiçoará." *A Gazeta Esportiva.* June 29, 1940. Print.
"USA Extend Lead, Brazil Slip." FIFA.COM. June 1, 2012. Web. August 12, 2012.
Ballariny, Humberto. "Por que a mulher não deve praticar o futebol." *Educação Física* 49. December 1940. Print.
Cabral, Juliana. Interview. *Universidade do Futebol.* August 31, 2012. Web.
Chantecler. "Comentarios risueños sobre football." *El Gráfico.* September 25, 1926. Print.
FIFA Circular No. 1232. July 9, 2010. Print.
FIFA Circular No. 1246. November 29, 2010. Print.
FIFA Circular No. 1254. January 21, 2011. Print.
Ocampo, Harvey. "Fútbol Femenino en Bogotá." *El Tiempo.* September 1, 1969. Print.
pandeportes.gob.pa/index.html#. Web. July 14, 2010.
Radar Deportivo. October 6, 1951. Print.

BOOKS, THESES, AND JOURNALS

Archetti, Eduardo. *Fútbol y Ethos.* Buenos Aires: FLACSO, 1984. Print.
———. *Masculinities: Football, Polo and the Tango in Argentina.* New York: Berg, 1999. Print.

Ballesteros, Frank, and Hans Schoggl. "Panama, List of Women Champions." *RSSSF.com*. Web. March 10, 2011.

Bestard, Miguel Angel. *Paraguay, un siglo de fútbol*. Asunción: Liga Paraguaya de Fútbol, 1981. Print.

Binello, Gabriela, Mariana Conde, Analía Martínez, and María Graciela Rodríguez. "Mujeres y fútbol: ¿territorio conquistado o a conquistar?" *Peligro del gol: Estudios sobre deporte y sociedad en América Latina*. Edited by Pablo Alabarces. Buenos Aires: CLACSO, 2000. Print.

Carreño Martinez, Maritza. "Fútbol femenil en Mexico, 1969–1971." MA thesis. Universidad Autonoma de Mexico, 2006. Print.

Christenson, Marcus, and Paul Kelso. "Soccer Chief's Plan to Boost Women's Game? Hotpants." *The Guardian*. January 16, 2004. Web. April 2, 2010.

Christopherson, Neal, Michelle Janning, and Eileen Diaz McConnel. "Two Kicks Forward, One Kick Back: A Content Analysis of Media Discourses on the 1999 Women's World Cup Soccer Championship." *Sociology of Sport Journal* 19 (2002): 170–188. Print.

da Souza, Marcos Alves. "'A Nação em chuterias': Raça e masculinidade no futebol brasileiro." MA thesis. University of Brasilia, 1996. Print.

de Souza Junior, Osmar Moreira, and Heloisa Helena Baldy dos Reis. "Discursos hegemônicos es representações sociais do futebol feminino no Brasil." Presentation. 36th Annual meeting of Associação Nacional de Pós-Graduação e Pesquisa em Ciências Sociais. October 21–25, 2012. Print.

Daniels, Elizabeth, and Heather Wartena. "Athlete or Sex Symbol: What Boys Think of Media Representations of Female Athletes." *Sex Roles* 65:7/8 (October 2011): 566–579. Print

Elsey, Brenda. *Citizens and Sportsmen: Fútbol and Politics in Twentieth Century Chile*. Austin: University of Texas Press, 2011. Print.

Fahmy, Mustapha. "Increase Participation and Competitions." FIFA. 5th FIFA Women's Football Symposium. July 15–17, 2011. Print.

Ferreira Campos, Priscila Augusta. "Mulheres tocedores do Cruzeiro Esporte Clube presentes no Mineirão." MA thesis. Federal University of Minas Gerais, 2010. Print.

FIFA. *Big Count 2006: Statistical Summary Report by Association*. Zurich: Fédération Internationale de Football Association, 2007. Print.

———. *Health and Fitness for the Female Football Player: A Guide for Coaches and Players*. Zurich: Fédération Internationale de Football Association, 2007. Print.

———. Goal Project Fact Sheet-Colombia, 2009. Web.

———. *FIFA U-20 World Cup Colombia 2011, Statistical Kit: Event Edition*. July 8, 2011. Print.

Filho, Mario. *O Negro no Futebol Brasileiro*. Rio de Janeiro: Civilização Brasileira, 1964. Print.

Franzini, Fabio. "Futebol é coisa para macho? Pequeno esboço para uma história das mulheres no país do futebol." *Revista Brasileira de História* 25:50 (December 2005): 315–328. Print.

Goellner, Silvana Vilodre. "Bela, maternal e feminina: imagens da mulher na Revista *Educação Physica*." PhD diss. Universidade Estadual de Campinas, 1999. Print.

Goellner, Silvana Vilodre. "Mulheres e futebol no Brasil: entre sombras e visibilidades." *Revista Brasileira de Educação Física e Esporte* 19:2 (April/June 2005): 143–151. Print.

———. "'As mulheres fortes são aquelas que fazem uma raça forte': Esporte, Eugenia e nacionalismo no Brasil no início do século XX." *Revista de História do Esporte* 1:1 (June 2008): 1–28. Print.

Hobsbawm, Eric. *Nations and Nationalism since 1780: Programme, Myth, Reality.* Cambridge, UK: Cambridge University Press, 2012. Print.

Kane, Mary Jo. "Sex Sells Sex, Not Women's Sports." *The Nation.* August 15–22, 2011. Web. October 29, 2012.

Kane, Mary Jo, and Heather D. Maxwell. "Expanding the Boundaries of Sport and Media Research." *Journal of Sport Management* 25 (2011): 202–216. Print.

Knight, Jennifer L., and Traci A. Giuliano. "She's a 'Looker,' He's a Laker: The Consequences of Gender-Stereotypical Portrayals of Male and Female Athletes by the Print Media." *Sex Roles* 45:3/4 (August 2001): 217–229. Print.

Knijnik, Jorge. "Femininos e Masculinos no Futebol Brasileiro." PhD diss. University of São Paulo, 2006. Print.

Lessa de Moura, Erribero José. "As Relações entre Lazer, Futebol, e Gênero." MA thesis. Universidade Estadual de Campinas, 2003. Print.

Lotina, Juan A., and Hernández Luján. "El fútbol femenino en Cuba en cuatro etapas." *CubAhora.* July 13, 2010. Print.

Marín Méndez, Edgardo. *Centenario: historia total del fútbol chileno, 1895–1995.* Santiago de Chile: Editores y Consultores REI. Print.

Martínez Vega, Carlos Alberto. "Federación Panameña de Fútbol celebra 70 años." Web. March 10, 2011.

Méndez, Carolina. "¡Futboleras!" *La Nación.* August 27, 1999. Web. September 10, 2012.

Messner, Michael A. "Sports and Male Domination: The Female Athlete as Contested Ideological Terrain." *Sociology of Sport Journal* 5 (1988): 197–211. Print.

Moreira, Ramon Missias. "A mulher no futebol brasileiro: uma ampla visão." *efedeportes.com* 13:120 (May 2008). Web.

Mosse, George L. *The Image of Man: The Creation of Modern Masculinity.* New York: Oxford University Press, 1996. Print.

Mourão, Ludmila, and Marcia Morel. "As Narrativas sobre o Futebol Feminino." *Revista Brasileiro de Ciência do Esporte* 26:2 (January 2005): 73–86. Print.

Mourão, Ludmila, and Sebastião Votre. "Women's Football in Brazil: Progress and Problems." *Soccer, Women, Sexual Liberation: Kicking off a New Era.* Edited by Fan Fong and J. A. Mangan. London and Portland, OR: Frank Cass 2004. Print.

Rigo, Luiz Carlos, Flávia Garcia Guidotti, Larissa Zanetti Thiel, and Marcela Amaral. "Notas acerca do futebol feminino pelotense em 1950: um estudo genealógico." *Revista Brasileira de Ciências do Esporte* 29:3 (May 2008): 173–188. Print.

Rojas, Moya. "Del fútbol femenino en Golfito." *La Nación.* February 19, 1952. Print.

Vogel, Arno. "O Momento Feliz. Reflexões sobre o futebol e o ethos nacional." *Universo do Futebol: Esporte e Sociedade Brasileira.* Edited by Roberto da Matta. Rio de Janeiro: Edições Piankotheke, 1982. Print.

Zeledon Cartín, Elias. *Deportivo Femenino Costa Rica, F.C.: Primer equipo de fútbol femenino del mundo.* San José: Ministerio de Cultura, Juventud y Deportes, 1999. Print.

CHAPTER 3

(F)Utopias: The Nationalist Uses of Soccer in Costa Rica

Sergio Villena Fiengo

Translated by Katherine Clarkson

In 1921 the first national soccer team was established in Costa Rica with the objective of participating in the Centennial Games, to be held in Guatemala to commemorate the first century of Central American independence. The undefeated triumph of the adult men's team, *la Sele* (short for "Selección Nacional" or "national men's team"), transformed soccer into a "patriotic game", as from then on the discursive construction of Costa Rican national identity would be fundamentally linked to the continual sequence of "nationalist dramas" staged by this representative of the nation-team. With the approach of the second centennial celebration of Central American independence, the link between nationalism and soccer remains undeniably valid, although as time passes it has acquired new nuances, modalities, and uses.

In this article we study the discursive developments in nationalist narratives associated with soccer, contrasting four specific moments: (1) the arrival of soccer to the country; (2) the first international victory and the resultant profound nationalization of Costa Rican soccer; (3) the first and most successful participation in the World Cup; and finally; (4) the qualification of the Sele for the World Cup a second time. Our hypothesis is that in national history, each of these moments was lived as an "event" (Badiou) or a "liminal moment" (Turner) in which the narratives of national identity turned out to be insufficient to account for what had occurred, making it necessary for the proclamation of a new "truth" about what it means to be "Costa Rican."[1]

ORIGINS: COFFEE FOR SOCCER

According to the sports journalist Rodrigo Calvo, beginning in the third quarter of the nineteenth century, a group of young men "from the best families of high society, working in the cultivation and exportation of coffee," including a future president of the republic, returned from England where they had been studying, bringing a copy of the rules book, as well as soccer balls and other equipment. On October 8, 1876, in La Sabana urban park, these young men, accompanied by members of the British colony who had settled in Costa Rica to do business and participate in the construction of a trolley system in San José, got together "with their strange and imported attire" to, for the first time in the country, kick a ball (*La Nación* 6/10/2001, sports section: 38–A).

The importation of soccer formed part of the desire for a mimetic, pro-European modernization perpetrated by the burgeoning coffee-growing elite, who not only constructed their own monument—the National Theater—but also promoted the establishment of new forms of entertainment, such as the development of a newer, more physical culture, in which exercise and sports would occupy a prominent place. Historical research registers the first journalistic account of a soccer game on July 4, 1899, when *La Opinión* published a story that undoubtedly accounts for the participation of wealthy social sectors in this practice from its beginnings, for the hygienic and moralistic context that marks that era, and also for the adoption of Anglicisms in the local jargon: "On Sunday we were watching [the soccer game] in La Sabana, put on by the people of our high society. It appears a fairly hygienic and rather fun distraction. **Very Well!!**"[2] (*La Opinión*, 4/7/1899: 3, qtd in Urbina 77).

The reception of soccer, embraced with enthusiasm by the erudite sectors of society—who considered it a positive vector of social and cultural change—wasn't immune to the polemic of civilization and barbarity that was being disputed in Latin America. In this context, where the slogan was "educate and populate," soccer seemed a valuable instrument to reeducate society and eradicate the "burden" of Hispanic cultural tradition inherited from the colonial era, along with local indigenous traditions seemingly still very embedded among working-class sectors:

> It is time to abandon the ridiculous routine and the tasteless tradition. Our local festivals, as they have been celebrated until now, are no more than a reflection of barbarity or at least of ignorance. These grotesque masquerades, the running of the bulls and sometimes even cows, the manner in which the people amuse themselves wildly under the influence of cane liquor; that happiness manifested in brawls and the savagery of the cacophonous, shrieks, stinking of anise and dark rum; that fever of illicit gambling and limitless abuse, in no way speaks favorably of the culture and morality of the nation. Bring on the carnivals where art radiates, the

delicate festivities, the *beneficial sports* and all that which doesn't evoke the dusty memory of the era of conquest and the life of the uncivilized Indians. (*La República*, 12/21/1899: 2; qtd in Gaitán Urbina 84)

Soccer soon benefited from governmental support and assumed the role of national representation: the first game between *Ticos*—as Costa Ricans are popularly called—and (English) foreigners took place in 1899. The setting was during local celebrations of national independence on September 15. Soon the highest authorities of the country supported the development of soccer as a healthy, physical, and moral practice as demonstrated by the presence of a president on a soccer field for the first time on December 25 of that same year, when those same rivals competed in another game: "To encourage the enjoyment of foot-ball and knowing that *this game develops the vigor of the body while also correcting bad habits* (the President) has offered his support in every sense to the young people who dedicate themselves to such healthy exercise" (*La República*, 12/25/1899; qtd in Urbina 79; emphasis mine).

Nevertheless, the practice of soccer would remain very little uninstitutionalized until 1921 when, after repeated and failed attempts, the National Soccer League—the precursor to the current Costa Rican Federation of Soccer (FEDEFUTBOL, FIFA Affiliated in 1927)—was finally established. Soccer, until recently an exclusively male practice, would celebrate its first national championship that same year, with the participation of seven clubs including its first champion, Herediano Sporting Club prevailing over the "dean of national soccer," the Sport Cataginés Club, founded in 1906. The uninterrupted annual staging of the top tier men's tournaments has transformed soccer into a routine component of the day-to-day life of Costa Ricans, a process that would receive an important impetus with the development of radio broadcasts in the country starting in 1924, followed by television in 1962.

The Nationalization of "Football"

Our traditional villages had a soccer plaza—in front of a church that looked toward the west—around which its vital downtown areas were located: some markets, a school, a political establishment [...] and some houses owned by the political bosses, the businessmen, the teacher, the priest and some of the wealthier neighbors
—Jaime González Dobles, *La patria del tico*, 78, emphasis mine

Soccer was acquiring important civic and political importance, as evidenced by its inclusion in the programs of celebration for national and even religious holidays, both at the local and national levels. On Christmas of 1899 President Rafael Iglesias attended a game between a team "representing" Costa Rica against a team of Englishmen living in the country. In 1903 soccer was incorporated into the civic festivities at the end of the year (cf. Enríquez). And on April 11, 1911, the celebration of the main foundational event of the nation, the Battle of Rivas, included a *match* dedicated to a very distinguished spectator: the president of the republic (cf. Urbina). The civic and political function of soccer would become sacred in the 1920s, when the sport would become institutionally linked to Costa Rican nationalism.

The year 1921 saw the formation of the first national team, which would represent Costa Rica in the first international sporting competition that took place in the region: the Central American Games of the Centenary of Independence, held in Guatemala City. This triumphant debut—they were undefeated champions—initiated a long history of over-the-top nationalistic celebrations of adult men's soccer matches that, via the media, reinforces not only a sense of belonging for Costa Ricans in their country, but also a sense of superiority over other Central American nations. The construction of the "supreme national coliseum," the "National Stadium," inaugurated in 1924 with the first international game occurring in Costa Rica, indicates the importance that this inaugural triumph had for the nationalistic goals of this country.[3]

The national soccer team's activities became a social drama of nationalistic proportions in a public arena of prime importance for the collective imagination of the nation and the invention of national tradition and identity. By speaking about and playing soccer, as stated by a television journalist in 2000, "a nation is constructed." Soccer became a "patriotic game" and la Sele became, in terms of sports, the symbolic arsenal of the nation along with the flag, the coat of arms, the national anthem (political symbols), the Virgin of Angels (a religious symbol), the *guraranthe skinneri* orchid and clay-colored thrush (natural symbols), and the *punto guancasteco* dance and the traditional peasant costume (ethno-folkloric symbols).

Soccer was incorporated into national culture during a period in which, according to historian Steven Palmer, "the Costa Rican state and its intellectuals had acquired the ability to represent, in a coherent and convincing way, the 'imagined political community' that [...] is the nation" (170). The nationalist intelligentsia had managed to configure the essential characteristics of national identity, for instance, by establishing the "National Campaign" of 1856 as a foundational event and designating the "simple and humble peasant" a national hero (170). Both elements, consecrated in the lyrics of the current national anthem composed in 1903 by José María Zeledón, are continually renewed in diverse civic rituals including professional soccer matches, since—in addition to public schools—it is in the stadiums where the national anthem is most often played.

In the process of its dissemination from the elite to the common people, soccer ceased to be considered a "modern" imported practice, acquiring the character of a "national tradition." This produced its discursive articulation in the typically idyllic style of the rural world, the symbolic womb of nationalism: the peasant tradition, constituted as the basis of national identity in the first quarter of the twentieth century. Once incorporated into the "metaphysical ethnic nationalist" imaginary (Jiménez), soccer became a vehicle to promote the updating of idyllic rural morality among the increasingly urbanized masses.

The civic and moral centrality of soccer corresponds with its location in the ceremonial topography. Unlike other countries where the practice of this sport tended to occur in urban periphery spaces, Costa Rican soccer fields often occupied the central square of the villages, surrounded by the local centers of religious, political, economic, and intellectual power, a conclusion supported by the affirmation that "it was in the rural festivals where soccer spread and was popularized" (Soto). This characteristic of rurality that Costa Rican soccer took on would constitute the fundamental base of its nationalization in a profound sense, that is, symbolically: its transformation into a patriotic or meaningful game is based on its connection to the ideology of the rural idyll.

The mainstream adoption of soccer and its incorporation into everyday life, which gave it a central role in the configuration of local identities, was paired with its "domestication" in two ways: it proceeded to make up part of rural life, but at the same time was stripped—at least partially—of its civilizing connotations, as one of the country's first professional philosophers noted. Luis Barahona, in his book *El gran incógnito* ("The great unknown"), elaborates an "internal vision of the Costa Rican peasant," in which soccer plays an important role:

> You could say that soccer is the only thing that attracts our attention [. . .] For kids this game encompasses their pride, their worth, their boundless enthusiasm. Each village has its club and its soccer team, which from time to time plays in the plazas of the neighboring villages. On Sundays, and predominantly on the patron saint's festival day, they organize meetings or **match[e]s'** [. . .] There is nothing that inspires the *concho*[4] as much as this ballgame; not horse racing nor gambling, not even political festivals are able to excite as much as a game well-played, a skilled and clever taunt or a frenzied shot that leaves the goalie stunned by the score that means final defeat. No one speaks about anything else all day, as if that game could save or sink the good name of the village. The heroes of the day are cheered madly and toasted to their health. (40–41)

Barahona combines this short mid-twentieth-century ethnographic description of rural life with moralizing and racialist commentaries regarding the sport, anticipating some aspects of the style and discursive content of certain commentators in the contemporary press. Nevertheless, this philosopher differs from optimistic assessments of football's civilizing and pedagogical potential to reinforce traditional morals and austere discipline, and to search for "lofty causes." Unlike late-nineteenth-century liberals, Barahona considers soccer less of an exemplary practice useful to educate the population in work ethic and sacrifice, and more a space that reproduces the entire catalog of national defects:

> Soccer really is frenetic liquor; if someone were to inject the public with the same enthusiasm for a profound cause, soon we would see major development in all our social institutions, but unfortunately nothing rivals its stimulating efficacy. In addition, it's worth noting the indiscipline and lack of coordination involved in personal efforts. Individualism and exhibitionism kill the life that the team could have; soccer being in and of itself a team game, harmonious, dependent upon reciprocal understanding, can't perform or exhibit its aesthetic, moral and physical possibilities—which are all present in the game—if each member becomes separated from the others, denying the cooperative role that he is obligated to play as a member of this dynamic society. From where does such [in]discipline, such snobbism in the game come? They are the results of innate temperament, racial malaise and bad upbringing. (41)

However, once culturally and morally connected with rural tradition, the sport would begin to be considered by its defenders as the urban depositary of rural virtues: the humility and simplicity of the farmers. That said, despite the correlation between soccer and peasant culture, with its virtues and its defects, the nationalistic discourse doesn't totally renounce the modernizing values so evident at the moment of the sport's introduction into the country, assigning soccer a mythic function of resolving, at least imaginarily, the tension between tradition and modernity. With its gradual professionalization and internationalization, soccer would become a privileged space for the pedagogical unfolding of the illusion of upward social mobility through personal merit and in favor of a modernizing national social transformation, in which one can accomplish great achievements and advance along the path to progress. This occurs by way of a selective incorporation of rural tradition: once promoting the adherence to values such as simplicity and humility, but repudiating the burdens of rural culture, among them the "lack of discipline and teamwork in personal efforts," in other words, the individualistic and anarchic tendencies considered to be characteristic of the "mountain peasant" temperament, according to its representation by another of the founders of national philosophy, Constantino Láscaris.

Nationalist Apotheosis: Italy, 1990

The concession of this prize [the Nobel Peace Prize to Óscar Arias in 1990] was one of two of Costa Rica's spectacular interventions in the international arena. The other (of higher importance to the popular masses than the Nobel Peace Prize, although no more so than peace itself) was the brilliant performance of the National Soccer Team in the World Championship celebrated in Italy in 1990.

—Iván Molina and Steven Palmer, *Historia de Costa Rica* 105

Toward the second half of the 1950s, the initial internationalization of Costa Rican soccer did not surpass the limits of its immediate neighborhood, which contributed to the strengthening of beliefs about Costa Rican uniqueness and exceptionality in the Central American and Caribbean context, a region in which soccer has competed as a national sport along with baseball and cricket. The recurring success in regional tournaments and the growing media coverage in world competitions, in which some "small" Latin American countries such as Uruguay achieved unimaginable triumphs on foreign fields, generated a certain haste to join the big circuits of world soccer and put to the test the possibility of national soccer. That anxiousness increased notably during Costa Rica's distinguished participation in the Second Pan American Championship (Mexico, 1956), when the national team, nicknamed the "Chaparritos de oro" ("Golden Shorties"), obtained a prominent third place, behind Brazil and Argentina.

Nevertheless, that ambition—highlighted by the fact that other Central American countries, including El Salvador and Honduras, had already participated in these tournaments (in both cases, Spain 1982)—was only recently realized on the occasion of the 1990 World Cup in Italy. The anticipated initial participation of the national team on the world stage presented itself as a great opportunity to demonstrate to the world that Costa Rica is a great nation. All Costa Ricans were called upon to participate in this national event, as evidenced by an announcement made by a local newspaper, in the name of an anonymous worker: "No worthy citizen and lover of his country should neglect supporting the Team" (*La Nación* 6/3/1990: 2C). It's the gold standard of national prestige, as a song, modified for the occasion, indicates: "The National Team is the honor of Costa Ricans" ("Agárrense de las manos," song performed by La Nota, 1990). Soccer, in this way, has evolved thoroughly into "deep play" (Geertz 7) not only because it connects with local tradition, but also because it projects the nation onto the international stage.

Surpassing the most optimistic predictions, the Sele debuted successfully: they made it to the round of 16 and were ranked number 13 in the world by FIFA. This performance, which constituted the highest achievement in the history of Costa Rican soccer to date, was experienced as the greatest accomplishment in Costa Rican history, as an admission into world history, as a landing on the "soccer moon," and even as "the greatest thing God has given us." Designated as a "heroic deed," a "feat," and a "lofty achievement," among other hyperboles, it inspired a profound and festive experience for the national *communitas*, acquiring the character of a formative moment of nationality for contemporary Costa Ricans.

The very worthy performance of the Sele, witnessed by the entire country in real time thanks to the live broadcast on television and the day off declared by President Calderón (*La Nación* 6/8/90: 12C), triggered public celebrations of epic proportions that, according to the press and the population in general, were never before seen. In an unprecedented crowd, just like any other citizen fan, the president of the republic took the streets in an air of profound communal emotionality. The euphoria of the head of state was such that he declared: "We have waited more than 30 years for this and they have given us the *most amazing thing that has occurred in Costa Rican history* [...] *the greatest thing God has ever given us*" (*La Nación* 6/21/1990: 10D; emphasis mine).

The enthusiasm of fan-citizenship reached maximum heights during the spontaneous celebrations that followed the victories of the Sele. Upon the team advancing to the round of 16, the capital city turned into a "carnival" and a "giant insane asylum" in an emotional national bash. The celebration not only encompassed "the whole country" and had the participation of "all citizens," but also called upon divine powers, as a veteran journalist expressed: "The look toward heaven to give thanks to *God and to the Virgin of Angels* for the victory was ever present" (*La Nación* 6/21/90: 18D; emphasis added).

The government was not at the margin of the massive, profound, and spontaneous experience of the nation. The celebrations to welcome the team were organized by a "welcome commission, in which the president, FEDEFUTBOL, and other sponsors also participated. The "triumphant reception" was an elaborate civic ceremony that started with the general call: "EVERYONE TO THE STADIUM!!," announced president of the Republic and other institutions (*La República*, 6/28/1990: 3-A). An aircraft from the national flag company transported the Sele, and the "national heroes" were welcomed in the diplomatic hall of the airport by the president, the first lady, members of the presidential cabinet, and sporting and ecclesiastical authorities. In "decorated and escorted" floats they crossed three of the country's seven provinces before arriving at the National Stadium for the main ceremony. On their journey they were cheered by "all Costa Ricans" and a general flag-waving enthusiasm spread across the country.

The "silver cup" (the nickname for the National Stadium) was the setting for the solemn civil-nationalist ceremony, which not only effusively celebrated the success of the national team, but also renewed the sense of belonging to the nation and the connection between the common people and its leaders (not only the sports heroes, but also the political and religious authorities). The ceremony included a speech by the president of the republic, words from the coaches and members of the Sele, religious rites officiated by the highest representatives of the Catholic Church, and cultural activities, including musical performances of both "high" and "popular culture," with an assortment of prominent patriotic content and a musical tribute to the host country of the World Cup.

When the initial events were over, the players went to their hometowns where local authorities and neighbors paid them tribute. They also paid a thanksgiving visit to the Sanctuary of the Virgin of Angels, whose image accompanied the team during the entire journey through Italy, as well as during the celebrations on Costa Rican soil (*La Nación* 6/29/1990: 3C). This symbol, still in common use, is one of the most evident signs of the link between soccer teams and the rural nationalist collective imagination, one of whose fundamental features is precisely the devotion to the "*Negrita*," as the Virgin of Angels is popularly known.

The celebrations, spontaneous or organized, publicly reaffirmed a sense of belonging and loyalty to the nation, its symbols, and its traditions. What convened and united the imagined national community was the national team, around which other national symbols of patriotism unfolded, including the traditional costume and the musical repertoire that became the soundtrack of the event and the festivities. During the entire celebration the name of the country was repeated like a litany: "Costa Rica, Costa Rica."

This rousing patriotic liturgy, at which all "worthy citizens and lovers of their country" were brought together, meant a profound immersion in the national *communitas*: feelings of wholeness, unity, solidarity, and equality were intensely experienced by all who identified themselves as Costa Ricans. The performance of "everybody's team" still evokes a profound patriotic pride and a singular emotion: two decades having passed, but many Costa Ricans in adulthood—regardless of social position, profession, gender, or geographic origin—report the most proud moment they have felt to be *ticos* and even the happiest day of their life, as the "great World Cup feat" of Italy 1990 (at least until 2014).

In the national collective imagination the "tricolor adventure" constitutes a socially heavy event, a producer of *communitas*; it is a liminal moment that establishes a divisive line between the "now" and the "after." This "change in history" is a ritual of reversal: "*Our ambassadors in Italy 1990 left as 'Cinderellas' and returned consecrated*" (*La Nación* 6/28/1990: cover; emphasis mine). "This small and poor country of only 51 thousand square kilometers and three million inhabitants." David defeated Goliath, personified by such soccer superpowers as Scotland, Switzerland...and Brazil.[5] It is a collective rite of passage in a far and unknown territory. The "extraterritoriality" of the event turns the players into ambassadors and the victory into a conquest: in the generalized perception among citizen fans, the Sele "made the grade," reached maturity, and won a place for Costa Rica in the world. Because of that it has become an allegory for the brightness of the future of the nation if every Costa Rican emulates the players, constituted as the "exemplary center" of the nation, whose heroic deeds point the way toward a glorious future.

THE RETURN TO THE BIG STAGE: KOREA-JAPAN 2002

Wednesday, September 5, 2001, 8:00 p.m. is the time. The nation plays on the green lawn. Saprissa Stadium, considered by locals to be "true hell" for any visitor, is packed with an enthusiastic public that has been following by radio the games prior to the decisive game. The teams line up in front of the national pavilions and a solemn voice sings the respective anthems. The Costa Rican hymn is sung a capella by Lencho Salazar, a traditional musician who is accompanied by a young girl who—we suppose—represents the future of the nation. An impressive chorus of fans accompanies the voices of this vernacular duo, dressed in old-fashioned Costa Rican peasant outfits, as established by the canons of official nationalism.

The final whistle sounds and jubilation erupts. The Sele has qualified for the second time in its history for the final phase of the World Cup. In the midst of the postgame media kaleidoscope, the president of the republic, who has accompanied the Sele in all matches of this elimination process, here and abroad, makes his appearance. Euphoric, "the number 1 fan of the team," announces a victory parade for the following day and declares a two-hour paid rest period for public administration and education workers. Then, he joins the players in the locker room delivering hugs and congratulations. The players give him a white T-shirt with the national flag printed on the front, accompanied by the phrase "My pride is Costa Rica." Rodríguez puts on the T-shirt and forms a circle with the players and coaching staff. They are all huddled together holding hands, praying with pious expressions and thanking God for the victory.

Outside of the stadium newspaper vendors distribute *La Nación* and *Al Día* as free souvenirs of the victory. 20,000 special edition copies. The front page of *La Nación* the following day shows a photo of the greatest hero of the day, Rolando Fonseca, celebrating one of his two goals with the giant headline in red letters: "Yes he could." On television, the head coach of the team responds to the hosts of the show "Buen Día [Good

Day]," who ask him to share the secret to the victory. The desire to know the details and consequences—sporting, civic, and moral—of making the cut will be an obligatory subject in the press, the radio, and the television for several days, whether for sports-themed sections or programs, or any other kind.

The presidential call for the victory parade was an absolute success: at 11:00 a.m. a euphoric public fills up the main streets of San José. The players, dressed informally, traverse the civic topography of the country perched atop a truck from the Ministry of Transportation decorated as a soccer cleat, receiving displays of affection and gratitude. The television cameras broadcast, without commercial breaks and in real time, the details of the parade throughout the country.

A crowd congregated in the Plaza of Democracy anxiously awaits the heroes. The musical group "la Selección" (!) enlivens the wait to the rhythm of *cumbia*, interspersed with cheers to the Sele echoed enthusiastically by the attendees and expressions of gratitude to the president of the republic, received with ironic smiles. The euphoria heightens among a mixed population of men and women, made up of students, bureaucrats, elderly people, and small children, some of them dressed in red with commemorative inscriptions printed on their backs. Street vendors of patriotic symbols and face painters conduct their business in competition with ice-cream and cold-drink vendors, among them those discreetly selling beer. The stage is saturated with Costa Rican flags, soccer administrators, high government officials, reporters, and musicians from the National Youth Symphonic Orchestra. Oddly, there is no national symbol alluding to rural tradition, nor any member of the church hierarchy.[6]

At around 12:30 p.m., arriving in a discreet manner, without a big display of security, the president arrives. His arrival is not announced and only civil servants of the presidential house even pay attention to the matter. This would be nearly impossible in any other Latin American country but is customary here, where, despite the loss of prestige of the political class, the country hasn't given up on pomp and circumstance. One hour later, the team arrives. Complete euphoria erupts and a tricolor cloud of balloons covers the radiant midday sun. The other "selección" sings "Agárrense de las manos" (Hold Hands), the unofficial anthem of the Sele. The players, ecstatic, throw soccer balls into the crowd, as a memento of the victory won. The crowd waves their flags and shouts cheers: "Yes, they could! Yes they could! Hey, hey, hey, hey, Ticos, Ticos!"

Amidst the rejoicing, the symphonic orchestra plays the national Anthem, sung in chorus by those present with notable enthusiasm. Act two: the three captains of the team—coincidentally all of Afro-Costa Rican descent—give short speeches without making any mention of the president of the republic, FEDEFUTBOL, or team sponsors. They alternate expressions of gratitude with promises of giving it their all in the final round of the 2002 World Cup in Korea-Japan. Then the head coach intervenes, thanking the fans and closing his brief address with the phrase that becomes the slogan of the moment: "A celebrar, carajo!" ("Now let's celebrate, dammit!"). The president of FEDEFUTBOL thanks the head of state for his support for the team, to which the public responds with indifference. In contrast to the spontaneous celebrations the night before (see Villena, "Fútbol y nación"), the speeches of the soccer officials don't include religious demonstrations.

The closing speech is reserved for the president of the republic. As a subject who is supposed to know, he will be in charge of stating the "truth" of the event. Amid a rumor of general disapproval, Rodríguez delivers a moralizing harangue to the crowd. He interprets the win as a milestone in national history, equating it the heroic events of 1856, in which he highlights the presidential figure Juanito Mora and fails to mention the popular hero Juan Santamaría. He also does not allude to the participation of the team in Italy 1990, forgotten also by the soccer officials who preceded him.

The president stresses, as key to the international success of the team, the adherence to various values expressed in business jargon, terms like excellence, discipline, teamwork, leadership, competitiveness, and so on. He sets aside the "classic" values of the "metaphysical ethnic" nationalistic discourse such as the humility and simplicity of farmers, whom he qualified as poor and ignorant, although visionaries, while referencing the founding of the nation. Reiterating what he expressed when he welcomed the swimmer Claudia Poll, winner of the gold medal in the 200-meter freestyle race in the Olympic Games in Sydney (the only gold medal won by a Costa Rican athlete in Olympic history), he renews the national axiology, replacing the values of bucolic nationalism with a set of values more suited to the demands of neoliberal globalization.

To ensure that there would be no doubts about the principles that the government was promoting, Rodríguez delivered to the president of the Legislative Assembly a reform proposal called the "Claudia Poll" law of medals, with the intention of increasing the reward that each player or athlete that stood out in an international tournament would receive. Unlike some who see the team as a substitute for the army (abolished in 1948), the president presented the national team as an exemplary model of corporate competitiveness. The declarations on a radio program by German Retana, an expert in management and "motivator" of the Sele, in addition to being a professor at INCAE Business School—the think tank of Central American neoliberalism—seemed to confirm that this discourse also formed a part of the management model of the team.

The president, who after every sentence inserts a "Yes, we can!," officially sanctions the sporting accomplishment, incorporating it among the historic deeds that led the way for the construction of the nation, but leaves out what Amoretti has called the "Costa Rican self-image," with which soccer had been associated since 1921: the humble and unassuming peasant seems to have become an anachronistic character, giving up his place to the dedicated entrepreneur that, under the direction of a providential and enlightened leader, is capable of achieving excellence without fear in international competition. The opening—that is, globalization—is presented as an opportunity to increase the glories of the nation, even when this implies renouncing cultural tradition or Costa Rican public patrimony, whose privatization was promoted by the Rodríguez administration.

Oddly, traditional values of official nationalism that were removed from the presidential discourse would be openly adopted by those creating the advertisements that were broadcast for the participation of the team during the qualification process and final phase of Korea-Japan 2002. In this way, the Costa Rican peasant was simultaneously removed from official discourse and appropriated by marketing discourse, which deployed the bucolic nationalism theme so as to position global brands locally (see Villena, *Golbalización*: Chapter 7).

The last hurrahs and harangues to Costa Rica from the president overlapps with the first notes of the "Costa Rican Patriotic Song," the theme song for the head of state's public performances. The victory parade is the headlining news item on the television news programs, as well as on the national presidential channel, broadcast in primetime, highlighting at every moment the image of the president alongside the players, as though he is a protagonist on the team.

Conclusion

In Costa Rica soccer rose up to form a part of national culture at a moment in which the government had affirmed its will to exist, expounding an official nationalist imaginary and facing the task of introducing it to the masses. In this context, soccer constituted a functional element for the elaboration and diffusion of nationalist discourse in a public arena that still operates today and to which diverse figures come together for the purpose of molding the nationalist collective imaginary in the image of its own visions of the world and its interests.

The link between soccer and Costa Rican nationalism spans distinct moments, with diverse ideological nuances. Initially it was a vehicle for the modernizing and civilizing aspirations of the liberal elites of the late nineteenth century, who insisted upon, like the majority of their peers in Latin America, constructing the nation with an eye turned toward the European capitals. Meanwhile, as soccer was spreading and becoming rooted among the working-class sectors, it became linked to the peasant tradition and experienced a profound nationalization, in terms of its symbolic connection with the nationalist collective imaginary of a bucolic nature. During this period, soccer played a fundamental role in the configuration and strengthening of local identities and in the linking of these identities to the national framework.

As a result of this process, soccer would be used by the elites to interpellate the growing urban masses, encouraging their adherence to traditional rural values such as humility and simplicity, in profound correlation to Catholicism, while also rejecting the traditional aspects of rural life they considered impediments to their modernizing aspirations. Nevertheless, the reception and appropriation of soccer by the popular sectors seems to have been achieved, at least in part, by stripping soccer off the civilizing stamp that the elites had impressed upon it, thus creating a role of social integration in which rural culture operated as a melting pot both at the local and national levels.

The internationalism that began with the victory in the Centennial Games (1921) would turn soccer into a tool to reinforce the working class's adherence to nationalist ideology. Nevertheless, the initial internationalization of Costa Rican soccer was limited—until 1956—to a regional context. The successful performances of the national team against its neighbors not only contributed to strengthening beliefs about Costa Rican uniqueness and exceptionality in the context of Central America and the Caribbean, but also generated aspirations toward joining the big circuits of world soccer, which was becoming more and more of a media spectacle.

The 1990 World Cup would be a tremendous moment in the search for international recognition, as it opened a new period in the geography of Costa Rican soccer. The entry onto the world stage was interpreted according to the values of "metaphysical ethnic nationalism." It's no coincidence that the most celebrated player—and more generally, the entire team, who became as a sort of exemplary model for the nation—came to be considered the very incarnation of the humble and unassuming peasant who, when it comes to defending the honor of the nation, becomes a virile fighter, willing to give his life on the playing field (Villena, *Golbalización*: Chapter 5).

Nevertheless, the team's elimination in the qualifying rounds in 1994 and 1998 showed that its access to global markets was not assured. Therefore, its qualification for the 2002 World Cup was lived as a nationalist drama of high intensity. But this development is also important because, in alignment with neoliberal globalization processes, notable variations were introduced into the nationalist discourses associated with the national team. The reaffirmation of a national sense of belonging that followed its performance in Asia was framed by the president of the republic and some influential sectors of national journalism through a process of developing narratives about national identity that sought to replace values of bucolic nationalism—except for its religious components—with values more in tune with the new functional imperatives of the globalized economic system.

The new discourse did not promote a critical revision of identity from a communicative rationale oriented toward expanding the boundaries of democracy or social inclusion, but rather sought to establish the foundations—intellectual, affective, and axiological—of a new hegemonic articulation and, therefore, of new forms of subjectivity that aimed to legitimize the process of transformation framed within the context of globalization. For the president, the peasant tradition, strongly associated with the collective imaginary of the welfare state, had become an obstacle for the economic, social, political, and cultural transformations demanded by the development of the globalized neoliberal model.

The connection between soccer and nationalism in Costa Rica has acquired distinct nuances according to the characteristics both of the social and political contexts that mark its limits and in the development and insertion of the national soccer field into international circuits. As a result, the early phases of importation and popularization are similar to those seen elsewhere in Latin America, including Brazil, Uruguay, and Argentina. As in these cases, soccer was initially an elite activity imported with the purpose of connecting national economies to the capitalist world economy, and associated with a nationalizing imaginary of pro-European civilizing style. Afterward, with the crisis of the liberal exporter model, soccer was an important tool for the formation of an imagined community that sought to incorporate—symbolically and, in certain ways, also materially—the working class, be it rural (in the case of Costa Rica), foreign immigrants (Uruguay and Argentina), immigrants from the provinces (Argentina), or ethnically marginalized populations (particularly those of African descent, as in the case of Brazil, where soccer was even designated one of the pillars of "racial democracy").

Nevertheless, unlike in the cases of Uruguay, Argentina, and Brazil, which joined the world circuits early and successfully, Costa Rica was a part of a second wave of nations to emerge onto the world stage, a generation that also includes Colombia, Ecuador, and El Salvador, to name just a few. Of the countries where soccer has been the national sport for a long time, Guatemala is the only one that still remains marginalized on the world circuit of men's soccer, along with the traditional baseball-playing countries like Cuba, Nicaragua, Panama, and Venezuela. In any case, Costa Rica's performances at the World Cups also place it at an intermediate Latin American level (along with countries like Ecuador and Chile), considering that it has yet to achieve a place of privilege (in contrast to Brazil, Argentina, and Uruguay), but it also has not had "disastrous" performances (as El Salvador and Bolivia have). This intermediate place, which implies possibility, but in no way assures success, helps to explain why in

Costa Rica—unlike Mexico, whose qualification is practically taken for granted and has been for a long time, although it has never placed near the top at a World Cup—the World Cup qualifying rounds are experienced as an intense nationalist drama, making it possible to politically accomplish the reworking of the nationalist collective imaginary according to the political and economic interests of the moment.

The reworking that was realized during the qualifying process for Korea-Japan, which is not unique to Costa Rica, has a bitter, ironic flavor, as it shows that precisely the moment when the country prepared to celebrate the bicentennial of its constitution as a nation-state was when the economic, social, cultural, and political transformations in process seriously called into question the very existence of the "nation-state," at least in its classic forms. More ironic still is that the continuing erosion of institutions and national identity make use, at least partially, of the same nationalistic passions, especially those associated with adult men's teams, to promote a series of values that enter into tension with those considered the very foundation of every nation-state, such as national sovereignty and cultural tradition.

World Cup 2014 Postscript

La Sele earned a spot to go to Brazil with the enthusiastic support of both the new president, Luis Guillermo Solís, and the body of citizen fans, who thanks to a recent feature film had recuperated the memory of Italy 1990. They set off for Brazil with the promise of showing that Costa Rica was capable of not only participating, but also truly competing in the big leagues. However, given their draw in the "group of death" and their modest results in previous Cup appearances, their possibilities of making a mark were seriously in doubt, leading their coach to appeal to the religious resources that underlie Costa Rican football and nationalism alike: "May divine providence permit us to achieve in the World Cup much of what we did against Ireland (1:1 tie)."

Brazil turned out to be a true event: la Sele was the revelation of the tournament, advancing for the first time ever to the quarterfinals, obtaining an overall ranking of eighth, and remaining undefeated. "Los muchachos" showed not only their commitment, physical strength, and technical conditioning, but also their religious faith: Costa Rica was the only team to kneel during penalty kicks.

The ensuing elebrations were tremendous. The country, president included, dressed in red and threw itself euphorically into the streets upon each victory. Something new this time around was that la Sele included for the first time a player born in Nicaragua, which provoked an unusual unity between the two nations, with many Ticos applauding the play of Óscar Duarte (who made a decisive goal against Uruguay) and many *nicaragüenses* joining eagerly in the revelry, both in Costa Rica and in their own country.

In Costa Rica, which has no national tradition of carnival, the fiestas came to border on the Dionysian, with their corresponding violent byproducts. The orgiastic tone of the celebrations mushroomed as the Sele advanced deeper into the competition, provoking a sort of moral panic among conservatives. Faced with Costa Rica becoming a new "Sodom and Gomorrah," some pious souls actually felt relief when la Sele was finally eliminated.

In sum, the 2014 festivities included a high dose of patriotic pride and explosions of hedonist excess, along with professions of religious faith, such as prayers, invocations, litanies, and a massive participation in the annual pilgrimage to the Virgin of the Angels ("la negrita"), wearing a read team jersey to thank her for la Sele's triumphs.

However, the telenovela of la Sele is not over. For now, an unfortunate episode has sullied the celebrations: a public polemic between the national coach, who has been nominated by some congressmen to be awarded honorary Costa Rican citizenship, and much of the rest of the team, who have brought to light a series of conflicts and antagonisms within la Sele, all while expressions of authoritarianism, chauvanism, and xenophobia among fans have come to light, with a certain tendency toward self-flagellation.

It's still too soon to assess all of the accomplishments of la Sele in Brazil 2014. We need only to wait for the clouds of the day to blow off to begin drawing out interpretations of the event and its consequences for Costa Rican society.

Notes

An earlier version of this chapter was presented at the annual meeting of LASA in 2012, held in San Francisco. The author is grateful to Héctor Fernández L'Hoeste and Robert McKee Irwin for their invitation to participate in this book, Katherine Clarkson for the translation, and Fidel de Rooy for the final review of the English version.

1. Our main source of information is the extensive discursive corpus published by the mass media—both printed and audiovisual, especially television—with reference to the team's participation at the two moments mentioned, complemented—in the case of the 2002 Korea-Japan World Cup—by our ethnographic notes. Fragments of this text have been taken from previous publications by the author, but they are used here for the first time as inputs for a long-term historical interpretation.

2. The expression "Very Well!!" appears already in English in the original text, as an Anglicism. From now on, any Anglicism will be highlighted in bold typeface.

3. The National Stadium, also known as "the little silver cup," was demolished in 2009 to make way for the "New National Stadium," donated by China. Opening activities of the new stadium (2011) included La Sele matches with its counterparts from China, Argentina, Brazil, and Spain.

4. "Concho" is the term by which urban dwellers designated peasants and, by extension, is still used today as a qualifier for those considered "rustic." This character became the "typical" foundation of the nation with the publication of the "Concherías" by Aquileo Echeverría (1905).

5. The loss against a powerhouse like Brazil would be, for local commentators, a moral victory: "1 to 0 is not a defeat," and even "the result against Brazil was a great victory!" (*La República*, special Italy 1990 issue, 6/17/1990: 15).

6. Perhaps the organizers of the event thought that due to recent scandals involving the church, coupled with the growing presence of evangelical Christian players on the team, it was best to abstain from Catholic rituals.

BIBLIOGRAPHY

Badiou, Alain. *El ser y el acontecimiento*. Buenos Aires: Manantial, 2003.

Barahona, Luis. *El gran incógnito: Visión interna del campesino costarricense*. San José: Ed. Universitaria, 1953.

Calvo, Rodrigo, and Gabriela Solano. "Aventura Tricolor." *La Nación*. San José: Ed. La Nación, 1992.

Enríquez, José. "Las fiestas cívicas en San José (1825–1930)." *Temas de Nuestra América* 25. Heredia: UNA, 1996.

Geertz, Clifford. "Deep Play: Notes on the Balinese Cockfight." http://uwch-4. humanities.washington.edu/~WG/~DCIII/120F%20Course%20Reader /CR5_Geertz_Deep%20Play.pdf, undated.

González Dobles, Jaime. *La patria del tico*. San José: Logos International, 1995.

Jiménez, Alexander. *El imposible país de los filósofos*. San José: Perro Azul, 2002.

Molina Jiménez, Iván, and Steven Palmer. *Historia de Costa Rica: Breve, actualizada y con ilustraciones*. San José: Editorial de la Universidad de Costa Rica, 1997.

Palmer, Steven. "Sociedad Anónima. Cultura Oficial: Inventando la nación en Costa Rica (1848–1900)." *Héroes al gusto y libros de moda*. Edited by Iván Molina Jiménez and Steven Palmer. San José: Porvenir-Plumsock Mesoamerican Studies, 1992. 169–205.

Rodríguez, Julio. "Fútbol: Vector Social." *Costa Rica Imaginaria*. Edited by Alexander Jiménez, Giovanna Gigliolli, and Jesús Oyamburu. San José: Editorial Fundación UNA, 1998. 219–234.

Sot, Rodrigo. "La Tierra Prometida." *La Nación. Revista Dominical*. San José: Ed. La Nación, April 25, 1999, http://www.nacion.com.dominical/1999/ abril/25/dominical12.html.

Turner, Victor. *El proceso ritual*. Madrid: Taurus, 1988.

Urbina Gaitán, Chéster. *Costa Rica y el deporte, 1873–1921: un estudio acerca del origen del fútbol y la construcción de un deporte nacional*. San José: Editorial Universidad Nacional, 2001.

Villena, Sergio. *Golbalización: Siete ensayos heréticos sobre fútbol, identidad y cultura*. San José: Norma, 2006.

———. "Fútbol y nación en América Latina." *Constitución de 1991 y cultura*. Edited by Alcaldía Mayor de Bógota. Bógota: Alcaldía Mayor de Bogotá D.C., 2011. 113–142.

CHAPTER 4

Race, Sports, and Regionalism in the Construction of Colombian Nationalism

Héctor Fernández L'Hoeste

The history of Colombian sports is tinged, I contend, with tensions emanating from the reiterated strain between rivaling national identity constructs for diverse regions of the country. Colombia is broken into a number of regions, geographically reinforcing the emergence of very distinctive cultures throughout its territory. In turn, these cultures have fostered essentialism, sponsoring reductive constructs within their boundaries, that is, the fact that to truly belong to one of these regions, inhabitants must favor certain kinds of food or music, and/or look, dress, behave, or talk according to a particular set of codes. In this way, in Colombia, regionalism has played a precursor role to nationalism, curtailing the potential development of more encompassing perspectives (Posada Carbó; Serje). If nationalism is the love of nation in the language of the state, regionalism stands as the expression of the love of region—an imagined community of lesser, more tightly knit proportions—in the language of the province. Amid these tensions, sports in Colombia have emerged along the lines of simplistic, dysfunctional articulations, according to which inhabitants from coastal regions, with a sultrier weather, excelled in disciplines like boxing and baseball, which required less bodily displacement, while inhabitants from the more temperate climates of the interior stood out in sports like track and field and bicycle racing, which usually involved more ample circulation. As I've stated elsewhere, such constructs found anchor in racialized readings by authors like José María Samper and Ricardo Pereira during the later nineteenth century. In conjunction with race, weather and geography were used to ratify rudimentary theories of identity, substantiating proficiency in particular pursuits. In these ways, the skills associated with each of these cultural practices were viewed as supportive of the theoretical features behind each of these identity constructs. If *costeños*, the inhabitants from the Caribbean basin, were good at boxing or baseball, it surely had to do with the idleness of their Afro-Colombian heritage (Deford). On the other hand, if *cachacos* or *paisas*—respectively speaking, the inhabitants of Bogotá and Medellín, the two largest cities in the country, located in the Andes—excelled at cycling or running, it surely had to do with the tenaciousness underlying their Amerindian/mestizo descent, never mind daily or historic context, in which cycling or running served as alternatives in service/transportation. In the end, it was through the eventual rise of soccer, which allowed for more comprehensive collective dynamics, that these constructs coalesced into that of a national entity, serving as an all-inclusive mapping of the nation. Thus, while many sports were visible, the tensions between who practiced each activity and what this meant to the nation played a huge role in the degree of support awarded by the national government and/or private sector. Initial efforts from the periphery of the country were barely funded or supported elsewhere (neighboring Venezuela or the United States), till the appearance of key sports personalities from the center of the country in the 1980s—chiefly among them, cyclist Luis Herrera—motivated interest from corporate sponsors (Rendell 187–203). In a way, the history of Colombian sports is the story of the evolution of an idea of nation and its implicit inequities.

I will discuss and analyze three main moments in the history of Colombian sports, which I believe play crucial roles in the understanding of sports' close alignment with nationalism in such a conflict-ridden setting. The first of these three moments is the emergence of Colombian boxers as international contenders in the 1970s, best personified in fighters like Antonio Cervantes (aka Kid Pambelé) and Rodrigo "Rocky" Valdez. A novelty in the national scene, this emergence brought about a newly found pride in things Colombian at a time when successful sports practices were not yet linked to an international profile. In the 1970s, prior to the boom in illegal drug trafficking of the following decade—Santa Marta Gold, a variety of Colombian marihuana especially popular in the United States, was just beginning to surface—the name of Colombia hardly elicited recognition in the worldwide scene. The second key moment is the accomplishment in European circuits of Colombian cycling squads in the 1980s, following decades of practice of the sport in the center of the country and best incarnated in racers Luis "Lucho" Herrera (aka El Jardinerito de Fusagasugá), Alfonso Flórez, and Fabio Parra. Herrera's success, in particular, brought about a golden age of Colombian cycling in Europe at a key time in national politics, when the country's international image was severely tainted by subversive exploits and the rise of the drug cartels. Thus, the Colombia he portrayed, connected to coffee culture and humble origins, contrasted deeply with the one associated with more nefarious elements, such as Pablo Escobar. Within this scheme, the heart of national representation shifted toward the interior of the country, seeking a balance between the popularity of a sports practice and governmental designs—not necessarily concerned with beneficial sports policies. Finally, the third and culminating moment in the consolidation of a relation between nationalism and a theoretical construct of nation is the rise and establishment of Colombian soccer as a consecrated form of national identity in the 1990s. In association football, Colombian culture recognizes a more integral, equitable representation of nation—the 11-player ensemble and its cohorts—readily available for trouble-free manipulation. The fundamental contention behind these three moments concerns the country's gradual adjustment to a construct of nation that more effectively integrates representation from all provinces, from all corners of the country, and thus provides a more integral expression of national identity, essentially overcoming the limitations implicit in regionalism. Within this process, following the neoliberal spirit of the times, the private sector increasingly contributed to the enactment of nationalism at the expense of the state, which failed to make its presence evident given added concerns (the drug war, subversive groups, etc.). The obvious motivation behind these dynamics was to benefit or profit from the commercialization of products associated with the official image of the nation. In a way, boxing and cycling serve as learning stages for the identification of a cultural practice that more appositely allows the consolidation of nationalism in the minds of Colombians. By way of a squad with players from all corners of the country, soccer provides an ideal template for the celebration of the idea of nation in the language of the state (visually: the colors of the flag, ultimately embodied in the national soccer squad's uniform; audibly: the playing of the national anthem prior to every single official match, thwarting deafening trumpet-like vuvuzelas), embracing the 11-player ensemble as the veritable summation of the country's population at the stadium field.

Blood, Sweat, and K.O.s: From the Slums to Glory

The history of Colombian sports suggests, from its very beginning, the evolution of a cultural practice according to the identity politics of an economically emerging nation such as Colombia. In 1961, as a prelude for the triumphs to come, a humble shoe-shiner named Bernardo Caraballo—from the Caribbean seaport of Cartagena de Indias, a location well known as a place with slave heritage—became the first

Colombian boxer to appear in the world ranking and to fight for the world NBA (National Boxing Association) title. He fought two world champions: Brazilian Eder Jofre and Japanese Masahiko Harada. In the first case, he lost due to a technicality; in the second, he was outpointed. Caraballo went into history as the champ that never was, but, along the way, paved a future for a lineage of prizefighters. Today, Cartagena's boxing coliseum bears his name.

Up to this point, sports practice and politics of identity evolved in a relatively uncomplicated fashion, legitimizing stereotypes and regional affinities. However, this pattern would soon be tested by events at the Olympics. Aside from its protagonism, boxing also figured in juxtaposition to sports of other varieties, enacting a hierarchy for identities. In 1972, the gradual rise of boxing as a successful sports practice added contrast to a circumstance that sharply contradicted established notions pertinent to sports and region. Shooter Helmut Bellingrodt and boxers Clemente Rojas and Alfonso Pérez, all from the Caribbean region, won silver and bronze medals (for the boxers) at the Olympics in Munich, Germany. Unlike the boxers, who further validated the notion that Afro-descendants of Caribbean extraction were ideal fodder for pugilistic aspirations, Bellingrodt represented an anomaly for prevailing constructs of identity. The thought of a middle-class, blonde *costeño* of evident German descent did not appear likely to many Andean Colombians, who at the time ignored the ethnic diversity of national seaports, and equated Caribbean identity almost strictly with African and/or mixed race heritage. On the other hand, the fact that a Caucasian—even a *costeño*—managed to debunk the early efforts of two boxers ratified prevalent racial prejudice. In the end, Rojas and Pérez fit neatly into the prescriptive mold of identity constructs of the time and anticipated the arrival of more triumphant figures to the Colombian boxing scene.

In terms of international presence, the big break comes when Antonio Cervantes, Kid Pambelé, a humble boxer from the runaway-slave village of San Basilio de Palenque, won the world light welterweight title on October 28, 1972. At the time, such was the degree of abandonment of Palenque by the Colombian state that, in the late 1970s, despite being honored for its heritage by UNESCO, it lacked running water and electricity. Having established his credentials as boxer in Venezuela, Pambelé's background evinced the measure of neglect of destitute segments of the population by the Colombian state. As a child, he worked as shoe-shiner and sold cigarettes for a living; as an adolescent, he commuted between Palenque and Chambacú, a now extinct slum by Cartagena's walled city. His rise, quite literally, splits the history of sports in the country in two, for it was the first time a Colombian national held a world title.

Cervantes's story is also one of the saddest chapters in the annals of Colombian boxing. Having conquered the world title by defeating Panamanian Alfonso Frazier, he successfully defended it ten times in four years, till he lost to a very young Wilfredo Benítez. Subsequently, Pambelé regained the title and held it from 1977 to 1980, defending it six more times. In the course of the 1970s, Pambelé managed to squander a sizeable fortune and, along the way, became a drug addict at a time when the marihuana boom and the disco lifestyle ravaged the fates of many personalities. It is possible to argue that Pambelé was a victim of the times, of the excesses of the late 1970s, and of the fact that Colombians were yet unaccustomed to the notion of a successful Afro-Colombian, giving in to much prejudice.[1] Throughout it all, Pambelé even made a reputation for himself as a sage of the masses for his laconic, commonsense aphorisms, like *"Es mejor ser rico que pobre"* (It is better to be rich than poor), which recapped his concern for rampant social inequity in Colombia. In fact, it was Pambelé who inaugurated the tradition—nowadays common among well-known Colombian boxers with international ranking—of wearing boxing shorts with the colors of the flag, capitulating to an exceedingly triumphalist strain of nationalism, an ironic fact as most of them emerged from poverty resulting from disdain by the state.[2] (To a fair extent, this circumstance speaks volumes about the average Colombian's failure to distinguish between nation, the imagined community, and state—the material expression of the idea of nation; thus, Pambelé's behavior betrayed his lack of awareness of the celebration of a state that persistently ignored his cultural tradition.) It was also a well-known fact in Colombian boxing circles of the time that, to fire up a rage in the boxer prior to combat, his agent, entrepreneur Machado, would launch into a tirade of ethnic slurs, seeking to hurt his pride and trigger an adrenaline rush, transforming Pambelé into a formidable foe. Pambelé's meteoric rise into a society unaccustomed to embracing blackness, which came to embody his estrangement as Afro-descendant, in due course fed many of his inner demons, as documented in Alberto Salcedo Ramos's *El oro y la oscuridad*. His rambunctious behavior validated many prevailing prejudices pertaining to Afro-Colombians, who, within a society unwilling to admit its ignorance, were stereotyped as undisciplined, boorish individuals, lacking refinement or restraint (Friedemann; Salcedo Ramos). Plainly, the times of Afro-Colombian musical prodigies and diplomats, like singer and composer Joe Arroyo, scholar Alfonso Múnera, and journalist Edgar Perea, were yet distant. After losing the title, Pambelé's life went into a tailspin and, eventually, he traveled to Cuba for drug rehabilitation. Most recently, he received psychological treatment, seeking to address years of abuse and alienation. Pambelé's folk-hero status has been epitomized in music ("Pambe," a song by *vallenato* star Carlos Vives), books (Salcedo

Ramos's *El oro y la oscuridad*, a winner of the King of Spain Journalism Award), and television (Caracol's *Genio y figura*).

Ironically, another Afro-Colombian boxer from Cartagena followed Pambelé's good streak. Like Pambelé, Rodrigo "Rocky" Valdez did not master the sport in Colombia. There most boxers toiled in poverty and facilities were near inexistent; the prevailing economic disparity between regions of the country—the Atlantic coast lagging conspicuously in terms of infrastructure—did not help. Instead, Valdez moved to New York—where he trained with renowned coach Gil Clancy. Valdez held the WBC (World Boxing Council) middleweight title from 1974 to 1976, and then unified the WBA (World Boxing Association) and WBC titles from 1977 to 1978. Unlike Pambelé, Valdez is a reserved, disciplined individual who, despite ensuing bouts with diabetes, enjoys financial stability and a congenial demeanor. To this day, he lives in Cartagena de Indias, where he keeps a low profile (Rodrigo). In the eyes of many Colombians, Valdez was the correct type of Afro-Colombian, one who "knew his place," and, in spite of his brushes with the political, economic, and social elite, was aware of his situation in a world of whites (Franco Altamar). Nonetheless, within the scope of regional identities, both boxers ratified Cartagena's preeminence as the setting for Afro-descendants, adding to the mythology of a sensual, urge-driven Caribbean basin. In this sense, unmatched, they held the stage of Colombian sports through the 1970s, projecting an image that, while celebrated, did not prove comfortable to the cultural establishment of the interior, unwilling to recognize itself either as Caribbean or black. Years later, once soccer sanctioned a more unified construct, the national team would play to the cry of "¡Sí, sí, Colombia; sí, sí, Caribe!" echoing the official anthem of the Festival of Caribbean Music in Cartagena. By then, it didn't matter whether the national soccer team included a sizeable contingent of players from the Andean region or the national periphery, as Caribbean identity—yet unaccepted in its entirety—was viewed in a different light. Cervantes and Valdez serve as forerunners to subsequent Caribbean boxers like Miguel "Happy" Lora (WBC bantamweight title, 1985–1988), Fidel Bassa (WBA flyweight title, 1987–1989), Jorge Eliécer Julio (WBA, bantamweight title, 1992–1993; WBO bantamweight title, 1998–2000), and Ener Julio (WBO light welterweight title, 2000–2001), who granted continuity to a national boxing tradition.

A Land of Cyclists, though Just the Andes

The first hints of Colombian bicycle racing date as far back as November 1929, when twelve Colombians and six foreigners embarked on a competition in what was, back then, a rough excuse for the word "highway" from the capital city of Bogotá to the northern provincial capital of Tunja and back. In this particular case, the event was suggested as a challenge between nationals and non-nationals. In the beginning, it seems, sports events were merely employed to ratify the difference between locals and "others," with little consideration of the intricacies of national identity (Galvis 19–30). In 1951, the first Vuelta a Colombia cycling race finally took place. This first stab at organized bicycle racing at the "national" level heralded the beginning of a tradition that only thrived when capital-city teams embraced it fully. Most of the route was limited to the interior of the country since, at the time, the better paved and more challenging roads only existed there. Consequently, lack of proper infrastructure in other corners of Colombia challenged the theoretically "national" nature of the event. Hence, from the very beginning there is an evident split in the way sports are practiced in Colombia, with certain practices strongly correlated with more sweltering climates, and others identified with more centrally located urban enclaves. In a way, the gap between these practices replicates the breach between the nation, which theoretically embodies most of Colombia's 47 million inhabitants, and the state, which happens to ignore 30.6 percent of the population, living below the poverty line.[3]

In 1970, Antioqueño racing cyclist Martín Emilio "Cochise" Rodríguez broke the world record for the hour, after winning the Vuelta a Colombia in 1963, 1965, 1966, and 1967, and winning gold at the Central American (1962), Bolivarian (1965), and Pan American (1967) Games. In 1973, he turned professional to race in Europe, where he won two stages in the Giro d'Italia, and finished twenty-seventh in the 1975 edition of the Tour de France. "Cochise's" nickname—granted, an Apache, rather than a more indigenous variety—further validated the bond between bicycle racing and Andean mestizo heritage. His European participation, though, preceded the boom of the 1980s by a decade and was accomplished through personal merit and with scant national support. Bianchi-Campagnolo, the Italian professional team, hired him for several seasons (1973–1975), though the team itself lasted from 1973 to 1977 (Rendell 97–111).

Nonetheless, in the world of Colombian sports, definite whitening came along in the form of a man who evokes Valdez's presence, not in physicality, but in demeanor. Luis Herrera, aka *Lucho* or *El Jardinerito de Fusagasugá* (the little gardener from Fusagasugá), was an unassuming climbing specialist who went on to start a veritable bicycling craze in Colombia, when, during the 1980s, he won three stages in the Tour de France, earning the King of Mountains jersey in 1985 and 1987, and the corresponding King of Mountains title in the Giro d'Italia in 1989 and the Vuelta a España in 1987 and 1991, having won this latter event in 1987, a first for a South American national. Unlike Cochise, who came from the Andean province of Antioquia, a natural antagonist to the whims of political circles in Bogotá, Herrera came from the small town of Fusagasugá, a place that, proudly evincing its indigenous heritage in its name, sits smack in the center of the country, only 40 miles away from the capital. In addition, Herrera's humble background spoke volumes about his mestizo roots, in a way much more compatible with the aspirations of the central cultural establishment, more at ease with Euro-American and mestizo heritage. Thanks mostly to him—and to the memory of a blood-covered Herrera (the cyclist had fallen dramatically at an early point) winning the Alpe d'Huez stage in the central French Alps in 1984, a heroic feat by many standards—a formidable gush of dollars became available to Colombian bicycling squads, like Pilas Varta or Café de Colombia, traveling to Europe to compete in grand tours, in sharp contrast with the lack of funding for sports like boxing, baseball, or even track and field, which, until then, seldom included participants from Bogotá's vicinity. It's important to note that all of the incarnations of the jerseys for all of these two teams sported the national colors visibly, usually in the form of triangle-shaped peaks, each in a different hue of the flag ("Cafe").

While Herrera practiced with a squad made up mostly of cyclists from the provinces neighboring the capital, a most remarkable feat was his duel with French star Bernard Hinault, a five-time champion of the Tour de France. It was in part thanks to Herrera's jovial relationship with Hinault—they challenged each other during mountain stages in France—that Colombian cycling became renowned in Europe (Rendell 175–186). Colombian media celebrated regularly how Herrera's humility and lack of fear for the Frenchman's stature had led to a contest of equals, taking national sports to a new level, on par with Europe's most esteemed cyclist (Cañón 101–104; Rendell 145).[4] Herrera's tête-à-tête with Hinault posited *colombianidad* in equal competing terms with *gallicité* (loosely translated, Frenchness), a remarkable feat in terms of the politics of identity. For a brief period of time, French bicycle racing became the Colombian Other. In the eyes of the national political establishment, so Colombian-centric (i.e., the whirlwind of global events allegedly turning with Colombia at its center), these circumstances brought the attention of the world to the country. In fact, the year before his retirement, Hinault visited Colombia and participated in the Vuelta, mostly as a gesture of recognition to the years of hard work by Herrera and his team (Pilas Varta, and later, Pilas Varta-Café de Colombia-Mavic) in European settings. Thus, from 1983 to 1996 it is possible to see a certain amount of continuity in Colombian efforts in participation in European grand tours, funded actively by the National Coffee Grower's Federation and Postobón, the Colombian beverage manufacturer owned by the Ardila

Lülle group. At the time—and even today—the team Café de Colombia's cycling jersey became a staple among cycling enthusiasts.

The rise in popularity of bicycling brought about a certain identity construct as the reigning paradigm for Colombian nationality in sports. Cycling, aside from highlighting the individual achievements of an athlete in categories like mountain climbing—an aspect at which Colombian bicyclists excelled, thanks to Andean ruggedness—brought much attention to the fact that, in the end, no individual endeavor was feasible without the support and hard work of an entire ensemble. Teamwork was highly visible in much of the TV coverage for any of the races of the *escarabajos* (scarabs, the Colombian cyclists' nickname) in Europe; key bicyclists seldom triumphed without the support of their corresponding squads.[5] This collective nature surely appealed to champions of nationalism in Colombia, who recognized in it the kind of team dynamics necessary to overthrow evils like the drug cartels and other armed groups, positing the idea of the entire country's population as one. Also, in an actual "mapping" of the nation, Colombians even grew accustomed to daily TV installments of European circuits, with beautiful panoramic shots of the French, Italian, or Spanish geography from helicopters, and eventually demanded a national equivalent from TV coverage of the Vuelta a Colombia, in an audiovisual survey of the country's unforgiving topography.[6] In the imagery, cities, highways, forests, mountain peaks, and river valleys were displayed strikingly amid a sport for which fans were required to study daily maps in an intensive review of the corresponding stage's geography. Thus, bicycling augmented the "collective" side of the enterprise both from the participant and the spectator's point of view and, with a few key figures as exceptions—the declared leaders of each bicycling team, enforcing order and the importance of rank—further consolidated the idea of national success as the product of collective effort and sacrifice. In other words, bicycling's "collective" construct was the type of "group" construct favored by the cultural establishments of the interior of the nation, at this point more interested in gaining political and social legitimacy for the struggle against drug cartels and guerrilla fighters (Salazar). In a country where the state failed to substantiate its presence in many key corners (the slums of Medellín, breeding ground of *sicarios* [young assassins] and subversives), sports could be embraced as national allegories and used to rally the general population in operations against kingpins (Pablo Escobar), revolutionaries (FARC [Revolutionary Armed Forces of Colombia], ELN [National Liberation Army]), and vigilantes or paramilitary groups (MAS [Death to Kidnappers], PEPES [Persecuted by Escobar], AUC [United Self-Defense Forces of Colombia]). In effect, by the time the Colombian bicycling squads in Europe reached their peak in popularity, *ciclovías* (bike ways)—the practice of closing key segments of the city grid to cars on Sundays and holidays, so the general population could go out and ride bikes, skate, or jog—had been implemented in most large metro areas of the interior.[7] During the late 1990s and early 2000s, Colombian cities like Bogotá and Medellín even integrated the bicycle into their growth patterns and planning, developing cycling corridors through which the population could traverse cities without any of the inconveniences of regular traffic. In due time, Colombia's urban experiment with bicycles was exported all over the world.

Nevertheless, the team's lineup was rather incomplete. A summary of the origin of winners of the Vuelta shows that its champions came from only seven departments—all Andean (following a French model, Colombia has thirty-two departments and one capital district)—Boyacá (23), Antioquia (14), Cundinamarca (11), Santander (3), Risaralda (2), Caldas (1), and Tolima (1)—evincing the event's limited appeal (*Federación*). On the coasts or plains, where weather was warmer and the topography of the land was less rugged, initiatives of this nature were not very appealing. The lack of mountains or an adequate highway infrastructure further hindered any possibility of participation from country folks from these corners of the nation. Colombia's highest peak, the Cristóbal Colón (5,775 meters high), is by its Caribbean coast, in the Sierra Nevada de Santa Marta, separated from the Andes, but its mountain range lacks proper roads. Theoretically speaking, better roads by the coast would augment the possibility of mountain-climbing cycling by locals. However, this has never been the case. At times, the route of the Vuelta a Colombia was modified, adding stages by the Caribbean or other provinces of the nation, yet the event was perceived and consumed as something extraneous, strictly for the enjoyment of audiences in the major Andean centers of the country (Rendell 76–96).[8] Thus, national urban politics, arising from Andean metropolitan areas, played a significant role in underscoring the relevance of sport as a cultural practice of national affiliation. Overall, bicycling impacted thoroughly the way of imagining Colombian nationality during a period of at least ten years, from the early 1980s to the early 1990s, even if in the end it did not manage to gain a truly national audience. Bicycles, it seemed, worked only in the mountains of the Andes.

THE CASE OF ASSOCIATED FOOTBALL: THIRD TIME'S THE CHARM

Associated football or soccer was first established in Colombia in the Caribbean port city of Barranquilla, where the influence of trade with Europeans—the British, in particular—was rather strong. In 1924, the Liga de Football del Atlántico was founded in Barranquilla; it was later admitted to FIFA (the world-governing body for the sport) in 1931

(Henshaw 134–136). From 1937 to 1947, the country first exported a soccer player: Alejandro Frigerio Payán, born in the Pacific coastal town of Tumaco, a place closely identified with African heritage, played for a number of European soccer clubs, including Lugano and Liverpool (Galvis 45–48). Though Payán was of European descent, the emergence of soccer from such a distant corner of the nation, by the Ecuadorian border, shows how a valid sports tradition arose from the periphery from the start. The event, however, hardly registered in national consciousness. From 1947 to 1948, once again, soccer was exported, though to a much closer, hemispheric location: Barranquilla native Efraín "Caimán" Sánchez played for San Lorenzo in Argentina. Sánchez's time in Argentina serves as introduction to a key period: the so-called era of El Dorado, the golden age of "Colombian" soccer.[9]

In 1948, shortly after turning professional, Colombia's ruling body for soccer, Dimayor, engaged in a dispute with Adefútbol, the existing amateur football authority. As a result, Dimayor broke from FIFA. In theory, this consigned Colombian soccer to a limbo, since its teams were suspended from international competitions and could not play against foreign teams (Taylor 166–171). In actual practice, it led to a most arresting development. At the time, Argentine soccer players went on strike against Perón, who was limiting their pay. Realizing the opportunity to operate without transfer fees, Alfonso Senior, founder of Dimayor and chairman of Millonarios F.C., sent the club's Argentine manager, Carlos Aldabe, to Buenos Aires with instructions to sign up a big name. Aldabe soon wired a response back to Senior, announcing soccer star Adolfo Pedernera's imminent arrival in Colombia to play with Millonarios in Bogotá for an annual salary of $5,000, a phenomenal sum in those days. Senior was no slouch. With the income from the sale of tickets, which could amount to $38,000 per game at Bogotá's El Campín stadium, he realized Pedernera's hire meant good business. Subsequently, Pedernera returned to Argentina and managed to convince others—including some of the best players in the world at this time, from *La Máquina* (The Machine), the River Plate's stellar lineup of the 1940s: namely, Néstor Raúl Rossi, Julio Cozzi, and Alfredo Di Stefano—to come with him to Colombia. At Millonarios, they played together and went on to create the Blue Ballet, a lineup that included ten extremely well-paid and pleased Argentines. As soon as other Colombian teams realized what was happening, they emulated Millonarios and started hiring foreigners. Deportivo Cali also brought in players from Argentina while Pereira brought in Paraguayans, Cúcuta imported Uruguayans, and Medellín hired Peruvians. Santa Fe, Bogotá's local team, imported British players and even modeled its colors on Arsenal, thanks to the Anglophilia of its chairman. Hence El Dorado was created, with five years (1949–1954) of exceptional soccer taking place in Colombia (166–171).

Millonarios, the main club benefitting from the boom, won the Colombian soccer tournaments in 1949, 1951, 1952, and 1953, gaining repute as one of the best teams in the world—the 1950 tournament was conquered by Deportes Caldas, which by then had fortified its squad with Argentine, Chilean, Peruvian, and even Lithuanian imports. In 1952, Millonarios even beat Real Madrid in the Spanish capital. In due time, the soccer federations from Argentina, Paraguay, and Uruguay realized how their leagues had been poached and sued Colombia's Dimayor for failing to pay international fees for the transfer of players. Eventually, a deal was struck whereby the Colombian league could enjoy its hires till 1954, after which it would pay transfer fees like anybody else in the world, returning to FIFA's fold (166–171). As a result of the deal, Dimayor also committed itself to the return of imported players and Millonarios' initial phase of unsurpassed glory began to fade. While the aforementioned foursome brought glory to Millonarios, teams from Cali and Medellín imported internationals of many kinds, nourishing specific styles of soccer. Coastal Barranquilla, in turn, imported Brazilians and eastern Europeans (Hungarians, mostly) with a brand of soccer very dissimilar to the one favored by players of the Southern Cone. By 1953, with Di Stefano's departure to Spain—he was transferred to Real Madrid, bent on hiring him after the 1952 defeat—El Dorado had effectively come to an end and Colombia had reestablished formal ties with FIFA.

In terms of identity politics, El Dorado contributed to a lasting relationship with alternate South American soccer traditions, particularly those of Argentina and Brazil, thus influencing the Colombian style of play for decades. However, rather than the Argentine way of playing, the *jogo bonito* made a lasting impression on Colombians, bent on producing a style of play that appealed to the eye. In the local context, nonetheless, soccer mainly became a matter of exploring a relationship with an "Other," as many players were imported. As a result, from the 1950s to the 1970s, soccer in Colombia was viewed as a cultural practice and sport designed for the acquaintance with foreign sports traditions, in an effort to assimilate techniques that would someday evolve into a "national" style. While Colombian professional teams incorporated a quota of national players, main positions and leverage were awarded to foreigners, who arrived with established credentials. Thus, though "Caimán" Sánchez traveled to Argentina in 1947 and 1948, Colombian soccer was still far away from signifying a more intimate problematization of national identity, that is, a practice where resolutions for inner tensions in a national construct could be explored.

By the late 1970s, a time at which the rosters of many teams began to look markedly national, there were escalating complaints about importing players who did not necessarily justify the amount of money paid for their transfers, as the gap in quality between locals and imports diminished drastically. By then, soccer began to look like what it is today—the eminent vehicle for nationalism in sports—though many things would have to take place before Colombian culture reached this stage. It is also important to note that while soccer continued to garner growing support, other sports—like baseball, emerging from the Colombian Caribbean—also underscored the collective nature of their practice. However, lack of appeal to the audiences from the interior of the country resulted in scant support for such alternatives. Occasionally, teams from the interior of the country would embrace baseball—Antioquia, with Medellín as its capital, competed capably—though as Joseph Arbena has pointed out, the holding of "national games" sometimes intensified rather than softened sectional identities and rivalries. According to Arbena, "such competition may also highlight traditional regional inequities which will intensify rather than diminish hostility toward the national metropolitan center" (145). In short, this is exactly what happened. Baseball tournaments engendered growing resentments in provinces that recognized a lack of official support. Soccer, on the other hand, allowed all regions of the country to participate in a more or less equitable basis, given lesser demands in terms of equipment and facilities.

By the 1980s, once it was evident that bicycling—already firmly established in the Andes—would fail to gain traction in areas outside the large metro centers of the interior, the eventual, organic rise of a substitute sports practice became foreseeable. It was only then, thanks to inroads made by the drug cartels, which allowed Medellín's Atlético Nacional to enjoy a formidable winning streak under the guidance of Francisco Maturana and Hernán Darío Gómez (1987–1990), that Colombian soccer surfaced as the potential candidate for the integration of the nation. In point of fact, it was through Maturana's work that Colombian soccer came of age and entered one of its most successful periods. Unlike boxing or cycling, soccer brought together Colombians from many provinces, ethnicities, and even social classes, handily supported by a league that, by the late 1980s, was beginning to include teams with a recruitment policy fiercely based on nationals rather than imports. This eventual maturing into a national style is clearly reflected in the evolution of the national squad's uniform, which gradually settled for the present standard, going from a blue and white ensemble in 1938 to a darker hue of blue and white (1957–1965) to an orange or white jersey with a tricolored stripe (1971–1984) to the nowadays celebrated tricolored kit (initially designed by María Elvira Pardo) in 1985, a time when a growing sense of identification with the uniform began to hold sway. In this way, thanks to greater empathy toward an official image, based on the colors of the state, soccer emerged as the ideal tool to forge loyalty to the national government and foster pride in the positive achievements of the community—in many occasions, poverty-stricken townships almost entirely forsaken by the central government, as in the case of the slums in Cali or Medellín. That is, for the most part, the evolution of the sport took place thanks to the private sector and in spite of the almost total neglect of the state.

In 1994, the Colombian national soccer team was ranked fourth in the world according to FIFA, its highest position ever.[10] This prominent position, it could be argued, resulted from phenomenal investment from drug cartels (Medellín and Cali) in solid support of soccer clubs with eminently national participation. That is to say, drug cartels played a very active role in the emergence of a successful Colombian soccer tradition, investing money in the sport in the magnitude necessary to bring about results. In 1983, justice minister Rodrigo Lara Bonilla stated bluntly, "The mafia has taken over Colombian football." In fact, by late 1984, shortly after Lara Bonilla's death at the hands of the Medellín cartel, Hernán Botero Moreno, chairman of Atlético Nacional, was extradited to the United States, where he was sentenced to 30 years in prison and fined $25 million for laundering drug money (Redacción). By 1987, journalist Ignacio Gómez claimed that "of the eighteen teams in the league at the time there were maybe two or three which didn't have links to drug trafficking...By 1987 there was hardly a leading drug trafficker who didn't have his fingers in football" (Taylor 154–155).

Unlike conventional private soccer clubs ruled by budgets and profit-oriented policies, the drug kingpins spared no expense to bring their players to world-class standards. At times, they even invited professional soccer players to their estates, where they would sponsor matches for huge sums of money. For these criminal organizations, legalization of funds (money laundering) was a must. Thus, investment in esteemed cultural practices such as soccer made good sense from a business perspective. While it allowed the return of big sums of money into the legal economy, it also provided key yields on investment in terms of prestige and image. Ticket sales at soccer stadia, generally unmonitored by government audits, allowed for the swift and speedy laundering of millions, since soccer teams could report inflated numbers, thus creating a channel for legalization. In addition, Pablo Escobar gained substantial goodwill in the slums of Medellín through the donation of soccer fields and equipment for community leagues that would serve as breeding grounds for the professional league. Not to be outdone, Miguel Rodríguez Orejuela, head of the Cali cartel, specialized in buying the registration—or *pase*—of top players. Rodríguez Orejuela not only owned the registration for his players at Deportivo América, one of the two teams in Cali, but also those for players in Argentina, Brazil, Peru, and other South American countries (Taylor 158–159).

Yet the effects of the cartels' influence on the soccer league were not exclusively on the legal side, making sense from a good "business" point of view. Investment in soccer also led to a parallel industry of bribing, betting, and corruption, as many of the drug barons bet against each other. As a result, referees, players, coaches, and managers received threats and were murdered. In 1988, referee Armando Pérez was kidnapped and harassed for 20 hours by armed men claiming to represent six professional clubs ("Fuera"). In 1989, referee Álvaro Ortega was shot dead in the streets of Medellín ("Algunas"). In January 1990, the president of Millonarios was shot by *sicarios* (Taylor 161). In the same year, the director of Cristal Caldas was killed ("Fútbol"). In June 1992, a vice-president of Millonarios was shot to death and, subsequently, his body was even run over by a car ("Asesinado vicepresidente"). In March 1993, the president of Difútbol resigned after receiving death threats. In 1995, Juan José Bellini, ex-chairman of América and then chairman of the Colombian football federation, resigned promising to clear his name from allegations ("Amistades"). By 1997, he was jailed for six years and fined $200,000 for illicit enrichment ("Orden"). In 1996, Felipe "Pipe" Pérez Urrea, a former player of Atlético Nacional, Envigado F.C., and the national soccer squad, was shot dead in Medellín, following his connection to the city's drug cartel ("Asesinado"). When it comes to keeping track of the unsavory side effects of drug-related money in the Colombian soccer league, the list is endless.

Four main teams, Atlético Nacional, Deportivo Independiente Medellín, Millonarios, and América, the first three linked to the Medellín cartel and the latter to Cali, are particularly notorious in relation to these events, though it could be argued that illicit funding was also tangible in many other squads (The Two). (In the case of América, the team was placed under watch by executive order of the US government, which froze its assets in the United States and forbade other companies from conducting direct business with the club [Quevedo].) It was through these teams, particularly Nacional and América, which made great strides in national and international soccer tournaments, that the drug cartels proved the viability of soccer as big business. By investing sums of money unseen in the national market, they demonstrated the national soccer scene's ability to achieve a world-class level, a feat yet unattained in the field of Colombian association football. Thus it can be said that, even within the interior of the country, regionalism played an active role in the evolution of sports: Pablo Escobar's men, a bunch of thugs from Medellín, sought to teach a lesson to the members of the Rodríguez Orejuela family, from the city of Cali, or even to challenge, on a friendly basis, the designs of José Gonzalo Rodríguez Gacha (aka El Mexicano), military head of the Medellín cartel, though based in the town of Pacho to the north of Bogotá (thus favoring an opposing team like Millonarios). In actual fact, the defensive backbone of the team that traveled to the United States to participate in the World Cup in 1994 came almost entirely from Nacional, the first Colombian winner of the Copa Libertadores de América in 1989 with an entirely Colombian squad (thus adding to the literal value of its name: national), given then national-team coach Francisco Maturana's familiarity with these players.

Hence, by the late 1990s, there was a shift in both the degree of support by the national government, avid for good news amid its struggle with drug cartels and guerrilla groups, and the private sector, seeking a better return than with the so-called *escarabajos* at the Tour de France, Vuelta a España, or Giro d'Italia. In first place, the government, previously conspicuous for the absence of a beneficial sports policy, began to associate itself more with the national soccer team. Second, the private sector, conscious of dwindling benefits from its investments in cycling teams, began to orient its support toward soccer. Also, since drug money was rampant in soccer, to a certain extent, there was a willingness to eradicate its presence through legal means—quite obviously, once soccer's viability as good institutional investment had been proved. As late as 1997, the Colombian Business Superintendence found that 80 percent of the shares of the country's top five clubs were in the hands of drug traffickers; 15 smaller teams were also suspected of drug links (Taylor 182). In this sense, the "legal" private sector came to the rescue. Soft-drink manufacturer Postobón, for example, stopped funding bicycle racing in 1998, the date when it decides to start sponsoring Atlético Nacional. Eventually, the Ardila Lülle group, owner of Postobón, bought the team. Bavaria, the national brewery and second largest one in South America, started sponsoring the national soccer team timidly in 1991—through its Águila brand—and gradually increased the profile of its support in this century, when it was clear that soccer represented a more dynamic and updated construct of the nation ("Águila"). After all, the national soccer team brought together players from all corners of the country. By June of 2007, Bavaria was investing $10 million for exclusive rights to the national soccer team, covering players of all ages and both sexes, as well as 15 billion pesos (now over $8 million) to sponsor six of the clubs in the Colombian soccer league.[11]

Thus, by way of injecting capital into soccer, the drug trade had the unintended effect of sanctioning a more inclusive understanding of national identity in sports, effectively incorporating soccer players from all regions of the nation and paying less attention to the importation of costly, overvalued foreign players. It wasn't that members of drug cartels had a more expansive understanding of identity. If anything, drug cartels were rabidly regionalist, sticking with men of their vicinities for reasons of trust. It was that, by way of bringing a better quality of training to the game, thanks to their fortunes, they heightened the profile of soccer as a more effective representation of the nation, literally bringing along—hiring—participants from every corner of the nation, thus covering all markets with one single cultural practice. When it came to soccer, sensible business acumen prevailed; the degree of regional affiliation, so relevant to drug deals, mattered little in terms of dribbling skills. As long as someone played well, his regional origin (and/or race) was a nonissue. After all, kingpins invested exclusively in players and teams of their choice. In a way, thanks to their millions, the lessons learned from the times of El Dorado to the 1990s came to fruition. Finally, in both the eyes of the government and the private sector, a single sports practice attained a stature relevant to a more cohesive construct of nation.

Coda

Nowadays, Colombian sports are in the throes of progress. In a country with one of the most ethnically diverse populations in the Americas, as well as one of the highest Gini coefficients, they remain a charged subject.[12] The political and social situation has evolved and, in many instances, things are better, but much remains to be addressed. Soccer has risen to prominence, but it's difficult to celebrate its inclusiveness, when most of its imagery and significance have been co-opted by the state apparatus and the private industry. The Colombian flag has never been as popular as when the national soccer team embraced it, and this has benefitted both the government and private interests, though much of the work and effort corresponds only to the latter. Through sponsorship deals (e.g., Bavaria covers traveling costs and fees; Adidas supplies uniforms), the rising popularity of soccer has involved a windfall for the image of the state.[13] Financially, though, many professional teams are struggling, given the vanishing of unrestricted sources of funding like the drug cartels. As late as 2011, Ramón Jesurún, head of the Colombian Dimayor, cited the obsolete legal framework imposed on teams during the exit of drug-related capital in the 1990s as the reason for a somber financial assessment. Stadium attendance has suffered and teams like América, Cúcuta, Once Caldas, and Deportivo Pasto are deep in red ink. According to an article from *El Tiempo*, Colombian soccer teams accumulated debts for $20 million, emanating mostly from taxes and obligations from labor benefits and social security ("Equipos"). Therefore, this is perhaps a good moment to reflect on what sports signify as a cultural practice and how they contribute to the way we imagine nationality in a place where guardianship of identity is as hotly contested as in Colombia. As is the case in many other Latin American countries, the evolution of a sports tradition in a place like Colombia says as much about how people like to enjoy their spare time following a particular kind of sports as it says about how they imagine their nation and its inhabitants through it, and their corresponding role within this construct.

NOTES

1. In *Blackness and Racial Mixture*, Peter Wade argues that Colombia is characterized by a racial order in which black people are both included and excluded: included as ordinary citizens, participating in the overarching process of *mestizaje*, and simultaneously excluded as inferior citizens, or even as people with marginal participation in "national society," and as individuals with whom whiter people might not want to actually practice *mestizaje*, especially in the most intimate sense of forming links not just of sex but of kinship.
2. For an image of these shorts, see Colprensa—*El País* http://www .eluniversal. October 12, 2012. Available at http: com.co/cartagena /deportes/pambele-de-vaina-estoy-vivo-95497.
3. The data for 2013 are by the Departamento Administrativo Nacional de Estadística (DANE). Available at http://www.dane.gov.co/files /investi gaciones/condiciones_vida/pobreza/bol_pobreza_13.pdf.
4. Matt Rendell states, "'Lucho' Herrera speaks quietly and in volleys that quickly tail off into silence. He belongs to Colombia's peasantry: unassuming, jovial, and of few words" (145).
5. Essentially a team sport, road bicycle racing relies heavily on collaboration between team members. For the most part, the ability of cyclists to maintain key positions is strongly correlated to squad support. In media coverage done from helicopters, a practice emulated by Colombian TV networks, team dynamics in a cycling peloton are explicit through jersey colors.
6. Though daily coverage of European cycling circuits started in Colombia in the 1980s via TV broadcasters like Radio Cadena Nacional (RCN), nowadays, coverage is handled by Señal Colombia. Coverage of the Tour de France for 2013 is noted at http://www.senalcolombia.tv /senaldeportes/2096-senal-colombia-se-alista-para-transmitir-la-edicion -100-del-tour-de-france.html.
7. Montezuma et al.; and Hernandez.
8. Rendell states, "The Tour of Colombia will never incorporate the forested expanse of Colombia's Oriente—departments like Vichada, Guanía, Vaupés, Putumayo—forested areas where State weakness and sometime ineffectual vigilance have allowed guerrilla activity and coca production to flourish" (77), acknowledging the limited nature of the event. In fact, he goes as far as demonstrating how so-called independent republics of subversives influenced the route of the 1964 Vuelta a Colombia (76–96).
9. "Colombia entra en la élite del fútbol mundial con 'la época de El Dorado.'" *El Tiempo*. December 20, 2012. Available at http://www.eltiempo.com/100/dk100/cronologia_centenario/ARTICULO-WEB-PLANT_NOTA_INTERIOR_100-7821763.html. While El Dorado is a welcome memory, its success was mostly limited to one Bogotá team—Millonarios—hardly qualifying as "national." If anything, El Dorado evinces Bogotá's penchant to equate itself with the country. The large number of imported players also detracts from national nature. That is why I've framed "Colombian" with quotation marks.

10. By late 2012, Colombia ranked among the top five teams in the world in FIFA soccer listings. See Willis, "Colombia Enters Top Five in FIFA Soccer Rankings."
11. Bavaria's investment denotes its awareness of soccer's potential, evident in http://www.colombia.com/actualidad/autonoticias/economia/2007/06/19/detallenoticia30602.asp.
12. The Gini coefficient or ratio measures inequality of income in a society. According to DANE, as of 2013, Colombia's ratio stands at 53.9 (high).
13. Marketing of nationality is explicit in both examples. For Águila, see http://www.cervezaaguila.com/Futbol_Aguila/Seleccion_Colombia. For Adidas, see http://www.adidas.co/Seleccion-Colombia.html.

BIBLIOGRAPHY

"Águila y los colombianos entregaron la 'Bandera de la Alegría.'" *Bavaria.com. co.* June 15, 2011. Web. April 16, 2013. Available at http://www.bavaria.com.co/internaNoticias.php?uuid=23766.
"Algunas perlas del fútbol colombiano." *Semana.* September 27, 2012. Web. April 16, 2013. Available at http://www.semana.com/deportes/articulo/algunas-perlas-del-futbol-colombiano/265457-3.
"Amistades peligrosas tumbaron a Bellini." *El Tiempo.* July 7, 1995. Web. April 16, 2013. Available at http://www.eltiempo.com/archivo/documento/MAM-360976.
Arbena, Joseph, ed. *Sport and Society in Latin America: Diffusion, Dependency, and the Rise of Mass Culture.* New York: Greenwood Press, 1988.
"Asesinado el ex futbolista Pipe Pérez." *El Tiempo.* October 19, 1996. Web. April 16, 2013. Available at http://www.eltiempo.com/archivo/documento/MAM-548223.
"Asesinado vicepresidente del club Los Millonarios." *El Tiempo.* June 22, 1992. Web. April 16, 2013. Available at http://www.eltiempo.com/archivo/documento/MAM-142647.
"Bavaria duplicó el patrocinio a las selecciones Colombia." *Colombia.com.* June 19, 2007. Web. April 16, 2013. Available at http://www.colombia.com/actualidad/autonoticias/economia/2007/06/19/detallenoticia30602.asp.
"Café de Colombia Jersey." Google. July 1, 2013. Web. August 12, 2013. Available at https://www.google.com/search?hl=en&site=imghp&tbm=isch&source=hp&biw=1257&bih=603&q=cafe+de+colombia+jersey&oq=cafe+de+colo&gs_l=img.1.6.0l10.60269.68063.1.70848.34.14.10.10.10.1.508.2055.4j6j1j1j0j1.13.0...0.0...1ac.1.11.img.4ViiUPe9ahU.
Cañón, Héctor. *Récords y hazañas de colombianos.* Bogotá: Grupo Editorial Norma, 2008.
"Colombia entra en la élite del fútbol mundial con 'la época de El Dorado.'" *El Tiempo.* December 20, 2012. Web. April 16, 2013. Available at http://www.eltiempo.com/100/dk100/cronologia_centenario/ARTICULO-WEB-PLANT_NOTA_INTERIOR_100-7821763.html.
Colprensa—*El País.* "De vaina estoy vivo." *El Universal.* October 12, 2012. Web. April 16, 2013. Available at http://www.eluniversal.com.co/cartagena/deportes/pambele-de-vaina-estoy-vivo-95497.

Cuadrado Mendieta, Efraín. "El título que más ha emocionado a Colombia." *El Heraldo*. October 27, 2012. Web. April 16, 2013. Available at http://www.elheraldo.co/deportes/el-titulo-mundial-que-mas-ha-emocionado-a -colombia-87131.

DANE. "Pobreza monetaria y multidimensional." March 21, 2014. Web. May 30, 2014. Available at http://www.dane.gov.co/files/investigaciones /condiciones_vida/pobreza/bol_pobreza_13.pdf.

Deford, Frank. "Tick Tock: Make the Serve, Pitch, Putt, or Shot." *NPR*. June 19, 2013. Web. August 12, 2013. Available at http://www.npr .org/2013/06/19/193086412/tick-tock-make-the-serve-pitch-putt-or-shot.

Elespectador.com. "Helmut Bellingrodt Wolf. Primer medalista olímpico de Colombia y único con dos podios." El Espectador.com. July 6, 2012. Web. April 16, 2013. Available at http://www.elespectador.com/especiales /juegosolimpicos/articulo-357841-helmut-bellingrodt-wolf.

"Equipos de fútbol colombiano, con deudas por $33,800 millones." *El Tiempo*. March 18, 2011. Web. April 16, 2013. Available at http://www.eltiempo .com/deportes/futbol-colombiano/ARTICULO-WEB-NEW_NOTA _INTERIOR-9032462.html.

Federación Colombiana de Ciclismo. July 1, 2013. Web. August 12, 2013. Available at http://ciclismodecolombia.com/spip.php?article61.

Franco Altamar, Javier. "El ritual de Rocky Valdez." *Narración periodística*. July 9, 2008. Web. April 16, 2013. Available at http://narracionperiodistica.blog-spot.com/2008/07/el-ritual-de-rocky-valdez.html.

Friedemann, Nina de. *La saga del negro: presencia africana en Colombia*. Bogotá: Pontificia Universidad Javeriana, 1993.

"Fuera de lugar." *Semana*. December 5, 1988. Web. April 16, 2013. Available at http://www.semana.com/nacion/articulo/fuera-de-lugar/11062-3.

"Fútbol y violencia, una larga historia." *El Tiempo*. July 3, 1994. Web. April 16, 2013. Available at http://www.eltiempo.com/archivo/documento/MAM -164658.

Galvis, Alberto. *Grandes hazañas deportivas de Colombia*. Bogotá: Ediciones Martínez Roca, 1997.

Henshaw, Richard. "Colombia." *The Encyclopedia of World Soccer*. Washington, DC: New Republic Books, 1979. 134–136.

Hernandez, Javier. "Car-Free Streets, a Colombian Export, Inspire Debate." *New York Times*. June 24, 2008. Web. April 16, 2013. Available at http:// www.nytimes.com/2008/06/24/nyregion/24streets.html?_r=1&scp=1&sq =Ciclov%C3%ADa&st=cse.

Montezuma, Ricardo et al. *Ciudadanos, calles y ciudades: las Américas unidas por una ciclovía*. Bogotá: Universidad del Rosario, 2011.

"Orden libertad de Bellini." *El Tiempo*. October 20, 1998. Web. April 16, 2013. Available at http://www.eltiempo.com/archivo/documento/MAM-832732.

Pereira, Ricardo S. *Les Etats-Unis de Colombie: précis d'histoire et de géographie, physique, politique et commerciale: contenant un grand nombre de renseignments utiles aux voyageurs et aux négociants, de courtes notices biographiques des personnages célèbres de la Colombie*. Paris: C. Marpon et E. Flammarion, 1883.

Posadá Carbo, Eduardo. *El desafío de las ideas: ensayos de historia intelectual y política en Colombia.* Medellín, Colombia: Banco de la República, 2003.

Quevedo, Norbey. "La piedra en el zapato del América." *El Espectador.* February 22, 2013. Web. April 16, 2013. Available at http://m.elespectador.com /impreso/cuadernilloa/investigacion/articuloimpreso-piedra-el-zapato-del -america.

Redacción Judicial. "La pelea del primer extraditado." *El Espectador.* July 11, 2009. Web. April 16, 2013. Available at http://www.elespectador.com /impreso/judicial/articuloimpreso150194-pelea-del-primer-extraditado.

Rendell, Matt. "The Sense of an Ending." *Kings of the Mountains: How Colombia's Cycling Heroes Changed Their Nation's History.* London: Aurum Press, 2002.

"Rodrigo Rocky Valdés." *YouTube.* September 7, 2010. Web. April 16, 2013. Available at http://www.youtube.com/watch?v=BXzNZ3cGnRk.

Salazar, Alonso. *La parabola de Pablo.* Bogotá: Planeta, 2001.

Salcedo Ramos, Alberto. *El oro y la oscuridad.* Bogotá: Debate, 2005.

Samper, José María. *Ensayo sobre las revoluciones políticas y la condición social de la república colombiana.* Bogotá: Biblioteca Popular de la Cultura Colombiana, 1945.

"Señal Colombia se alista para trasmitir la edición 100 del Tour de Francia." *Señal Colombia.* May 23, 2013. Web. April 16, 2013. Available at http:// www.senalcolombia.tv/senaldeportes/2096-senal-colombia-se-alista-para -transmitir-la-edicion-100-del-tour-de-france.html.

Serje, Margarita. *El revés de la nación: territories salvajes, fronteras y tierras de nadie.* Bogotá: Ediciones Uniandes, 2005.

Taylor, Chris. *The Beautiful Game: A Journey through Latin American Football.* London: Phoenix, 1998.

The Two Escobars. Dir. Jeff and Michael Zimbalist. All Rise Films/ESPN Films, 2010. Film.

Wade, Peter. *Blackness and Racial Mixture: The Dynamics of Racial Identity in Colombia.* Baltimore, MD: Johns Hopkins University Press, 1995.

Willis, Simon. "Colombia Enters Top Five in FIFA Soccer Rankings." *Colombia Reports.* December 19, 2012. Web. April 16, 2013. Available at http://colom biareports.com/colombia-news/sports/27473-colombia-enters-top-5-in -fifa-soccer-rankings.html.

Sports as Intranational Mediation

The Players of the Brazilian Football Team as a Model of Culture: Life Stories Mediated by Television News

Vander Casaqui

INTRODUCTION

This study deals with football and its intrinsic and complex relationship with Brazilian identity, mediated by the imagery presented in testimonies of the very protagonists of the spectacle, the members of the national men's team.[1] It analyzes, specifically, a series of interviews with the players of the Brazilian football team that participated in the 2010 South Africa World Cup, carried out by the National Journal of TV Globo, a major news program of Brazilian television. The series is based upon life stories mediated by the aesthetics of journalism, in which the players' trajectories are presented as models of overcoming, as examples of people who are bound to the national spirit, and as incarnations of the spirit of the warrior and worker, which represents the country (in accordance with the advertising concept of *seleção guerreira* (warrior team), developed in the campaign of Brahma beer, the official sponsor of the 2010 Brazilian team). These personal stories become allegories of a transformation of the whole nation; the overcoming of obstacles and challenges in their lives is a metaphor for a country achieving advances in social, cultural, and economic spheres.

The interest in studying this particular period through the national imagery around football, at a time of economic euphoria in Brazil, is supported by our working hypothesis. We believe that this moment represents a turning point in the national context, in which entrepreneurial culture exercises a growing influence on notions of Brazilian identity. The narratives of the national team introduce themes that become recurrent in social discourses, in various media products, in political speech, and in everyday life.

An expression of contemporary individualism manifests itself in these players' life stories, which incorporate other key themes that form part of this new national image: the idea of the Brazilian fighter, the significance of work, the enterprising spirit, the neoliberal subject and the ideal of authenticity. These narratives produce meanings in the mediatic world, constituting models of culture susceptible to becoming projections and inspirations for common subjects in their everyday life.

The relationship between Brazilians and football tends to be framed in terms of "being" or "not being" Brazilian. Even in times of nations and nationalism in decline, the sense of nationalism in the context of football would seem to reflect totalitarian discourses that represent all Brazilians in a unified connection with football, the national team, and the country. This discourse becomes hegemonic in periods of World Cup competition; however, this does not mean that there are no dissonances and oppositions. We understand the idea of "Brazilian spirit" in alignment with the theory of the new spirit of capitalism. According to Boltanski and Chiapello, the spirit of capitalism is a rhetoric, cyclically renewed, that promotes engagement in the system. We see the same sense of engagement in discourses that promote the "national spirit" as an enticement to participate in a media event (the World Cup) as a patriotic fan and a consumer, through the consumption of culture models, symbols, and goods.

The Brazilian Nation and the Mirror of Football

The nationwide propagation of football was initially realized through radio transmissions and later television broadcasts, which presented local championships and, every four years, the World Cup, which quickly became the apogee of patriotic sports euphoria. Football cannot be dissociated from its process of mediatization, a process that implies the construction of idols who serve as culture models, examples of success, aggregators of the values, and imaginaries of their time.

The story of great Brazilian football idols goes back to a distant past. One of the first to become famous and be associated with the culture of consumption was a player who became legendary following his outstanding performance in the 1938 World Cup: Leônidas da Silva, nicknamed the *Diamante Negro* (black diamond). His fame as a goal-scorer led to the creation of a chocolate brand of the same name, which remained commercially successful for decades. At a time when racial discrimination was more explicit in Brazilian culture, Leônidas was respected, worshiped, and envied. His career was certainly stimulated by his mediatic presence, through radio transmissions and journalistic coverage, that narrativized his exploits on the playing field and his stories off of it.

Pelé belongs to another time, in which the matches of the World Cup were transmitted live, via satellite, to locations worldwide. His goals and plays for the Brazilian team in 1970 continue to be broadcast again and again, with this permanence on the mediatic scene also contributing to the endurance of his myth. It would seem that his image as the greatest player of all time will never be forgotten.

Pelé and Leônidas da Silva, like more recent global stars, such as Romário and Ronaldo, are examples of the cult created around top sports idols in Brazil. Edgar Morin (2007) identified in the context of the Hollywood star system a process that maintains an association with classical mythologies, reinvented by a predominantly visual culture and organized in accordance with its own aesthetic principles. The Olympians, following Morin, are beings who transcend their humanity by inhabiting the media and serving as projections for their fans, maintaining a presence in the everyday life of common people; they serve as points of identification and inspirations for life trajectories. A significant number of these figures in Brazil, as well as in other countries, originate in sports, especially football. There is an important common element in the construction of these images in Brazil: many of those who attain success come from poor families, from poor communities from the interior of Brazil, and from economic conditions that offer no other paths for social mobility.

It is this route from difficult origins to international success that characterizes the testimonies of the players of the 2010 Brazilian team. Their 23 narratives were transmitted the day before the beginning of the competition, a moment in which patriotic feeling, often expressed in excessive terms, sets the tone for media coverage and its accompanying advertising communication linking commercial brands to sports. This process of associating football with the rhetoric of consumption is carried out in a direct way, by means of official sponsorships as well as through links to specific players, elevated to the status of world athletes who transcend the image of the nation. Those athletes are recruited for the globalized sports team sponsored by powerful international brands, such as Nike and Adidas, among others.

The narratives of the self (Sibilia) of the athletes construct meanings about the world of labor, based upon the cult of performance (Ehrenberg), appropriated into a Brazilian imagery that portrays football as a means of social mobility for young people of humble origin. These national team players, who attained positions on important professional teams around the world, particularly in European clubs, are mirrors that reflect and refract (Bakhtin, *Marxism* 46) the image of the Brazilian, an image mediated by the developmental imagery that surrounds Brazil's recent emergence in international media, mainly in economic news. The economic and corporate logics highlighted in journalistic and business discourses converge to give meaning to sports through its main actors: the players and their stories. These narratives are elevated to the status of models of a Brazil that projects its future through media storytelling. Local and global meanings are presented as complementary in order to structure the narratives, which are a sample of Brazil's cultural diversity, in connection with the world scene, where football is a spectacle within the contemporary entertainment industry.

Inspiring Narratives between Heroic Life and Everyday Life

In the current Brazilian context, the presence on the mediatic scene of inspiring narratives, of testimonies of famous and common people sharing their life stories with the public, is quite recurrent. They are narratives of overcoming, of transformation, and of the subjects' exposure to the obstacles and adversities of life, which result in a form of success based upon merit, personal effort, devotion to a dream, and persistence. Martín Barbero's reflections on the way in which Latin American culture draws from the cultural industry through a process of appropriation, translation, and negotiation, arriving at a mediated identity, sheds light on the way in which the characters of the worlds of football fit into this never linear process of projection and identification associated with the idea of the nation. In his analysis of the hero from a historic perspective, Buonanno differentiates everyday life from heroic life as follows:

> Everyday life is the domain of common existence, of common sense, of regular habits and at the same time (more and more) of the internal horizon of the quest for wellbeing and personal achievement; heroic life, on the contrary, is the reign of unique experiences, of uncommon actions, in which great individual virtues sensitive to the enchantment of transcendence are put to the service of objectives for the common good. (69)

The Brazilian World Cup team's autobiographical testimonies present a curious relationship between heroic and everyday life. The athlete—who earns high wages, becomes a celebrity, and traverses frontiers in order to attain international success—is presented as someone who shares the everyday life of any Brazilian but who struggled very hard to reach the status of a contemporary heroic life constructed through great mediatic events. The process of legitimizing his wealth and success is part of a transformation of the meaning of Brazilian nationality around the 2010 World Cup.

The question of nation is discussed again every four years as the formation of a national team is also a way of reformulating what it means to be Brazilian. The Brazilian team is constituted by discourses of its time—according to Bakhtin, every new enunciation is another link in the discursive chain (*Estética* 270). Bakhtin's language theory suggests that every World Cup produces slippages of meanings in that the Brazilian team is characterized not only by how it performs on the field, but also through its entry into the mediatic scene and into the quotidian dialogues that construct common places, shared opinions, and popularized judgments. These discourses start to define the set of athletes and specific traits—and, by extension, the common Brazilian people themselves in relation to them.

In the recent past, the mirror that served for the projection of the Brazilians' image was a team of famous players, stars of the major clubs of the planet, some of them chosen as the best players of the world by FIFA: for example, the team that went to the 2006 World Cup was considered to be the favorite to win the title. The early defeat of this "dream team" of Brazilian football generated a reaction that led to the construction of a counter-concept, nourished by an advertising campaign, for the following competition. Called "*seleção guerreira*" (warrior team), the team that participated in the 2010 World Cup became an explicit projection of the image of the Brazilian as a fighter in everyday life, represented by players who exhibit the same spirit. One of the advertisements of the traditional Brazilian beer brand Brahma used the voice of actors as fans manifesting what they expected from the players, with one of them expressing the synthesis of the connection between the athletes and the common Brazilian: "I want players who fight on the playing field like we fight in our lives."

In his analysis of the recent economic and sociocultural transformations in Brazil, which generated a national debate about the existence (or not) of a new middle class that emerged from the success of social inclusion policy during the government of President Luiz Ignácio Lula da Silva (2002–2010), Jessé Souza discusses the work ethic that characterizes the sector of society that identifies itself with the idea of the "Brazilian fighter." As the author puts it, "The fighters, in their overwhelming majority, do not have the privilege of experiencing a whole important stage of their lives divided between playing and studying" (Souza 51). Thus, the imposition of the necessity to work predominates as the most important element in this sector's characterization as a class, which differentiates it from a traditional middle class (and, obviously, from the classes that are more privileged economically) that has greater access to education.

The image of a Brazilian who fights for survival in everyday life to maintain his family, to provide better living conditions to his children, is a strong feature in Brazilian identity. This causes a certain tension in the way in which some figures, who attain success and who have media visibility, present themselves to the public in general when they speak about their trajectories that focus on their struggles to reach the top and attain success.

This not-always-conscious strategy of narrating one's own life, in the case of the players of the Brazilian team based upon the logic of overcoming, is a way to preserve one's roots, the "national spirit", and the connection with the imagery of "being Brazilian," in a discourse of identity delimitation. This characterization collides with the contemporary process of mediating football and the way in which players became millionaire actors of a global mega-spectacle. This mise en scène involves the exhibition of the actors as *garotos-propaganda* (advertising-boys) of brands of sporting goods and of other paraphernalia who aim to associate themselves with these athletes' image. Sponsored individually and celebrated in European clubs, the athletes are known beyond their national context, some eventually becoming figures whose wearing of the national uniform is questioned. Damo points out that these subjects go through a naturalization process of human trafficking since the players are treated openly, without ethical restrictions, as if they were material goods. The merchandising of football derives from its spectacularization and professionalization, which can be seen in three major milestones:

> a) the emergence of remuneration, which took place at the turn of the 20th century, in the spectrum of the disputes between amateurism and professionalism; b) the regulation of remuneration, or legalization, that took place by 1930; c) production and promotion of, and speculation on football players as a lucrative business, which started in 1970 and has intensified with the globalization process of the last decades. (Damo, *Do dom à profissão* 70)

This naturalized vision of the football players' work as a good is suspended when they are called upon to join the national team. As Oliven and Damo have pointed out, fans' distrust of those players who have scaled the mediatic Olympus is due to the way in which money is symbolized: these athletes' considerable earnings are very often perceived as something that breaks with the romantic vision of selfless devotion, of unconditional attachment to the struggle concerning the whole country. In this case, "the law of the market again takes the place of the law of national belonging" (Oliven and Damo, 111–112).

Paradoxes remain when we consider the meanings of work that come into play. On the one hand, work treated as a good—particularly understood in the athletes' relationships with their clubs, that is, based upon links to their workplace—in a certain way follows a model, established by capitalism from the Industrial Revolution on, in which labor is sold by the worker and consumed as merchandise by the productive processes. This notion of work reduces human activity, in a broad sense, to what

Schwartz calls "work *stricto sensu*," characterized by the dimension of employment and the link to an organization. On the other hand, sports activity is the basis of what Ehrenberg calls *the cult of performance*, that is to say, the logic of the management of life as a whole toward the goal of maximizing performance, overcoming one's own limits, an idea that derives from the neoliberal vision that makes subjects directly responsible for their successes or failures. High performance sports inspire a whole management vision applied not only to work but to everyday life, and even leisure, converting itself into a social illness.

Thus, we have two meanings of work that combine, although generally in conflictive ways. The athlete worker is made into merchandise for an institution, depending on a working team and on management by superiors, such as trainers, agents, and others who are responsible for the player's career, while being simultaneously subjected to a business-oriented system of evaluation, in which he is judged to be a good or bad manager of his own body, and of its performance. The player for the national team does not escape from this paradoxical way of perceiving his activity, which oscillates between devotion to the team spirit that represents the country and attention as an individual to individual exigencies and evaluations of his performance, which go beyond activities on the field, encompassing character, personal life, media image, and so on. Both these ideas enter into debates, whether in round-table discussions on sports television or in daily conversations in pubs and other public places.

Biographical Space and Life Stories of the Players of the Brazilian Team

Arfuch defines the concept of *biographical space* in relation to a "multiplicity of forms" (testimonies, life stories, voices, and images of common people) in which all *"relate*, in different ways, a story or a life experience" (111). Sustained by Bakhtin's dialogic theory, Arfuch's focus with regard to the narratives that compose biographical space takes into consideration the decentered character of the subject; although, the place of speech is characterized by a multiplicity of voices—that is to say, the one who says "I," assumes a discourse and in this way speaks, but is also being spoken by the social discourses of the time. The location from which a football player speaks in telling his life story in the media must be considered in terms of production conditions and any guidelines established during the creation of the self-referential narrative for its television format, the athletes' interactions with the interviewer (even if they are suppressed in the editing process); and the way in which the subject who assumes the discourse establishes the dialogue with the social audience. The other speech acts that contribute to the construction of the narrative—from relatives, acquaintances, people from the player's past and present life, also interviewed in the filming—sustain the legitimacy and the truth effect of the biographical discourse as part of a strategy of orchestration of voices.

The question of social audience cannot be underestimated; members of the national team craft a public persona based not only on their own ideas and those of their backers, but also on the identities and values of the Brazilians to whom they address their speech. This means that the presence of the image of the Brazilian fighter in his discourse is the result of this dialogic process, in which the subject elaborates the narrative of his own life in a calculation that adjusts itself to the worldview of his interlocutors. The result of this interaction is paradoxical: the same narrative concerns a subject's life story, with its peculiarities and unique experiences, while also being projected within the imagery of a nation, whose ideals regarding labor and the legitimacy of success determine the speaker's strategies in evoking authenticity. Authenticity here refers to Taylor's theoretical perspective, which discusses the moral idea of our times, articulated in terms of a search for self-realization and self-satisfaction in a quest for happiness, which implies the capacity to "hear one's inner voice" and reach a harmony in being (39).

ANALYSIS OF THE TESTIMONIES

Of the 23 roughly five-minute testimonies that convey the stories of the 2010 Brazilian players, we privilege those of the twelve starting players of the team (including Daniel Alves, a backup player who assumed starting status following Elano's injury during the competition): goalkeeper Júlio César (Internazionale); defenders: Maicon (Internazionale), Lúcio (Internazionale), Juan (Roma), Michel Bastos (Lyon), and Daniel Alves (Barcelona); midfielders Felipe Melo (Juventus), Elano (Galatasaray-Turkey), Gilberto Silva (Panathinaikos-Greece), and Kaká (Real Madrid); attackers Luís Fabiano (Sevilla) and Robinho (Santos).[2] The team's composition illustrates its globalized character: only one player (Robinho) plays for a Brazilian club.

The stories exhibit the realistic register of documental style aesthetics, along with graphic interventions. These visual resources provide a referential anchor of childhood photographs and images from personal archives, as well as images already known from the media world covering matches of the national team, the players presented in private and public life, and the players performing their job on the stage of the sports spectacle.

The stories are not necessarily presented in chronological order: a mixture of voices speaks about past and present, and reveals future expectations. Nevertheless, there are two very well-delimited temporal axes in the narrative construction: the first, situated in the distant past, traces origins, from birth through childhood, to the discovery of the vocation and the beginnings of professional trajectory. The second axis is concerned with recent history, already known by fans, presenting a portrait of the present situation and pointing toward the future in the context of the Brazilian team.

Family memory is key: the figure of the mother is the most prominent in most of the stories in which the difficulties of the origins, the fragility of past times, and the humanity of the high-performance athlete are exposed. An important element at this stage is the revelation of the nicknames, attributed to them by family members, through which they are known in their private lives. Some are diminutives of their first names, a common and affectionate form of address in any intimate relationship. Others are nicknames created in a given circumstance of life, such as that of the defender Maicon, known as "Pingo" ("small amount"; in Portuguese, this word is related to water droplets) because he was very small and fragile as a child. Maicon and Lúcio's mothers reveal practices that characterize this family figure as the religious, mystical center of her son's trajectory: both buried the umbilical cord of their newborn babies, one on the football field and the other near the entrance of the club of their small town. Dona Olindina, Lúcio's mother, explains: "Since I wanted him to be a football player, I took his little umbilical cord and buried it as the door, at the entrance of the stadium."

In this sense, the mother is the spiritual stimulator, the initial force that blesses the football player's trajectory—an element that appeals to both Brazil's Catholic tradition and the increasing bonds of some Brazilians to neo-Pentecostal religions. This family faith centered on the mother figure implies a sense of preservation of roots, of bonds to the homeland, which can be understood as local markers in the stories of players of global fame who act abroad. This is to say, local and global meanings permeate the audiovisual narrative.

The father figure assumes the role of cultivating the love for football, of having served as an inspiration and model, or even early amateur trainer. The presentation of affective relations, as in the case of the player Kaká, whose mother figure is the grandmother who took care of him when he was a child, exploits the human aspect of the performance, including the mediation of the family as a link between the story of these characters and the millions of Brazilians who have had similar experiences. The link between success and maternal love is thus constructed: Kaká, who at the time of the 2010 Cup had been signed by and presented as the great star of Real Madrid, dedicates his first shirt, from one of the greatest world clubs, to his grandmother. His story is interesting compared to the other player's lives because he was born in a family that was not poor, yet his difficulties in childhood emerged from class conflict. In a popular sport practiced by so many young people from lower classes, Kaká, a "rich" kid, was viewed with suspicion; he had to show talent above others to be respected and accepted. More commonly, stories of poverty, survival difficulties, obstacles to the practice of sports, and the need to work at other jobs to contribute to the family's income are told in an openly emotional tone. Tears, repressed voices, and earnest expressions nourish this first moment, which serves as a counterpoint to the victories of the present. The narrative structure is established from the knowledge already acquired about success in order to deconstruct it. This image of the Brazilian fighter and his reified individual trajectory conceals the obstacles that make access to a better social level difficult for millions of people. In this context, individuals are responsible for their success or their failure; the ideology of meritocracy dissimulates social barriers of class prejudice or racism.

This emphasis on hard work applied to reach the top brings the distant star (Morin's Olympian) down to the level of the everyday struggles of common subjects. The spirit of the Brazilian fighter emerges as the mark of the team, anchored in the story of each player. The totality of private experiences serve as a symbol of a whole nation, as their diversity invites fans to identify with these everyday struggles, dramas, and obstacles overcome. In this sense, these trajectories of success become exemplary life stories, according to Buonanno's theory, as we can see in the following passage from the story of Daniel Alves:

Off screen: "He never talked too much; he always lived on modest means."

Alves's brother: "My father always was a farmer, and we spent our childhood helping him to work in the fields."

Alves's brother: "At four a.m. we woke up, at five we went to the fields."

Alves's father: "He worked a lot, from Sunday to Sunday. Six months with plenty of water and six months of drought. So it's quite difficult."

Reporter: "In the dry land of the *sertão* [an arid region of the northeast of Brazil] of Bahia, Mr. Domingos [Alves's father] managed to plant and harvest melons and onions for sale. And he hoped that in these fields, composed of soil and stone, the most precious seed would grow."

In the passage quoted here, we clearly see the mediation of the life story through journalistic language in which a plurality of voices is woven together to construct the legitimacy and the authenticity of the narration. The scenario is visually spoken and portrayed, in a homology between picture and sound. The arrangement of these voices around the subject of journalistic discourse is evidenced in the reporter's synthesis, by the editing of their speech, by the way the theses about what it is to be Brazilian are organized on the basis of the footballers' private stories.

Alves's story depicts the most backward and inhuman aspect of Brazil: the suffering of the inhabitants of the northeastern *sertão*, who fight for survival in a desolate scenario, in precarious conditions. It is within these extreme difficulties that hope is planted, then transformed into success due to good luck, a combination of chance and competence. This narrative is recurrent in the national imaginary, constituting a model of a country that itself wants to overcome marginality in the present time: a country of improbable heroes, of people who fight against adversity without being able to count on social policy and structures that would allow most Brazilians' access to full citizenship, to constitutional rights, and to an existence of human dignity.

In this context, faith and hope are indispensable elements of the daily life of millions of people waiting for miracles. Some of these heroes, coming from the poorest strata of the population, represent this possibility of upward mobility through football. Here, impoverished Brazil is situated in the past, in the origins of the trajectory that at the present time is one of success and points toward a future of victories. Due to the recurrence of this narrative structure, the construction of a thesis based upon life stories mediated by journalistic language becomes evident: the thesis that Brazil has overcome its underdevelopment and is experiencing a moment of international acknowledgement, progress, and competitiveness in the global sphere. Nonetheless there are links to the origins that must be maintained in order to reinforce the imaginary of the nation. This reinforcement emphasizes the players' role as representatives of all Brazilians—thus there is the deconstruction or genealogy of the success of the national team's football players, which emphasizes the trajectory of overcoming. This becomes evident at the beginning of Gilberto Silva's story, through the voice of Globo Television's reporter, Tino Marcos: "From the Luciânia train station to Lagoa da Prata there are six kilometers; from Lagoa da Prata to Europe, there are a few chapters. Beto's story begins here, in the west of the state of Minas Gerais."

The successful millionaire athlete stands in for any common Brazilian, overcoming traumas, difficulties, and obstacles. The figure of the potential player rejected many times during his trajectory emphasizes a sense of resilience and perseverance: if he obtained his place in the sun, he struggled very much to get there. He counted on the support of family, experienced sacrifices, and had the blessing of someone's trust in his potential. In this sense, his trajectories evidence the revelation of his authentic being: his "inner self" flourishes with time passing, with dedication, with faith, and with the support of the family (Taylor 38).

The narrative of overcoming emerges from traumas that were avoided: the player Michel Bastos, for example, carries with him the loss of his twin brother, run over right in front of him, while his four year old brothers were playing on the street. This tragedy was transformed into a tattoo and into the religious discourse that identifies him as the angel that protects Bastos in the struggles of life. The midfielder, Elano, manifests his emotion when speaking about his motivation to win and realize the dream of giving his parents, who work cutting sugar cane and harvesting oranges in a rural area of São Paulo state, a better standard of living. Likewise, Bastos is applauded by his family for offering them a better life.

This role of "the family's savior," who assumes the duty of realizing his relatives' social ascension, reinforces some elements that compose the profile of the legitimately successful Brazilian soccer player: a strong attachment to his origins; a humble character, appropriate to the traditional family structure; faith; and a fighter's perseverance. This moral and psychological outline guides all the narrated stories; their effect is to promote the authenticity of national representatives, who are elevated to exemplars of behavior and mirrors of a country that aims to achieve social progress. They are models of success with a Brazilian "look." They conquer the world but cannot lose their original character; they are stars who are generous and responsible, good sons, good fathers, and good workers.

The figure of the player is exalted to gigantic proportions due to the difficulties he has faced in the past that are put in parallel with the other temporal axis that shows the recent past, the present, and the perspective of the future. If the prior moment is that of the apparently insurmountable challenges of everyday life, enveloped in emotion and faith, in a belief that transcends rationality in its perspective on social ascension, heroic life appears in all the splendor of performance. The images of the remote past, presented in a naturalistic register and very often in slow motion, lead into the accelerated rhythm of the players' maneuverings for the Brazilian team and for major world clubs, accompanied by their record of successful careers. If at first there was the rejected aspiring professional player who attempted to accomplish other functions and failed (as in the case of Luís Fabiano, who tried to work in a mechanic's workshop, but was fired as he "had not the least aptitude for it"), now there is the high performance athlete, exhibiting power over his own body, success on world-class teams in Brazil and abroad, and admission to the national team that has won more world titles than any other. Statistics abound (number of goals, matches played on the national team, years playing abroad), proof of the efficient management of the player's career and talent for playing football.

The role of the soundtrack in the narrative is fundamental to mark the transition from the past, in which the tone is melodious, discreet, like in the melodies of the guitar that accompany the memory of family life, to the present moment, in which the music becomes intense, accelerated, and grandiose, producing the heroic tone of recent professional accomplishments. This is the scenario or the mediatic scene of the World Cup, in which the players of the Brazilian team are protagonists. In the present time, the family joins the ranks of the fans, cheering on and admiring the high performance worker, considered an exceptional case in the place he came from. The focus is on the subject and on his individual successes. There is clearly a neoliberal spirit associated with the football player when the narrative deals with his victorious performances on important teams or him wearing Brazil's green and yellow shirt. Now, the indisputable results are at the forefront, amplified by the mostly unknown stories of overcoming hardships. This is exemplified in the story of Kaká, who was elected as the best player in the world by FIFA in 2007: "In 2002, the youngest world champion: twenty years old. Today, twenty-five years old. Twenty-five goals for Brazil." The focus is similar in a passage of the narrative about the goalkeeper Júlio César: "Seventeen years old, starting player of the Flamengo Squad. Thirty years old, the great starting player of the Brazilian team. Forty-seven matches. As goalie on the Internazionale FC team, he is one of the stars of the team."

From a historical perspective, it is important to observe the transition of the imaginary surrounding the Brazilian player. Figures such as Garrincha and Pelé, who represent the golden age of the Brazilian team (1958–1970), when Brazil won three of four World Cups, were symbols of the art of football, of "playing beautifully," which would differentiate theirs from the playing style of opposing teams. Until recently, the Brazilian football school privileged its virtuosos, who fascinated the public with their ability and also achieved victories. After a long period of defeats, the conquest of the 1994 World Cup in the United States was marked by pragmatic football, by the predominance of the tactical application more identified with European style—with the exception of two skilful attackers, Romário and Bebeto. In the profiles of the 2010 players, the focus is on earnestness, application, and efficacy: the legacy of joy, dribbles, and the *ginga* (a sway combining agility, flexibility, strength, and speed) of the football of former times is reserved only for a few attackers, such as Luís Fabiano and Robinho. According to an ex-trainer, the latter was "irreverent, creative…many times I removed him from the match because he dribbled a lot—the opponents wanted to hit him." But what stands out is the reading of the Brazilian player who adapts himself to the contemporary neoliberal spirit. In the narratives that make up this research, there is an interesting homology between personal profile and playing style, between the individual's story and the role he plays on the team. In counterpoint to the irreverence of the two attackers mentioned earlier, the great majority of the group is composed of earnest players, devoted to the mission to win with willpower and determination, echoes of a corporate culture that has integrated itself into the spirit of the Brazilian team. Symbols of a spirit of competitiveness, the defenders have an introspective way of being; they are indefatigable in the fight and in their obsession with victory. Team leader Lúcio's mother evokes this spirit when she declares herself an unconditional fan of her son, "mainly when he scolds the players... [demonstrating] much determination, this will to win."

CONCLUSIONS

This study identifies the meanings of the personal narratives of Brazilian football players, and the composition of the spirit of the warrior team that participated and was defeated in the 2010 World Cup. From a diachronic perspective, the role of the origins, stories of overcoming, and family mediations are ways of linking the international football stars to an interpretation of what it is to be Brazilian. The cultural models propagated by journalistic discourse build the scenario in which Brazil overcomes the difficulties of the past and achieves success in the present time. The cult of performance appears in the portrait of each player's present moment, in which the quantification of achievements emphasizes their efficacy and competitiveness in a globalized and demanding market. The myth of the art of football, of a glorious past, gives way to a new myth of the warrior team, which corresponds to the profile of the Brazilian fighter, who experiences difficulties but is also capable of overcoming adversity and achieving glory. In accordance with the neoliberal performance-based perspective, these players were evaluated according to their results; the pre-Cup moment depicted in these testimonies is when the expectations surrounding the Brazilian team took on notes of exaggerated patriotism, an intensified national spirit, and the idea that we are "the country of football." Nevertheless, the reality of the defeat in the quarterfinals against Holland led to the discredit of the concept of the warrior team; the players were stigmatized, silently deprived of their role as models of character and of behavior for the nation.

The neoliberal framework of the contemporary Brazilian team is however still sustained by a results-oriented culture: in the country that has conquered more world titles than any other, victory is always expected, whether the team "plays beautifully" or not. With each new World Cup, the media scene reinvents the meanings of what it is to be Brazilian, in mirrors that reflect and refract history, memory, and nation. Personal life and national spirit are intricately entwined in the spectacularized euphoria that creates audiences, sponsorships, and merchandise. This logic of consumption has resulted in the players' heroic lives, as promoted in journalistic discourse, being discarded because of defeat in the competition.

The analyzed models are a metaphor of the idea of the nation before and after a great transformation. The Brazil of the interior—rural, backward, underdeveloped—appears initially as the place of origin of a subject who, in normal conditions, could advance very little beyond the poverty line, or the circumstances of any common Brazilian. The image of the Brazilian fighter is then enhanced, as can be seen in Gilberto Silva's narrative: according to him, personal success is to be "a good son, a good brother and a good worker." The illnesses, the traumas, and the will to win, based upon faith and not reason, are associated with the past. At this moment of the narrative, family ties are linked to the image of the nation, the mother country, the never forgotten origins.

Nevertheless they are narratives of overcoming, success stories, at a second moment linked to the present and the future. The image of the nation is individualized, personalized in the great player's performance, which led him to the conquest of a privileged place in the soccer market, that of an athlete able to overcome the most difficult historic adversaries (in various narratives, the goal or the unforgettable victory came against Brazil's greatest rival: the Argentine team), and capable of performing on the world scene.

Defenders such as Lúcio are earnest, quiet, and responsible; the team's captain has manifested his vocation since he was very young, as his mother says he was "fierce" and never liked to lose. Attackers, on the contrary, like Robinho and Luís Fabiano, are extroverted, good-humored, polemical, and irreverent. In this way, the narratives project the image of a team that combines the tradition of the art of football, magic of dribbles, and improvisation of the past with the exigencies of technique, earnestness, and physical vigor, which were formerly specific attributes of European teams, such as Italy or Germany, and which today are requirements of sports in general.

The narratives trace the profile of the ideal worker, defined by his personality. They reinforce the idea of his talent and unequivocal vocation for his chosen activity, and of the extrapolation of these characteristics to ideals of life in general. The role of sports celebrities, then, is to disseminate and legitimize culture models aligned with a project of nation, guided by the discourse of change. In this sense, the individual's transformation is an allegory of change in the country; this project is invitation to Brazilians to engage in the "new spirit" of Brazil. The ideology of meritocracy advocates, categorically, that the success of culture models is proof of the possibility that anyone can achieve his goals through effort and willpower. More than that: in this move from the Third World to the First World, from the unfavorable conditions of underdevelopment to victory in high performance sports, the image of a country that strives to be another, that glorifies success models and improbable trajectories, is being constructed. The "national spirit," updated by the logic of neoliberalism, calls for all Brazilians to overcome their limits and win. However, this image also exposes what remains of its backwardness, of what has still to be overcome so that there will be less mystique, less faith, and more logical opportunities of upward social mobility, not only for a few, but for the great majority of Brazilians. In this regard, there is still a great deal of narrative to be constructed.

Notes

1. Thanks to Juliana Doretto for her help with the translation and final review of this article, as well as to the editors for their review of the translation.
2. The analyzed material can be found on the YouTube channel of the Brazilian Flamengo club: http://www.youtube.com/user/FlamengoFutebol (accessed June 17, 2012).

Bibliography

Arfuch, Leonor. *O espaço biográfico: dilemas da subjetividade contemporânea.* Rio de Janeiro: EdUERJ, 2010.
Bakhtin, Mikhail. *Estética de la creación verbal.* Buenos Aires: Siglo XXI, 2008.
———. (Volochinov) *Marxismo e filosofia da linguagem.* São Paulo: Hucitec, 1997.
Boltanski, Luc, and Ève Chiapello. *O novo espírito do capitalismo.* São Paulo: Martins Fontes, 2009.
Buonanno, Milly. "Histórias de vidas exemplares. Biografias." *MATRIZes* Ano 5:1 (Jul./Dez. 2011): 63–84.
Damo, Arlei Sander. *Do dom à profissão: formação de futebolistas no Brasil e na França.* São Paulo: Aderaldo & Rothschild Ed., Anpocs, 2007.
———. "A magia da seleção." *Rev. Bras. Cienc. Esporte* 28:1. Campinas, 2006: 73–90.
Ehrenberg, Alain. *O culto da performance: da aventura empreendedora à depressão nervosa.* Aparecida, Brasil: Idéias & Letras, 2010.
Martín Barbero, Jesús. *Dos meios às mediações: comunicação, cultura e hegemonia.* Rio de Janeiro: UFRJ, 2003.
Morin, Edgar. *Cultura de massas no século XX: neurose.* Rio de Janeiro: Forense Universitária, 2007.
Oliven, Ruben George, and Arlei Sander Damo. *Fútbol y cultura.* Bogotá: Norma, 2001.
Schwartz, Yves. "Conceituando o trabalho, o visível e o invisível." *Trabalho, Educação e Saúde.* 2011. Web. September 18, 2011. http://www.scielo.br/scielo.php?script=sci_arttext&pid=S1981-74620110004000002&lng=pt&nrm=iso.
Sibilia, Paula. *La intimidad como espectáculo.* Buenos Aires: Fondo de Cultura Económica, 2008.
Souza, Jessé. *Os batalhadores brasileiros: nova classe média ou nova classe trabalhadora?* Belo Horizonte, Brasil: Ed. UFMG, 2010.
Taylor, Charles. *A ética da autenticidade.* São Paulo: É Realizações Editora, 2011.

CHAPTER 6

Nationalism and Public Policies of Sports in Brazil

Renata Maria Toledo and Maria Tarcisa Silva Bega

Translated by Cassandra White

INTRODUCTION

At the end of the twentieth century, a series of social changes came to influence the relationship between politics and sports in Brazilian society. With the end of the military dictatorship, a set of political and institutional reforms was included in the country's political agenda, culminating in the formulation of a new Federal Constitution in 1988. In this new constitution sports were included as a "right of everyone," to be guaranteed by the state (Brasil, 2011). This was not the first time Brazilian legislation adopted a principle of expansion of access to sports practices. The military regime had made a move in this direction, with the development of the legal concept of "mass sport." The 1988 Constitution, however, restructured this idea by presenting sports as a right for everyone, as a social good to be democratized through Brazilian public policies of sport.

The inclusion of the "right to sports" in the 1988 Federal Constitution created an expectation of significant changes within public policies of sports. Before these changes, ideological use of sports as national symbol and an emphasis on high performance sports (Veronez, 2005) prevailed. The latter were defined as connected to the international sports system and as part of the national and international sports federations and confederations, as well as the Brazilian Olympic Committee and the International Olympic Committee (Brasil, 1998).[1] With the new Constitution, the hope was that the Brazilian state would give priority to the democratization of access to sports practices.

Nonetheless, these expectations were not ratified by the subsequent historical process (Veronez, 2005; Boudens, 2008). On the contrary, the new constitutional rules came into conflict with bureaucratic and symbolic guidelines that underlay sports policies in Brazil. Considering that what stands out in these guidelines was the political and ideological use of sports as a national symbol, in this article we set out to spell out how the symbolic association between sports and nationalism conflicts with the premise of sport as a "right of everyone," as stated in the Federal Constitution. We firstly present a historical retrospective of sport policies in Brazil, highlighting the connection between sports and nationalism in the country. Next, we examine the social conditions for the emergence of the concept of "right to sports." Finally, we analyze the conflicts between the symbolic construction of sport as a national symbol and the principle of democratization of sports practices.

The Politics of Sports and Nationalism in Brazil: Some Historical Background

The first major state regulation of the sports sector in Brazil came about during the Getúlio Vargas Government (1930–1945) through Decree 3199 of April 13, 1941. Among other provisions, this decree established that "sports take on a patriotic character" (Brasil, 1941). In addition, it restricted the participation of foreign managers and coaches in sports organizations. Since then, sports have been considered a matter of national concern, as reflected in a set of cultural policies the state developed in order to achieve its project of nation-building. The national identity and the sovereignty of the country became topics of intense social and intellectual debate in Brazilian society in the early twentieth century. Brazil was seen as going through a crisis, evident in the difficulty of populating its vast and empty territories, as well as in its fragile position on the international stage, all of which brought the demand for national organization to the forefront of intellectual concerns.

In view of that diagnosis, conservative intellectuals defended the idea that the strengthening of the state was the only possible solution for saving Brazil from what they considered to be the crisis of the country (Oliveira, 2003). The idea of the centralization of the Brazilian state found fertile ground with the rise of Getúlio Vargas to the presidency of the republic in 1930. Under Vargas, the issue of national identity and sovereignty was given a new foundation that included concerns about the appreciation of Brazilian culture, the construction of a national sentiment, and the production of political legitimacy for the government (Velloso, 1987). This resulted in the implementation of measures in several cultural arenas, for example, in formal education, literature, music, and cinema, among others, with the goal of constructing a Brazilian national identity.

Sports was one of the focal areas for such cultural policies, as the Vargas government incorporated it into its nation-building project, not just conferring upon it the status of being a genuine expression of Brazilian popular culture and patriotic character. Since the end of the nineteenth century, there had been a symbolic connection between modern sports and the nation. Houlihan (1997) asserts that sports contribute to the fusion of different characteristics of national states, including their territorial organization, the active participation of the population in the life of the nation, the setting up of national guidelines for the construction of citizenship, and cultural homogenization through mass education.

These assertions are relevant in our context because they suggest important reasons why different countries/governments seek to appropriate the sports phenomenon as an instrument of political legitimacy, both domestically and in international relations. According to Houlihan (1997), this political use of sports tends to be the most useful and effective in countries without a strong, historically rooted ethnic identity where, without significant historical symbols, the population tends to choose athletes and athletic achievements to affirm the glory of the nation and national identity. This is because a modern sport is organized in a system that "provides a number of emotionally charged occasions for citizens to be made aware of and express their common identity within the nation. The participation in major sports events as spectators has the element of ritual and emotional appeal capable of sustaining the 'imagined community' of the nation" (121). Thus the attribution of a patriotic character to sports by Vargas's government, especially considering that the social and intellectual debate at the time, and even beyond (Carvalho, 2003; Schwarcz, 2003), was that the national component was notably fragile in Brazil, so that the country was said to be formed as a state with no nation.

Vargas's government also imposed a rigid control over sports organizations, determined by Decree 3199 (1941). However, if on one hand this legal control restricted civil liberties, on the other hand it opened up material support for the development of sports in the country. Indeed, in its Chapter 7, entitled *On the Measures for the Protection of Sports*, this decree established a funding policy for sports, based on two primary principles: (a) grants for the construction of sports facilities and the maintenance and development of sports activities; (b) tax exemptions for imported sports equipment. The new Vargas measures established a standard for sports policies in Brazil, characterized by administrative centralization, government control and oversight of sports associations, the provision of public funds, the labeling of sport as a national matter, and the political-ideological use of sports. These guidelines were mostly maintained by subsequent governments.

Indeed, during the military dictatorship that ruled the country between 1964 and 1985, the symbolic association between sports and the nation continued to be a mandate for sports policies. However, the military government introduced some new elements in the process of policymaking for the sports sector, among which, notably, is the fact that these policies came to be understood as "social policies." In 1971, the government published a diagnostic study about physical education and sports in the country. In it, Arlindo Lopes Corrêa brought forward the following concerns:

> The activities of Physical Education and Sports are then intimately tied to health and education policies, given their influential role in shaping the physical and mental aptitude of the population; they have, moreover, ties with policies of well-being, as they relate to leisure and recreation; in addition to these implications, that alone justify carrying out this study, we cannot ignore the psychosocial aspects linked to this sector, that also have an influence on the international political level. (Corrêa, 1971, 7)

This excerpt includes two central principles of sports policy of the military regime. First, it indicates the key connection between physical education/sports and social policies, with the example of health, education, and leisure. Second, it involves the influence of sports on external policy. Both contributed to the formation of the *National Policy of Physical Education and Sport*, instituted in 1975, which stated that sports could be "one of the instruments used by the State and by the community to solve contemporary problems, created by modern industrial society, with more time devoted to leisure and the diminished need of physical effort in human labor" (Brasil, 1976, 27). By attributing a social character to sports policies, the military established new guidelines for sport policies in Brazil that resulted in the development of mass sports. Therefore, the *National Policy* set out, among other goals, to implement and intensify mass sports, conceiving "physical education in the schools as a cause and high level sports as an effect, with mass sport as an intermediary" (53). The perspective, then, was that the expansion of sports for a significant part of the population, including those who were already out of school, would allow the sports system to broaden the selection pool of athletes for high performance sports.

Another noteworthy element in *The National Policy of Physical Education and Sports* was the premise that sports could be an instrument of social and national cohesion. This brings up two questions: (a) what were the motives of the military government in concerning itself with "social and national cohesion"?, and (b) why were sports understood as an instrument that could attend to this concern? With regard to the first question, it is necessary to consider various social and economic tensions during the military dictatorship. During the 1960s and 1970s, there was intensive economic and industrial development which resulted in a demographic shift, so that urban populations exceeded those in rural areas for the first time in Brazilian history. The sudden and uncontrolled growth of the large urban centers exposed the precariousness of national infrastructure in areas such as basic sanitation, transportation, and public security. In addition, there was a progressive change in labor distribution, with a significant drop in the availability of jobs in the agricultural sector and a correspondent increase in the industrial sector. This, however, did not alter the structure of social inequality that had become a prominent feature of Brazilian society. On the contrary, this great economic expansion deepened this inequality (Carvalho, 2001). These changes and the tensions due to the authoritarian regime manifested primarily in the restriction of the civil and political rights of the population. Such was the context for the preoccupation with social and national cohesion, expressed in *The National Policy of Physical Education and Sports*.

Regarding the second question, it is worth considering, as mentioned before, that sports constitutes one of the most effective means of making the "nation" palpable to people, strengthening national sentiment and bringing it to the surface (Hobsbawm, 1990; Houlihan, 1997). This symbolic strength of sport as an instrument of political and social legitimacy was acknowledged by the military in the diagnostic study as well as in the *National Policy*. And it was recurring not only in the documents, but also in the political acts of the government, which made use of sport for ideological purposes in many occasions. One of the most significant was when the national soccer team won the 1970 FIFA World Cup (Carvalho, 2001). This ideological use of sports and the emphasis on high performance within sport policies did not obstruct the dissemination of sports as a right, which was echoed by individuals and sport organizations. Important changes in the political framework would create the conditions for that idea to take hold.

The Restoration of Democracy: Sports in the New Brazilian Constitutional Order

A set of government measures partially reversing the restrictions on civil and political rights, culminated in the return, in 1982, of direct federal elections and the choice, in 1985, of the first civil president after 20 years of military rule. Running parallel to these measures, civil society reorganized itself, creating political parties, unions, and social movements, staking a claim in the restoration of democracy in the country.

Indeed, the so-called New Republic, which governed Brazil after the military regime, was a period of intense reform activity. Spanning several social areas, the proposals for changes were also directed toward the sports sector. To reform it, the Brazilian government created a commission in the Ministry of Education, in charge of sport policies in Brazil, to "carry out studies about national sports and to present related proposals" (Brasil, 1985a). The work of this commission was published under the title *A New Policy for Brazilian Sport: Brazilian Sport as a State Matter*. It included suggestions for sport policies in the country and provided two central guidelines: (a) administrative autonomy was granted to sport organizations, as the state should only guarantee and stimulate the conditions allowing the sport sector to operate as a free market; (b) sport was stated as a social right, to be guaranteed by the Federal Constitution. This document proposed an end to state interference in terms of the administrative organization of sports, but it did not suggest an end to funding. Though affirming free enterprise as a basic principle of performance sports, it suggested the continuation of dependence on the state for the provision of necessary resources and infrastructure to sport organizations (1985b).

The work of this commission did not produce concrete results in the formulation of sport policies. According to Sônia Draibe, the commissions put together by the government served more to bolster the constitutional debate on how to build a new legal framework for the country. The new Federal Constitution was introduced on October 5, 1988, bringing important institutional changes. Built from the perspective of broadening rights, its Article 6 defined that social rights, in Brazilian society, are "education, health, work, leisure, safety, social insurance, protection of motherhood and infancy, assistance to those in need" (Brasil, 2011). Even though sports was not listed in this article, it is apparent that the constitutional text comes close to including it, especially in its Article 217, described in the following terms:

> Article 217. It is the responsibility of the State to promote formal and informal sports activities as *a right of everyone*, respecting: I—the autonomy of controlling sports entities and organizations, as much in terms of their organization as with their operation; II—the provision of public resources with priority to educational sport and, in specific cases, for high performance sports; III—differential treatment for professional and nonprofessional sports; IV—the protection and encouraging of the creation of new forms of sport created in the country [...] § 3° The government will encourage leisure, as a means of promoting social welfare. (Brasil, 2011; emphasis added by the authors)

The connection between sports and social right was established not only by giving sports the status of a right, but also by placing Article 217, which rules sport practices, in the same part of the Federal Constitution which regulates other social rights, such as education, health, and social insurance. In addition, by declaring the encouragement of leisure, it connected sports practices with one of the social rights listed in the aforementioned Article 6.

In view of this, the following question arises: what is the sociological meaning of this connection between sports and social rights, as outlined in the 1988 Federal Constitution? In other words, what is meant by this claim about sports practices as a "social right"? In order to answer these questions we need to conceptualize the latter. From a sociological point of view, social rights can be understood not only as abstract legal constructs, but as historical and social phenomena. According to Thomas Marshall (1967), social rights make up an integral part of social citizenship, which has to do with the extension of the right of participation in social wealth to every citizen who belongs to a given society. It is officially established in the nation's legal framework and guaranteed by institutions that make up the modern nation-state. In the context of capitalist societies, the historical emergence of social rights represented a decrease of individual performance in the market as a requirement to acquire goods and services related to social welfare, since these would come to be provided by the state (Esping-Andersen, 1991).

Thus, the connection between sports and social rights in our society lies in its conception as an integral part of social wealth, guaranteed by the Brazilian state, as a "right of everyone." Nonetheless, it is important to consider that this was not the only meaning of sport within public policies in that period of our history. As we mentioned before, sports became a national symbol, and this symbolic connection was a recurrent theme in Brazilian sport policies since the 1940s. Both meanings were not necessarily mutually exclusive; on the contrary, they coexisted in the representations of sports inside the political arena. How then have these two meanings fit in to the public policies of sports in Brazil?

To outline an answer to this question, we firstly consider that both social rights and nationalism are modern phenomena, the historical development of which has distinct symbolic dimensions. Norbert Elias (1997) pointed out that the emergence of the modern nation-state had effects on social relations, giving them a dual orientation. On one hand, modernity was based on a code of moralistic humanism, founded on the principle that this could be applied universally, granting an ontological equality to individuals and assigning the greatest value to human beings. On the other hand, modernity was based on a code founded in nationalist belief, that is, not on equality and whose most important value was the collectivity formed by individuals that make up the nation. This dual orientation tends to result in a series of conflicts, especially when taken as guiding principles of human action.

The theoretical arguments of Elias (1997) help us understand the distinction of the symbolic dimensions of social rights and nationalism. The former, representing a concern that minimum social standards be established and shared by the whole society, correcting the excessive inequalities that class stratification imposes on individuals, can be identified with the humanistic code. Different from it, nationalism suggests the primacy of the nation over any other value, including, in certain circumstances, as in wars, over its own people. Therefore, after the advent of the 1988 Federal Constitution, sports was connected, even though not in the same proportion, to the two symbolic camps discussed earlier. Actually, when considering the historical development of sport policies in Brazil, it is clear that they have deeper roots in the symbolic dimension of nationalism, given sport's use as a national symbol, even though not necessarily incorporated into the institutional framework of the country. This situation explains why public policies of sports continued to operate primarily according to the nationalist code and not according to the humanistic perspective privileging the association of sports with social rights in our society.

This scenario becomes more complex if we consider the historical circumstances which resulted in the economic exploitation of sports. We mentioned the reformist debates of the mid-1980s in which sport organizations called for an end to state intervention with regard to sports governance but not with respect to their funding. The organizations supported the idea that high performance sports were an integral part of the "social right" to sports. This created a dual conceptual space in which sports was referred to as both a social right (which presupposed detachment from the market and a legitimate claim to public funding) and as a commercial activity, suggesting free enterprise and the adoption of the supply and demand law of the market.

These two principles proposed by the commission established in the Ministry of Education to reform sport policies in Brazil during the New Republic were assumed by the 1988 Federal Constitution. Indeed, it adopted the principle of ensuring the autonomy of sports organizations as well as guaranteed the distribution of public funds for high performance sports, although it gave priority to educational sports. While sports practices were promoted to the status of a right, sports did not lose its status as national symbol. This gave rise to tensions that influenced sport policies in the following period, as we will discuss in the next section.

Sports and Public Policies Post-1988: The Dominance of Symbolic Nationalist Values over the Humanistic Perspective of Democratization

On the twentieth anniversary of the enactment of the Federal Constitution, Emile Boudens (2008) analyzed the impact on sport policies in Brazil of the inclusion of sports and leisure in the constitutional text. The author not only pointed out the failure of different governments to observe the constitutional guidelines, but also stated that there was a "betrayal" of those principles. Concluding his analysis, Boudens advocated a set of institutional arrangements for the Brazilian sport sector, in order to follow that law. Boudens's article brings to the surface some topics that are also relevant for a sociological study of public policies: (a) the differences between legal principles and their application within social relations; (b) the influence of different interest groups in the formulation of a given public policy; and (c) the institutional fragility of sports as a fundamental right in the country.

Let us examine the first topic. Boudens's conclusions, referring to the failure of different governments to follow the constitutional guidelines, are not surprising. It is important to recognize the presence of different interest groups within the political process producing diverse public policies of sport. Identifying these groups will allow us to better understand the conflict between the humanistic and the nationalist code in the formulation of those policies. As mentioned before, the boundaries between the civil society and the state have been historically unclear in Brazilian society, especially from the enactment of Decree 3199 (1941) on. However, if this proximity implied a decrease in administrative autonomy for the sports organizations, it also gave way to a kind of legacy for these organizations, particularly those connected with high performance sports. As a result, these entities gained a privileged position of access to the government, in a way that placed their interests in the political agenda above those of other interest groups.

A significant example of this privileged condition is the composition of the National Council of Sport, responsible for developing and promoting mass sport, as well as managing quality and transparency in Brazilian sport (Brasil, 2002). This council is currently composed of five representatives of the federal government, two from subnational government and fifteen from nongovernmental organizations. Among the last group, seven are directly or indirectly connected to high performance sports: the Brazilian Olympic Committee, the Brazilian Paralympic Committee, the National Commission of Athletes, Social Clubs, the Brazilian Military Sport Commission, the National Organization of National Sport Entities, and the Brazilian Soccer Confederation. One seat belongs to a professional association, the Federal Council of Physical Education; another to a scientific organization, the Brazilian College of Sport Sciences; and six are occupied by "representatives of national sports." This last group is composed of members of civil society who had or still have connections with high performance sports in Brazil (2014). Considering this distribution, it is clear that high performance sport is better represented in the National Sport Council than any other interest group of the sport sector.

The aforementioned strategic position is also evident with respect to state funding policies. In general terms, there are four financial sources for sports in Brazil: (a) the federal budget; (b) the national lottery; (c) tax waivers; and (d) sponsorship by companies under state control. Although there has not been much research on sports-financing in the country, the few studies that focus on this theme come to the same conclusion: high performance sport is the primary beneficiary of federal funding (Veronez, 2005; Almeida, 2010; Castelan, 2010; Almeida et al., 2012). Revenue from the national lottery goes exclusively to high performance sports, according to Law 10.264 (2001). This law earmarks 2 percent of the gross income from the national lottery to Brazilian sports, divided as follows: 85 percent to the Brazilian Olympic Committee and 15 percent to the Brazilian Paralympic Committee. This law also establishes that both committees will receive resources from the federal bank in charge of the national lottery (Brasil, 2001).

Therefore, besides selecting the Brazilian Olympic Committee as its principle beneficiary, the law determines that the resources generated from the national lottery be transferred directly to this institution. The law gives another advantage to the Brazilian Olympic Committee: though variable over time, lottery funds are a strong source of guaranteed revenue, while those coming from the federal budget are subject to the vagaries of economic crises, fiscal adjustments, and changes in the country's political scene. The third source of funds mentioned was created by Law 11.438 (December 29, 2006), authorizing individuals and companies to deduct money spent on sponsorship of all kinds of sports activities for tax purposes. Finally, the last source is the sponsorship through companies controlled by the state, whether they operate as public monopolies or in accordance with free market rules. Though sponsorship of other types of sports exists, most of the investments are allocated to high performance sports, especially to the national teams. The most long-lasting and successful of this type of financing is the Brazilian volleyball team, sponsored by the Bank of Brazil since 1991 (Banco do Brasil, 2013).

In view of this, the centrality of high performance sport is evident in the public policies implemented since the introduction of the Federal Constitution of 1988. This can be partially understood as a result of the historical development of sport policies in the country creating the conditions in which sport entities linked to high performance sports gradually acquired a strategic position in the sports-politics arena. However, this may be also explained by the symbolic association of sports as a national symbol. Given that the events that reinforce this connection are related to high performance sports, the latter is considered by the legitimacy-seeking state as the most profitable sport dimension.

This statement could be challenged by two ends of the twentieth century trends that, in some ways, affect the symbolic connections between sports and nationalism: (a) the decline of the nation-state and of nationalism; and (b) the economic exploitation of sports.

Despite the expansion of economic and cultural globalization, the figure of the nation remains an important element of state cohesion and identity production, though sharing space with other makers of identity. Because nationalist beliefs remain, governments continue to use sports to symbolically construct the image of their respective countries, both domestically and internationally. In the Brazilian case, this perspective becomes apparent in the official discourse of public policies related to the sports industry. One example of this trend can be found in the following excerpt from the report of the commission of the National Congress that shows support for the Law 10.264 (2001), which states:

> As is apparent, the amount allocated for Olympic sports is extremely limited and insufficient, *taking into account its importance for the promotion of Brazil's image to a prominent position in the international scene.* In its different manifestations, far from being a second-tier activity, Olympic sports represent a socially relevant activity, which should, for this reason alone, make it a permanent focus of attention of the Brazilian parliament. (Brasil, 2001, 4; emphasis added by the authors)

In terms of the economic exploitation of sports, we note that, mediated almost exclusively by political concerns until the beginning of the twentieth century, the relationships between sports entities and the state in Brazilian society came to concern economic interests as well, especially in the last 30 years. The conceptual duality of sports in the constitutional text, as discussed earlier, is an example of this process. However, this process did not cause a rupture in the symbolic association between sports and the nation, though it might seem this way at first glance. Instead, there was an appropriation of this connection between sports and nationalism by the companies that operate within the sports marketplace, in order to make it more profitable. And this tendency is currently so prevalent that some researchers (Silk et al., 2005; Scherer and Jackson, 2007; John and Jackson, 2011; Kobayashi, 2012) have been focusing on studies of *corporate nationalism.* Coined by Silk et al. (2005), this concept refers to a process by which global corporations associate their products with national/local culture, in order to capitalize on the powerful symbolism of the nation and, consequently, to broaden the identification of potential consumers with their products. In this process, sports and their double status of global commodities and national symbols play an important role. In summary, as Damo (2006) asserts, national symbolism is used as a decoy for consumers of sports and its associated products and services.

The third and final element underlying Boudens's analysis (2008) is the institutional fragility of sports as a "fundamental right." Even though public policies of sports have become institutionally stronger with the creation of the Ministry of Sports in 2003, it is not possible to say that sports have, in the Brazilian institutional framework, the official status of a social right. In contrast to what has happened in areas such as health and education, in the sports sector, there is no national public system that connects all of the administrative levels of service provision as well as the groups that work with the needs of the population. As a result, sports policies are founded on a transience that is nearly permanent; the political decision-making process starts often from scratch, or rather, from the precarious situation of sports in the country and the demand for more resources or for a more rational organization of the Brazilian sports system.

CONCLUSION

Our goal was to identify, by means of legal document-based research, how the symbolic connection between sports and nationalism came into conflict with the principle of sport democratization, deriving from the Federal Constitution of 1988. The affinity between sports and the nation resulted in the former becoming one of the most important factors helping the "national community" come into being. Meanwhile, unlike the flag, the national anthem, and even the official language of the country, sports are national symbols of a "private" nature, since their institutional and bureaucratic structure is not integrated with state organizations. This situation creates an increase in the social interests involved in the symbolic production of sports and in the process of formulating public policies of sport.

In this sense, in the historical development of sport policies the symbolic association of sports with nationalism resulted in the primacy of high performance sport, the state manipulation of which served as a tool in the project of nation-building. From the forging of Brazilian national identity in the 1940s, to nationalist ideology in the 1970s, sports has had an important role in the expression of national sentiments in our society. This came about through a focus on high performance sports in public policies, so that sport, by virtue of the rituals it involves, offers the best opportunities to efficiently mobilize affective ties between people and the nation. In this way, since the beginning of the first regulatory framework for Brazilian sports, during Vargas's government, sports policies have been focused primarily on stimulating high performance sports. And, aside from some changes introduced by subsequent governments, high performance sports have continued to be the primary beneficiaries of state efforts and resources.

Even after the formulation of the principle of sports democratization, during the military regime—which became official with the new Brazilian constitution in 1988—this historical trend did not change. An examination of the sport policies after the creation of the Federal

Constitution of 1988 shows that high performance sports still occupies a strategic position in the formulation of public policies in our society, not only in the political arena, but also in the distribution of public funds. This strategic position could be understood through two basic evidences: (a) the historical pattern of sports policies in Brazil, that gives high performance sports and related institutions, and their representatives, the role of protagonists in the relationship between the state and sports in the country; and (b) the strength of the symbolic connection between sports and nationalism that, even in the face of historical changes to the nation-state system, as well as the economic exploitation of sports, remains unchanged.

The set of public policies analyzed in this article indicates that in the symbolic conflict between sports as a national symbol and as the "right of everyone," Brazilian public policies of sports tend to prioritize the former and only peripherally take into account the latter.

NOTE

1. Law 9.615 (March 24, 1998), establishes that: "Sport can be recognized in any of the following ways: I—educational sport, practiced in educational systems and systematic forms of education, [...]; II—participatory sport, or those practiced voluntarily, including the sports that contribute to the richness of participants' social lives, to the promotion of health and education, and to environmental preservation; III—performance sports, practiced according to the general rules of this Law and the rules of national and international sport practices [...]" (Brasil, 1998). We will base our analysis on these categories of Brazilian legislation. Nevertheless, we consider that, from a sociological point of view, it is important not to take this legal typology in a rigid way, so that we may avoid the dualistic opposition between high performance sports and, on the other hand, educational or participatory sports, since these three forms are often intertwined in social practice.

BIBLIOGRAPHY

Almeida, Barbara Schausteck. *O financiamento do esporte olímpico e suas relações com a política no Brasil.* 122fl. Dissertação (Mestrado em Educação Física). Departamento de Educação Física da Universidade Federal do Paraná. Curitiba, 2010.

Almeida, Barbara Schausteck, Jay Coakley, Wanderley Marchi, Jr., and Fernando Augusto Starepravo. "Federal Government Funding and Sport: The Case of Brazil, 2004–2009." *International Journal of Sport Policy and Politics* 4:3 (2012): 411–426.

Banco do Brasil. *BB e CBV anunciam renovação do contrato de patrocínio ao vôlei brasileiro por mais cinco anos.* Disponível em http://www.bb.com.br /portalbb/page118,3366,3367,1,0,1,0.bb?codigoNoticia=33503 Acesso em 12 jan.2013.

Boudens, Emile Paulus Johannes. Desporto e lazer—legislação infraconstitucional: a Constituição traída. In: VVAA. *Ensaios sobre impactos da constituição federal de 1988 na sociedade brasileira.* Brasília: Câmara dos Deputados, Edições Câmara, 2008, 235–253.

Brasil. Conselho Nacional de Esporte. Membros que integram o CNE. Poder Executivo, Brasília, DF. Disponível em http://www.esporte.gov.br/conselho Esporte/membros.jsp Acesso em 20 fev. 2014.

———. *Constituição da República Federativa do Brasil:* texto constitucional promulgado em 5 de outubro de 1988, com as alterações adotadas pelas Emendas Constitucionais n°s 1/92 a 67/2010, pelo Decreto n° 186/2008 e pelas Emendas Constitucionais de Revisão n°s 1 a 6/94. Brasília: Senado Federal, Subsecretaria de Edições Técnicas, 2011.

———. Decreto 91.452, de 19 de julho de 1985. Poder Executivo, Brasília, DF.19 jul. 1985a. Disponível em http://www2.camara.leg.br/legin/fed /decret/1980-1987/decreto-91452-19-julho-1985-441587-publicacaooriginal -1-pe.html Acesso em 07 jan.2013.

———. Decreto 4.201, de 18 de abril de 2002. Poder Executivo, Brasília, DF. Disponível em http://www.planalto.gov.br/ccivil_03/Decreto/2002/D4201 .htm Acesso em 07 jan.2013.

———. Decreto n° 3199, de 14 de abril de 1941. Poder Executivo, Brasília, DF, 10 abr. 2003a. Disponível em http://www6.senado.gov.br/sicon /ExecutaPesquisaLegislacao.action Acesso em 20 abr.2010.

———. Lei 10.264, de 16 de julho de 2001. Presidência da República. Poder Executivo, Brasília, DF. Disponível em http://www.planalto.gov.br/ccivil _03/leis/LEIS_2001/L10264.htm Acesso em 07 jan.2013.

———. Lei n° 9615, de 24 de março de 1998. Poder Executivo, Brasília, DF, 24 mar. 1998. Disponível em www.planalto.gov.br/ccivil_03/Leis /L9615consol.htm Acesso em 13 out.2010.

———. Ministério da Educação e Cultura. Departamento de Educação Física e Desportos. *Lei n° 6.251/75, política nacional de educação física e desportos, plano nacional de educação física e desportos—PNED.* Brasília: Departamento de Documentação e Divulgação, 1976.

———. Ministério da Educação. Secretaria Educação Física e Desportos. *Uma nova política para o desporto brasileiro:* esporte brasileiro, questão de estado. Relatório conclusivo da comissão de reformulação do desporto. Brasília: 1985b.

———. Parecer da Comissão de Educação, de 15 de maio de 2001. Senado Federal, Brasília, DF. Disponível em http://www.senado.gov.br/atividade /materia/getPDF.asp?t=29472&tp=1 Acesso em 07 jan.2013.

Carvalho, José Murilo de. *Cidadania no Brasil:* o longo caminho. Rio de Janeiro: Civilização Brasileira, 2001.

———. Nação imaginária: memória, mitos e heróis. *A crise do estado-nação.* Adauto Novaes (org.). Rio de Janeiro: Civilização Brasileira, 2003. 395–418.

Castelan, Lia Polegato. *As Conferências Nacionais do Esporte na configuração da política esportiva e de lazer no governo Lula (2003–2010).* 2010. 139fl. Dissertação (Mestrado em Educação Física). Faculdade de Educação Física da Universidade Estadual de Campinas. Campinas, 2010.

Corrêa, Arlindo Lopes. Apresentação. In: COSTA, Lamartine Pereira da. *Diagnóstico de educação física/desportos no Brasil.* Rio de Janeiro; Ministério da Educação e Cultura: FENAME, 1971.

Damo, Arlei Sander. O ethos capitalista e o espírito das copas. In: GASTALDO, Édison; GUEDES, Simoni Lahud. *Nações em campo:* copa do mundo e identidade nacional. Niterói: Intertextos, 2006. 39–72.

Draibe, Sonia Miriam. As políticas sociais brasileiras: diagnósticos e perspectivas. In: IPEA-IPLAN. *Para a década de 90:* prioridades e perspectivas de políticas públicas. Brasília: IPEA-IPLAN, 1990. 1–66.

Elias, Norbert. *Os alemães:* a luta pelo poder e a evolução do habitus nos séculos XIX e XX. Editado por Michael Schröter. Trad. Álvaro Cabral. Rev. Técnica: Andréa Daher. Rio de Janeiro: Jorge Zahar, 1997.

Esping-Andersen, Gosta. As três economias políticas do *Welfare State. Lua Nova,* nº 24, 85–116, set.1991.

Hobsbawm, Eric J. *Nações e nacionalismo desde 1780*: programa, mito e realidade. 5ª ed. Tradução: Maria Célia Paoli, Anna Maria Quirino. Rio de Janeiro: Paz e Terra, 1990.

Houlihan, Barrie. "Sport, National Identity and Public Policy." *Nations and Nationalism* 3:1 (March 1997): 113–137.

John, Alistair, and Steve Jackson. "Call Me Loyal: Globalization, Corporate Nationalism and the America's Cup." *International Review for the Sociology of Sport* 46:4 (2011): 399–417.

Kobayashi, Koji. "Globalization, Corporate Nationalism and Japanese Cultural Intermediaries: Representation of *bukatsu* through Nike Advertising at the Global-Local Nexus." *International Review for the Sociology of Sport* 47:6 (2012): 724–742.

Marshall, Thomas H. *Cidadania, classe social e status.* Introdução de Phillip C. Schmitter. Trad. Meton Porto Gadelha. Rio de Janeiro: Zahar, 1967. 57–114.

Oliveira, Francisco de. Diálogo na grande tradição. In: Adauto Novaes (org.). *A crise do estado-nação.* Rio de Janeiro: Civilização Brasileira, 2003. 443–464.

Scherer, Jay, and Steve J. Jackson. "Sports Advertising, Cultural Production and Corporate Nationalism at the Global-Local Nexus: Branding the New Zealand All Blacks." *Sport in Society: Cultures, Commerce, Media, Politics* 10:2 (2007): 268–284.

Schwarcz, Lilia Moritz. Estado sem nação: a criação de uma memória oficial no Brasil do Segundo Reinado. *A crise do estado-nação.* Adauto Novaes (org.). Rio de Janeiro: Civilização Brasileira, 2003. 349–393.

Silk, Michael L., David L. Andrews, and C. L Cole. "Corporate Nationalism(s): The Spatial Dimensions of Sporting Capital." In: *Sport and Corporate Nationalisms.* Eds. Michael L. Silk, David L. Andrews, and C. L Cole. Oxford and New York: Berg, 2005. 1–12.

Velloso, Mônica Pimenta. *Os intelectuais e a política cultural do Estado novo.* Rio de Janeiro: Centro de Pesquisa e Documentação de História Contemporânea do Brasil, 1987.

Veronez, Luis Fernando Camargo. *Quando o Estado joga a favor do privado*: as políticas de esporte após a Constituição Federal de 1988. 2005. 386fl. Tese (Doutorado em Educação Física). Faculdade de Educação Física da Universidade Estadual de Campinas. Campinas, 2005.

CHAPTER 7

The Nation in the Strike Zone and Reality at Bat: Bodies, Voices, and Spaces of Cuban Baseball in Sport Documentaries

Juan Carlos Rodríguez

In 2005, a group of young Cuban filmmakers arrived at the National Exhibit of New Filmmakers dressed as baseball players to protest the exclusion of a documentary entitled *Fuera de liga*, a film directed by Cuban filmmaker Ian Padrón about Havana's Industriales, Cuba's most emblematic revolutionary baseball team (Arreola). Apparently, the film had been excluded from the National Exhibit because it included interviews with Cuban players who had abandoned the island to play Major League Baseball in the United States (Padrón). Completed in 2003, *Fuera de liga* circulated clandestinely in portable digital drives for five years, but it was not publicly released until 2008, when it was transmitted only in Havana by a provincial television station (Vicent). Until its release, the topic of Cuban baseball defections was taboo in Cuban media. By the time of its premiere, one of the protagonists of the film, Industriales's first baseman Kendry Morales, rookie of the year in the 2002–2003 National Series, had abandoned Cuba to pursue his dream of playing Major League Baseball.

As *Fuera de liga*'s censorship reveals, the Cuban revolutionary state has invested many efforts not only in transforming Cuban baseball into an amateur sport but also in controlling the very discourse on Cuba's national game. But this tendency of controlling baseball discourse in

Cuba may be changing. In 2013, the Cuban government TV station transmitted the first US Major League Baseball game in over 50 years (Latimer). One could argue that *Fuera de liga* and other sports documentaries on Cuban baseball produced after the Special Period have played a key role in pushing for changes in Cuban media policy regarding Major League Baseball. In doing so, these documentaries, as I will argue, have also served to expand the horizons of the Cuban baseball nation.

In this essay, I will discuss the representation of the Cuban baseball nation in sport documentaries made by Cuban and foreign filmmakers after the Special Period. According to Zachary Ingle, "While sports documentaries share with the television coverage of sporting events the nonfictional component, the sports documentary differs from a televised game in that the former seeks to interpret a sport story, to make sense of it, and to explain its significance" (xi). Baseball documentaries offer a cinematic interpretation of the diverse situations that shape and transform the meanings of Cuba's national sport. I would like to argue that sport documentaries play an important role in the development of Cuban baseball as a national and transnational discourse.

In the first section of the chapter, I will explain the emergence and transformations of Cuban baseball as nationalist and revolutionary discourse, focusing first on its moment of consolidation during the 1960s and 1970s and then on its crisis during the Special Period. In the second section, I will discuss how the glorious period of Cuban revolutionary baseball is captured by *Redonda y viene en caja cuadrada* (Rolando Díaz, Cuba, 1979), a film that constructs Cuban baseball as a choreographic visual spectacle, to highlight the role of the sport in the creation of a national collective body. In the next section, I will analyze two post–Special Period documentaries on Cuban baseball, *El juego de Cuba* (Manuel Martín Cuenca, Spain, 2001) and *Fuera de liga* (Ian Padrón, Cuba, 2004), which examine the history of Cuban baseball in light of the social crisis of the 1990s. Through testimonies and interviews, these documentaries reveal the role of the sport as a discourse that projects conflicting national imaginaries. Finally, in the last section of the chapter, I will analyze one more recent documentary that opens a path toward a more inclusive version of Cuban baseball history by exploring Cuba's national game from the standpoint of a marginalized perspective: *The Lost Son of Havana* (Jonathan Hock, United States, 2009) focuses on the return to Cuba of exilic player Luis Tiant. By exploring the fissures within the Cuban baseball nation, these documentaries not only highlight the conflictive views of players, fans, and officials but also provide an opportunity to restore those perspectives that have been excluded from Cuban baseball culture after the revolution.

Cuban Baseball as Nationalist and Revolutionary Discourse

When Cubans adopted baseball from Americans at the end of the nineteenth century, it became a national sport associated with the Cuban anticolonial struggle against Spain. Baseball's expansion in Cuba was part of the modernization of the island, a process in part assisted by the US government in connection with American companies. In 1959, Fidel Castro adopted baseball in the name of the Cuban revolution when he organized a baseball team named Barbudos for a series of games against a team of Batista's ex-military officers.[1] Two years after the revolution, Castro eliminated pro baseball and inaugurated a national amateur baseball league (González Echevarría 589), in effect nationalizing baseball, substituting a privately owned league with a state-operated system. Castro himself created a slogan to consolidate the role of amateur baseball as revolutionary national policy: "el triunfo de la pelota libre sobre la pelota esclava" (the triumph of free baseball over slave baseball) (quoted in Jamail 125).

Castro's nationalization of Cuban baseball altered the national imagination of the sport. From being a sign of the Americanization of Cuban national culture, baseball became one of the emblematic cultural practices of the revolution, playing a dual role in socialist Cuba. At the national level, revolutionary baseball expanded beyond Havana to cover the entire island, serving as an instrument of collective participation because it incorporated the provinces to a baseball landscape that had previously been exclusively *habanero* (during the republic, Cuban pro baseball was entirely located in Havana). At the level of international competitions, the success of the Cuban Baseball National Team served to create a sense of national pride. In the context of Cold War politics, a baseball victory of the Cuban team over the US team meant not only a triumph of socialism over capitalism but also a victory in a sport created by an old friend who turned into an enemy. In other words, the victories of the Cuban baseball national team were those of a cultural practice substantiated by the Cuban socialist state, differing from the American baseball system and its national team, so influenced by private initiative.

Playing revolutionary baseball and representing Cuba in international competitions have been considered revolutionary acts equivalent to the defense of the nation (González Echevarría 580). As González Echevarría points out, the Cuban baseball national team tends to be considered by revolutionary officials almost like a military unit at the service of the nation (631). This ideal image of the national team began to change when some Cuban baseball players abandoned the island during the Mariel exodus of the 1980s, becoming the first sign of a crisis of Cuban baseball that would reach its peak in the Special Period of the 1990s, with the collapse of the Soviet Union and the intensification of the US embargo. In the context of the economic crisis of the 1990s, revolutionary baseball suffered from a scarcity of resources and some Cuban baseball players began to look for better opportunities. Some players abandoned the island to become baseball stars in the Major Leagues.

After the Special Period, revolutionary baseball suffered a crisis of legitimacy because it could no longer attract the best Cuban baseball talent, and fans began to lose interest in the Cuban amateur league. For many years baseball operated as an instrument of collective participation, regional and national pride, but after the Special Period baseball has become an index to measure the economic crisis and its consequences, underscoring the multiple perspectives it has created as well as the diverse Cuban responses to its devastating effects. In the context of the Special Period, the crisis of Cuban baseball can be interpreted as a part of a general crisis of the revolutionary value of collectivism and egalitarianism (Fernandes 24). As a team sport, baseball became one of the cultural platforms from which to question the legitimacy of revolutionary collectivism and egalitarianism. Speaking about Cuban baseball in the Special Period has become an opportunity for Cubans to redefine their sense of collectivity and egalitarianism.

In spite of the new economic realities, revolutionary authorities have continued to promote a nationalist view of Cuban baseball, excluding any referent that does not belong to the state-promoted revolutionary baseball league. If a Cuban baseball player abandons the island to become a professional in the Major Leagues, he is considered by default a traitor to the nation (González Echevarría 632). Until very recently, neither Major League Baseball nor Cuban baseball "defectors" were covered in Cuban official media networks (Jamail 71). That explains why Cuban authorities censored *Fuera de liga*, a film that included interviews with Cuban baseball "defectors" and conversations among fans about these polemic figures.

But, as *Fuera de liga* and other sport documentaries on Cuban baseball suggest, Cuban baseball fans do not endorse the official erasure of professional baseball. For many Cubans, talking about baseball involves referring to a complex history that goes beyond revolutionary sports; it includes exchanging information on key aspects of the Cuban republic's baseball culture (amateur and professional leagues), as well as conversations about professional Cuban players from the US Major, Minor, and Negro Baseball Leagues. At their *peñas deportivas* (sport gatherings), Cuban baseball fans also talk about those players and teams that are currently reshaping the history of Major League Baseball. Aside from failing at home, at the level of Cuban fans, state control over Cuban baseball discourse is also incapable of containing the international perspectives on Cuban baseball elaborated by academics and filmmakers, some of whom belong to the Cuban diaspora. Since the end of the 1990s, when two Cuban brothers, Liván and Orlando "El Duque" Hernández, abandoned Cuba and participated in subsequent baseball World Series, various books and documentaries analyzing Cuban baseball have drawn local and international attention. As a consequence of all this, the role of Cuban baseball as a revolutionary discourse has been questioned, while the imaginary cartography of Cuban baseball as a national and transnational discourse that includes but goes beyond the revolution has been expanding in recent years. The polemics within the contemporary discourse on Cuban baseball are part of what Rafael Rojas has labeled the symbolic war over the cultural heritage of a Cuban nation (15). According to Rojas, it is a symbolic war between the Cuban government and other sectors of Cuban society (in the island and in exile) for the control of the politics of memory regarding the republican and revolutionary periods.

Cuban Baseball as Choreography in *Redonda y viene en caja cuadrada*

Sport documentaries on baseball display the choreographic qualities of the sport. Most of them include sequences that explore the athlete's body movements in detail, making visible the theatrical and performance elements that constitute baseball as a spectacle. Recent documentaries on Cuban baseball explore the game's choreography in a way that resembles the visual style of *Redonda y viene en caja cuadrada* (Rolando Díaz, Cuba, 1979), a sport documentary that focuses solely on the choreographic dynamics of Cuban baseball as they are performed in Havana's Estadio Latinoamericano. Díaz's film is one of the best Cuban sport documentaries because it offers a satiric view on Cuban baseball choreography; it captures the typical gestures and distinctive movements executed by the emblematic figures of the game, a complex mix of social actors that includes pitchers, batters, runners, coaches, umpires, and fans. The film becomes a collection of fragmented swings, pitches, and gazes performed by different agents, suggesting that the completion of each play involves the articulated actions of the collective body participating in the game. Some movements and gestures are successively repeated to emphasize their typicality as well as their ritualistic quality. The repetition of the same gestures and body movements creates an interesting effect: it defers the outcome of the play to build expectations and create suspense. At times, it also appears as if some baseball plays documented in the film are purely cinematic events created by mixing and repeating fragmented views of the same action at different stages of its completion and as performed by different agents in a single edited sequence. In this way, the acts of playing, pitching, swinging, cheering, or calling out are no longer represented as belonging to each of their individual performers, they express instead the transformation of Cuban baseball into a cinematic embodiment of the nation: a collage of mixed gestures, a flow of images combining different movements and bodies that work together like an assemblage in order to affirm the collective agency, and athletic achievements of revolutionary baseball.

The cinematic body of Cuban baseball constructed by the editing techniques of *Redonda y viene en caja cuadrada* is a collective body that defies the rules of the game and the circumscription of the baseball spectacle to the competition that takes place on the baseball field. The film ends when a slugger bats a winning home run in the last game of the National Series and the fans jump from the bleachers to the field to celebrate the victory before the game is officially over. Due to the celebration, the confusion of players' and fans' bodies in the field is so intense that it ends up interrupting the slugger's trajectory to home plate. In the end, it is never clear whether or not the slugger reached the home plate to end the game officially. This last sequence cannot make its point more clearly: Cuban baseball is about a multitude of bodies participating in an interactive choreography that blurs the boundaries between players and fans, questioning the limits between game and victory, infield and outfield, competitive actions and social pleasures, nation and revolution. It is no surprise that the collective unconscious of Cuban Baseball comes to surface in the form of a choreography when it is well known that baseball clubs played a dual role in Havana during the nineteenth century, serving as sports facilities but also as grounds for dancing parties. According to González Echevarría, both Cuban baseball and *danzón* emerged at the end of the nineteenth century as embodied social practices representing the modernist sensibility of Cuban culture (175–180).

Redonda y viene en caja cuadrada tells us something about the nature of mass mobilization in Cuba during the 1970s. After the baseball choreography, the film ends with a spontaneous mass mobilization that resembles the improvised spirit of the masses that received the revolutionaries in Havana in the 1960s. By the 1970s, however, the collective spontaneity of Cuban masses had moved from the political to the cultural field. Instead of the highly planned militaristic rituals that characterized political mass mobilizations in Cuba during the 1970s, the mass mobilization represented in *Redonda y viene en caja cuadrada* assumes the form of a carnivalesque festivity. If the strict organization of political mass mobilizations in the Cuba of the 1970s represents the consolidation of an immutable revolutionary order, the improvised celebration of a baseball victory in Díaz's film represents, in contrast, the role of sports as a safe channel for the manifestation of collective spontaneity in revolutionary Cuba. The carnivalesque atmosphere of the National Series captured in

Redonda y viene en caja cuadrada also differs from the militaristic image associated with the Cuban national baseball team that participates in international competitions.

Díaz combines two different modes of documentary making to express the interactive and choreographic qualities of Cuban baseball: the observational approach in which the filmmaker "adopts a peculiar mode of presence 'on the scene'" while trying to remain "invisible and non participatory" (Nichols 112), and the poetic approach in which the filmmaker manipulates the filmed material "to explore associations and patterns that involve temporal rhythms and spatial juxtapositions" (102). Aside from a brief interview with a fan at the beginning of the film, *Redonda y viene en caja cuadrada* does not adopt the participatory mode of documentary making in which the verbal interaction of social actors with the filmmaker is mostly captured through interviews. Instead of documenting his interaction with players and fans, Díaz is more concerned with the gestures, body movements, and interactions of players, coaches, umpires, and fans. Díaz's observational and poetic exploration of the Cuban baseball choreography contrasts with the representational strategies observed in more recent documentaries on Cuban baseball, all of which tend to privilege a particular combination of the observational, participatory, and expository mode of documentary making.

The contrast in the documentary modes of representation could tell us something about the main difference that exists between *Redonda y viene en caja cuadrada* and the more recent sport documentaries on Cuban baseball. Díaz's film reconstructs Cuban baseball as a corporeal spectacle, as a choreographic performance formed with the gestures and movements of the different social actors participating in the filmed games. In other words, Cuban baseball in Díaz's film is represented as a corporeal discourse involving the transformation of the collective into a national body. In contrast, the more recent sport documentaries on Cuban baseball explore the national game mainly as a verbal discourse involving the participation of many different voices. The testimonial interventions and linguistic performances of players, fans, and officials highlight the importance of *discutir de pelota* (speaking about baseball) in Cuba as well as in the Cuban diaspora, an emblematic practice that defines Cuban baseball culture (Carter 188). While the national body represented in Díaz's documentary appears in a Cuban setting, Havana's Estadio Latinoamericano, the multiple locations of the speaking bodies included in more recent documentaries suggest that the voices participating in the conversations about Cuban baseball belong to a national and transnational network.

Ian McDonald reminds us that

> sport documentaries are key to placing sports in their social context and in the process reveal that sport is more than simply about the performance

on the field of play. They illustrate how sport has significance beyond the specificities of the game itself, and it is the exploration and analysis of this significance that represents the domain of the sports documentary. (222)

In *Redonda y viene en caja cuadrada*, the social context evoked through the cinematic display of the sport adopts the shape of a collective body whose choreographic performance transcends the realm of sport competition because it represents the Cuban baseball nation as a festive community. More recent documentaries, however, highlight the importance of speaking about baseball in the construction of cubanidad, and because this social experience goes beyond the realm of sport competition, it also provides some keys to understanding the role of Cuban baseball in the projection of Cuban national and transnational dilemmas.

CUBAN BASEBALL'S NATIONAL AND TRANSNATIONAL DILEMMAS IN TEAM-BASED DOCUMENTARIES: AFFILIATION AND RIVALRY IN *FUERA DE LIGA* AND *EL JUEGO DE CUBA*

Fuera de liga and *El juego de Cuba* revise the intertwined history of baseball in Cuba and the United States. *Fuera de liga* focuses on the history of one of Havana's baseball teams, Industriales, particularly after the hardest years of the Special Period. The film offers a detailed account of Industriales's fan culture, including cheering rituals at the Estadio Latinoamericano and conversations at the peñas deportivas that gather in Havana's Parque Central. Padrón follows Industriales during the 2002–2003 National Series; this specific temporal frame serves as an anchoring point to evoke the history of the team and of revolutionary baseball. *Fuera de liga* also explores the transformations of revolutionary baseball and its crisis in the 1990s, when various players from Industriales left the island to pursue their dream of playing in the Major Leagues. At the end of the film, René Arocha, El Duque Hernández, and other Industrialistas in exile confess their emotional bond with Havana's blue team, transforming a local landmark into a transnational sign. By incorporating the testimony of Cuban Major League players, *Fuera de liga* challenges the conception of Cuban baseball as a nationalist discourse exclusively constructed by those who speak from within the revolution.

In contrast, *El juego de Cuba* offers a broader view of the history of baseball in Cuba that covers but goes beyond revolutionary baseball and its crisis. It begins with the arrival of the game to the island in the nineteenth century, when it became a symbol of modernity immediately associated with Cuba's anticolonial struggle against Spain (Cluster and Hernández 92–94). It continues with the development of professional baseball in Cuba and the participation of Cuban players in the Major Leagues. And then it covers the history of revolutionary baseball and its crisis during the Special Period, exploring it from the perspective of the Cuban national baseball team. The film uses as its anchoring point a two-game series between the Cuban national team and the Baltimore Orioles. Since it explores the changing meanings of baseball in Cuba from a historical perspective, *El juego de Cuba* highlights the difference between baseball as national sport and baseball as revolutionary tool.

By focusing on specific teams, both *Fuera de liga* and *El juego de Cuba* tell the story of Cuban baseball from the perspective of a collective protagonist: Havana's Industriales and Equipo Cuba. The story of the collective protagonist operates as an allegory of a Cuban baseball nation that has to redefine its sense of collectivity in the Special Period, at a time when Cuba is experiencing social disintegration and Cubans are embracing individualism in order to survive the crisis. Both documentaries highlight the diverse social meanings and specific roles of each team in the construction of Cuban baseball as a national sport. As team-based documentaries, both films build their drama by exploring the networks of affiliation and rivalry created by each team. They provide alternative geographies of Cuban baseball by offering cinematic explorations of the symbolic territories and real spaces and places that mark the history of the sport as a national and international spectacle. The main affiliations and rivalries of Cuban baseball presented in these films are structured by sociocultural and geopolitical tensions that are local as well as global.

Fuera de liga's emphasis on the national rivalries that have characterized the history of Industriales serves to project an imaginary geography of revolutionary baseball in which the team representing Havana, the nation's capital, has to defend its protagonic role against provincial teams such as Pinar del Río and Santiago de Cuba. Padrón's road trip with Industriales to Santiago de Cuba at the beginning of the film includes traveling shots of the journey that contextualize the expansion of revolutionary baseball in the Cuban national landscape, adding a road movie flavor to Industriales quest. This sequence also include takes that reveal the poor condition of the baseball training field assigned to Industriales by the authorities of the Santiago branch of INDER (Instituto Nacional de Deportes, Educación Física y Recreación). Industrialistas interviewed by Padrón consider the poor conditions of the training facilities as a sign that Havana not only has to compete against Santiago's baseball team but also has to overcome the unfair disadvantages created by the Santiago INDER officials.

The landscape of Cuban baseball is also explored in *El juego de Cuba*. According to this documentary, baseball's arrival to Havana is associated with a Cuban refusal of Spanish rule, while its expansion to the country's interior at the beginning of the twentieth century is associated with the expansion of American sugar cane companies. A series of traveling shots on top of a train serve to display the Cuban cane landscape in which baseball proliferated under the tutelage of American corporations. The local affiliations and rivalries created by professional baseball in Cuba also take the form of a cinematic exploration of space in *El juego de Cuba*. Martín Cuenca takes us to the space where the Almendares Park used to be located. The stadium was the setting of one of the most intense rivalries in Cuban baseball, the one between the Almendares and Havana teams. As the film shows some photographs of the Almendares Park, an old player shares his memories of the games played there. But later in the film, when the same old player navigates through the space where the Almendares Park used to be located, he has difficulties identifying its location. This act of memory reveals that even if the witness remembers one of Cuba's pro baseball emblematic places, today vanished, he can no longer locate it in space due to the dramatic transformations of the island's baseball landscape implemented by the revolution.

Although it covers the local development of Cuban pro baseball, *El juego de Cuba* focuses extensively on the international development of revolutionary baseball. The film's central conflict is between the Cuban national baseball team and two American teams, the US national baseball team and the Baltimore Orioles. In this and other accounts of Cuban baseball, the rivalry between Equipo Cuba and the US national baseball team serves to underscore the success of Cuban revolutionaries in international competitions. But the story of the games between the Cuban national team and the Baltimore Orioles operates differently because, even before taking place, it suggested different connotations. On one hand, the games against the Orioles were perceived as a test to prove the talent of Equipo Cuba against a much better team than those in the amateur leagues (Jamail 144). On the other hand, the games suggested a clash between two different systems of playing baseball that reproduced the Cold War ideological divisions between Cuba and the United States: professional versus amateur baseball ended up being equated to capitalist versus socialist baseball (Carter 96). Finally, the Cuba and US sport agreement was seen by some as an achievement in "baseball diplomacy" (93) and by others, particularly Cuban exiles in the United States, as a step backward in their symbolic struggle against Castro (92). Aside from building suspense through the cinematic display of the baseball spectacle, *El juego de Cuba* creates suspense by exploring the political drama implicit in the confrontation of Cuban and Cuban American perspectives, highlighting as well the transnational scope of this highly emotional controversy.

In *El juego de Cuba*, Cuban baseball star Omar Linares defends amateur revolutionary baseball and confesses that he disapproves of playing baseball for money. His interview is juxtaposed with another interview in which El Duque invites Cuban players to open their eyes and seek inner freedom. This sequence also includes an interview with an ex-minister of INDER who explains that Cuban athletes playing baseball in the Major Leagues are traitors, an opinion contested in another interview of the same sequence by El Duque's brother, Cuban Major League star Liván Hernández. Edited together, these conflictive positions create the illusion that a debate is taking place among subjects who otherwise may refuse to speak to each other in person.

Fuera de liga and *El juego de Cuba* explore the situation of Cuban baseball players, a group that for a long time did not have the same privileges of other Cuban cultural workers. While Cuban artists, writers, and musicians are allowed to receive honoraria in hard currency, Cuban players who are active in the National Series make a very modest salary in Cuban pesos.[2] That explains why so many Cuban athletes find attractive the possibility of playing professional baseball.

Both documentaries discuss the financial hardships of Cuban baseball players as well as the difficult conditions they face while participating in revolutionary baseball, including lack of equipment, deteriorated infrastructures, heavy traveling schedules, and inappropriate lodging facilities. None of the films, however, discuss a policy implemented in Cuba after the Special Period that promoted early retirement among baseball players who could then work as players or coaches at the Italian or Japanese professional leagues and receive a modest salary in hard currency.

These films also offer a multiperspective view of the controversial case of Rey Vicente Anglada, an ex-Cuban player who was suspended and served time in jail for apparently participating with other Industrialistas in pre-arranging baseball game results to benefit gamblers. Anglada was later vindicated, returning to Cuban baseball and becoming the coach of Industriales in the early 2000s. In both films, Anglada's testimony is accompanied by interviews with players, fans, sports journalists, and even state officials who offer diverse opinions about Anglada's suspension and vindication. Anglada's story operates in both films as an alternative public trial in which spectators have the opportunity to examine Anglada's testimony and compare it with the opinions of fans, players, and even the statements of those officials who participated in Anglada's suspension. By participating in the public vindication of a suspended Cuban player, each film collaborates in an effort to revise Cuban baseball history.

Both documentaries also explore Havana's fans' debates on Cuban baseball issues as they are performed in *la esquina caliente*, the hot corner, Cuba's main baseball discussion point, located in Havana's Parque Central. *Fuera de liga* documents the reactions of Havana's fans to the defections that have affected Industriales's team composition and baseball performance. Some fans reproduce the tactic of the revolutionary state, that of erasing or considering traitors the ex-Industrialistas playing in the Major Leagues. Other fans, however, defend the defectors' legacy or take advantage of the presence of the camera to question the exilic players' loyalty to Industriales. *Fuera de liga* promotes a transnational dialogue between Industrialistas when it gives El Duque an opportunity to deny that he is a traitor and to respond to the question of a Havana fan about whether or not he still considers himself an Industrialista, to which he responds affirmatively. Padrón invites Cuban players and fans to consider the inclusion of baseball "defectors" in Industriales's history, an element that tends to be excluded from the official version of Cuban baseball history promoted by revolutionary sports media.

The incorporation of Cuban defectors in the island's baseball culture, however, does not simply take the form of verbal endorsements; it also involves a series of gestures and performance acts that contribute to restoring a national baseball bond between players and fans, a bond partially broken by exile and by the severe policies of revolutionary baseball. In *Fuera de liga*, fans proudly show a poster of El Duque pitching with the New York Yankees, while El Duque, at the end of the film, opens his New York Yankees jacket to show his blue shirt, affirming his loyalty to Industriales's color and uniform. As this sequence suggests, *discutir pelota* becomes a performance act and also a cinematic spectacle in which players and fans manipulate and exchange sport symbols. But the sequence also highlights the role of sports and media in the new international division of cultural labor. Rowe, McKay, and Miller explain that "the new international division of cultural labor, combined with media globalization, means that sports and athletes are now moving around the world both in person and as signs in ways that open up issues of race, gender and nation in the interest of capitalist expansion" (130). In this sequence, El Duque is not simply an Industrialista that has become a New York Yankee; he is also an exilic Cuban baseball player that returns to the island as a subversive sign, but only in the form of a commodity that evokes global capitalism.

El juego de Cuba registers the aggressive reactions of baseball fans, gathered at the Parque Central's peña deportiva, who discuss INDER's announcement stating that the tickets for the game between the Orioles and Equipo Cuba in Estadio Latinoamericano will be distributed by invitation only. From the Cuban baseball fans' perspective, this arbitrary decision functions to exclude from the game authentic baseball aficionados and to affirm the privileged social position of bureaucrats, members of the party, and pro-revolutionary families invited to the game. As this sequence suggests, the presence of the camera serves as a provocation to speak about baseball but also stimulates debates about Cuban revolutionary policies in areas that transcend the realm of sports competition.

Fuera de liga's and *El juego de Cuba*'s exploration of affiliations and rivalries open the door for the examination of Cuban baseball's passion politics, institutional practices, and economic challenges. Through the use of the participatory approach based on interviews and testimonies, both documentaries capture the symbolic layers, disputed meanings, and conflictive perspectives of baseball players, fans, and institutional officials that participate in the performance of discutir pelota in Cuba. By framing baseball as a polemic field of unsolved tensions regarding the cultural legacies of the republic and the revolution, both *Fuera de liga* and *El juego de Cuba* become manifestations of a broader symbolic war for the control of the politics of memory of the Cuban nation. These two films seem to confirm Zach Saltz's idea that "the cinematic examination of baseball not only reveals details about the internal workings of a complex network of athletes, fans, managers and team personnel but also places baseball as a cultural artifact with significance that is bolstered by the collective society and the fandom that promotes its ubiquity and popularity" (111). As both documentaries suggest, Cuban baseball is constructed by many voices that speak from different locations (capital city-interior province; island-diaspora), revealing the overlapping of national and transnational dilemmas within its discourse.

Speaking from the Strike Zone: The Marginalized Voice of the Cuban Baseball Nation

Instead of focusing on a collective protagonist, *The Lost Son of Havana* develops its plot through the figure of an individual hero, Cuban pitcher Luis Tiant, Jr., who, after having a memorable career in the Major Leagues with the Cleveland Indians, the Boston Red Sox, and other teams (1964–1982), decides to return to Cuba in 2007 to visit his relatives. The drama constructed in the film involves a sports hero who intertwines family and baseball memories across borders. Tiant's return to Cuba occurs after 46 years in exile. As documented in the film, Tiant's story represents one of the fissures of the Cuban baseball nation, the perspective of the exilic player excluded from the Cuban baseball culture created by the revolution. *The Lost Son of Havana* symbolizes the reconciliation of an exilic player with his nation.

Although the film covers the elimination of pro baseball in Cuba and refers to certain elements of revolutionary baseball today, this documentary is less about Cuban baseball than about the careers in the United States of Luis Tiant, Jr. (1940–) and his father, Luis Tiant, Sr. (1906–1976), also known as Lefty Tiant, a Cuban pitcher with an extraordinary trajectory in the Negro Leagues. For the Tiants, baseball is a family drama, and also a photo album: a photograph of Lefty Tiant wearing a baseball uniform is carried like an amulet by Luis Tiant, Jr. through the course of his trip to Cuba; the image becomes Tiant's way of evoking the past and of establishing contact with relatives, friends, and fans eager to know more about Tiant's relationship with his father. The focus on baseball as a family affair helps to humanize these baseball legends and underscore key aspects of their personalities, but it also displaces baseball to the terrain of melodrama, making it into a strategic narrative to contain substantial critiques of the corporate system that sustains Major League Baseball as a professional sport.

American sports hero documentaries tend to develop various lines of conflict through the rise and fall narrative structure, sometimes complementing it with the comeback or social redemption plot. *The Lost Son of Havana* is a sports biopic that develops a series of conflicts around a father and son relationship marked by a mutual devotion to baseball. The story of Luis Tiant, Jr. is the story of a man who had to abandon his family to pursue his dreams of playing in the Major Leagues and then had to struggle against his own body to continue his athletic career. Tiant's rise as a sports hero occurs in exile within a historical context marked by political tensions between Cuba and the United States. For Tiant, choosing pro baseball is both a sign of freedom and suffering; his victories on the diamond are bittersweet because, as an exilic subject separated from his family, he cannot share his baseball achievements with his parents.

In the film, the story of Luis Tiant, Jr. is intertwined with the story of his father, Lefty Tiant. As the story goes, Lefty Tiant also dreamed of playing in the Major Leagues, but his dream was broken by the baseball color line existing in the United States at the time in which he played in the Negro Leagues. The story of Lefty Tiant's relationship with baseball adopts a rise and fall structure that later assumes a redemptive twist when Luis Tiant, Jr. begins to play pro baseball. Lefty Tiant's story becomes an explicit critique of the social consequences of baseball segregation in the United States, while Tiant, Jr.'s story assumes the form of a Cold War plot whose protagonist is an Afro-Cuban athlete who escapes socialism to succeed as a free agent in the desegregated job market of American pro baseball. *The Lost Son of Havana* in a way reinforces "the ideology of sport as a route to success" (McDonald 221). Although the film discusses some issues of power (racism and baseball segregation), it never questions the post-Negro Leagues pro baseball system.

Even if Tiant, Jr. also suffers racial discrimination in the early stages of his career in the United States, his rise to Major League baseball operates as a social mobility plot, but the family redemption is far from complete because Tiant's father cannot witness the success of his son. Full redemption for Lefty, Tiant's father, comes later, when he and his wife are finally able to meet his son in the United States and he is invited by the Boston Red Sox, his son's team, to throw the first ball in a Major League game. But before narrating the family reunion, *The Lost Son of*

Havana focuses on Luis Tiant, Jr.'s own fall and comeback story as a result of an injury that put at risk his baseball career. As happens in other sport hero's films, this documentary incorporates a couple of sequences chronicling the hero's health condition, injuries, and rehabilitation process, all of which lead him to alter his athletic performance. Tiant, Jr.'s comeback to glory occurs when he wins two games in the 1975 World Series, a crucial moment in which he redeems himself and achieves the status of legendary baseball figure. Baseball glory for Tiant, Jr., however, does not necessarily mean full social redemption.

In addition to the intense drama of some baseball games played by Tiant, Jr., this documentary constructs its suspense by creating expectations about Tiant, Jr.'s encounter with his family and friends in Cuba. In a way similar to other sports hero's films, the hero's victory in a sports competition is only his first step on his path to solve the social conflicts that haunt him. Instead of using a baseball event as an anchoring point from which to organize its temporal frame, as happens in *Fuera de liga*'s observational sequences of game action, *The Lost Son of Havana* organizes the plot around observational sequences of Tiant's trip to Cuba. The hero's comeback to his native country and his reconciliatory encounter with aunts, cousins, and old friends occur outside the baseball field but serve as anchoring points to frame the narration of the Tiants' baseball careers in Cuba and the United States. The Cuban trip also serves as a redemptive quest for a hero whose dream of playing pro baseball came at a very high cost, because it meant leaving his family behind. Redemption is finally completed beyond the baseball diamond, when Tiant declares that he is a free man after having achieved a symbolic reconciliation with his homeland and his family. *The Lost Son of Havana*'s redemptive comeback plot leads the hero to exorcise his demons through social reconciliation; together with the story of Tiant's comeback to baseball after physical rehabilitation, this narrative format differs from the affiliation and rivalry plots that structure *Fuera de liga* and *El juego de Cuba*. Even if they differ in narrative frame, all these documentaries explore the sociopolitical dramas, emotional states, and affective constellations generated by baseball among Cubans from the island and the diaspora.

The Lost Son of Havana emphasizes the transnational dimension of Tiant's story by framing the film shooting as a travelogue in which Tiant's trip to Cuba is juxtaposed to baseball events in the United States. In order to create a travelogue effect, the film includes various sequences in which we see Tiant packing his luggage while preparing himself mentally for the trip, scenes that also project the confessional tone of similar segments in reality shows. *The Lost Son of Havana* could be considered a travel film with some on-the-road sequences in which the hero navigates through public and intimate places that are meaningful signs of how much things have changed in Havana since he left the city 46 years ago. The exploration of the baseball landscape in Cuba and the United States through the travelogue and road movie conventions is a key element of the more recent documentaries on Cuban baseball.

In a way similar to *El juego de Cuba* and *Fuera de liga*, *The Lost Son of Havana* examines Cuban baseball and its connections to American baseball in an attempt to articulate a politics of memory of the Cuban national sport that differs from the official version of Cuban baseball history promoted by revolutionary authorities. Director Jonathan Hock tests the collective memory of Cuban baseball fans when he arrives to la esquina caliente and asks the fans: "Who was the best Cuban pitcher in Major League Baseball?" The filmmaker captures the enthusiastic reaction of fans yelling at each other the names of Cuban pitchers, including José Luis Contreras, Liván, and El Duque Hernández, until a fan with a soft voice mentions the name of Luis Tiant. It is only at that moment when Hock introduces Tiant to the fans gathered in la esquina caliente, offering them a unique chance to greet and discuss pelota with a Cuban star from the Major Leagues. Tiant takes the opportunity to share with fans key aspects of his and his father's careers, at times making jokes, at other times affirming the quality of Cuban players. Tiant's encounter with Cuban baseball fans in la esquina caliente is a performance for the camera in which discutir pelota and exchanging baseball memories become major spectacles that also constitute a mutual reconciliatory gesture: for Tiant, it is a reconciliation with the past and the future of Cuban baseball; for the Cuban baseball fans, however, reconciling with Cuba's baseball past also means honoring a Cuban star who made it as a pro in Major League Baseball and, for that reason, was excluded from the official version of Cuban baseball history.

All the recent sports documentaries on Cuban baseball share the same interest in capturing the vivid discussions in la esquina caliente, one of the most emblematic social spaces of Cuban baseball. But each documentary explores this scenario through different angles, displaying not only the cultural meanings that circulate in such a space but also the various frames through which that space comes to signify different ways of assuming cubanidad. La esquina caliente in *El juego de Cuba* becomes a public space to question revolutionary policies relating to access to the international game. In *Fuera de liga* and *The Lost Son of Havana*, la esquina caliente functions as a place that facilitates the exchange of memories between Cuban baseball fans and Cuban baseball stars in exile. Through these sequences, the negotiation of cubanidad assumes a local but also a transnational character, revealing the role of Havana as a Caribbean global city.

CONCLUSION

Sports documentaries on Cuban baseball seem to confirm Thomas Carter's argument about the social role played by baseball discourse in

Cuba. According to Carter, baseball is an embodied spectacle and discursive platform through which Cubans constantly redefine their national identity: "baseball embodies and projects a specific version of what it means to be Cuban, not only through swinging a bat or throwing a ball but through its delineation of social space and the everyday talk informed by such spaces" (3). For Carter, "how Cubans create and interpret the cultural meanings of the actions on the baseball diamond shapes the narrative discourses of Cuba and cubanidad" (16). He argues that baseball is one of the social scenarios in which the concepts of Cuba and cubanidad take the shape of a language of contention, "a tacitly agreed upon symbolic framework that connects discursive and social fields of force through which contestations for power are articulated" (22). In all the documentaries discussed in this chapter, baseball operates as a discursive platform to negotiate the symbolic boundaries of Cuba and cubanidad as they refer to local and global processes that expand the perspectives of the baseball nation.

While *Redonda y viene en caja cuadrada* displays Cuban baseball as an instrument of collective participation and national pride, more recent documentaries represent Cuban baseball as an ongoing conversation about the consequences of the Special Period in the realm of sports. Instead of projecting the Cuban baseball nation as a corporeal and festive communal bonding, the baseball documentaries produced after the Special Period allow for the reconstruction of the Cuban baseball nation as a multiplicity of voices engaged in polemic discussions about the history and future of baseball in Cuba. Post–Special Period baseball documentaries invite Cuban players and fans to question the role of revolutionary baseball in the context of the economic crisis as well as the impact of its policies in the history of Cuban baseball. As they invite viewers to explore the ways Cubans reinvent or question their sense of collectivity in times of crisis, these contemporary documentaries also highlight the struggle for the control of the politics of memory associated with the cultural heritage of Cuba (both republican and revolutionary).

The transformation of Cuban baseball into a revolutionary discourse involved a series of breaks associated with revolution's own ruptures. First, the revolution's rupture with the republican past was experimented in the Cuban baseball context as a break with the history of the island's baseball pro league. Second, as a result of the revolution's rupture with the United States, American pro sports, including Major League Baseball, were banned in Cuba, which consequently disconnected many Cuban fans and players from the transnational networks of pro baseball, a vibrant sphere to which many Cubans contributed in substantial ways. Third, parallel with the nationalization of baseball by the revolution came the exclusion of Cuban pro baseball players from revolutionary baseball, which certainly was experienced as a split of the Cuban baseball nation, a rupture associated with the exodus of Cubans after the revolution. If the first rupture could be considered a historical one, the second could be characterized, among other things, as a geocultural rupture, while the third could be described as a communal split that refers to the separation existing between Cubans in the island and Cubans in exile.

In the Special Period, revolutionary baseball experimented dramatic changes. For many players and fans, speaking about baseball in the context of the crisis not only offered the opportunity to perform a critical reevaluation of revolutionary baseball policies but also to renegotiate the meaning of the Cuban baseball nation in the Special Period. For Cuban and foreign filmmakers, speaking about baseball opened the door not only to question the foundational ruptures of Cuban revolutionary baseball but also to investigate the historical and geocultural gaps as well as the social divisions they created.

Films such as *Fuera de liga* examine the consequences of baseball revolutionary policies, underscoring the need to reevaluate the legacy and shortcomings of revolutionary sports institutions. Other films like *El juego de Cuba* and *The Lost Son of Havana* can be seen as vehicles to reconnect Cuban players and fans with the history of Cuban prerevolutionary baseball. These two documentaries, together with *Fuera de liga*, also contribute to the reestablishment of cultural bridges between Cuban and American baseball. In addition, they accomplish the ethical task of promoting discussions between Cubans in the island and in exile. Some of these exchanges highlight the split of the Cuban baseball nation after the revolution, while others suggests that the Cuban baseball nation can be imagined, particularly after the Special Period, as a series of national and transnational networks that operate within but also beyond the realm of revolutionary sports. Overall, these documentaries offer official as well as alternative views of Cuban baseball that complicate the foundational boundaries of the Cuban baseball nation created by the revolution.

Notes

1. According to Thomas Carter, the Barbudos game series constituted a "metaphoric reenactment of the struggle against Batista's forces" because in some early games "revolutionary leaders played against a team of former military police officers from Batista's regime" (105).
2. It is important to clarify that Cuban baseball players do not receive salaries for their participation in the Cuban amateur baseball league but instead are assigned regular jobs in state institutions. Players receive a license from their regular jobs that allow them to use their labor time to participate in training sessions and games. This structure of indirect compensation

allows the Cuban government to claim that revolutionary baseball is amateur in spite of the fact that players receive salaries.

BIBLIOGRAPHY

Arreola, Gerardo. "Exhibe la televisión cubana polémico documental sobre equipo de béisbol." *La Jornada*. January 14, 2008. Web. March 25, 2013. Retrieved from: http://www.jornada.unam.mx/2008/01/14/index.php?sec tion=mundo&article=028n2mun.

Carter, Thomas. *The Quality of Home Runs: The Passion, Politics, and Language of Cuban Baseball*. Durham, NC, and London: Duke University Press, 2008.

Cluster, Dick, and Rafael Hernández. *The History of Havana*. New York: Palgrave Macmillan, 2006.

Fernandes, Sujatha. *Cuba Represent: Cuban Arts, State Power, and the Making of Revolutionary Cultures*. Durham, NC, and London: Duke University Press, 2006.

González Echevarría, Roberto. *La Gloria de Cuba: Historia del béisbol en la isla*. Madrid: Editorial Colibri, 2004.

Ingle, Zachary. "Introduction." *Identity and Myth in Sports Documentaries: Critical Essays*. Edited by Zachary Ingle and David M. Sutera. Lanham, MD: Scarecrow Press, 2013. ix–xii.

Jamail, Milton H. *Full Count: Inside Cuban Baseball*. Carbondale, IL: Southern Illinois University Press, 2000.

Latimer, Brian. "First MLB Game Broadcast in Cuba in over 50 Years Is 2 Months Old." July 3, 2013. Web. September 5, 2013. Retrieved from: http://nbclatino.com/2013/07/03/first-mlb-game-broadcast-in-cuba-in-over-50-years-is-2-months-old/.

McDonald, Ian. "Situating the Sport Documentary." *Journal of Sports and Social Issues* 31:3 (August 2007): 208–225.

Nichols, Bill. *Introduction to Documentary*. Bloomington and Indianapolis: Indiana University Press, 2001.

Padrón, Ian. "A todos los artistas cubanos." *Penúltimos días*. November 13, 2007. Web. March 25, 2013. Retrieved from: http://www.penultimosdias.com/2007/11/13/ian-padron-protesta-por-la-censura-de-su-documental-fuera-de-liga/.

Rojas, Rafael. *Tumbas sin sosiego: Revolución, disidencia y exilio del intelectual cubano*. Barcelona: Anagrama, 2006.

Rowe, David, Jim McKay, and Toby Miller. "Come Together: Sport, Nationalism and the Media." *Mediasport*. Edited by Lawrence A. Wenner. London and New York: Routledge, 1998. 119–133.

Saltz, Zach. "Blurred Boundaries across the Caribbean: The Transnational Experiences of Dominican Baseball Players in Documentary and Docudrama." *Identity and Myth in Sports Documentaries: Critical Essays*. Edited by Zachary Ingle and David M. Sutera. Lanham, MD: Scarecrow Press, 2013. 109–122.

Sánchez Rodríguez, Felix "¿Qué ocurrió con el jonrón decisivo de Kendry Morales? (Carta abierta a la comentarista deportiva Julia Osendi)." *Convivencia de Cuba*. September 13, 2009. Web. March 25, 2013. Retrieved from: http://convivenciacuba.es/index.php/debate-pblico-mainmenu-58/380-qu-ocurri-con-el-jonrn-decisivo-de-kendry-morales.

Spinoza, Benedict de. *Ethics*. Translated by Edwin Curley. London: Penguin, 1996.

Vicent, Mauricio. "Peloteros con cara y ojos en Cuba." *El país*. January 14, 2008. Web. March 25, 2013. Retrieved from: http://elpais.com /diario/2008/01/14/deportes/1200265227_850215.html.

PART III

Sports and Alterity

"Can I please have a ramp with that Gold Medal?": Colombian Paralympics and the Prosthetic Lim(b)inality of Nation

Chloe Rutter-Jensen

In their article "Come Together: Sport, Nationalism, and the Media Image," Rowe, McKay, and Miller argue that: "There is surely no cultural force more equal to the task of creating an imaginary national unity than the international sports-media complex" (133). Casual reflection on the World Cup of 2006 in Germany, which left Germans imbued with an unthreatening sense of national identity for the first time in decades; the 2012 Summer Olympics; and, importantly for this paper, the Paralympics that followed them in England, which left a depressed and cynical population aglow with a sense of accomplishment and potential, would seem to confirm this view, and this in contexts and populations whose nationness would seem to be well established. More compelling confirmation of the power of sports in crystallizing national sentiment comes from places that only enjoy a more tenuous claim to nationness. My focus in this essay is on some of the ways in which the sports-media complex in Colombia co-opts the performances and victories of the so-called dis-abled athlete in an effort to represent a more inclusive national sentiment. On the one hand, we are witnessing a real attempt to symbolically expand the purview of the nation, following its iteration in the Constitution of 1991 as a diverse community of difference. It would seem that the Paralympic media is a cultural force capable of creating imaginary national unity. On the other, nonetheless, I show how this effort is symbolic, and how, at the material level, the nation in Colombia remains the redoubt of the able bodied. In other words, the recognition in national discourses allows for a visibility that only symbolically and momentarily includes people with disabilities and yet still excludes them materially.

In the following pages, I show some of the tensions present in the relation between sports, nation, and social justice. I briefly elaborate on the national in a globalized world and on the micropolitical biopower of sports. Then, I interrogate the ways in which bodies are included and excluded in Colombian national mythmaking through sports. I argue that the representation in the media of Paralympic sports, the national and international sporting venues of bodies with disabilities, tends to give the impression of national belonging yet actually masks national exclusion. These reflections on representation emerge empirically from my own personal daily practices of training with the Paralympic swim team. I see first-hand the contradictions between the symbolic inclusion of my swim mates in the media and their material exclusions from other types of national participation. My experiences of training with the Paralympic swim team in Bogotá (I am a conventional swimmer)[1] allow me to see two stories, the story of national unity or inclusion that the media represents and the story of exclusion that the swimmers themselves tell. Through our daily routine, I am made aware of the hypocrisy of the self-congratulatory national recognition of athletes with disabilities in media events and of the "real" conditions in which they live. For example, while Mario (swimmer, double leg amputee, 18 years old) is proud to compete for Colombia, "it is a beautiful country with warm people," he adds, "the support for Paralympic athletes is not as complete or equal as for conventional athletes." Furthermore, it is "difficult to access most of the spaces [in the city of Bogotá] because they have no ramps" (translations of personal interviews are mine).

While my Paralympic swim teammates only briefly share membership in the city or nation as a whole, they create an example of the symbolic belonging that imagines national unity through the sports media complex. Their own mini nation expresses an ideal closer to the Colombian constitution's discourse of creating a "pluricultural and diverse nation." The athletes I train with seem to be part of an idealistic nation where they are symbolically recognized, participate in the public sphere, and even receive economic benefit through national sponsorship. One of the affirmative and inclusive phenomena observable in the group is an integration of its members from heterogeneous backgrounds, as opposed to the usual segregation along regional, class, gender, sexuality, and racial formations. These athletes come from very poor to upper-middle-class socioeconomic backgrounds. Their parents work in diverse fields such as bus driving, farming, and engineering. They live in vastly different neighborhoods of Bogotá and in home spaces that range from 40m² to 200m². While in a normative Colombian context they might never meet each other, not in educational institutions nor in social gatherings, which are sharply divided by class, as athletes they belong to the same team and the same community. They are dressed uniformly in the city's track suit or in the nation's tricolor track suit (they are both on the Bogotá team for national games and the Colombian team for international games). Not only are they outfitted similarly, many of them eat in the athletes' dining room where their food is subsidized by the city or nation, and some even live in athletes' housing, also sponsored by the city or nation. The close proximity creates a culture of commonality, in which their diverse family/ethnic/racial/class ties fade into the background and give way to that of their primary identities as swimmer.

On a symbolic level their identities as persons with disabilities allow for this unusually heterogeneous community whose relationship of affect is precisely because of, or through, their non-normative bodies. They are their own "swimming nation." In the day-to-day trainings with them, they occasionally refer to their disabilities, perhaps in the context of getting a new prosthesis, or sometimes to joke about who swims faster than me (the conventional body). Mario accuses me of cheating because since I have two legs I can push off the wall for more speed and impulse. Rather than imagining Mario as the body that doesn't fit, I, the two-legged body, am the problem. They even more infrequently mention other people's disabilities but when they do it is often to establish belonging to the group. Viviana, a swimmer with only one foot, comments on a new member of the team to the coach asking: "what is wrong with her?" The new woman looks like a conventional swimmer, and in Viviana's explanation of this comment to the coach, she says that the new member is weird since she has no identifiable disability: the "wrong" in her sentence is not a normative wrong, but rather, a wrong of not having a disability.

More often, the subject of conversations concentrates on other topics such as swim times (one of my repeat conversations is with a young woman, Adriana, with Down syndrome who asks me each week what my 50m butterfly time is to see if she has beaten me yet or not) or upcoming races, complaints about being tired and hungry, later trainings in the day, the weather, and lots of jokes about sex and romance (after all, the average age is early 20s). Their non-normative bodies provide their entrance into this group and swimming (sport) bonds them together as a group (the latter establishes my own ties to the group). Discussions about class, race, politics, and religion might, in other situations, easily divide them into individuals and erase their collectivity, but, in this community confronting uncomfortable ideas (or spaces) is part and parcel of life; after all, the city is inherently uncomfortable due to the man-made obstacles to their mobility.

Eliding race and class factors and only concentrating on the anatomical bodies, the team looks something like this: Mario's legs reach down from his trunk to his upper thighs. Jairo, Michael, Marvin, and Angie each have one leg. Nico has one arm. Viviana has one foot. Alejandro, John, Leonard, and Ximena are Deaf and communicate through sign language. For all of them, their disabilities form the basis of their entrance into high performance athletics. But once they are in the pool they are identified as experts in butterfly, backstroke, breast, or freestyle. They only have their specific non-normative bodies outside the pool, in their daily nonswimming activities.

At the pool, they train alongside several other teams, including "the cognitives" (Adriana and Duvan, people with cognitive disabilities), the "visuals" (Leider and Juan Felipe, visually impaired people), and "the conventionals" (Hernán and Carlos, in the morning workouts; the conventionals are elite triathletes and the subaquatic team). The sponsored athletes in all of these groups eat in the same dining room. Different identity categories share the same social space doing the same activity. One could almost even talk of integration between able and 'dis'-abled bodies in the cafeteria. The thread that ties them together is that of "athlete" and, more specifically, of "national athlete." The Olympic committee and regional support they receive subsidizes their food and part of their transport, and some even receive a monthly stipend depending on their recent competitive results. This makes sports a place of inclusion and integration, an idealistic form of community, in which the normative and non-normative bodies swim, eat, and earn money side by side. They seem to embody the "participative" and "pluralist" nation manifested in Article 1 of the Colombian Constitution. But this space of idealism basically ends up on the exit from the pool or dining room, and they return to a society riven by unjust social distributions.

Examining the sporting events and activities of people with disabilities allows us to identify some of the specific tensions of Colombian nationhood.[2] Disability, as Michael Davidson (2006) explains, can be used to bring into focus structurally determined inequities in society. He suggests we use a "disability optic" as a category of analysis; disability functions not only for issues of an individual body, but also for problems of social injustice on a broader scale. The objective is not to study the ways in which the disabled body is individually marginalized, but rather to use representations of the disabled body as a theoretical axis from which to study dominant discourses related to social injustice.

The disability optic reveals, on the one hand, the ways in which athletes with disability are finally included in the nation. This would seem to be the obvious use of a "disability optic." Yet it can also be used beyond the limits of the disabled body to interrogate the continuing existence of international sporting events between sovereign nations in an era of neoliberal transnational culture and economic flows. One of the critiques present in the concept of the national in a globalized world is that the nation no longer occupies the same role that it had earlier in our histories. The nation has traditionally generated enough imagined community in individuals to guarantee the shedding of tears at medal ceremonies upon hearing their national anthem and crowds unified in shouting their country's name. Yet, the idea of nations competing at sports in a neoliberal global economy is somewhat anachronistic. In this economy, interchangeable workers' bodies make up assembly lines that are distant from production lines. Consumer products and services are no longer national and are in fact porous over borders. Thus, sporting bodies and events are part of the consumer/service industry and frequently dependent on interchangeable athletic bodies.[3] So, one could conjecture that in the future rather than competing for nations we may eventually see Olympic Games in which *xyz* multinational conglomerate competes against *pqr* company, much like professional soccer leagues in Europe.

Nonetheless, it is perhaps rushed to symbolically eliminate national/international sporting events when finally people with disabilities, who were excluded from conventional games, have a venue in which to participate. Through these national/international competitions people with disabilities now also belong to the national community, they wear the national uniform, and they are lauded as national heroes. They are accorded the perceived privilege of competing in hierarchies of superior and inferior bodies and becoming members of a community. Once liminal participants in the nation, lacking social status, they are now included. Finally ramps have been installed at the swimming pool so that wheelchair users can enter and train hard to compete for the nation.

Before moving on to the specifics of belonging and not belonging, I'd like to point to another of these overarching tensions of sport and nation, in the same vein as the newly won "right" of Paralympic athletes to participate in a discriminatory system that constitutes superior and inferior bodies. One of these forms of understanding such hierarchies is through a Foucauldian model of biopower, in which the state fulfills its mandate to "foster life" while at the same time "letting die" those who are not productive (Foucault). If one observes the system of the categorization of bodies in the Paralympic Games, one sees the minutiae of micropolitical body management. Categories from T1 to T42 distribute bodies on a scale of disabilities. For example, T11 through T13 are the different degrees of visual impairment, and T11 runners do not compete with T13 runners. In swimming, S14 swimmers with intellectual impairments do not compete against S13 swimmers, with visual impairments. This micromanagement of bodies establishes the "fairest" competition possible in the Paralympics. Competition between a swimmers from the "global north" and "global south" is in itself questionable, because of the differences in material resources available for training, and highlights the tensions of national belonging and sports competitions not only in Paralympic competition, but in general. Yet, the access athletes with disabilities have to national sporting events through these categorizations is perceived as a balancing of the scales, instead of the micromanagement of bodies.

Having briefly elaborated some of the general tensions of sports, nation, and disability, I now draw on the social justice theories of Nancy Fraser and Martha Nussbaum to study the contradictions of visibility/invisibility and symbolic belonging/material nonbelonging to the nation. Fraser's concepts of redistribution, recognition, and reframing, as well as Nussbaum's social contract theory as related to citizens with disability, offer theories from which to examine the inconsistency between the visibility of an athlete with a disability as Colombia in the extraordinary sports events and the invisibility of this same person in the ordinary everydayness of the nation. For example, lack of accessibility or, as Mario puts it, the "impossibility" of using Bogotá's public mass transportation system Transmilenio for many swimmers illustrates the double standard that constitutes these athletes' lives. On the regional and national levels they have recognition as high performance swimmers, but when it comes to equal opportunities of education, jobs, mobility in the city, and participation in the public sphere in general they face systematic marginalization. This is the liminality, the threshold of belonging to nation: the symbolic recognition of the athlete and the breach between that recognition and his/her ability to participate materially in the community.

The opportunity to participate is constructed and standardized according to criteria that value people's contribution to society or their position in social hierarchies dependent on ability. Nussbaum's rejection of the notion of strict reciprocity as expected of heteronormative bodies (able bodiedness) as a basis for social welfare changes the whole social contract. Perhaps it even eliminates the contract and allows for other social systems to emerge. Fraser's notion of reframing further interrogates the social contract.[4] By reframing, she returns to the concept of representation to investigate *who* put the frame in place and *how* and *why*. The *who, how,* and *why* emerge as important questions for the construction of nation. In reframing the reciprocal, able-bodied social contract as problematic for community belonging, one questions the hierarchy of positions, inclusions, and exclusions in such a national structure. In reframing the bodily structure of the citizen, that is, thinking of the body in diverse ways or including the body with disabilities as central, not marginalized, the social contract would need to renegotiate belonging. A social "body" would include all types, both symbolically and materially. In the following section, the unbalanced contract of symbolic versus material belonging will become clear through the representation of athletes with disabilities in Colombian media.

Successes in the arena of international sports are most often manifested through conventional "able" bodied sports events, such as the Pan American Games, Olympic Games, or World Cup soccer. These are all shown on publicly broadcasted television, available to all who have access to television. Yet, recently there has been some coverage of the Paralympic version of these events in Colombia: both the Para Pan American Games 2011 in Guadalajara and the Paralympic Games 2012 in London received limited national television coverage (on state-financed channels), thus including nonconventional bodies as possible generators of positive national feelings.

Like conventional sporting events, the Para Pan American Games, Paralympic Games, and World Deaf Games[5] emerge as major cultural forces, as well as big business.[6] Television, sports venues, and advertising move multi-million dollar contracts as well as national fibers. On television, through music and interviews, the commentators stage dramas in which a viewer, consciously or not, participates as a nationalist. Without the media representation of sporting events, spectators could not form a community of affect for the athletes. Many people spend enormous amounts of hours and intense emotions devoted to sports on television, and the popularity of this is collective, based solely on how many channels and programming hours are exclusively devoted to sports. In these hours watching, the viewer appropriates the body of the athlete or the team of athletes and imbues it with a feeling of participation in the nation, whether elated at winning or devastated at losing. Intense emotions are projected onto the body as a site of national belonging, at least symbolically.

The body as central to these passions evokes the notion of "biological citizenship." Whyte and Ingstad define this organizing principle in their article "Disability Connections" as "people's sense of belonging and relations to each other and the state…based in a biological condition" (15). Perhaps the spectator does not identify through region, language, or social class, but does through the body. In the normative case, the biological connection would imply that an able bodied person can identify with the able bodiedness of a swimmer at the Pan American Games and that his or her medal will bring happiness to the viewer, not just to the medalist. There is no direct relationship between these two people;

they don't actually know each other, but the swimmer's biological body is a synecdoche for the nation. One can question the ways, or even if, this happens when the notion of biological citizenship is constituted not through the normative body but through the non-normative body. While Colombian media portrayals of para and conventional sports may be very similar (they frequently use the same music and same close-ups of triumph and defeat), the consumer could set aside the disability and belong together with the para-athletic body in the nation, in the same way one does with the conventional body. In this way, the important thing would be the national affirmation that the winning athlete, para or conventional, gives the viewer, either establishing a broad reading of biological citizenship that in fact includes all bodies, normative and not, or suggesting that citizenship might be based positively on other national constructs. This is particularly noticeable in the case of the Paralympic swimmers at the pool, Mario, Viviana, Alejandro, and so on. They have a different kind of biological citizenship, one based on the non-normative. I suggest that this distinct biological citizenship is not an exclusionary one, but rather one that includes the varied forms of disability in one single team (as we saw earlier, a heterogeneous community). So, while the Deaf person is not biologically similar to the double amputee, their experiences in a nonaccessible social space unite them.

While this may function within a community of bodies with disabilities, erasing biological differences between the able body and disabled body eliminates the biologically lived, different experiences of national belonging. The physically or cognitively non-normative body does not live united with the normative one. Thus, the affirmation or positive national cohesion the audience feels glosses over the material challenges a body with disabilities faces in a normative society and merely recognizes symbolically an inclusion of that body, briefly, on television, during a moment of success. Or to put it rather glibly, it is easy to get along when one is winning, but creative ties of solidarity when confronted with struggles of equality is a whole other ball game.

The positive national feeling in the case of Paralympic athletes resides in a world of narrative fantasy or at the threshold of belonging, and not in material sociocultural contexts of the body with disabilities' daily life. Perhaps the amputee swimmer or wheelchair tennis player represents an inclusion of the disabled body in the national rhetoric and the spectator cries with the athlete during the medal ceremony, but the presence of such athletes in the public sphere outside of sports is minimal, at best. The individual Paralympic athlete with a gold medal from London 2012 receives the same awards from the government as the conventional athlete from London 2012, but this does not translate into access and participation in Colombian public life for a disabled collective. I suggest that media representations of athletes with disabilities actually capitalize on this momentary collective national affirmation, this grasping for asser-tion of Colombian-ness by showing how "in spite" of the hardships of being disabled (or the negativity associated with being Colombian), peo-ple do make it, do get ahead.[7] Yet, beyond the symbolic recognition, the story is different; this is a body made disabled and excluded from archi-tectural and material spaces.

Alejandro is an example of both symbolic exclusion (people assume he is foreign) and material exclusion in the form of nonaccessibility in most places for Deaf people. He writes to me in an email communication (because I lack the ability to sign): "sign language is weird for people, they don't include me, they look at me weird when I speak, and they imagine I am from another *nation* and don't understand me."[8] When Alejandro speaks sign language he becomes foreign. He is all of a sud-den not Colombian and not understood. While on television in a race he may represent Colombia, off television, in real life, he is made alien. The athlete with disabilities, while most certainly privileged, with access to resources such as a pool and a coach, international travel, and minor fame in the media, loses these privileges when returned to the realities of a city and a nation. He or she is not included in the everyday common activities and faces little protection and few facilities for people unable to use their arms, legs, eyes, or ears in the demanding and limited ways the city requires. In the case of Bogotá, the city is designed based on a standard of a normative able bodied model. This artificial standard rep-resents an ideal, not a reflection of society. It is in fact an ideology, one that implicitly ranks bodies from superior to inferior by their capacity to use the city's public spaces. Alejandro notes that the public transporta-tion system Transmilenio is more of an obstacle than a help for people with disabilities. These spaces disable bodies and naturalize what types of bodies have access to what types of spaces.

The story becomes dismal when we study the 2005 Colombian census, which shows that the "majority of the population with disabilities lives in poverty and that 70% of them are unemployed" (Ángel, 39). Disability studies by law researchers in Colombia emphasize the right to work. *Discapacidad y derecho al trabajo*, a project from the Centro for Juridical Studies (CIJUS) at the Universidad de los Andes, states that "the right to work is fundamental for personal achievement and socio-economic stability, as well as essential to access other human rights" (Rodríguez and Rico, 18, translation mine). This study shows that 74 percent of the population with disabilities considers itself poor as compared to 66 per-cent of the population without disabilities. Additionally, only 22 percent of the population with disabilities has a formal work situation (45). This small number of working people is brought about by various factors: the accessibility of transportation to the workplace or educational institu-tion, accessibility at the workplace or educational institution, and the accessibility of proper education and job training to enter the institution or workplace. Because of the unavailability of accommodations, children frequently remain at home, a situation that isolates them from educational opportunities (52). The list of obstacles ranges from inaccessible public transportation to unnavigable sidewalks (or lack of sidewalks altogether) to the absence of bathroom facilities or ramps. Laws designed to combat these barriers exist, but as the Universidad de los Andes study shows, a major breach occurs between laws and their implementation. These obstacles to full participation in national citizenship are the lived experience of 6–10 percent of the population. At the local level, in Bogotá the marginalization of the disabled body from public spaces arises from a city landscape that refuses access to any but the most able bodied people, and this is the first barrier to participative parity for a person with disabilities. Public space in Bogotá repudiates the non-normative body, depriving people of opportunity and participation in the "world at large."

Susan Wendell, in her text on feminist philosophy of the disabled body, writes: "The public world is the world of strength, the positive (valued) body, performance and production" (40). In this case, the absence of possible mobility in the public sphere implies weakness and uselessness. The brief public appearances of the body with disabilities in sports events is a rare moment of access to this "world of strength" and productivity, but does not mean that beyond recognition the person with disabilities has a share in material rewards. Again, that positive national feeling is like the adding of a prosthetic leg to a body, rather than adapting the environment to make it usable by the person with only one leg. The liminality is the lack of full participation.

Fraser argues that participation in the political realm means deciding *who* the subjects of struggles for justice are and *what* those subjects can claim. People with disabilities are subjects of this struggle, as they are denied full distribution, recognition, and representation. And justice, as Fraser puts it, "requires social arrangements that permit all to participate as peers in social life" (*Scales*, 16). If people with disabilities receive insufficient education to be active in a labor market, formally or informally, they are devoid of tools with which they can act in social life or make claims against the state. Not participating means not contesting the current social and institutional limitations imposed on them, which in turn forces them to accept the claims and concepts of others who decide for them. Even if athletes with disabilities are hailed as national heroes, this status does not necessarily translate into participation in the broader national life, indeed perhaps they are confined to the symbolic arena in order to avoid the effort it would take to rethink public spaces from inclusive perspectives. They are at the threshold of belonging, symbolic, but not material.

Clearly, athletes with disabilities are not entirely invisible, and there is a relationship of national affect with sports consumers, but if we look closer at the representation in the media we can see many subtle differences and erasures in the treatment of conventional "able" bodied athletes and Paralympic athletes. First, on a global level, the amount of press devoted to London 2012 in the largest dailies of Colombia (Bogotá-based newspapers) was eight times that of Para London 2012. That means for every article about the Paralympics that *El Tiempo* published there were eight articles about the Olympics during London 2012. In addition, the editors buried most of the Paralympic articles in the last pages of the sports, whereas the Olympic articles led the sports section. Also, a good portion of the para stories were from outside news sources, revealing a lack of their own representation in London, yet for the conventional Olympics, the Colombian media companies each had correspondents in attendance directly reporting the news items. Similarly, Caracol, one of Colombia's dominant television/radio networks, bought the rights to show London 2012, but did not show Para London 2012.

In another example of inclusion and exclusion, the local Colombian media is seen to celebrate athletes with disabilities when it serves the positive image of the nation. According to Lobo in *Colombia: algo diferente de una nación*, any type of positive image of Colombia counts for national celebration, whether it reflects a common reality of the country or not. An example of this appears in the Bogotá daily *El Espectador*. An article written during the Para Pan American games praises the increase of medals won in Guadalajara 2011 compared to previous competitions: "Coldeportes, in an official press release, qualified the event as a historical *vanquishing*" (11/17/2011, translation and emphasis mine). The language evokes conquest and Colombian empowerment as a nation through its athletes with disabilities, *when they are winning*.

In fact, when they "vanquish" the opponent and win, they are reported as *being* Colombia. The winning tennis players are equated with Colombia when the press states that in doubles *Colombia* won—not the Colombian players, but the nation itself. Yet, if they do well, but don't win, as in the case of the swimmer Daniel Giraldo at Para Pans 2011, they are reported as "the great figure *of* Colombia" (*El Espectador* 11/16/2011, translation and emphasis mine). Soccer 5 (five person, visually impaired), with their loss to Argentina, is described as the national *team* losing, not the nation itself losing. Whereas during the same week in a World Cup soccer classifier, the Colombian national soccer (conventional) team *is* Colombia; the language even collapses the division between representation and reality. In a press article about the match, the journalist writes that the players have all arrived "according to the press office of the national team. In their first match in the South American qualifiers, *Colombia* debuted as the winner as the visitor in La Paz against Bolivia"

(11/6/2011, translation and emphasis mine). While in the first part of the quote the national *team* is mentioned, in the following sentence the team is elided into the nation. Colombia replaces the official title of the "national team *of* Colombia," and thus the country, not the group of 11 players, won, and it beat, not another 11 players, but the nation of Bolivia. Perhaps by distancing the language from the direct link in the news story of Paralympic Soccer 5 and only saying the Colombian *team* lost alleviates Colombia itself from being perceived as a loser. However, as much as any of the athletes with disabilities can *be* the nation, these same athletes cannot participate *in* the nation because they cannot freely transport themselves to a voting station and vote.

The collapse, between team/individual and nation, is a narrative strategy of masking the sociocultural conditions that allow people to attain success in a society. The intense national sensation identified with the medal winner serves to encourage the myth that personal hard work or will power (not one's sociocultural context) allows one to succeed. The language of individual triumph found in the stories of persons with disabilities ignores the sociocultural, economic, and political conditions that create inequality. Furthermore, it assigns credit or blame to the individual, thus eliminating the structural discrimination against non-normative bodies. For example, in the case of Moisés Fuentes, London 2012 silver medalist in 100-meter breaststroke, a report from the Paralympic Games in *El Espectador*, the news source with the second highest circulation in Colombia, tells of his achievements in life as unaffected by disability. He attributes getting the silver medal to his extraordinary optimism and desire to live, implying that these two things were enough to overcome the obstacles that a person in a wheelchair faces in an architecturally inaccessible society like Colombia. The article calls his life a "normal" one: "Even though he is in a wheelchair, he has continued life with *normality*. He completed a triple major in college and is the executive secretary of the Santander League of Disabled Athletes" (*El Espectador* 8/27/2012, translation and emphasis mine). Not only is a silver medal and three university majors not a "normal" Colombian life, but the violence that made him disabled is de-emphasized with the only briefest mention that he was the victim of an assassination attempt in which Moisés's "brother died from the impact of a bullet, and Moisés became paraplegic" (ibid).

Moisés is represented as an individual unaffected by the social structure, as if the bullet that disabled him was not a result of endemic violence, and as if he could overcome the structural (literally and figuratively) barriers and inequality in Colombia. In this paradox he is immune to the social conditions of Colombia, while simultaneously being disabled by them. Instead of recognizing the violence that disabled him, he actually thanks Colombia: "I owe so much to Colombia and to my family, that maybe I won't have enough time in my entire life to return the happiness it has meant to me to represent my country" (*El Espectador* 8/27/2012). He paid his legs to Colombia, and in return he feels gratitude to represent the very same national structures that disabled him. I suggest that for Moisés to express this undying loyalty to nation because of his medal demonstrates clearly what Lobo argues is a practice of "grasping" at positive activities to feel a secure national identity. To reconcile a secure national identity with being disabled by armed violence is no easy feat (pun intended). Finally, the article fails to mention what his ordinary daily life might be like or that of the many people in wheelchairs who are not Paralympic athletes. By winning a silver medal, Moisés seems to fulfill the social contract of belonging and being productive.

As mentioned earlier, Martha Nussbaum argues that the social contract is a highly problematic tool for analysis of social justice when the contract is not perceived as reciprocal, as is the case of people with disabilities. Nussbaum, in *The Frontiers of Social Justice*, examines the social contract in a society that assumes mutual benefits in its interactions among equals. She proposes that through the lens of disability studies, the social relationship of reciprocity cannot be formally contracted if some bodies are considered more productive (normative) and others a high cost to society (the non-normative or disabled). The productivity of a body is ascertained through its ability to fulfill capitalist market needs—in other words, its role as a wage earner independent of state help. Nussbaum interrogates the measurements of productivity derived from a normative standard. She writes that when gauging the output or efficiency of a person with disabilities in the market, "their relative lack of productivity under current conditions is not 'natural'; it is the product of discriminatory social arrangements" (113). A body, therefore, is only efficient in the current social arrangement in which competence is judged by the physical ability of the body to earn money, or, in the case of sports, medals. Moisés, then, is returned into the traditional social contract because he is a high performance swimmer or, as Susan Wendell proposes, through strength and productivity, and therefore the positive national feeling he brings to Colombia is perceived as holding up his end of the bargain. This might seem to imply inclusivity but, again, the status he attains is liminal, symbolic, and individual, and does not change the structural exclusion of most people with disabilities from most areas of public life. Moreover, the nonconventional athletes may be shown on television or briefly discussed in the newspaper, implying a symbolic belonging, but, in the case of Moisés, the media gloss over the material conditions that created his disability and maintain his lack of independent mobility in a non-wheelchair-accessible public life.

While many of the stories of individual athletes show their exceptional narratives of triumph, overcoming poverty, overcoming illness and accident, and overcoming pain, thanks to their chosen sport, as we see in the case of Moisés Fuentes, these individual scenarios reaffirm the systems as they are. I suggest that this is another example of symbolic recognition in national discourses that allows for symbolic visibility but sustains material exclusion. This type of media attention allows one to imagine that the nation is behind the double amputee swimmer and that when he or she wins a medal it is also for everyone. We can love the swimmer but disown the responsibility to think about the economic and social structures of injustice highly visible in the nation.

Thus, our sporting relationship to the nation is uncritical and passive. The participation of athletes with disabilities in sporting events conveys the idea that Colombian nationhood includes all types and capabilities of bodies, to the extent that the athletes dress in a national uniform and represent the nation in Para Pan American and Paralympic games.[9] This establishes a paradox in which individuals with disabilities who train for national sports in Colombia experience glory, travel, media attention, and standing on the podium, whereas the nonathlete disabled body is excluded from most participation in citizenship.

Michael Davidson, in his article "Universal Design," writes that disability is located "not in the individual's impairment but in the environment—in social attitudes, institutional structures, and physical or communicational barriers that prevent full participation as citizen subject" (119). The problem lies not in the body, but in the design of physical and social structures that ignore the possibility of different bodies or impose a vertical hierarchy of superior and inferior. What is merely a human body becomes abled or disabled depending on its environment. If there is such a thing as nature, then we can see that people are created in different ways, thus the disabled body *is* natural. Nobody genetically engineered disability; when it isn't the result of landmines, war, or accidents, it occurs naturally in our environment. The normative body is naturalized, but not necessarily any more natural than the disabled body. All bodies can become different (be naturalized or denaturalized), due to illness, accident, age, or other life events. All people can be remodeled from normative to non-normative bodies—and bodies can be naturalized as national and denaturalized as national as well. What is merely a human body becomes abled or disabled depending on its environment.

For example, in the swimming pool, Mario moves just as well as a person with two legs and during those moments he is an extraordinarily abled body, swimming 100 meters in a fast time, yet out of the pool steep steps or high curbs create a disability where previously there was none. Clearly the physical design of public space is what disables him, not his body itself. He wears two prostheses, one on each leg, and lifting them higher requires much effort. If the stairs or curbs are lower, all of a sudden he moves with ease, and again, he becomes more abled. Thus it is the design of spaces and social standards that brings into existence disability. In other words, Mario is not inherently disabled, he is differently abled than the standard, and the social structures work against him instead of for him, in effect dis-abling him and excluding him from first class citizenship.

For Alejandro, speaking a different language from verbal Spanish alienates him from the larger community, even though it is the larger community that doesn't understand him, not Alejandro who doesn't understand Spanish. Alejandro too is dismembered from the nation (even thought of as foreign). His entrance into the national community through the sport media complex is prosthetic and universalist. In contrast, Fraser calls for the "ability" to occupy an identity category through one's particularities without conforming to a universalist identity. Fraser advocates a situation in a "difference-friendly world, where assimilation to majority or dominant cultural norms is no longer the price of equal respect" ("Social Justice," 3). Redesigning the nation to be accessible would require restructuring based on concepts of recognition, redistribution, and political representation in all areas, not merely in the pool. In the end, it is not just geographical and material space that needs ramps, but also the concept of the nation itself.

Notes

1. In a continuation of the previous dichotomy, I include myself, as being both symbolically part of a collective, but materially different. My participation as an insider/outsider allows me insights in to the inner social workings of the group and observation of their lives outside of the pool. My age (20 years older) allows me to remain distant from their personal power struggles or friendship regroupings. My economic earnings are not related to swimming (I am a university professor and earn my salary teaching and researching), so therefore I am not in competition with them on any level. My primary identity is not that of an athlete as is theirs, thus making me an outsider to the collective, yet, I am an insider in the direct area of swimming.
2. For an interesting and elaborate discussion of nation and Colombia and the ways in which national coherence is frequently achieved through violence, that is, the negative, instead of through positive national feeling (in this essay, e.g., sports), see Gregory Lobo's *Colombia: algo diferente de una nación*.
3. European soccer leagues used to have a rule of a maximum of four foreign players. Within the European community, Europeans from other countries are not considered foreign, which means a team from an English city, such as Manchester, could have no English players in games. A side could be made up of four Spaniards, three Germans, two Italians, and, say, two Brazilians.
4. If we were to exercise reframing perhaps the next step, after outlining the injustices that I have attempted to do here, would be to contest the patriarchal notions of competition, both at the national and international levels.

The race to the finish line might not be about who was fastest, but who had the most fun.

5. See Hilde Haualand's article on the World Deaf Games in Rome for an excellent study of the business of sports events and the community ties that these create.

6. In August during the Paralympics London 2012, the Eurosport channel announcers commented that some of the venues for the Paralympics sold more tickets than during the Olympics.

7. For an interesting study of the campaign "Heroes DO exist in Colombia," see Gregory Lobo's article "Spectacular Nationism in Colombia: Making War Make Sense."

8. "el lenguaje de señas es raro para las personas, no me incluyen en actividades comunes, me miran con extrañeza y como bicho raro cuando hablo, siempre se imaginan soy de otra nación y no me entienden"; emphasis added.

9. The amount of people made disabled by landmines brings the topic of disability to the forefront in a country that might usually ignore the issue. The newspapers and magazines have frequent stories about the heroes of the nation, those soldiers who have lost limbs to landmines, "fighting" for the nation. I explore this topic further in a separate article (work in progress).

Bibliography

Ángel Cabo, Natalia. "*La convención de Naciones Unidas sobre los derechos de las personas con discapacidad: dejando atrás el modelo médico.*" Bogotá: *EGOB* 5 (September 2010): 39–41.

Davidson, Michael. "Universal Design: The Work of Disability in an Age of Globalization." *The Disability Studies Reader.* Edited by Lennard J. Davis. New York: Routledge, 2006. 117–128.

Eagleton, Terry, Fredric Jameson, and Edward W. Said. *Nationalism, Colonialism, and Literature.* Introduction by Seamus Deane. Minneapolis: University of Minnesota Press, 1990.

Foucault, Michel. *History of Sexuality.Volume 1: The Will to Knowledge.* London: Verso, 1990.

Fraser, Nancy. "Social Justice in the Age of Identity Politics: Redistribution, Recognition, and Participation." The Tanner Lectures on Human Values. Delivered at Stanford University April 30–May 2, 1996. tannerlectures.utah.edu/_documents/a-to-z/f/Fraser98.pdf.

———. *Scales of Justice: Reimagining Political Space in a Globalizing World.* New York: Columbia University Press, 2009.

Haualand, Hilde. "The Two-Week Village." *Disability in Local and Global Worlds.* Edited by Susan Reynolds Whyte and Benedicte Ingstad. Berkeley: University of California Press, 2007. 33–55.

Lobo, Gregory. *Colombia: algo diferente de una nación.* Bogotá: CESO, 2009.

———. "Spectacular Nationism in Colombia: Making War Make Sense." *Nationalism, War and Sacrifice: Dying for One's Country.* Edited by Richard Koenigsberg. Elmhusrt, NY: Library of Social Science, forthcoming.

Nussbaum, Martha. *Frontiers of Social Justice: Disability, Nationality, Species Membership.* Cambridge, MA: Harvard University Press, 2006.

Rodríguez, César y Laura Rico. *Discapacidad y derecho al trabajo.* Bogotá: CIJUS, 2009.

Rowe, David, Jim McKay, and Toby Miller. "Come Together: Sport, Nationalism, and the Media Image." *Mediasport.* Edited by Lawrence Wenner. London: Routledge, 1998. 119–133.

Wendell, Susan. *The Rejected Body: Feminist Philosophical Reflections on Disability.* New York: Routledge, 1996.

Whyte, Susan Reynolds, and Benedicte Ingstad. "Disability Connections." *Disability in Local and Global Worlds.* Edited by Susan Reynolds Whyte and Benedicte Ingstad. Berkeley: University of California Press, 2007. 1–29.

CHAPTER 9

Women Boxers and Nationalism in Mexico

Hortensia Moreno

Translated by Luis Lorenzo Esparza Serra

Can a female athlete embody the spirit of a nation? The study of sports teaches us that the essence of the practice traditionally lies in the construction and consolidation of masculinity. The accomplished vigorous male athlete who, wearing the colors of the flag, cries as he listens to the national anthem is also a proud national warrior. What happens when a woman occupies that place in the podium?

Boxing is one of the most popular spectator sports in Mexico. Along with soccer, it inspires a deep feeling of pride and dignity closely related to nationalism. Male boxers are truly popular idols, worshipped by their fans in international tournaments.

In 1999, women's professional boxing became legal in Mexico City after Laura Serrano, amateur boxer and law student, brought a lawsuit against the boxing regulations that banned women from the practice. A small sector of female boxers began to develop in spite of the scarcity of training facilities, the open hostility of their male counterparts, and the scarcity of tournaments and fights open to women.

My research project on women boxers in Mexico City has taken me to gyms and boxing arenas. From 2005 to 2008, I interviewed male and female boxers, trainers, managers, seconds, officials, and physicians. In this chapter, I try to decipher the gender implications of the national values and meanings that surround the boxing arena. The mere presence of women in sports—especially in combat sports—challenges the ways in which the human body is constructed as a receptacle of national symbols.

In the first section, I look at the place of boxing in the imaginary of the nation in Mexico in the context of the internationalization of a statutory base for sports originated in the countries of the North and imposed on those of the South, in a center-periphery movement. In so doing, I trace the transformation of boxing from an elite to a popular sport whose immense following many wouldn't hesitate to attribute to an inherent trait in the nature of the "Mexican soul."

In the second section, I review some historical data on women boxers in Mexico in an attempt to discern the main obstacles to the consecration of female figures as national boxing idols. I examine in particular the figure of Ana María Torres in the context of what I see as the four dimensions of social life in which athletic heroism finds a link to the imagination of nationalism: "the people," the state, private enterprise, and the media.

In the third section, I question whether the consolidation of masculinity is as essential a component of the practice of boxing as it is of nation-building. If sport serves to masculinize and affirm male identity, women's combat sports constitute a deviant practice that acutely challenges the sensitivity of Mexicans.

Boxing in Mexico

The development of each sport as a social phenomenon depends on a number of historical, economic, educational, political, institutional, cultural, climatic, ecological—and even biological, anatomical, and psychological—variables, so that it is legitimate to ask why a certain athletic activity thrives in a certain time and place, how it becomes a "national sport," and how it affects the lives of those who engage in it. One can speculate that the elevation of a sport to a national status expresses the ethos of a country and reveals a great deal about the character of a community. Mexico's "national" sports are soccer, baseball, and boxing. All three enjoy great popularity, although this might not necessarily be true from coast to coast and border to border, nor has it been the same at every stage in Mexican history (for a detailed review, see Arbena, "El mapa").

In Mexico and Latin America, research on boxing—and especially on nationalism and boxing—is still little developed. A very important precursor is Sugden, who conducted a comparative study of the practice of boxing in three cities: Hartford (United States), Belfast (Ireland), and Havana (Cuba). The main source of information on Mexico's boxing is the sports printed media. Some journalistic essays on the subject appear in Garmabella and Toledo, and the research of Maldonado and Zamora, based on a documentary collection of journalistic sources, provides a basic framework. An ethnographic research thesis appeared in Jerónimo Jiménez. For research on female boxing in Mexico, I refer primarily to the documentaries of de Lara and del Paso, as well as the newspaper articles of Hernández Carballido and my own research. At present, Teresa Osorio is compiling a history of women's boxing in Mexico.

Boxing was introduced in Mexico in the late nineteenth century. Several institutions adopted boxing; the army considered it an important element in military instruction; the martial academies saw it as one of several combat techniques cadets should master; and gyms, schools, and sports organizations (such as the YMCA, which brought "muscular Christianity" to this country in 1892) made it a point to include it on the sports menu. Moreover, the spectacle of boxing quickly became a very popular pastime, even though municipal authorities repeatedly banned it in an attempt to put an end to the gambling business.

Maldonado and Zamora state that around 1893, high society gentlemen practiced boxing as a martial art "to resolve conflicts of 'honor,'" in clear imitation of European elites. In the early twentieth century, at the end of the Porfirio Díaz regime, boxing gyms proliferated and academies emerged in scores, among them the Mexican Olympic Club, the Metropolitan Academy, and the Military School gym. These had "adequate facilities, light filled rooms, dressing rooms and showers," and were intended to "teach the new athletes to care for their appearance" as a "complement to the precepts acquired in the lyceums" (14–15).

Despite the existing bans on the practice of boxing, clandestine fights were organized in Mexico City in the early twentieth century, with substantial participation of young aristocrats as amateur athletes, as audiences, and as gamblers. However, boxing would soon lose its aristocratic vocation as its violence levels became unacceptable to the standards of the dominant classes in what Norbert Elias called the "civilizing process" (see Elias and Dunning), and the discipline, with the relatively cheap investment it requires, went on to acquire what is now one of its distinctive features over time and geography: being a sport of the poor.

The move from an elite to a popular practice can be linked to the existence of a deeply stratified society where the "lower" classes are identified with mestizo (mixed race) ethnic backgrounds (the "*nacos*"), while the "upper" classes strive to preserve their "racial purity" in an imaginary that never really managed to impose a physical barrier to racial mixing.

In the mythology of boxing, young people engage in its practice out of a need to overcome an adverse class condition: all that is needed to achieve the miracle of social advancement is strong will, a touch of fortune, and a good coach. The Golden Age of Mexican boxing coincided with a period of economic and cultural boom (the 1940s and 1950s) and was clearly depicted in the film industry, where actors such as Pedro

Infante and David Silva personified the legendary boxer. But the image of the hero was most effectively embodied in real popular idols and celebrities like Rodolfo "Chango" Casanova, Luis "Kid Azteca" Villanueva, Juan Zurita, and Raúl "Ratón" Macías, who inhabited the sports media and gossip with stories of courage, bravery, and sacrifice—but also ruin and adversity brought about by squandering fortunes, alcoholism, and dark ties with the underworld.

One of the reasons I maintain that boxing can be considered a "national sport" in Mexico is the number of medals it has gained for the country at the Olympics. The following two tables illustrate this. Table 9.1 presents the prospects of the Latin American region in the international Olympic context, the only real power being Cuba, which ranks second in the world after the United States. Next in the list is Argentina, occupying a distant ninth position, followed by Mexico, with a twenty-first position. However, within the regional context, Mexico certainly stands out with an honorable third place. Table 9.2 shows the ranking of sports in the national context. Until the Beijing Olympics in 2008, boxing was the sport that had given most medals to Mexico (21.81 percent), but in London 2012, it came second after diving.

In my ethnographic research with active subjects in gyms, training parks, arenas, sports fields, and offices in Mexico City (see *Orden discursivo*), some informants' theories about the affinity between boxing and

Table 9.1 Latin American countries and their Olympic medals in boxing

World ranking	Regional ranking	Country	Gold	Silver	Bronze	Total
2	1	Cuba	32	19	12	63
9	2	Argentina	7	7	10	24
21	3	Mexico	2	3	7	12
30	4	Venezuela	1	2	2	5
41	5	Dominican Republic	1	0	1	2
49	6	Puerto Rico	0	1	5	6
52	7	Chile	0	1	2	3
61	8	Colombia	0	0	3	3
65	9	Brazil	0	0	1	1
65	9	Guyana	0	0	1	1
65	9	Uruguay	0	0	1	1

Source: Built with information from http://es.wikipedia.org/wiki/ Categor%C3%Ada:Medallistas _ol%C3%ADmpicos_de_boxeo, and Wallechinsky and Loucky (2008).

Table 9.2 Medals obtained by Mexico in Summer Olympic Games

Sport	Total	Gold	Silver	Bronze	Percentage
Diving	13	1	6	6	20.97
Boxing	12	2	3	7	19.35
Track and Field	10	3	5	2	16.13
Equestrian	7	2	1	4	11.29
Taekwondo	6	2	1	3	9.68
Swimming	2	1	0	1	3.23
Archery	2	0	1	1	3.23
Cycling	2	0	1	1	3.23
Polo	2	0	0	2	3.23
Weightlifting	1	1	0	0	1.61
Fencing	1	0	1	0	1.61
Wrestling	1	0	1	0	1.61
Shooting	1	0	1	0	1.61
Basketball	1	0	0	1	1.61
Football	1	1	0	0	1.61
Total	62	13	21	28	100

Source: http://es.wikipedia.org/wiki/M%C3%A9xico_en_los_Juegos_ Ol%C3%ADmpicos; see Wallechinsky and Loucky (2008).

Mexican nationality introduced the ideas of genetic predisposition and historical conditioning as important factors to the development of boxing as a national sport:

> Traditionally, and according to some studies conducted at our top university, Mexicans are winners by genetic predisposition, but only in individual sports. You see, for example, over 89 percent of our Olympic medals are in boxing, diving and athletics—walking—while in team sports only in basketball; outside those sports it seems that athletes do not meet our expectations. Under these conditions, and without neglecting the masses, the government should channel its efforts more specifically to those who traditionally, genetically and historically, can give a greater chance of success. (Interview with Ricardo Contreras, president of the Mexican Federation of Amateur Boxing, November 28, 2005)

In testimonies collected in the field, along with an expression of a need to legitimize the practice of boxing in terms of masculinity values, citizenship, and "chivalry," there is a tendency to see in boxing a reason for national pride. The legitimation is of course paradoxical, as the chronic failure (until 2012) of national soccer, another "Mexican" sport, is very hard to justify:

> Well, definitely, Mexico is a football country, but also, a country of boxers. Proof of this is that currently thirteen of the professional boxing world champions are Mexican, and more are on their way. In the university community, these great achievements of professional athletes are a source of inspiration, and we are glad to see that boxing is the most practiced sport—well, after football—and that boxing is the sport that has given our country—and, consequently, the university community—the most Olympic medals. Given the characteristics of the Mexican national, this sport is ever more widely practiced; proof of it is the number of students enrolled. (Interview with Antonio Solórzano, head coach of the National University's boxing team, October 14, 2005)

In the realm of boxing there is a wide consensus in attributing the practice's popularity to the socioeconomic conditions in which it takes place. This establishes an almost linear relationship between sports and social class. Indeed, the decision to commit to an athletic discipline is not a free act open to individual choice, since there are material restrictions to overcome:

> In Mexico there is a lot of hunger, a lot of need. And this is a great opportunity for young people with few resources. Moreover, boxing is going to require from you an excellent physical condition. It will not allow you to stay up late, or binge drink, nor do drugs; it will not allow you anything of the sort. If you want to get ahead, it's up to you, it depends on you, not on a team: that's the nature of Mexicans [...]. Boxing is a great opportunity for humble individuals who have a heart and who are prepared to die right there; rather than intimidating him, a blow inflames the boxer, and the pain gives him the strength to punch back. This is a feature common to most Mexicans. (Interview with Alberto Reyes, industrial and promoter, November 30, 2005)

WOMEN'S BOXING IN THE NARRATIVES OF THE MEXICAN NATION

The entry of women into sports is not entirely new. In parallel with the expansion of women's access to the world of work and politics, the sports world has had to gradually open up to a more or less acceptable balance of women's inclusion. However, this inclusion—as it happens with the whole social organization—is still a peculiar phenomenon in the twenty-first century: outside their confinement in domestic space, women's bodies are still read as if they were "out of place."

Though it represents the last bastion of an imagined male exclusivity, boxing is no exception: since its inception it has had an irregular female presence. Jennifer Hargreaves has gathered evidence of women's boxing activity from the eighteenth century onward. As stated in the final note of her captivating essay, many of her sources are not identified, which expresses the inherent difficulty in the task of writing an almost clandestine history, in contrast to men's boxing, which has been documented in reasonable detail in different registers (Oates; Fleischer and Andre).

In her review of the history of women's boxing in Mexico, Teresa Osorio tells the story of the Mazatleca boxer Margarita "La Maya" Montes (1913–2007), who as a teenager excelled in baseball and bullfighting. At the age of 17, with the sponsorship of Chano Gómez, she won two fights to ten rounds at Mazatlán's Teatro Rubio (now Ángela Peralta), against Josefina Coronado, for a purse of 150 pesos. The Maya was then crowned as "Female Champion of the Pacific Coast." She also fought in the United States. In total, she held 38 professional fights, only 6 of them against women. It is unclear when she retired and whether she did because of marriage or because women's boxing was banned in Mexico on December 5, 1946, by presidential decree.

This explicit prohibition allows us to infer that women's boxing has had a significant presence in social life: what cannot be done needs not be prohibited. The desire to box has then been present in Mexican women throughout the twentieth century, probably for the same reasons that lead men to the ring, one of which is the existing link between sports effort and the construction of the idea of nation. The legalization of female boxing in Mexico in 1999 opened the door to a marginalized sector of society for a renewed participation in this collective, imagined project.

However, the possibility to practice a sport does not automatically lead to the creation of narratives about the nation, since the sports hero—a crucial element of the nationalist imaginary—can only be produced through the combination of the following four dimensions of social life: (i) "the people" (i.e., the fans, but also—and especially—the immediate social networks that constitute the athlete's springboard to obtain resources and support), (ii) the state (i.e., the ideological, bureaucratic, and administrative structure responsible for the institutionalization of sport as an element of a national project), (iii) private enterprise (i.e., the economic interest apparatus that "oils" the sports machinery by directly investing in sports entertainment, be it through advertising or through outright manipulation of competitions), and (iv) the fourth power (i.e., the media—the press, television, radio, film, and, more recently, Internet). None of these dimensions operates independently of the others, and each one of them has a specific weight in the process of "imaginarization" of a public figure. I will try to explain how these factors have operated in the national imaginary of boxing, taking Ana María Torres's career as a key point of reference.

The People

The trajectory of Ana María Torres confirms how a good physique and strong discipline are essential for success in sports: she has a "natural talent" for boxing and has worked devotedly and consistently for more than a decade in the construction of an athletic body with an outstanding performance. Her vocation is, undoubtedly, a necessary—albeit not sufficient—condition for achievement in sports.

In order to transcend mere entertainment space and proceed toward competitive practice, every sportsperson requires a social support and resource base—"social capital." In the so-called Third World countries—if not in all countries—the first step in any athletic career takes place in the family circle. Without this support, it is very difficult—if not impossible—to excel in the field of sports. In Torres's case, it was her mother who urged her to enter boxing:

> At first it was my mother who watched boxing on TV, and we [Torres and her siblings] didn't like it. I'd practiced taekwondo before; it was available close to home in Neza, and I liked it. I began working with a trainer at age 17. I went to two tournaments where I won two first places—well, thank God—but my parents—my mom basically—had no more money to pay for the training, it's very expensive. Then she said, "I'm taking you to boxing, to the gym where they practice boxing, so that you continue to practice self defense because you must know how to defend yourself." (Interview with Ana María Torres, November 17, 2005)

In *La Guerrera* (The female warrior), a documentary by Paulina del Paso on the life of Torres, each trip and each fight will either light up or darken in an intense emotional swirl caused by the constant oscillation between admiration and blackmail, support and disapproval of relatives. One example is the social pressure coming from relatives on her mother's side coercing the athlete to observe Catholic marriage standards in her intimate relationships (Torres travels with her professional and sentimental partner, Roberto Santos, to whom she isn't married). These regulatory mechanisms are not applied to the behavior of male athletes: the double standard of sexual morality continues to permeate gender conventions in Mexican society.

Directly linked to the aforementioned standard is the notion that attributes responsibility and mobility to male figures, while female figures are reduced to domestic space. In Del Paso's documentary, Torres breaks these conventions symbolically for the first time when she brings flowers and a mariachi band to her mother's house on Mother's Day, a move that is received with either disapproval or ambiguity, because of its gender meaning. In traditional Mexican society, women cannot take this kind of initiative because they are not supposed to leave home and because they lack the money to incur such an expense. In the gender imaginary of "deep Mexico," squandering money is something totally unacceptable from a woman, while in a man it may be read as a gesture of kindness, generosity, and magnanimity.

Here, the idea of the nation does not correspond to its modern definition, but rather to a traditional notion detached from the concept of citizenship and dependent on gender roles in several fundamental ways, the main one of which has to do with the legitimacy of offspring, closely linked to women's sexual behavior. In this way, boxing for Torres becomes a possibility for economic independence, a gateway to loosely regulated forms of sexual behavior and a reversal of gender roles.

Although quite effective from the symbolic point of view, all these transgressions have a limited impact on the field of Mexican boxing, a world with a traditionalist and stubbornly conservative nature. Moreover, entry into training spaces does not depend on personal choice, but rather on contacts—usually family ones—that open the possibility of integration to new members. The initiation process includes a number of tests of varying difficulty, and male and female novices are expected to have the endorsement or sponsorship of someone who belongs to the field:

> In many cases the contact exists before entry into boxing is attempted, for one of the pathways is precisely membership into a family of boxers, and in many interviews we have recorded how the sons and brothers of more or less established boxers and coaches become boxers and coaches themselves—the list includes sometimes female boxers too—and thus, the mechanism of reproduction of the practice depends on access to the places and the secrets that determine the configuration of the field through family relations. (Moreno 231)

For the vast majority of female boxers I interviewed, entry came by way of a family member: the father, a brother, a cousin, or an uncle—or even a husband or a boyfriend. This means that social control over women is reproduced in the field in a systematic way—although, as with all social phenomena, there are interesting exceptions. In this regard, the participation of Roberto Santos in the development of Ana María Torres's career is not just about providing the support a world-class athlete requires, but also about social control: the full-time monitoring of the young woman who has left home and yet in so doing has not acquired the status of an autonomous citizen. Simultaneously romantic partner (albeit illegitimate in the eyes of her family), coach, and manager of "La Guerrera," Santos's constant presence as custodian contributes to constructing for the athlete a public image of "respectability," in sharp contrast to what happens with male athletes, who often use travel as an opportunity to satisfy sexual desires.

The next step in the consolidation of a sports career has to do with the recognition of talent by the second layer of the social network on which every athlete depends; namely, coach and peer group. The first time I interviewed Torres, what most caught my attention was her notoriety in the small space where she trained. In November 2005, her fighting record included eleven wins, one loss, and one draw. I interviewed her in a makeshift gym on the median strip of Avenida Eduardo Molina, eastern Mexico City. These poor facilities were crowded with young hopefuls, all men, but the training revolved around the only woman present: La Guerrera.

Coach Miguel Ángel González ran a sparring session with one of his own pupils and the female boxer. A whistle by González indicated the beginning and end of each round and this synchronized the activities of each and every one of the attendees of that day. About 30 boys beat speed bags or the heavy bag, jumped rope, or simply cast their shadows at different points in that space, but the spotlight was on Torres sparring, so that each period was governed by the start and end of her rounds. The entire gym responded to that rhythm, engaging in frenetic activity during the two minutes she was sparring, and resting during the minute she recovered.

Consisting of only four posts in the hard asphalt to support the strings, with no wood platform or canvas as buffer, the ring was surrounded by diverse spectators: the coach himself, one of his assistants, reporters, photographers, and general observers—and, of course, the ubiquitous Roberto Santos.

During that first meeting I realized that, in addition to her natural talent and the physical capital she was developing painstakingly, the character of La Guerrera—as suggested by Wacquant (36–38)—had already developed a unique style, a personal characterization—"a mask, a tragic mask, a ritual mask"—that was unmistakable and could lead her in her path to becoming a popular heroine. Like most famous athletes, Torres was already deploying "a way that affirms, establishes, testifies to [her] uniqueness and [her] ability to create [herself]" (35).

During Torres's following two championship fights, both at the Deportivo Nueva Atzacoalco (one on May 13, 2006, against Susana "Toluquita" Vázquez, and another on August 16, 2006, against Gloria "Dinamita" Ríos) I could find clear evidence of the consolidation of her style. In Mexico, the boxing public is definitely of a "popular" class. The tickets to stadiums and boxing gyms are cheap and audiences are massive. Despite the skepticism still surrounding the practice of female boxing, attendance at both fights was large and enthusiastic. But more enthusiastic still was the public's reaction when confrontations culminated with the triumph of Ana María Torres by unanimous decision in the tenth round over Vázquez, and by technical KO over Ríos in the sixth. The fighters were convincing. They showed what in the boxing milieu is called "heart." To my surprise, at the end of the fight against Toluquita, people threw coins at the center of the ring in appreciation. The winner collected the money in a handkerchief and thanked them with her arms raised. A fervent cheer filled the precinct.

The State

Controlled as it is by private entrepreneurs, professional boxing in Mexico occupies a marginal place among government-sponsored sports. Amateur boxing, on the other hand, is taken care of by government agencies—such as those responsible for administering major international events. The relationship between these two modalities is somewhat perverse. Since amateur boxing is not profitable, it is taken as a starting point for "real" boxing, and entry into its practice is controlled by a bureaucratic structure that in principle rejects women.

This is so because the authorization for women's fights that Laura Serrano achieved in 1999 through a claim of constitutional controversy affects precisely the Professional Boxing Regulations Code of the Federal District, and not that of the Mexican Federation of Amateur Boxing. When I interviewed Ricardo Contreras, president of the federation, it became evident that authorities maintained a stubborn resistance to the acceptance of women's boxing:

> We men are structurally better prepared for punishment, because we have no ovaries, nor do we have a womb, nor do we have breasts [...] in our sport it is not only physical integrity that is exposed when going to compete, but life itself. There have been deaths in professional boxing recently and I think that is a matter to be reckoned with by the ladies who are going to practice this sport, right? (Interview with Ricardo Contreras, November 28, 2005)

Indeed, Ana María Torres's professional development has received minimal government support (at the time of our first interview, she said she had won small scholarships from the city governments of Nezahualcóyotl and Toluca), and her ability to compete in international tournaments depends more on private sponsorship.

Nonetheless, Torres's participation in world championships has always taken place "in the name of the Mexican nation." The athlete carries national symbols without any doubt of her right to represent her country and win—or lose—titles as a quintessential Mexican. This means that no explicit government sanction is needed for a boxer to compete in the international sports arena, and no special authorization is required to wear the national insignia on the uniform.

In *La Guerrera*, she appears not only displaying the colors of the flag, but also experimenting and acting the nationalist ethos at several levels of meaning. One of the most touching scenes of the documentary shows the shipment of canned foods (chilies, tuna, sardines) the athlete stores in her hotel room in Korea "to abate food 'home sickness'"—though it is also true that she might not be able to afford eating in restaurants. In addition, Torres and Santos play with Mexican imagery abroad when, for example, they carry sombreros as gifts to their hosts.

At another level of meaning, the athlete's phenotype certainly reveals her ethnicity: the high cheekbones, the olive color of her skin, her smile with perfect white teeth. Her long black hair has to be combed thoroughly before each fight. And in the last shots of the film, the athlete strives to stand out publicly by wearing a huge plume headdress of green feathers—a replica of Moctezuma's *penacho*—with which she simultaneously reinstates the myth of indigenous origin and the myth of *mestizaje* (see Gutiérrez, *Mitos*).

Gutiérrez (*Mitos, Mujeres*) has stressed the decisive influence of the state in the formation of a national consciousness. In the field of women's boxing, two examples of this influence seem particularly relevant in contrast with the case of Torres: those of North Korean boxers and of Jizelle Salandy in Trinidad and Tobago.

In her work, Jung Woo Lee reports how "the media coverage of sport in the Western World tends to sustain the notion of hegemonic masculinity by marginalizing and sexualizing women athletes," while North Korea "at least in theory, emphasizes equality between the sexes and the liberation of women" (193). "Red feminism" claims that sexism is a product of bourgeois capitalism, while "women's liberation and equality between the sexes characterize gender relations in a communist society" (195).

However, a more detailed analysis allows Lee to conclude that, in international competitions, sport in general and boxing in particular play a crucial role in the regime's propaganda as central themes for a nationalist, militarist, and patriarchal discourse where the images of "active and assertive women are highlighted insofar as they function to maintain the social order and fortify their national leader" (199) as the father of the nation. Thus, like *paterfamilias* in premodern society, "the leader is the central figure who represents every individual in the country" (201–202).

Female boxers' achievements are exploited to sustain the patriarchal system, and there is no indication that their personal expectations to succeed in the sport led these women to autonomy. Although these athletes are active agents in the sports field, in the political structure they appear as passive individuals who rely on the authority of the father (the leader) and thus help maintain a gendered social order where male dominance prevails. Female boxers should express their gratitude to their "symbolic father." Moreover, media discourse reinforces an extreme nationalism where "the media discourse of the female boxers consists of a number of nationalistic features that demonstrate the political excellence of the nation via sport" (Lee 204).

On the other hand, the boxer from Trinidad and Tobago illustrates the enormous importance of the liberal state in the promotion and legitimization of sport. Unlike what happens in Mexico, in Trinidad and Tobago "boxing, and sport in general has been used [...] as a public policy instrument to help deal with disaffected youth as part of a broader strategy of social inclusion and community revitalization" (McCree 341).

Between 2005 and 2008, Trinidad and Tobago's Ministry of Sports and Culture granted Jizelle Salandy, a first-line athlete of humble origin (orphan, raised in welfare institutions), US$80,000 "to help with her training and general preparation for competition" (McCree 341). Not surprisingly, the sudden death of the athlete on January 4, 2009, in an automobile accident, brought about great general commotion and the government honored her with a true state funeral. In time, Salandy's figure ended up being absorbed by the state and integrated into the narrative of the nation as a symbol, model, and heroine:

> This demasculinization of sport nationalism which Salandy engendered was reinforced further 7 months later when she was awarded posthumously the nation's highest honor, the Order of Trinidad and Tobago (*Trinidad Guardian*, August 31, 2009), at the country's annual independence awards, although the historical problems that beset female as well as male boxing persist in spite of her near canonization. (342)

Both North Korea and Trinidad and Tobago stand in stark contrast to Mexico in their ability to turn women's boxing into a symbolic space for the construction of the nation. Unlike female boxers in those countries, Mexican female boxers in general, and Ana María Torres in particular, have to make do with meager resources and put up with a still-entrenched hostility in official and extraofficial circles.

Private Enterprise

As noted elsewhere (Moreno, *Orden discursivo*), the way in which the practice of boxing, essentially a money making business, is structured leads to exploitation and abuse of its labor force, and the possibility of making a living out of boxing depends on the organization of public fights that generate income within a complex interest apparatus, in which managers, trainers, sponsors, venue owners, and promoters all take a cut.

Ultimately, a boxer—and of course, a female boxer—is an investment. Negotiations to schedule fights are anything but simple and depend on very delicate power balances that greatly influence not only boxers' careers but also their integrity and physical well-being. Here, the coach/ manager is a key figure for the fate of a boxer:

> Promoters don't want to risk. Today they're called matchmakers, and they are in charge of organizing fights. They have taken the bad habit of organizing fights on the spot. They say: "Ah, well, I call manager X two days before and tell him: 'I need a featherweight, I need Y, I know you have a featherweight.' 'Hey, but he's not ready.' 'I need him to fight on Saturday'—and today is Wednesday or Friday. 'No, but he is not ready and does not want to fight.' 'If he doesn't fight, I'll freeze you and will not contract any of your fighters.'" That's the way they operate. As for the boxer, well…they're all young, and they always say they will be able to win: "No, no I do not, no matter that I have not done my jogging, no, I will win." But once in the ring things are different, because they face a rival with the same conditions and characteristics and well, sometimes fights do not turn out so good. (Interview with Alberto Reyes, industrial and boxing promoter, November 30, 2005)

In an environment so controlled by money interests and opaque dealings, subject to so many indeterminate factors, a female boxer has little chance to thrive. Talent and discipline are pushed to a secondary role, while the hostile environment and the systemic obstacles acquire a solid consistency. It is unthinkable that a female boxer should receive minimal compensation to contend for a world-class prize:

> Oh no, much money no way! No, purses are very small. This time I got paid 2,000 US dollars. It's nothing. Moreover, when I fought for the national championship here I won 5,000 US dollars, 50,000 Mexican pesos […]. No, really one cannot [live off boxing]. I give my colleagues my advice, to those who are studying, to better finish their careers and work very hard. (Interview with Ana María Torres, November 17, 2005)

Also, as in all labor markets, there is a salary gap so deep that it seems impossible to overcome. Laura Serrano, a pioneer of women's boxing in Mexico, has suffered this disparity personally:

> If you're a male, super! You have a king's life. But if you're a woman, forget it. Only if you are in one of three cases can you live off boxing as a woman: if your name is Christy Martin, you are blonde and North American, if you are the daughter of a famous boxer named Mohammed Ali, or if your name is Mia and have posed for *Playboy* magazine with your gloves on. Otherwise, no chance. What women get paid is ridiculous, really, purses are derisory. For example, in a world championship a man of my category, featherweight, I think gets paid about 75,000 US dollars minimum. I do not know, it depends on the categories, it depends on the projection you

have internationally, it depends on many things, but I would think around that figure. For my world championship in 1995, as featherweight, I won 1,500 dollars, I mean, it's ridiculous, it's like I was paying them to let me fight. You cannot live off boxing as a woman. (Interview with Laura Serrano, October 5, 2005)

The Media

News and sports programs are extremely important sources for the formation of a national consciousness, and their continued tendency to ignore or marginalize women's sports helps maintain the myth that sports are for men, are about masculinity, and have an audience made up exclusively of men.

In 1990, the research team of Michael A. Messner published their first report on "Gender in Televised Sports." The study concluded that the ridiculous 5 percent of news coverage devoted to women's sports in television belied a misconception about this sports category. Twenty years later, the data for the United States are:

> In 1971, only 294,000 US high school girls played interscholastic sports, compared with 3.7 million boys. In 1989 [...] high school boy athletes still outnumbered girls, 3.4 million to 1.8 million. By 2009, the high school sports participation gap had closed further, with 4.4 million boys and 3.1 million girls playing [...] In 1972, the year Title IX was enacted there were only a little over 2 women's athletics teams per college. By 2010, the number had risen to 8.64 teams per NCAA school [...] However, during this two decades of growth in women's sports, the gap between TV news and highlights shows' coverage of women's and men's sports has not narrowed, it has widened. Women's sports in 2009 received a paltry 1.6% of the coverage on TV news, and an anemic 1.4% on ESPN's *SportsCenter*. (Messner, Cooky, and Hextrum 22)

The exclusion from the sports field goes beyond simple negligence. For some authors, at the present time it is through sports that the nation is represented, as "mediated sporting bodies are critical articulators in the construction of the symbolic making of the nation" (von der Lippe 373); "few other cultural forms lend themselves as easily as sport to being used as an indicator of national identity. National identity is established through the achievements of male sports teams and individual male athletes. As such, male sports stars emit the masculine status of the nation's men" (Harris and Clayton 402).

A country's sports "might create national identities if hegemonic cultures interpret the victory as a profound cultural experience" (von der Lippe 374). However, instead of providing them access to this space for the creation and definition of identities, the mass media exclude women's bodies and deny them the space and time for their sports expressions, and by marginalizing and trivializing women's sports performance they contribute to "preserve sports as a male domain" (King 187).

This common view results in a continued invisibility of female boxers in image-building spaces. Examples abound of sexualization, trivialization, and ridicule of women's sport in the media. Boxer Clara Pérez Segovia denounces the media portrayal of women's sports as a model that influences behavior and criticizes the media's inability to adequately interpret her personal stand as a female athlete:

> They even branded it as "pink boxing" because when we get to the ring—not all of us, of course, and it doesn't have to be that way, but—the moment a woman climbs into the ring her neatness, her body care, her personality, become evident; even the way they wear the uniform is evidently much more careful. They sometimes told us that we were kind of flirty, right? They used to tell me at times: "please pose for a picture," and the boxer always made an identifiable gesture, and then when I saw myself in the pictures I realized I was kind of flirting, and then I'd say: "well, it wasn't flirting, simply it is my style." (Interview with Clara Pérez Segovia, September 9, 2005)

Yvonne T. Caples conducted a survey to "identify the general public's knowledge, perceptions and attitudes towards women's boxing" in downtown Las Vegas (43–44). Overall, the survey found that male viewers support women's boxing due to the sexual image and femininity of female athletes, while female viewers are rather inclined to support women's boxing for the sake of sport:

> *Showtime*, one of the major cable networks that show boxing [,] recently announced that it will be broadcasting a show called "Model Boxing" on August 6, 2004. On this show models who have been trained for a few months in boxing will put on boxing gloves and headgear and compete against one another. *Showtime* may have gotten it right in terms of what will initially attract a male audience, but this will not develop a long-term fan base, and it will work to damage the legitimacy of women's boxing as a sport. (56–57)

Among the strategies female boxers turn to in order to ensure media visibility for themselves is sexualization—that is, a recourse to sex appeal with an emphasis on body stereotypes—along the same lines through which actresses and models construct their performance in any show. Among the boxers I interviewed, the one who most obviously resorts to this strategy is Mariana "la Barbie" Juárez (whose professional nickname alludes to the famous doll figure so much criticized by feminism). Juárez's body, hair, and tattoos undoubtedly emphasize femininity and sex appeal for media notoriety.

In this way—and in combination with many others—the image of female athletes in the media move from invisibility to objectification, without ever really consolidating themselves in the public consciousness as representative figures of national reverence.

THE NATION DIVIDED

Can a woman embody the meaning of the nation in sports performance? As a champion in a boxing match, can a female body carry the national values of the country? If, as claimed by Gutiérrez (*Mujeres* 24), national discourse is constituted by successive exclusions, and nationalism has a long history of excluding women, the body of the female boxer poses then a series of challenges to the national consciousness.

On the one hand, "nationalism is an ideological construct that delineates and determines the differential roles of men and women" (Gutiérrez, *Mujeres* 23) and "gender relations are critical to the understanding and analysis of the phenomenology of nations and nationalism" (Yuval-Davis 67). On the other, sport is characterized by its explicit intention of masculinizing boys in order to affirm male identity, in a clear nexus with the warrior ethos. Boxing, in particular, is the "combat sport" par excellence.

The image of femininity in the Mexican nation is in contradiction with the figures of women who dare to cross the boundaries of the "acceptable." The field of sports in general and of boxing in particular—along with all "combat" sports—represents a transgression that deeply affects the sensibility of Mexicans, because it undermines stereotypes that are "gender signs in a unified community identity discourse" (Palomar Verea 25–26).

Women are placed in a "dual citizenship" of sorts, such that, on the one hand, they are included "in the general group of citizens of the state and its political and legal practices, and on the other there is a separate legislative body, more or less developed, which specifically refers to them as female" (Yuval-Davis 73). This duality establishes a dichotomy in the areas of social life: "war, diplomacy and high politics are gender concepts, because it is precisely in the exclusion of women from their scope that they establish their crucial importance, their power, the reasons and the fact of their superior authority" (Mejía Núñez 26).

In Mexico—and most probably in the whole of Latin America—the practice of female boxing is marginal and has not yet fully established itself in any of the dimensions of nation-building discussed earlier. Although women's boxing in Mexico is accepted in formal terms, there is a more or less overt hostility in the field that effectively keeps female boxers at bay. All my informants seem to have a more or less defined consciousness of invading a territory. They all know they are crossing a border, and their very insistence that they are "welcome" in gyms reflects this sense of estrangement with which males mark the acceptable limit for the presence of women in the social arena of boxing. "It in itself...is a sport for men, right? And we women are usually thought of to come to hang out and see who, you know, to see who we can pick up, as they say. Once I told one of them: 'you know what, I'm going to come and train, not to waste time'" (Interview with María Elena Villalobos, April 15, 2008). In the social arena of boxing, along with hyper-feminine female boxers, one runs into types of femininity that might be characterized as "new," "different," or perhaps "non-traditional"—that is, with forms of female subjectivity that are overtly opposed to conventional ones. However, the emergence of these identity deployments does not disturb hegemonic masculinity because generic differentiation processes persist and the female athletic body is still primarily valued for its aesthetic and expressive qualities.

Female boxers *have* to explain their involvement in boxing. Their testimonies reveal the need to adjust to dominant thinking patterns regarding what is basically perceived as a "deviant" position. They usually use discursive tactics that allow them to simultaneously downplay ("I feel that boxing is a sport like any other" [Elizabeth Sánchez López]) and assert their presence in a heavily gendered field. They express a sense of belonging ("My family is one of boxers, my dad was a boxer, my brothers" [Elizabeth Sánchez López]), of personal pride ("I've come to the conclusion that for me it will be a great honor to die above the ring" [Clara Pérez Segovia]), and a diffuse conviction of transgressing limits ("I am dedicated to boxing because I really like the sport, because I like difficult things" [Citlalli Lara]) by engaging in a trade that, ultimately, occupies a particularly prestigious place in the social imaginary, precisely because it is so strongly gendered.

The main result of this marginalization can be found at the institutional level, with Mexican women's boxing not receiving the kind of support required by any athlete who aspires to engage in international competition. Thus, Mexican women who box are in a structurally disadvantageous position vis à vis their counterparts elsewhere:

The fight where I won the world championship was in 1995, against an Irish fighter. It was my second bout. Then I had problems with my manager, and he sent me to Las Vegas alone. I did not know English, and then I'm told I will fight at the 59 kilos category and not at the 61 one, so I had to lose two kilos fast, imagine, with no coach, no one to help me in the corner. So fortunately I met people there in Las Vegas who helped me at the corner, who helped me lose weight, who accompanied me. It was a tough fight, but I won. Then I became the first Mexican and the first Latin American to win a world championship in women's boxing. (Interview with Laura Serrano, October 5, 2005)

The national pride a Mexican boxer deploys when he wears the colors of the national flag is linked to the mythology of the warrior. Boxing imbues a deep sense of nationalism and its champions become true popular idols. Mexican male boxers receive official recognition and are supported by the massive state or entertainment apparatuses to enhance their performance.

In contrast, Mexican female boxers face outright hostility within the field, a chronic resource shortage and a reception still doubtful on the part of the general public, even though there is an increasingly greater acceptance of the practice, and some female boxers, like Ana María Torres, enjoy a significant presence in the popular imaginary.

BIBLIOGRAPHY

Arbena, Joseph L. "El mapa deportivo de América Latina." *efdeportes* 4:14 (June 1999). http://www.efdeportes.com/efd14/mapa.htm.

Caples, Yvonne T. "Public Perception, Attitudes and General Knowledge of Women's Boxing in Central Las Vegas." Master's thesis. Las Vegas, Nevada: United States Sports Academy, 2004.

del Paso, Paulina. *La Guerrera*. Film on DVD. Mexico: Ambulante, 2011.

de Lara, María del Carmen. *Más vale maña que fuerza?* Film on DVD. Mexico: Conaculta/Calacas y Palomas, 2007.

Elias, Norbert, and Eric Dunning. *Deporte y ocio en el proceso de la civilización.* Mexico: Fondo de Cultura Económica, 1995.

Fleischer, Nat, and Sam Andre. *An Illustrated History of Boxing*, 6th ed. New York: Citadel Press/Kengsington Publishing Corp., [1959] 2001.

Garmabella, José Ramón. *Grandes leyendas del boxeo.* Mexico: Debolsillo, 2009.

Gutiérrez Chong, Natividad. *Mitos nacionalistas e identidades étnicas: los intelectuales indígenas y el estado mexicano.* Mexico City, Mexico: Instituto de Investigaciones Sociales, National Autonomous University of Mexico, 2001.

———, coord. *Mujeres y nacionalismos en América Latina/de la independencia a la nación del nuevo milenio.* Mexico City, Mexico: Instituto de Investigaciones Sociales, National Autonomous University of Mexico, 2004.

Hargreaves, Jennifer. "Women's Boxing and Related Activities: Introducing Images and Meanings." *Body and Society* 3 (1997): 33–49.

Harris, John, and Ben Clayton. "Femininity, Masculinity, Physicality and the English Tabloid Press/The Case of Anna Kournikova." *International Review for the Sociology of Sport* 37/3–4 (2002): 397–413.

Hernández Carballido, Elina. Column "Atletas." *fem magazine.* México, 1998, 1999, 2001, 2002.

Jerónimo Jiménez, Alejandro. "El sacrificio en la ideología del boxeo como sistema cultural/El caso de los boxeadores del gimnasio Miguel Ángel 'Ratón' González." Bachelor's degree dissertation. Mexico: National Autonomous University of Mexico, 2012.

King, Christopher. "Media Portrayals of Male and Female Athletes/A Text and Picture Analysis of British National Newspaper Coverage of the Olympic

Games since 1948." *International Review for the Sociology of Sport* 42:2 (2007): 187–199.

Lee, Jung Woo. "Red Feminism and Propaganda in Communist Media: Portrayals of Female Boxers in the North Korean Media." *International Review for the Sociology of Sport* 44:2–3 (2009): 193–211.

Maldonado, Marco A., and Rubén A. Zamora. *Pasión por los guantes/Cosecha de campeones: Historia del box mexicano* (2 vol.). Mexico: Clío, 1999/2000.

McCree, Roy Dereck. "The Death of a Female Boxer: Media, Sport, Nationalism, and Gender." *Journal of Sport and Social Issues* 35:4 (2011): 327–349.

Mejía Núñez, Gerardo. "Reconceptualización de los discursos de nación desde las fronteras geoculturales." Bachelor's dissertation in International Relations. Mexico City, Mexico: Facultad de Estudios Superiores Acatlán, National Autonomous University of Mexico, 2011.

Messner, Michael A., Cheryl Cooky, and Robin Hextrum. "Gender in Televised Sports/News and Highlights Shows, 1989–2009." Research report, Center for Feminist Research, University of Southern California, 2010.

Moreno, Hortensia. *Orden discursivo y tecnologías de género en el boxeo*. México: Inmujeres, 2011.

Oates, Joyce Carol. *On Boxing* (expanded edition with photographs by John Ranard). New York: ecco (Harper Collins), 2002.

Osorio, Teresa. 2012. "Las reinas del ring, una historia del boxeo femenil en México." Paper presented at the Colloquium Noveno Diplomado de Relaciones de Género del Programa Universitario de Estudios de Género. México: National Autonomous University of Mexico, 2002.

Palomar Verea, Cristina. "El juego de las identidades: género, comunidad y nación." *La Ventana, revista de estudios de género* 12 (2000): 7–42.

Sugden, John. 1996. *Boxing and Society/An International Analysis*. Manchester and New York: Manchester University Press, 2000.

Toledo, Alejandro. *De puño y letra/Historias de boxeadores*. México: Ficticia/ Ediciones del Boxeador, 2005.

Von der Lippe, Gerd. "Media Image: Sport, Gender and National Identities in Five European Countries." *International Review for the Sociology of Sport* 37:3–4 (2002): 371–395.

Wacquant, Loïc. "Carisma y masculinidad en el boxeo." *debate feminista (cuerpo a cuerpo)* Annum 18, 36 (October 2007): 30–40.

Wallechinsky, David, and Jaime Loucky. *The Complete Book of the Olympics*. London: Aurum, 2008.

Yuval-Davis, Nira. "Género y nación," in Natividad Gutiérrez Chong (coord.), *Mujeres y nacionalismos en América Latina/de la independencia a la nación del nuevo milenio*. Mexico City, Mexico: Instituto de Investigaciones Sociales, National Autonomous University of Mexico, 2004. 67–81.

CHAPTER 10

"You Have the Right to Surf!": Riding Waves of Modernity, Decolonization, and National Identity in Peru

Dexter Zavalza Hough-Snee

Glossing Peruvian culture as civil rights, a promotional film produced by the Peruvian government's Commission for Promotion of Exportation and Tourism (PromPerú) prominently highlights the cultural elements traditionally associated with Peru: the rich and varied cuisine; traditional music and dance; colorful Andean dress and artisanry; and, of course, surfing (Maldonado). That's right, after a feast of *comida criolla* and a foray into *huayno* and *festejo* dance, professional surfer Gabriel Villarán exclaims, "You have the right to surf!" opening a minute-long segment of tarp-surfing. While tarp-surfing—which simulates a surfer's tube ride on flat ground by pulling a vinyl tarp in the motion of a hollow wave breaking over a skateboarder riding through the open space created—is a less-than-faithful approximation to surfing, the message is clear: Peru is surfing, and surfing is Peruvian.

Initiating PromPerú's 2011 *MarcaPaís* campaign, the segment clearly, and perhaps, strangely, to the unacquainted viewer, privileges surfing as Peru's hallmark sporting pastime. Notably absent from the segment is *fútbol*, a sport in which Peru enjoys only marginal competitive success. Instead, Villarán is accompanied by national celebrity Sofía Mulanovich, the Association of Surfing Professionals (ASP)[1] 2004 World Championship Tour (WCT) Women's Champion, 2005, and Peru's most heralded competitive surfer. As the segment rolls, Villarán declares more rights of the Peruvian, exclaiming, "You have the right to surf good waves"; "you have the right to surf the longest left-hand wave in the world," a reference to Chicama, a three-kilometer-long pointbreak in La

Libertad region; and "you have the right to pull into some huge tubes," a reference to Peru's renowned barreling waves.

Working among textuality, media, and surfing's material life, this essay seeks to explore the discourses that render surfing Peru's dominant national sporting tradition in the wake of recent political stability and economic growth while contributing to twenty-first-century constructions of *peruanidad*. Whereas Peru is perennially absent from the FIFA World Cup (last qualifying in 1982) and has accrued only four Olympic medals, it has enjoyed 50 years of international surfing success since Felipe Pomar captured gold at the International Surfing Federation's (ISF) 1965 World Championships.[2] Most recently, Piccolo Clemente claimed the 2013 ASP Longboard World Championship, following Peruvian victories at the 2010 International Surfing Association (ISA) World Surfing Games and 2011 World Junior Surfing Games on the beaches of Punta Hermosa. Sponsored by preeminent global surf brands, the IOC-recognized ISA bills these events as the apex of this non-Olympic sport, and the Peruvian media heralds these victories as some of Peru's greatest sporting achievements ever. In addition to providing a platform upon which to construct a national sporting identity, the growth of surfing industry and culture also signals the country's self-perceived emergence as a proprietor of late-capitalist modernity, as demonstrated by lavish beachfront homes south of Lima, cutting-edge surfboard technologies in Miraflores, exclusive seasonal surf fashions, and the pervasive marketing campaigns that aggressively promote them from billboards along the *Panamericana Sur*.

Given this propensity for associating surfing with global Western and localized *limeño* modernities, how does one account for the fact that the promotional materials for the Peru-hosted 2010 ISA Games depict a pre-Columbian warrior surfing atop a 3,000-year-old *caballito de totora*? This essay contends that as a symbol of national identity, surfing sheds its long-standing associations with California to render Peru a sporting empire, simultaneously deploying ancient and modern local surfing histories to resist negations of Peru's sporting sovereignty and cultural modernity. Peruvian mediation of surfing history opposes what Dipesh Chakrabarty and Mark Thurner have termed "not-yet narratives," refusals to acknowledge cultural sovereignty originating in the residual hegemony of Spanish colonialism and contemporary Western cultural imperialism (Chakrabarty 8; Thurner 141). To borrow Thurner's brilliant words about the postcolonial historicist wagers of Sebastian Lorente, I argue that discursive mediation of surfing practice and culture provides "the political community of Peru with a positive and persuasive historicist narrative of its own modernity and contemporaneity as a sovereign historical subject" that transcends "the standard negative or "not-yet" plots of most narratives of Peru," past and present (141). Drawing from

Enrique Dussel, I understand modernity as "the culture of the *center* of the world-system" in which "modernity is not a phenomenon of Europe as *independent* system, but of Europe as 'center'" (4; original emphases) relative to the colonized periphery exemplified by Latin America. As I will argue, Peruvian understanding of surfing as a local, pre-Columbian practice exported to Oceania and, later, the Anglophone world rejects Peru-as-periphery narratives and renders Peru a global center, claiming material and cultural expressions of surfing's modernity as its own.

Although these articulations suggest contradictions (invoking concurrent notions of mass-mediated Western modernity and proto-*indigenista* ancient Peruvian surfing origins) and come at the expense of international scrutiny, I will introduce how hyperbolic discourses permeate Peru's popular surfing history to construct an identity of sporting primacy, consolidating Peru not only as sovereign historical subject but also ludic-cultural empire. Furthermore, this essay builds upon David Wood's assertion that surfing "emerges as an effective medium for addressing the tensions inherent in binary visions" of Peru ("On the Crest of a Wave" 241), suggesting that surfing's symbolic integration of Western modernity and pre-Columbian history attempts to render it a sporting tradition compatible with diverse notions of contemporary peruanidad.

A Brief History of Surfing in Peru

Before proceeding, it is necessary to provide an abbreviated history of modern surfing in Peru. Here I use the term "modern surfing" to refer to surfing practice as recreational or competitive sport practiced during the twentieth century. This is in opposition to "ancient surfing," which refers to precolonial ceremonial or navigational waveriding forms in Hawai'i and Peru, respectively. My discussion of the sport's local history privileges Magoo de la Rosa Toro's *Huellas en el mar*, the most rigorous history of Peruvian surfing to date. Former professional surfer turned Peruvian surf industry mogul, De la Rosa provides a valuable popular history of the sport's local practice and evolution deploying archival material dating to the 1930s. Although written for general audiences and strongly nationalistic in tone, his text serves as necessary supplement to the history found here.

Carlos Dogny Larco is attributed with bringing surfing to Peru from Hawai'i in 1937 (De la Rosa Toro 104). The Peruvian-born son of a French military official, heir to a family of powerful agriculturists on Peru's north-central coast, and cousin of archaeologist Rafael Larco Hoyle, Dogny studied in Europe and the United States before arriving in Hawai'i in 1934 alongside the French water polo team. There, he met Waikiki beach boy and famed Hawaiian surfing ambassador Duke Kahanamoku. An Olympic champion swimmer credited with introducing surfing to the

Western world, Kahanamoku is said to have personally given Dogny his first surfboard (102–106). Dogny took up surfing under Kahanamoku's tutelage and later trained under legendary waterman Rabbit Kekai, cementing relationships with two of Hawai'i's most important local figures during the global infancy of modern surfing. After several years in Hawai'i Dogny returned to Lima, introducing the first surfboards to Peru (104).

Surfing then exploded through the 1940s as wealthy Peruvians accustomed to summering at the beach quickly took up the sport. The exclusive Club Waikiki was founded on Lima's shores in 1942, providing a social outlet for affluent surfers and socialites. Heralding surfing as its primary activity, Karin Sierralta, vice president of the ISA and executive director of Peru's Federación Nacional de Tabla (FENTA), maintains that "Club Waikiki is the oldest surf club in the world dedicated exclusively to surfing" (interview). Surfing flourished through the 1960s with the advent of local and international surfing competitions under Dogny's leadership—including the 1965 ISA World Championships—and the exploration of the coastline beyond Lima, yielding early encounters with now world-renowned waves throughout Peru. The 1970s yielded the first Peruvian surfing brands as the sport's growth generated commercial possibilities given an ever-larger domestic surf market.

Peruvians held a privileged place in early international surfing due to their competitive activity and frequent travel to Hawai'i. During the 1960s and 1970s competitive "rules were created [in Lima] among Peruvians, Hawaiians, Australians and Californians" as heightened international competition demanded stable judging criteria (Sierralta, interview). However, the onset of armed conflict and political uncertainty greatly diminished international surf traffic in the 1980s, and surfing again became a practice exclusive to the Peruvian elite. As Sierralta states, "The Peruvian surfer achieved an international renown that was lost during the eighties, and limited until the nineties by the military governments who cut imports and limited the entry and construction of boards" (interview). Relative political stability and significant economic growth through the 1990s and 2000s, Mulanovich and Clemente's ASP titles, Peruvian ISA victories, and increased media coverage have enabled the sport to flourish and slowly spread to an expanding middle class and coastal working class through conscious promotional efforts by FENTA and the Instituto Peruano del Deporte (IPD) financed by multinational and local surfing brands.

Peruvian Surfing Demographics

Acknowledging the veritable absence of reliable ethnographic information enabling a portrait of the contemporary Peruvian surfing population, this abridged history highlights several key elements of Peru's

surfing demographics. Given the affluence of Lima's early surf community and the continued protagonism of Club Waikiki and other elite
social clubs (such as Club Regattas and Club Terrazas) in surfing culture, urban surfers are still largely "white upper-middle class males"
(Wood, "On the Crest of a Wave" 227) generally residing in Lima's
exclusive districts. Surfing has long implied having access to the equipment necessary to surf year-round in Peru: a surfboard, wetsuit, and private transportation. This latter element is crucial for accessing the Costa
Verde or the beaches outside of Lima that serve as primary surf zones
for those residing in inland districts nearer the Panamericana Highway
than the Circuito de Playas. Historically, limeños surf around professional obligations within 100 kilometers of Lima and surfers of such
means frequently travel nationally and internationally as their professions allow, often with friends or family. Additionally, for many limeño
surfers, owning vacation homes south of Lima in Punta Hermosa, San
Bartolo, Puerto Nuevo, or Asia, or near northern surfing destinations
such as Ancón, Huanchaco, or Lobitos is requisite for social acceptance
among peers and heightened access to quality surf beyond the mediocre
waves of the Costa Verde.

At the risk of reducing a complex practice with diverse participants to
an overly simplistic binary caricature, Peruvian surfers tend to be either
of the aforementioned class or provincial residents of coastal zones of significantly lesser socioeconomic status. The coastal resident group consists
largely of working-class, non-European-looking Peruvians who reside in
proximity to popular surf zones. Demonstrating lesser geographic and
social mobility, their surf travel takes place almost exclusively within
Peru. Often employed within informal economies, coastal residents' geographic and temporal access to the surf is less restricted by professional
obligations although their economic power is considerably less than their
urban counterparts. Consequently, their quotidian surfing radius is more
limited, often surfing within a few kilometers of their homes. These surfers will inevitably share waves with more affluent surfers, although likely
only when limeños visit the beaches where they reside. Greater availability and affordability of surfing equipment has improved access to the
sport for coastal residents and expanded their ranks. Some provincial
surfers from the working class have even enjoyed some professional success, evidenced by 2011 Peruvian National Champion and ASP Junior
competitor Juninho Urcía and 2007 ASP Junior Women's Runner-Up
Analí Gómez, known as "*la negra.*" The son and daughter of fishermen
from Huanchaco and Punta Hermosa, respectively, Urcía and Gómez's
competitive activity depends largely on sponsorship by multinational surf
brands. Although Wood suggests that Gómez's success "has broken the
hold of white elites on the practice of the sport" ("Representing Peru"
426), this demographic produces few competitive surfers and most of

Peru's 200-something professional surfers pertain to the upper-middle class.

Both groups surf more frequently in the summer when the water warms and longer daylight hours, end-of-year festivities, and school recesses facilitate extended beach excursions. In these months, a high density of young surfers, both male and female, flock to the beach. Although surfing remains a predominantly male practice worldwide, Peru's young surfing population reflects a significant, expanding female demographic, and there is substantial media attention to female competitive surfers in Peru, especially after Mulanovich's and Gómez's competitive successes (Wood, "Representing Peru"). Female surfers pertain to both groups though, like their male counterparts, the dominant female surfing population is relatively affluent.

Statistically appraising Peru's surfing demographics is veritably impossible. Given that neither FENTA nor the IPD collect comprehensive data about surfing participants or practice, quantifying the surfing population rests on unofficial, politically motivated estimates. Tellingly, the statistics that do exist are tied to the economic productivity of the surfing industry and focused on generating tourism revenue and investment in beachfront development. Two such fiscal studies provide demographic estimates: the congressional proposal of Peruvian Federal Law 27280 (the *Ley de Rompimientos*) and a 2007 FENTA study. Ratified by Congress in 2000 and signed into law by President Ollanta Humala in 2013, Law 27280 seeks to officially conserve coastal surfing spaces and charge the Peruvian Navy with the law's enforcement in order to sustain and expand the economic benefits of surf tourism and development. The law's preliminary language estimates that 100,000 Peruvians practice some modality of surfing while 12,500 foreign surfers, mostly American and Brazilian, visit Peru each year.

The 2007 FENTA study projects a considerably smaller national surfing population of 15,000–20,000 local surfers and 10,000–12,500 visiting foreign surfers—a figure revised to 19,124 visiting surfers in 2012 ("PromPerú interesado")—while estimating that the surfing industry could potentially generate $485 million annually and create 21,000 full-time jobs. Sierralta repeats the Ley 27280 figure of 100,000 surfers in a 2010 *El Comercio* feature appraising Peru's surf industry at $80 million annually ("El surf es rentable"). Supporting the assertion that Peruvian surfers largely pertain to the upper-middle classes, said article places the average annual cost of surfing equipment—excluding transportation—at 7,000 soles, corroborating that surfing is prohibitively expensive for many Peruvians, especially those who earn the federal monthly minimum wage of 750 soles ($270). In spite of such speculative figures, it is clear that at least two socioeconomic groups of surfers exist in Peru although the majority pertains to an affluent, urban, professional demographic.

SURFING'S CULTURAL WEIGHT AND PERU'S "RELATED LOCALS"

Tellingly, the aforementioned studies are as concerned with attracting foreign tourists as they are with local diffusion of the sport. This highlights the global nature of surfing, but also suggests inherent tensions between local and foreign surfers as the sport transcends cultural and political boundaries. As living discourse, surfing is, as Krista Comer cogently contends, "a globalist trope" (12) related to neocolonial subjectivities that are imposed by the frequent search for "new" places to "explore" through surfing and the colonizing rhetoric that accompanies what Henri Lefebvre has termed the "consumption of space" (58). To the surfer from the industrial West, Latin America is rendered what Lefebvre terms "a 'non-work' space" for leisure and rest that "has been subjected to a sort of neocolonization" (58). Since the 1960s, the international surfing bourgeoisie has gone "in global pursuit of the perfect wave" (Comer 20) and accompanying coastal leisure spaces, rearticulating haphazard, neocolonial notions of civilization, modernity, and otherness everywhere they go. As Comer writes: "The white, western protagonist of so many cultural tales co-opts features of indigeneity (he 'goes native') and becomes a border crosser to critique normative WASP discourse. But that process compromises the very places and peoples he admired and needed to formulate different visions of white manhood" (20–21). Through such forays into the so-called wild, underdeveloped, and often postcolonial world in search of new waves, surfing has been introduced to veritably every coastal country, usually by white males from the industrial West looking to "go feral" in lesser-developed regions perceived as politically and economically precarious. Since incipient postwar surf exploration best exemplified by Bruce Brown's film *The Endless Summer* (1966), surfing has historically been a product of white Westerners arriving, surfboards under arm, to ride the "unexplored" waves previously ignored by locals (see Ormrod 49; Comer 23, 53–65; and Lawler 142–146). Like Brown and friends in *The Endless Summer*, a naïve ignorance of the social spaces in which these waves exist is pervasive.

Keeping in mind Allen Guttman's assertion that ludic diffusion is a reflection of larger power relations, Western surfers practicing the sport outside of their home countries represent more than sport and leisure: they represent the hegemonic political, economic, and cultural legacies that the Anglo bourgeoisie exercise worldwide (171–188). Surfing then ought to be understood as a practice defined by local and global colonial subjectivities dependent on manifestations of political, economic, and cultural power. Ongoing through the present, surfing's postwar diffusion is analogous to a colonizing process. According to Comer, a "renewable western American regional identity" imbues surfing with its metaphoric and cultural power and is responsible for surfing's projection into the global sphere (18). Defining the regional American west as the unified cultural space of Hawai'i, California, and the southwestern borderlands, Comer posits that surfing's global charge depends on a western American identity embodied and broadly disseminated by Anglo surfers and Western commercial iconography, regardless of long-standing local histories or practice.

However, this theory encounters resistance when considering surfing's global diffusion prior to 1950. Given foundational figures such as Dogny, active prior to the postwar American surfing boom, I would like to suggest that local Peruvian surfing history enables a national identity reflective of broad notions of modernity and cultural autonomy without relying on the cultural weight afforded surfing by the sport's associations with the regional American west. Peruvian surfing discourse confronts and rejects the model of hegemonic, unilateral, Anglo transmission of surfing to the rest of the world, instead privileging limeño surfers as pioneers of the modern sport and representatives of leisure practices common to international elites.

In spite of a long Spanish colonial past that left little residual sporting culture, surfing did not arrive to Peru through the neocolonial ludic diffusion realized throughout Latin America. An ancient Hawaiian ritual practice, surfing's initial export from colonial Hawai'i to the Americas and Australia through the 1940s was not a Western imposition upon the culturally "weak," but rather a case of Guttmann's "two-way" ludic diffusion (173) in which white elites from more powerful nations—Dogny among them—exported the Hawaiian tradition to their home countries. In rethinking surfing's diffusion, one must admit that "receptivity to 'exotic' sports has been limited to the more affluent and better educated sectors of the population" (174), this consistent with Peru's dominant surfing demographic. Dogny's introduction of modern surfing to Peru precedes surfing's 1950s commercialization and the onset of widespread foreign surf "exploration" in the 1960s that lend surfing its current neocolonial character. Peru's foundational modern surfing history thus asserts that global power imbalances did not generate a neocolonial transmission of surfing emanating from the Anglo metropolis prior to the 1950s. Only after Western appropriation of Hawaiian beach culture and the United States' emergence as a global political force could surfing's cultural power be associated with a regional American west.

Comer's concept of surf culture's "related locals" (22–23; 57) further elucidates how modern surfing resists connotations of Anglo cultural hegemony in Peru, instead envisioned as a local practice associated with local identities. Comer proposes that the international cultural power of surfing as metaphor—and by extension, as political discourse, cultural text, and marketing gold—relies on "a renewable western American regional identity" (18), that is, California and its most intimately related local space, colonized Hawai'i. However, given California's relative absence from Peru's appropriation of modern surfing, Peru's most important related local is a *non-Western* Hawai'i. Though Comer considers Hawai'i part of the regional American west, Peru's construction of national identities through localized readings of global surf history are based on self-identification with a politically and culturally autonomous Hawai'i predating colonization and American statehood.

California's diminished role as a related local in Peru results from the early arrival of the sport and Peruvian views of the territory of Hawai'i outside of American iconographies indicative of Anglo cultural hegemony. Dogny visited the self-governed Territory of Hawai'i over two decades before Hawai'i's 1959 statehood and was an intimate of Hawaiian royalty opposed to the territory's 1898 annexation. Additionally, Dogny and renowned promoter Carlos Rey y Lama began inviting native Hawaiian surfers (such as Kahanamoku) to visit Peru in the 1940s—a time when surf travel between California and Hawai'i was slowed by World War II—locally privileging indigenous Hawaiian surfing (De la Rosa Toro 136–139). Eduardo Arena then continued this practice through the 1960s. A by-product of this, even today Peruvian surfers historically associate surfing practice and culture—though not necessarily commercial iconography—with Hawaiian cultural and political autonomy rather than postwar Anglo beach culture. Evincing such ties, two of Lima's central beaches were named after Hawaiian surfing landmarks Makaha and Waikiki during surfing's introduction to Peru. In homage to Hawaiian culture, Club Waikiki still hosts an annual *"Gran Luau"* founded by Dogny in 1956. Long-standing outrigger canoe clubs—an indisputably Polynesian practice—on Lima's Costa Verde further reflect Hawaiian influence on Peruvian beach culture.

In understanding surfing's cultural distance from California in the Peruvian context, one must acknowledge that modern surfing developed simultaneously in the "founding nations" of Peru, Hawai'i, Australia, California, Brazil, and South Africa and that Peru ostensibly claims the first modern surfing culture in Latin America.[3] Given this history, Peru heralds an unprecedented modern surfing subculture distinct from those found in the rest of Latin America, complete with its own practical and linguistic codes. The prevailing idiom for referring to surfing is *corriendo tabla*, literally "running board," a term first found in Peruvian print media in the 1940s, predating the sport's practice throughout Spanish America. In the rest of Latin America, the anglicization *surfear* (*surfar* in Portuguese) is the dominant idiom derived from the English infinitive "to surf," which accompanied the sport's Anglo introduction. As the act of riding the huge wooden surfboards contemporary to Dogny's generation literally implied walking the length of the board, *correr tabla* is a lexical remnant of the sport's inception by Peruvians who devised a Spanish neologism describing waveriding mechanics instead of deriving a cognate from English terminology. *Tabla* itself is shortened from the more formal, exclusively Peruvian term *tabla hawaiiana* used in official literature on surfing. Demonstrative of a broader, definitively Peruvian surf culture, local idiom subordinates anglicizations and invokes Peru's unique foundational position in Latin American surfing history.

Accompanying this register, surfing's cultural power in Peru is founded on local perceptions of the Club Waikiki founders as global sporting innovators and cultural ambassadors responsible for inviting and hosting foreigners for international competitions and surfing expeditions. This stands in contrast to suffering cultural hegemony by wandering foreign or expatriate surfers lacking firm domestic ties, as frequently occurred elsewhere in Latin America. Strong relationships between limeños and Hawaiian, Californian, and Australian surfers were consolidated prior to the postwar commercialization of the sport, and Peru's identity as an independent surfing nation precedes the cultural hegemony that introduced the sport elsewhere post-*Endless Summer*. The heavily documented exploration of the Peruvian coast was initiated by first-generation Peruvian surfers in the 1950s, not by foreign visitors in the 1960s. The inaugural 1965 ISF World Championships were actually just another installation of the Peru International Surfing Championships—the first international surfing competition outside of the United States—organized by Club Waikiki between 1956 and 1974, not a production engineered from overseas. The 1967 discovery of Chicama, the famed pointbreak referenced by Villarán in the PromPerú segment, was the product of exploration by Club Waikiki members on a trip popularly known as "the great discovery" (De la Rosa Toto 72–75). Though globetrotters introduced surfing in much of Latin America, leaving an indelible and often contentious foreign presence, Peru's surfscape was charted principally by Peruvians.

However, if the global power imbalances responsible for introducing surfing to Latin America post-1950 are not characteristic of Peru, then local power imbalances certainly are. Apparent throughout Peruvian surfing histories, early surfers pertained to the national elite, claiming familial ties to prominent politicians, entrepreneurs, and intellectuals. To this day, most limeño professional surfers maintain direct links to Club Waikiki's socially distinguished membership, linking surfing a priori to local notions of exclusivity and status.[4] Modern surfing connotes modernity and cultural power not because foreign travelers disseminated western American regional values through surfing practice, but rather because local surfers continue to pertain to a coastal elite historically associated with Western modernities.

Resulting from popular consciousness of local surfing history, Peruvians of all backgrounds today associate surfing first with Peru, its athletes, and surf industry, then with the related locale of Hawai'i, and only then with Western marketing iconographies of multinational surf brands.[5] Furthering this popular consciousness, the international competitive success of Sofía Mulanovich has created what FENTA has termed "the Sofía effect" (Vásquez 21): an association of surfing with Peru as a result of Mulanovich's competitive accolades. Marco Antonio Cabezudo, professional coach and figurehead of working-class surfers in Lima's Barranco district, affirms: "there aren't people that don't know Sofía [...] in Peru. She's, so to speak, like Pelé in Brazil, something similar here in Peru. Because of her, one identifies surfing with Peru" (interview). Sierralta also states, "Common people know that we have world champions. Sofía is the pioneer and the 'queen' of the sport, the entire country knows her; you could say that she's one of the three most esteemed people in Peru, for which people identify surfing with Sofía and her triumphs" (interview).

Mulanovich's laurels and the Peruvian ISA victories have resulted in further domestic recognition of the sport as a *producto bandera* and national pastime, regardless of most professional surfers' elite upbringing and the prohibitive cost of surfing for many Peruvians. Although Mulanovich, like Dogny, comes from an admittedly affluent background, her reverence by the Peruvian masses is testament to Loïc Wacquant's assertion that athletes "are folk heroes, not transcendent figures. [...] not *other-worldly* but *this-worldly*. They are not violators of tradition but expressions of it; not innovators but ritualists" (27; original emphasis). Though still secondary to soccer stars, Peru's professional surfers are popular figures that transcend their privileged backgrounds, commonly becoming national symbols of sporting primacy resonant across diverse sectors of Peruvian society. Such icons of national sporting success also serve as foci for celebratory reflection on Peru's self-proclaimed role as a global sporting pioneer.

By way of local history and culture, surfing serves as an effective symbol of Peruvian contemporaneity and cultural autonomy. This is no small claim for Peru as both a former colony and a lesser-acknowledged national actor in an Anglo-dominated modern surfing world characterized by neocolonial notions of North/South difference and the sport's diffusion on the grounds of a pervasive Western cultural power. Within political economy, surfing history inserts Peru equally alongside the United States, United Kingdom, and Brazil—nations historically held as imperialist threats to Peru—allowing Peru to compete for cultural capital with forces that wield disproportionate shares of political and economic power in the arena of late capitalism. In this regard, Peru's centrality in the global development of modern surfing and the primary role of Peruvians in the exploration of their coastline render surfing as strong a symbol of Peruvian autonomy and modernity as any. Thus when Peru's surfing community, media, corporate advertisers, and government agencies (MINCETUR, PromPerú, IPD, etc.) employ surfing as national symbol, they project identities of Peruvian late-modernity through a long, localized surfing heritage built upon affluent, urban elites independent of the cultural power of an Anglo metropolis. Of greater political consequence, modern surfing's symbolism enables Peru to shrug the weight of Western cultural hegemony and celebrate a sporting practice whose local history is certifiably *tan peruano como el ceviche.*

From Cultural Sovereignty to Cultural Empire: Ancient Surfing and Hyperbolic Discourse

The present understanding of modern surfing as an historically Peruvian tradition and, as I've argued, a mechanism for articulating Peruvian modernity-as-center and cultural decolonization through a narrative of sovereign ludic subjectivity runs parallel to theories of pre-Columbian surfing traditions in Peru. In 1987, Felipe Pomar (the aforementioned 1965 ISF World Champion) proposed to California's *Surfer* magazine that for more than 3,000 years Peruvians had practiced a form of wave-riding on *caballitos de totora*, prehistoric reed rafts still used for fishing and transportation along Peru's north-central coast near Huanchaco, La Libertad. Unconvinced that Peruvian waveriding outdated Hawaiian surfing, the editors nonetheless permitted Pomar to expound his theory in print.[6] Though widely contested by foreign surf journalists, Pomar's article reflects long-standing Peruvian popular consciousness of the ocean-going ways of ancient peoples on Peru's north-central coast. Relying on Thor Heyerdahl's 1947 Kon-Tiki raft expedition from Peru to Polynesia as primary evidence, an expedition that attempted to prove the navigational possibility of ancient east-to-west nautical exchanges between coastal Peru and Oceania, Peruvian professional surfers, surf industry figures, and politicians continue to vocally support the claim that surfing originated in ancient Peru before spreading to Polynesia. Prominent surf personalities have sought to substantiate the theory by citing Spanish colonial chronicles and pre-Columbian ceramics although Peruvian academics seem reluctant to comment on the caballito de totora's relationship to modern surfing.[7] Proponents of the theory also frequently co-opt scholarship in support of the ancient Peruvian surfing hypothesis, such as De la Rosa's recurrent citation of tangential anthropologies of pre-Columbian coastal Peru.

Although rebuked overseas, surfers' sustained, vocal support for Pomar's hypothesis has garnered considerable Peruvian public recognition of surfing as an ancient local practice. Following decades of activism by prominent limeño surfers under Pomar's lead, in October 2012 Huanchaco was dedicated the first World Surfing Reserve (WSR) in Latin America. The honor accompanied countless publications linking *caballitos* to surfing, ranging from pseudo-academic ethnographies to illustrated children's fiction (e.g., Sabogal; del Águila Miñano). If the caballito de totora resonated as a relic of *huanchaquero* identity before Pomar and the WSR, it has since become a national symbol of Peruvian coastal indigeneity-come-modernity and a trope of national surfing culture.

My intention here is not to discredit Pomar's hypothesis—Warshaw has already done so at length. Rather, without fully endorsing its validity I hope to highlight that the claim to Peruvian ancient surfing origins constitutes a political discourse that places Peru at the center of modernity—3,000 years ago—à la Dussel's non-Eurocentric world-system view of modernity. I concede that advocates of Peruvian surfing origins "appear to be motivated by cultural-political concerns, or perhaps simply by economic interest" (Wood, "On the Crest of a Wave" 228). However, the global surf industry's rejection of Peruvian claims to surfing's primordial origins results from an inversion of the process of ludic diffusion outlined by Guttmann, comprising an attempt to refuse Peruvian modernity by relegation to the world-system periphery (Dussel 3). As Peru has lacked the surf industry power (reflective of broader economic and political power) of the United States, Australia, or Brazil, the international surf community has largely rejected Peruvian claims to surfing's ancient origins as unfounded nationalist fervor. Instead, international media retains colonized Hawai'i as surfing's mecca within the regional American west. In spite of this, the Peruvian government, media, and surfers continue to defiantly assert national identity by claiming Peru's oceangoing historical evidence of cultural empire.

Maintaining constant opposition to foreign "not-yet" narratives of Peruvian modernity, claims to caballito surfing origins display elements of what Estelle Tarica has termed "intimate *indigenismo*," a form of *indigenista* discourse that "is not the bearer of an exclusively repressive power operating externally or from above on those whom it takes as objects" (xxiv), but rather promotes the identification of nonindigenous subjects with indigenous subjects. In the way that "*indigenista* discourses build on and modify existing racial discourses to nationalize identity" (xviii), Pomar—described by Warshaw as a "Peruvian aristocrat" (*Encyclopedia* 470)—forges a connection between the urban, white, limeño surfer and coastal residents descendent from the Moche (100 BC—700 AD) and

Chimú (900—1470 AD) civilizations. Coincidentally, many Huanchaco surfers, including Juninho Urcía, proudly claim descent from the Moche/Chimú, understanding surfing to connect them to their ancestral heritage ("Surf y caballitos").

A form of indigenismo that substitutes the north-central coast for the Andes as the space of identity formation, the claim to Peruvian ancient surfing origins "influence[s] the racial and cultural construction of national selves" (Tarica xxiv) by identifying the urban surfer with coastal indigenousness and, through invocations of the Inca conquest of the Chimú and contemporary Andean migration to the coast, the Andean world. Most importantly, the connection of the caballito to modern surfing forms historically associated with limeño elites constructs a "national subject [that] proclaims an intimate affinity with Indians" (xxii), a discourse absent from other spheres of contemporary Peruvian cultural production.

Surfing's coastal indigenismo "becomes a discourse of liberation and redemption, both individual and collective" (xxi) on two levels. It first serves to construct a relationship between the coastal fisherman (Urcía/Gómez) and the urban surfer (Dogny/Pomar) built on collective affinity for the ocean, by default connecting nonindigenous Peruvians to indigenous Peruvians, redeeming each subject for past difference through their intimate oceanic bond. Second, it counters Anglo surfing hegemony by connecting the Peruvian practice to indigeneity, an identity predating Western adoption of the sport by millennia. Peruvian surfing's vein of indigenismo renders Peru "unique with respect to the United States and Europe, [. . .] independent of the imperialist and neo-colonialist designs of such global powers" (2–3), a form of Étienne Balibar's "fictive ethnicity," subordinating internal Peruvian difference to international difference, "the symbolic difference between 'ourselves' and 'foreigners'" (Balibar and Wallerstein 93–94).

Projecting professional surfing onto coastal indigenista discourse, competitive surfers such as Mulanovich and José "Jarita" Gómez (elder brother of Analí Gómez) have engaged in exhibitions aimed at proving that ancient fishermen indeed rode waves on caballitos de totora. Notwithstanding the fact that the caballito was traditionally navigated while seated or kneeling with little evidence of stand-up surfing, both surfers successfully surfed waves upon modified caballitos, Mulanovich at San Bartolo (2010) and Gómez at big wave Pico Alto (2009). Shortly after his famed session at Pico Alto during which he pinned a Peruvian flag around his shoulders, Gómez addressed the media about his feat. His interview clearly demonstrates the varied and at times contradictory discourses that surfing employs in constructing Peruvian identity (Tramontana Figallo; "Sofía"). The muscled fisherman from Punta Hermosa promotes the belief that caballito-riding ancient Peruvians comprised the first surfing civilization. Following Pomar and De la Rosa, he declares that ancient Peruvians populated Polynesia and spread the original practice to Hawai'i through maritime exchanges. Gómez then paradoxically discusses the "minimal" high-tech modifications made to his caballito replica using space-age composites pioneered by NASA. He then announces plans for a number of Hawaiian and Peruvian surf product manufacturers to produce and market caballito replicas in North America (a venture that never happened). Throughout the interview, claims to surfing's premodern origins are interspersed with expressions of the technological sophistication of Peruvian composites and claims of a genetically founded Peruvian propensity for big-wave surfing. Calls for the Peruvian people to embrace domestic surfing tourism accompany calls to propel local surf brands into overseas markets. The Quechua language is proposed as a linguistic precursor to the Hawaiian language. He reiterates that Peru possesses the oldest, longest, and biggest waves in South America, if not the planet. Gómez paradoxically refers to riding waves on the technologically advanced caballito as the arrival of "the time to evolve our history." He concludes by thanking both God and "our Inca Tupac Yupanqui, who sent me his energy in order for all of this to happen" (Tramontana Figallo).

Gómez's comments illustrate how exercising a modern form of surfing on the ancient caballito de totora constitutes the simultaneous mediation of (1) discourses of modernizing national identity, (2) surfing's construction of a Peruvian imperial imaginary, and (3) a coastal form of Tarica's intimate indigenismo. Gómez's statements also serve to introduce the hyperbolic discourses—absolute claims to Peruvian surfing primacy and ingenuity—common in media, government, and the surfing community's celebration of surfing as national symbol. For example, hotels and *cebicherías* around Punta Rocas exclaim, "Punta Rocas, the most consistent wave in the world!" proclaiming an unparalleled consistency of the waves found in the area. In the PromPerú segment, Villarán declares Chicama the longest wave in the world, anticipating limeño Cristobal de Col's 2012 Guinness World Record of 34 maneuvers on a single Chicama wave. Gómez comments that Pico Alto is the biggest wave in South America. Likewise, while Peru won the 2010 ISA Open and 2011 ISA Junior, surfing's most important amateur team competitions, the Peruvian media continues to expound *"Peru, campeones mundiales de tabla."* This last discourse is complicated by the fact that both the ISA and ASP crown "world champions," the ISA as the IOC's officially recognized surfing governing body and the ASP as the definitive professional surfing organization. Although ASP professionals compete in ISA events, to date Peru was yet to qualify a male surfer for the elite ASP WCT. These details are overlooked locally in favor of politically empowering hyperbole: Peru, world champions of surfing.

I argue that the accuracy of these claims is unimportant, but rather that such broad categorical claims about Peru's surfing legacy serve to unify Peruvians around a consolidated identity as a surfing people as the nation seeks to demonstrate international cultural power through surfing. At a national level, hyperbolic discourse attempts to unite dissonant, localized identities resulting from sociopolitical polemics and economic disparities around unifying claims to Peruvian sporting primacy and surfing's genesis. Internationally, hyperbolic discourse resonates as nationalist discourse, demanding that more politically powerful surfing nations acknowledge Peru's foundational surfing identity. While conspicuous for their absolute nature, the wagers of hyperbolic discourse strive to generate national cultural power while foreign surf media continue to deny that Peru demonstrates the economic and political power indicative of such cultural power.

Highlighting regional political rivalries, a primary target of hyperbolic discourses is Brazil. As evidenced earlier, hyperbolic discourses transcend the political metaphor of competitive success by privileging surfing geographies as treasured natural resources. Peruvian stakes to the biggest, longest, and most consistent waves in South America and the world are equally directed at eastern neighbor Brazil as the Anglo world. Touted as the region's economic leader, Brazil has long been Latin America's most prominent surfing nation. Boasting the most developed non-Anglo surf industry and several generations of ASP WCT competitors, Brazil eclipses Peru in both surfing's economic productivity and competitive success. However, international commentators have long derided the quality of Brazilian waves, regarded as offering short rides in small conditions. In fact, Brazilian surfers frequently travel to Peru for the variety and quality of waves found along the Peruvian coastline. Avoiding mention of competitive surfing or industry power, hyperbolic discourses of surfing geography simultaneously privilege Peruvian waves as unparalleled natural resources and undermine Brazil's regional hegemony by denigrating their surfing landscape.

Consolidating such sentiments is naturally easier domestically than internationally, and I would like to reemphasize the value of hyperbolic discourses for unifying Peruvians around a surfing identity representative of a decolonizing process. A 2006 interview with De la Rosa demonstrates the unifying, decolonizing power of hyperbolic claims to surfing origins. Echoing Mariátegui, De la Rosa faults the Spanish—and, revealingly, the Indians' poor adaptation to Europeanized society—for the presence of poverty in Latin America:

> The Spanish [...] came and they took everything and they left [...,] they came here to take, not to build something, [...] and probably it was hard for the Indians to adapt to a different society and for that we

[contemporary Peruvians] are suffering. There are million[s] of things that could have happened but the fact is that most of the countries of Latin America are in a third world situation. (*Peel*)

Upon attributing Peru's political and economic difficulties to its post-colonial position, De la Rosa emphasizes the importance of ancient Peruvian waveriding as a mechanism for the construction of cultural power:

[W]e have the [ceramic] proof [...] of the *caballito* [from] many years ago and [it] definitely is one of the first form[s] of surfing and that's something to us, as Peruvians, that we feel proud about [...] And we have to grab from there to present [to] the world that we are a part of an ocean culture. (*Peel*)

Transcending surfing, De la Rosa returns to the fundamental debates of Peruvian coloniality that centuries of intellectuals have attempted to resolve through demonstrations of sovereign peruanidad. The objective of this claim—as with all hyperbolic discourse—is to decolonize Peruvian identity from "not-yet" narratives of sovereign Peruvian sporting subjectivity and assert that Anglo cultural and commercial hegemony are not responsible for Peru's surfing success or industry growth. Surfing, like peruanidad, has always existed in Peru independently of outside forces, Spanish, Hawaiian, American or otherwise.

Propagating Imperial Imaginary and Imagery at the ISA Games

De la Rosa's sentiments would be echoed while hosting the 2010 ISA World Surfing Games and the 2011 ISA Junior World Surfing Games at the adjacent beaches of Señoritas and Caballeros in Punta Hermosa. After all, international surfing competitions, like the Olympics and the World Cup, are often "used by the host nations both to celebrate an historical legacy and to aspire to the expression of their modernity" (Tomlinson and Young 5). However, the discursive value of hosting surfing events is complicated by the fact that although every surfer must officially declare their nationality in ASP competition,[8] most professional surfing events feature no team scoring as participants compete for individual purses, thus reducing the sport's national stakes. However, invocative of Olympic team scoring, ISA events privilege national results over individual performance. Given a decade of dramatic economic growth, the completion of Lima's Metropolitano transit system, and an upcoming presidential election, FENTA and the IPD wielded a seminal opportunity to issue a statement through the internationally focused ISA competitions.

Convening the opening ceremonies in historic Lima, the lone official publicity image startled the international surf community: a Moche fisherman riding a massive wave atop a caballito de totora beneath a beachfront huaca and a background of Andean peaks. Flanked by the bright colonial facades of Lima's 500-year-old plaza, the billboard-sized image clearly conveyed Peru's pre-Hispanic and colonial history to the international field. Though the events were sponsored by Volkswagen affiliates, surf giants Billabong (Australia) and Quiksilver (United States), and Spanish telecommunications power Movistar, this image by limeño surfer-artist Flavio Caporali defiantly favored notions of ancient Peruvian cultural empire and indigenista discourse over those of surfing's mass-mediated Western modernity. Though the modern Peruvian surfing community has long been synonymous with white limeño elites and the symbols of modernity that they parade—oversized 4 x 4 trucks, beachfront vacation homes, personal watercraft, and international surf fashions—FENTA and the IPD elected an indigenous fisherman as their icon of choice, directly confronting the surfing world's "not-yet" narratives of sovereign Peruvian sporting subjectivity. It was under this banner that Peru's Open and Junior selections would both claim decisive victories over the international field, modern competitive success vindicating the disputed image of ancient Peruvian surfing.

The question of Caporali's artwork is not one of phenotypic representation, of whether the pre-Columbian fisherman-surfer is analogous with limeño figures such as Dogny, Pomar, or Mulanovich, but rather of reasserting ancient Peruvian surfing identity in order to reject that Peruvian surfing is akin to a modern ludic form of Homi Bhabha's notion of mimicry (85–92). This image, as with the Peruvian imperial cultural imaginary constructed by Pomar's hypothesis and supported by Gómez's caballito big-wave surfing exhibition, does not seek to contest Peru's place within a Western surfing tradition. Rather, it seeks to place Peru at surfing's center independently of the West, sustaining visions of ancient cultural empire and enabling a contemporary identification of Peruvian national subjectivity with indigenousness.

Flattening the "Not-Yet" Wave: Contradictions and Conclusions

Returning to the assertion that a decolonized Hawai'i is Peru's closest related locale in the modern surfing context, the veracity of where surfing originated in the ancient context, Polynesia or Peru, is insignificant. Rather, the import of the wager lies in constructing an historical imaginary with Peru at the helm of cultural empire. Suggesting that ancient Peruvians populated the Pacific Rim in antiquity, introducing surfing to Polynesia before autonomously contributing to modern surfing's development in the twentieth century effectively relocates Peru at the center of global surfing history. Read between the lines, Pomar's theory implies that although the Inca Empire fell to the Spanish, this was not before lasting dissemination of ancient Peruvian culture—represented by surfing—throughout the Pacific Rim by pre-Incan peoples. While Gómez's gratitude to God and Inca demonstrates considerable popular association of contemporary peruanidad with Andean identity, discourses on Peruvian surfing imagine a globally reaching pre-Hispanic Peruvian imperial cultural system as Peru seeks to consolidate a position in the contemporary surfing world and global economy. Although "not-yet" narratives declare Peru a product of Spanish colonialism and attribute modern surfing's tremendous cultural power to Californian commercial forces, the Peruvian surfing community envisions Peru's surfing heritage and the entire surfing world, multibillion dollar industry and all, as products of this expansive and ancient Peruvian imperial cultural system.

This construction of an imperial Peruvian cultural imaginary, embodied by Gómez surfing a caballito de totora in seven-meter waves, accompanies significant (if overstated) Peruvian competitive surfing success. Such victories of the colonized over the colonizer might seem to indicate a reversal of cultural power, Bhabha's mimicry-turned-victory. However, assertion of Peruvian surfing empire far supersedes colonized mimicry or "beating Westerners at their own game." Rather, recent competitive success is read as a return to that ancient order in which Peruvians formed an imperial (waveriding) polity. Metaphorically transcendent of surfing, competitive victories augment imperial imaginary, signaling broader efforts to tout Peruvian modernity and autonomous cultural identity to regional rivals and former colonizers alike.

Reflection on surfing's metaphoric political and economic power invites reassessment of the PromPerú film that opens this essay. Thinking beyond the film's privileging of surfing as a Peruvian national pastime, PromPerú dispatches a detail of Peruvian celebrities (Mulanovich and Villarán among them) to the provincial US hamlet of Peru, Nebraska, to educate residents about their rights as "Peruvians." Like discourses of surfing nationalism, the film, too, envisions a Peruvian imperial cultural imaginary that inverts neocolonial notions of Western hegemony. As Pomar's seafaring ancient Peruvians spread surfing to Hawai'i in 3000 BC, PromPerú's cultural ambassadors transmit Peruvian popular culture to the unenlightened residents of the bucolic US interior. The bright red PromPerú bus becomes the vehicle of Peruvian cultural empire, its occupants "question[ing] the master narratives of modernity produced in the north" (Thurner 245) by notifying rural Nebraskan "Peruvians" of their rights through autarchic cultural transfer.

As the hallmark sport of PromPerú's campaign, mediation of surfing as an expression of Peruvian imperial cultural system and its confrontation of deep postcolonial "not-yet" narratives inscribed upon peruanidad calls upon diverse sites and structures, emanating from the union of ritualesque quotidian surfing practice, ceremonies such as caballito waveriding and international competition, and institutions such as Club Waikiki, PromPerú, and FENTA. While I suggest that these histories declare Peruvian modernity and autonomy, participating in larger nationalist projects asserting Peruvian cultural power to the world, surfing nationalism demonstrates no shortage of contradictions in its negotiations of history. By its absolute nature, hyperbolic discourse, like nationalism, breeds contradiction. Though I intentionally limit my discussion of these contradictions, one ought to acknowledge some blindspots of Peruvian surfing nationalism: Dogny's canonization as Peruvian sporting icon despite his elite status, the articulation of a singular national identity through a predominantly elite practice restricted to coastal environs, coastal intimate indigenismo in the face of prevailing class and racial tensions, identitarian discourse's emphasis on surfing's economic potential, and surfing's opposition to foreign cultural impositions although local surf culture demonstrates the neocolonial tendencies of privileged surfers worldwide.

In spite of these contradictions, discourses of surfing in Peru transcend emancipation from an absolute Western modernity by repositing the very center of modernity, constructing a Peruvian national countermodernity forged through an intimate, millenial bond with the ocean. As metaphor for economic and political power, surfing reconfigures notions of national identity founded upon this uniquely Peruvian modernity. Peru's resignification of surfing practice through renarrativization of surfing histories thus proclaims pre-Hispanic Peruvian identity to be modern and hegemonic. Peruvian mediation of surfing throws occidental, neocolonial modernities under the now-iconic Marca Perú bus, so to speak. Forging a local, national modernity based on the diverse historical valences of peruanidad—indigenous and elite, ancient and contemporary—and employing sport and national identity to construct sovereign historical subjectivity, surfing flattens "not-yet" waves of Peruvian contemporaneity.

Notes

I would like to thank Estelle Tarica, Michael Iarocci, the volume editors, and the anonymous reviewer for their comments. All translations are mine unless otherwise noted.

1. As of 2015, the Association of Surfing Professionals (ASP) has been renamed the World Surf League (WSL).
2. If popular culture is any indication, Peru's proudest mainstream sporting feat was arguably earning the silver medal in women's volleyball in the 1988 Seoul Olympics. Peru's most recent sporting success is men's WBA interim Light Flyweight Champion Alberto "Chiquito" Rossel, who has defended his title four times as of March 2014. Rossel is the second Peruvian WBA World Champion after Kina Malpartida, who defended her Women's WBA Super Featherweight title five times from 2009 to 2013 before retiring. The 1996 Peruvian Women's Surfing Champion and daughter of the late three-time Peruvian Surf Champion Oscar Malpartida, Malpartida formerly trained and competed with Sofía Mulanovich. While boxing has become a Peruvian sporting tradition, *blanquiroja* international success is limited compared to the country's competitive surfing legacy and Peru remains overshadowed by long-standing boxing traditions in Latin America. See Wood, "Representing Peru" (429–430).
3. Warshaw dates Americans surfing in Brazil to 1928, Brazilian surfers emerging by 1939 (*Encyclopedia* 81). He also unexplainedly suggests that surfing was practiced in Lima circa 1923 and arrived with Dogny after 1938 (159). I adhere to De la Rosa's archivally substantiated chronology.
4. Gabriel Villarán is the nephew of Lima mayor Susana Villarán. See Wood, "Representing Peru," for a portrait of Kina Malpartida and Sofía Mulanovich's class ties.
5. Peruvian surfboard and wetsuit brands such as Klimax, Wayo Whilar, and Boz are infinitely more popular than their foreign counterparts. Overlooked here for brevity's sake, the Peruvian surf industry embraces nationalist discourses ranging from "Made-in-Peru" marketing to indigenista-informed brand names such as Inti Surf and Accesorios Etnia.
6. See Pomar, "Surfing in 1000 B.C." and Warshaw, *Encyclopedia* 469–470. For Peruvian appropriations of the theory, see De la Rosa 81–99 and Sabogal 73–87; for an Anglo rebuttal, see Warshaw, *History* 17–22.
7. To my knowledge, late historian José Antonio del Busto Duthurburu's *Túpac Yupanqui: Descubridor de Oceanía* is the only scholarship engaging the topic.
8. In a nod to decolonization, competitive surfing enables athletes from former colonies and disputed territories to represent their communities instead of the parent nation. For example, Hawaiians represent Hawai'i and not the United States. Puerto Rico, Guam, Tahiti, Guadaloupe, Réunion, the Canary Islands, and the Basque Country are autonomous in ASP events (the first four in ISA events as well).

BIBLIOGRAPHY

Balibar, Étienne, and Immanuel Wallerstein. "The Nation Form: History and Ideology." *Race, Nation, Class: Ambiguous Identities.* London: Verso, 1991. 86–106.

Bhabha, Homi. *The Location of Culture.* London: Routledge, 1994.

Brown, Bruce. *The Endless Summer.* Monterey Media, 1966. Film.

Cabezudo, Marco Antonio. Skype Interview. January 21, 2012.

Chakrabarty, Dipesh. *Provincializing Europe: Postcolonial Thought and Historical Difference.* Princeton, NJ: Princeton University Press, 2000.

Comer, Krista. *Surfer Girls in the New World Order.* Durham, NC: Duke University Press, 2010.

De La Rosa Toro, Magoo. *Huellas en el mar.* Lima: Editorial Elefant, 2010.

Del Águila Miñano, Eduardo. *Antik y Tup: Viaje a la Polinesia.* Lima: Lealtad, 2012.

Del Busto Duthurburu, José Antonio. *Túpac Yupanqui: Descubridor de Oceanía.* Lima: Fondo Editorial del Congreso del Perú, 2006.

Dussel, Enrique. "Beyond Eurocentrism: The World System and the Limits of Modernity." *The Cultures of Globalization.* Eds. Fredric Jameson and Masao Miyoshi. Durham, NC: Duke University Press, 1998. 3–31.

"El surf es rentable: las ventas de ropa y tablas hawaianas en el Perú crecen al año 30%." *El Comercio,* June 7, 2010. Web. May 25, 2014.

Guttmann, Allen. *Games and Empires: Modern Sports and Cultural Imperialism.* New York: Columbia University Press, 1994.

Lawler, Kristin. *The American Surfer: Radical Culture and Capitalism.* New York: Routledge, 2011.

Lefebvre, Henri. *The Production of Space.* Malden, MA: Blackwell Publishing, 2011.

Maldonado, Ricardo. *Perú, Nebraska.* PromPerú, 2011. Film.

Ormrod, Joan. "Endless Summer (1964): Consuming Waves and Surfing the Frontier." *Film & History* 35:1 (2005): 39–51.

Peel: The Peru Project. Dir. Wes Brown and T.J. Barrack. Monterey Media, 2006. Film.

Pomar, Felipe. "Surfing in 1000 B.C." *Surfer* 29:4 (April 1988).

"PromPerú interesado en posicionar al Perú como paraíso para los tablistas." *OlasPeru.com.* January 31, 2014. Web. May 25, 2014.

Sabogal, Ricardo. *Los antiguos y originales surfers de Huanchaco.* Trujillo, Peru: Universidad Nacional de Trujillo & CEPRODE, 2003.

Sierralta, Karin. Interview. February 8, 2012.

"Sofía Mulanovich más peruana que nunca: surfeó sobre un caballito de totora." *El Comercio.* May 28, 2010. Web. May 25, 2014.

"Surf y caballitos de totora en Huanchaco." *GravedadZero.tv.* November 2, 2013. Web. May 25, 2014.

Tarica, Estelle. *The Inner Life of Mestizo Nationalism.* Minneapolis and London: University of Minnesota Press, 2008.

Thurner, Mark. *History's Peru: The Poetics of Colonial and Postcolonial Historiography.* Gainesville: University Press of Florida, 2011.

Tomlinson, Alan, and Christopher Young, eds. *National Identity and Global Sports Events: Culture, Politics, and Spectacle in the Olympics and the Football World Cup.* Albany: SUNY Press, 2006.

Tramontana Figallo, Óscar. "Correr Pico Alto en Caballito de Totora, por José 'Jarita' Gómez." *OlasPeru.com.* September 8, 2009. Web. May 25, 2014.

Vásquez, José. *La tabla como actividad económica: relevancia y visión a futuro.* Lima: FENTA, 2007. Print.

Wacquant, Loïc. "From Charisma to Persona." *The Charisma of Sport and Race.* Berkeley: Townsend Center Occasional Papers Series, 1996. 21–30.

Warshaw, Matt. *The Encyclopedia of Surfing.* Orlando: Harcourt, 2003.

———. *The History of Surfing.* San Francisco: Chronicle, 2010.

———. "Representing Peru: Seeing the Female Sporting Body." *Journal of Latin American Cultural Studies* 21:3 (2012): 417–436.

Wood, David. "On the Crest of a Wave: Surfing and Literature in Peru." *Sport in History* 29:2 (2009): 226–242.

Sports as Transnational Mediation

PART IV

Sports as Transnational Mediation

CHAPTER 11

Guillermo Vilas, "Tennis's Sexiest Man": The Argentine Dictatorship in the US Tennis Press, 1974–1982

Robert McKee Irwin

Guillermo Vilas has been called the "foremost Latin American male" player in tennis history (Collins 655). Emerging as a contender on the international tour by winning the year end Masters Grand Prix championship in 1974, Vilas went on to forge an illustrious career, winning four major ("Grand Slam") championships, ranking in the worldwide top ten from 1974 through 1982, and setting numerous all-time records that hold to this day. His success was the inspiration for Argentina's tennis boom, and he remains a beloved celebrity in his homeland. A charismatic star, the long-haired, dark, and muscular Vilas became an international sex symbol in the late 1970s, as was confirmed by *Playgirl* magazine in 1978 when it named him "Tennis's Sexiest Man." His rise to fame coincided roughly with the escalation of Argentina's "dirty war," a story from which Vilas was kept at a distance in the US sports press. Notwithstanding Argentina's surprise victory in the World Cup in 1978, Vilas was quite likely the best-known Argentine in the United States throughout his prime, and yet his image in the United States was never reconciled with that of his homeland, even as the latter's human rights abuses provoked well-publicized tensions with the Carter administration. This study looks at Vilas's image in the US sports press (including specialized tennis magazines, as well as more mainstream journals) and the more generalized image of Argentina constructed around him in relation to violence of the guerrilla warfare and state-sponsored campaigns of genocide that assaulted his homeland during the years of his international stardom. Vilas, a 1970s style "Latin lover," indeed conjured up an exotically attractive and inoffensive international image of Argentina that rarely hinted at the reality of Argentine politics and everyday life under military dictatorship, a phenomenon that reflects not on the apolitical nature of sports in the United States, but rather on the parochial politics of a US-centric sports press that remained actively uninterested in all but a few international issues, reducing cultures abroad to well-established, easily digestible stereotypes, and that expressed a nationalism constructed in mostly white and sometimes black terms that ignored the United States' own growing Latino population.

This study is realized in the tradition of "media sports" studies (Rowe), focusing the images and meanings media (in this case print media) communicate in their elaboration and dissemination of sports stories. While media sports studies thrive in both the United States and in Latin America, their history is not long; writes David Rowe in 2009: "it was only relatively recently that the importance of the subject was matched by academic attention to it" (7). And while tennis has at different moments ranked fairly high in terms of participation and spectatorship in the United States (the 1970s, treated here, indeed saw a boom in its popularity) and has produced some of the most well-known sports stars of the past decades (Billie Jean King, John McEnroe, Maria Sharapova, and Roger Federer are without a doubt international superstars), it remains one of the least studied sports. Indeed, in spite of several intriguing elements about the sport (its class significations, its production of iconic stars, its history of controversies related to gender and race, its broad international popularity), there is no definitive study of tennis as media spectacle. The 1970s, a key moment in the sport's history, as will be made clear in this chapter, has been particularly neglected. At that time, while tennis, like many other sports, was in the midst of a process of mediatization, prior to the rise of cable television, US air time dedicated to tennis was relatively insignificant (with the sport often relegated to the low profile Public Broadcasting System, or PBS), especially when compared with sports such as American football or baseball; it was therefore the print media—two major specialized journals (*World Tennis* and *Tennis*), *Sports Illustrated*, and newspapers, along with occasional feature stories in journals not specialized in sports—that were most influential in shaping the image of tennis stars and therefore provide the main archive for this investigation. This study of Guillermo Vilas's rise to the status of media darling in the United States—at a moment when professional tennis was beginning a period of outward growth and quickly becoming one of the most broadly international of professional sports in terms of both athlete participation and competitive venues—aims to draw attention to this key period of the sport's mediatization, and some of the ways tennis was made to signify through the Argentine idol.

This study approaches its subject not specifically from questions of nationalism, but from a very particular transnational context in which the internationally influential media of one powerful nation construct a national image of another nation through their representations of an internationally popular sports star from the latter country. Specifically, Vilas's case illustrates how the US sports media seek to cast foreign sports stars within convenient categories corresponding to existing archetypes circulating in the United States, producing images that have little to do with the nationalist propaganda of foreign nations, nor with their day-to-day realities. It would not have been favorable to the relatively new and increasingly profitable tennis wing of the US sports entertainment complex to absorb Argentine sports stars through the public image of Argentina best known to readers of international news, that of a repressive and violent dictatorship, nor did the US sports press have the knowledge or motivation to promote a greater understanding of Argentine or other foreign cultures through its sports coverage. Instead, it was easiest to turn to existing tropes, in this case the well-known and eminently alluring archetype of the Latin lover. At once in line and in contrast with Vilas's image in Argentina, co-opted by the military regime to support nationalist pride at a time when Argentina's national psyche was severely damaged by violently divisive internal conflict and brutally repressive politics, a particular transnational ideology was at work in the US press that rather than use Vilas's positive image to boost that of the Argentine government, instead radically detached the tennis star from (and utterly turned a blind eye to) the increasingly discomforting image of his country's military government, one that ensured that sports entertainment in the United States would remain uncontaminated by the complications of international politics. His familiar Latin lover image also maintained a nonspecific foreignness that reinforced the United States' own image as white (and black), but not Latin.

THE RISE OF GUILLERMO VILAS

Vilas was born in 1952 in Buenos Aires into a well-to-do family. Growing up in the seaside resort of Mar de la Plata, Guillermo was a talented student and athlete. Discouraged by his father from engaging in the "low class" sport of soccer (Robbins 43), he quickly developed into a promising tennis player. By 1970, already Argentina's top tennis player, he chose to try his luck as a professional on the just-forming international men's tour (see Evans). He made his first splash in late 1973, winning a professional tournament before a home crowd in Buenos Aires with a victory over the rising Swede Björn Borg. Then in 1974, he ascended rapidly, winning six tournaments, finally upsetting Rumanian Ilie Nastase to take the men's year end championship—"the upset of the decade" (*SI* 5/29/1978). His success was received eagerly back at home where a rebroadcast of his August victory over Chilean Jaime Fillol in the final at Louisville was the first televised emission of tennis ever (*LAT* 8/26/1974: D1; 12/16/1974: D3). *Sports Illustrated* was already declaring him "the best non US-trained South American male player of all time" (9/9/1974). Over the next two years, the left-hander won eleven more tournaments, becoming a "national monument" in his home country (*WT* 12/1975: 24) and an international star.

Down to earth and accessible, he fascinated the US press, proving especially interesting for the unusual profile he represented. Vilas was a writer—in 1975 he had already published a volume of poetry—who referred in interviews to his readings in philosophy and his love of music. Long-haired and soft spoken, Vilas came across as gentle and cerebral; indeed his pacific nature was revealed in his fashion choices, including his habit of wearing MIA and POW bracelets, symbols of support for troops missing in action or prisoners of war in Viet Nam, a gesture also meant "to protest all wars" (*T* 1/1975: 39). An early profile portrayed him as an "Argentine author and bongo drummer" (*SI* 9/9/1974).

Tennis's Latin Lover

Vilas's most-often repeated nickname in the US tennis press was "the mild bull of the pampas," after the 1920s Argentine boxer Luis Ángel Firpo ("the wild bull of the pampas"), who had perhaps been Argentina's most world renowned athlete prior to Vilas. Vilas was the "mild" bull because he was, as rival Jimmy Connors would attest, ferociously "tenacious" (Smilgis), but also, as Vilas himself put it, "sentimental" (*Tennis* 1/1975: 40). However, from his earliest profiles in the US press in the summer of 1974, his image was constructed as an object of desire as Vilas left "fans spellbound" with his "twisting torso," "tumbling hair," and "sweat drenched back" (*LAT* 8/26/1974: D1). As a poet, a lyricist and an avid reader of Asian philosophy, he was presented as "a refreshing change" from the typical jock, a "rare individual" (*Tennis* 1/1975: 40), a sexy and exotic mix of traditionally masculine ("muscular torso," "thick legs") and feminine (gentle demeanor, contemplative nature) characteristics that aligns with the "Latin lover" archetype, well known in the United States since the early years of Hollywood.

Rudolph Valentino is often cited as the original Latin lover, a dark, handsome, seductive, physically fit, but debonair and always exotically foreign (in terms of both his swarthy looks and his pronounced accent) figure (Hansen). Charles Ramírez Berg cites the Latin lover as one of six main stereotypes that have shaped the history of representation of Latin Americans in Hollywood cinema, defining him through his "romantic promise" fueled by a combination of "eroticism, exoticism, tenderness" and "danger" (76). While the image of Vilas in the 1970s tennis press does not incorporate any element of danger—in fact, it emphatically portrays him as harmless, except to his competitors—he possesses every other attribute of the archetype and is often referred to by the term in more recent representations (Herrerías; Puce435; Leonardi).

Miriam Hansen emphasizes that a key element of the Latin lover archetype is that it represents a male object of desire, in opposition to the dominant visual coding of classic cinema, for which the camera assumed the position of the heterosexual male voyeur; Vilas was constructed through both words and images as a sex symbol, much more so than his greatest rivals, the temperamental and often boorish Connors or the impassive and scruffy-looking Borg, in line with the Latin lover dynamic. From early on, his handsomeness is described through a paradox of feminized hypermasculinity: "With his square build, muscular chest and shoulders and thick legs, Vilas could pass as a football player. But soft facial features seem to reflect the poetic side of his nature [...] Vilas's face may be gentle, but his tennis is intimidating" (*NYT* 9/5/1975: 23). These early profiles dwell upon Vilas's tendency to adorn his body with "headband, bracelets, rings, beads" (*SI* 9/9/1974) or "numerous necklaces, medallions and assorted baubles" (*T* 1/1975: 40). Just as had been the case with Valentino, this romantic image attracted "groups of young female admirers," with the difference that, in the case of Vilas, his "build of a halfback" ensures that there is no doubt about his heterosexuality: as one early interviewer succinctly puts it in *World Tennis*, where he earned his second cover story in late 1975: "He likes girls" (12/1975: 24).

It is impossible to guess the precise politics behind his bracelets. He states in an early interview that he wears them to express pacifism: "I am happy I never had to fight in a war. War is so bad. When I think things are wrong for me, I look down at my bracelet and remember how lucky I am" (*WT* 12/1975: 22). However, it is unclear just how politically oriented his conviction is. Was he also making a militant statement against the war in Viet Nam? Or more of a gesture of sympathy to the young soldiers sent to fight in it? Or does his solidarity with this US cause signal instead a mere token affiliation with transnational youth culture? In the United States these bracelets did not necessarily symbolize a left (antiwar) or right (prowar, anti-Viet Cong) politics; instead they communicated a more politically ambiguous statement in sympathy with those who were captured or disappeared in a controversial war. In the context of Argentina, their precise political implications are even more obscure, and the US press did not pursue the question at a time (the war effectively concluded in 1975) when many readers wanted nothing more than to forget about Viet Nam. US sports journalists expressed no curiosity about Vilas's positions on the Viet Nam War or on any other political matter.

Apart from these bracelets, the Argentine remained detached from politics—unlike South America's second-best player of the time, Chilean Jaime Fillol. Indeed en route to Vilas's Canadian Open win in August of 1976, he played a semifinal match against Fillol for which tournament officials had received bomb threats, directed against Fillol. This was not the first time Fillol had been publicly threatened due to his alleged allegiance to the Pinochet regime after having participated in a locally symbolic, government-sponsored Youth Day event (Cavalla 163). Vilas, who apparently had stopped wearing bracelets right around the time of Argentina's 1976 military coup, despite being much more internationally prominent than Fillol, would never be accused of collaborating or even sympathizing with the Argentine military dictatorship.

Argentina in the Mid-1970s

It is ironic that Vilas's rise to fame coincided with one of the most violent periods in Argentina's history as both leftwing guerrilla groups and rightwing paramilitaries took advantage of the weakened government following the death of Juan Perón in mid-1974 and the assumption of the presidency by his politically inexperienced widow, Isabel, with groups of both persuasions engaging in violent acts with shocking frequency. Indeed, perhaps more prominent in the pages of some major US newspapers in 1975 than Guillermo Vilas was another Argentine with the same last name, General Acdel Vilas, who was charged early that year by Isabel Perón with putting down a rebel insurgency in the northern province of Tucumán. The "dirty war" carried out by Acdel Vilas in 1975 (this is the term Vilas himself is quoted as using: *NYT* 3/21/76: 184) would serve as a model for the state-sponsored campaign of kidnappings, tortures, disappearances, and murders that would characterize the military dictatorship's crackdown on leftist opponents following their 1976 coup d'état. Acdel Vilas, who is not known to be related to Guillermo, founded the first concentration camp of the era in Tucumán and is remembered as one of the most notoriously ruthless military leaders of the period (precursor to the more infamous Antonio Bussi). Acdel Vilas's positions, laid out in detail in a campaign diary, were extreme even for military leaders, who relieved him of his duties through an early retirement at the end of 1976 after international outcry following Vilas's orders for the arrest of 48 Argentines, including 17 university professors and a former minister of education, in order to check into "ideological penetration" of Marxism at universities and other sites (*NYT* 8/7/1976: 4; see also Vilas's chapter on "La guerra cultural" in Tucumán).

In the summer of 1974, when Guillermo Vilas was first identified as "a star on the rise" (*LAT* 8/26/74: D1), Argentina was intensely divided. Readers of international news were likely alarmed the increasing frequency of reports of such occurrences as leftist "urban terrorism" and assassinations of prominent leftist intellectuals by rightwing guerrillas (e.g., *NYT* 6/25/1974: 36; 8/2/1974: 4). Vilas's long hair and potentially politically charged bracelets might easily have labeled him as a radical leftist in his country just around the time that the University of Buenos Aires, where he had briefly studied, was being taken over by conservatives as the institution had, according to its interim rector, become a hotbed of "subversion against the national powers" (*NYT* 9/19/1974: 12). *Sports Illustrated*'s conclusion that Vilas's style had more to do with "taste in fashion rather than rebellion" (9/9/1974) distances a figure that might easily have been associated with leftwing militancy from the increasingly violent political conflicts that otherwise dominated news reports on Argentina.

On the very same day as Vilas's breakthrough 1974 victory over Nastase, a report summed up the first months of Isabel Perón's presidency as a period marked by a steady stream of kidnappings and raids by leftwing guerrillas; a precipitous increase in rightwing terrorism, the latter apparently sanctioned by the government; political assassinations occurring at the rate of one a day; and over 170 deaths due to political violence in less than six months, in an article ominously titled "The Right's Guns Give Argentina 'Stability': The Spirit of Fascism Lives in Mrs. Perón's Regime" (*NYT* 12/15/1974: 231). By the time of the publication of his second *World Tennis* cover story in late 1975, violence in Argentina had escalated significantly, with reports of over 1,100 deaths in 1975 and the threat of a military coup looming (*NYT* 12/29/1975: 24), an especially frightening thought given the recent rhetoric of military leaders, who had been quoted expressing their desire to "fumigate" leftwing "scoundrels" and to "annihilate extremism" (*NYT* 10/27/1975: 5; 11/30/1975: 21). Yet no tennis journalist wondered whether when Vilas declared, "War is so bad," he was not referring to the "underground miniwar" being waged in his homeland (*NYT* 11/23/1975: 215)—or indeed why he would care more about POWs in Viet Nam than the terror that had become part of everyday life for his compatriots.

Open Tennis and the Boom of the 1970s

Guillermo Vilas, as Latin lover, did not summon up references to revolutionary insurgency, political violence, or state repression in the US sports press of the mid-1970s, where the semiotics of tennis signified in other directions. The 1970s was the era of a major tennis boom in the

United States, its rise in popularity brought about to a large degree by the introduction of "open" tennis beginning in 1968 (Evans). Prior to that time, the elite sport had largely been a game of wealthy amateurs; in fact, the four major international championships, those of Australia, France (Roland Garros), England (Wimbledon), and the United States, were open only to amateurs until that year. Prior to that, those who were not independently wealthy and wanted to compete internationally had to renounce amateur status—and the chance of playing in major championships—and to get by playing on a somewhat makeshift professional tour. Open tennis changed things radically by incorporating the four major championships into a larger worldwide professional tour. Tennis suddenly assumed a new image in the United States as homegrown stars such as Arthur Ashe, Billie Jean King, Jimmy Connors, and Chris Evert protagonized tennis's launch as a commercialized professional form of athletics and entertainment. Its elite country club image would be radically transformed as major championships became important media events, and the sport's new stars challenged all kinds of hierarchies once associated with the game.

Arthur Ashe, the 1968 US Open champion, was an articulate African American, just as Evonne Goolagong broke racial boundaries by rising up as Australia's first aboriginal sports heroine. A new breed of champions (Connors, Nastase) were well known for their brazen vulgarity, contradicting tennis's image as a gentlemanly game of the upper classes. While King, protagonist of the 1973 "Battle of the Sexes," a major television event in which she defeated macho trash-talking Bobby Riggs, was a feminist activist, the stoic Evert emerged as a sex symbol, the sport's blonde "girl next door." As tennis became a more media oriented sport, with colorful stars that appealed to multiple audiences, it also took on a new glamor. In this atmosphere, Vilas was appreciated by tennis journalists, comparing favorably with his main competitors: Connors, brash and rude, and Borg, silent and aloof (*WT* 12/1975: 22), himself signifying, despite his own upper-class background, another aspect of the democratization of the game in the 1970s—its potential for producing Latin American (nonmetropolitan, Third World) stars.

It should be noted that the mediatization of tennis was gradual and that media coverage in the United States, very much the center of the world's tennis boom at the time, was quite US-centric, with US major network television coverage limited to Wimbledon, the US Open, and a few other major North American tournaments. European tournaments or other events held outside of North America, including majors such as the French and Australian Open, were not covered at all on TV. On the other hand, many smaller US tournaments were televised in those days, often on public television—indeed Vilas first became well known to US television audiences after following up his 1977 French Open victory (reported to US fans in newspapers and magazines) by winning tournament after tournament on the televised (on PBS) US summer circuit.

Tennis's popularization was media driven, which meant that it was both professionalized and defined more clearly than ever before as entertainment. The "Battle of the Sexes" was not so much tennis competition as media spectacle, incorporating all kinds of Las Vegas style showmanship, with King, after being carried onto the court by shirtless male "slaves," giving opponent Bobby Riggs the gift of a live piglet, symbol of his posture as "male chauvinist pig." The highly publicized spectacle drew the largest live audience ever for a tennis event, as well as a television audience rivaling that of the United States' greatest sporting events: 50 million in the United States alone—approximately the same number who saw the Superbowl that year (Collins 167). Tennis was part of a 1970s zeitgeist that built on *Roe v. Wade*, the mass release of porn movie *Deep Throat*, Burt Reynolds's *Cosmopolitan* centerfold, and the publication of *The Joy of Sex*, all of which coincided roughly with "The Battle of the Sexes," linking tennis in the popular imagination to a new sexual freedom. Tennis was billed as a sexy sport, an attractive activity for young heterosexual singles during the era of disco. An article titled "Now Everybody Has the Bug" declared that "tennis is, indisputably, the passion sport of the '70s" (*SI* 11/11/1974). Vilas, who would a few years later become romantically involved with Princess Caroline of Monaco, was a glamorous, sexy figure, his image molded by the media, whose tendency was and is to shape sporting story lines to include "many of the same melodramatic elements that characterize soap operas" (Kinkema and Harris 32), crafting interesting, colorful, and appealing characters.

VILAS'S SPECTACULAR YEAR

The year 1977 was when Vilas's status changed from that of a talented second tier player to a big time champion. It began in early May in Buenos Aires with Vilas leading Argentina to its first Davis Cup victory ever over the United States. Several weeks later, Vilas won his first Grand Slam singles championship at Roland Garros, dominating his final round opponent Brian Gottfried of the United States 6–0, 6–3, 6–0, the most lopsided score ever recorded there in a men's final. He set several other records that year, winning 16 tournaments and 130 match victories, records that stand to this day (Lupo 422). Among his wins was his second Grand Slam tournament, the US Open, which he achieved over archrival Jimmy Connors by a decisive score of 2–6, 6–3, 7–6, 6–0, earning him a number one ranking for the year from *World Tennis* magazine.

His phenomenal year earned him numerous print media feature stories, not only in tennis journals and on newspaper sports pages, but also in *People, Esquire, Penthouse,* and *Playgirl.* These latter journals moved beyond questions of tennis, delving more deeply into what was already known about Vilas's endearing personality: his esoteric readings, his poetry, his fascination with rock music (including collaborations Argentine rock superstar Luis Alberto Spinetta), and above all his personal life, including his dalliances with various women: *People* declared that he was a "classy sex symbol" (Smilgis) while for *Playgirl* he was "tennis's sexiest man" (Robbins 43).

People's 1978 profile reported on his affairs with Latin American beauties including possibly Bianca Jagger (Smilgis). In May of 1978, *Esquire* featured Vilas on its cover and in an article portraying him on the one hand as a relentlessly hard working athlete, an image reinforced by numerous photos of him shirtless displaying his muscular physique, and on the other as a "reflective and sensitive" poet. Its author, Philip Taubman, dwells on Vilas's "incredible eyes—large, soft, soulful hazel eyes that women find irresistibly sexy and men find trusting and relaxing. The eyes are the man. They speak of distant, secret places, of dreams and andante tempos, of ripples silently spreading across a still pond. They soothe and caress" (41). Taubman's fanciful approach carries over into his descriptions of Vilas's tennis training. Under the "scorching" sun, Vilas works out on the court, "sweat streaming down his body, small rivulets feeding larger tributaries that flow into rivers of perspiration running down his chest and back" (39), pushing the limits of his "muscular arms and chest, taut stomach, and powerful tapered legs" (42) in his seven-days-a-week, six-hour practice sessions. Herculean, but sensitive, Vilas, utterly desirable, is very clearly cast as a contemporary Latin lover.

This image is confirmed and expanded upon a few months later in a *Playgirl* interview with Fred Robbins. *Playgirl,* oddly, features only one color photo of Vilas squinting into the sun as he waits to receive serve, an image that neither emphasizes his strapping physique nor his sensitive eyes, which are lost in shadows. However, he is constructed to be even more sexually desirable than in the *Esquire* article. *Playgirl,* in its very selection of Vilas for a feature story, takes as a starting point his role as object of desire of the magazine's mostly female readers. In contrast with the *Esquire* article that describes Vilas's interactions with his 16-year-old girlfriend, *Playgirl* focuses on Vilas's sexual tastes and availability. Robbins asks if Vilas "ever manage[s] to fall in love" while on tour, if "those empty arms get filled up in every city" and how he handles groupies (44–45). He also asks about the "type" of woman Vilas prefers and the "special qualities" he seeks in the opposite sex, as well as how he feels about sexually aggressive women and older women. Robbins focuses his questions very directly on Vilas's sexual availability, asking, for example:

"How much of a sex life [...] can a player have during a tournament?" to which Vilas responds that in the less demanding early stages of a tournament "I do have a sex life" and that "I like [groupies]." He adds that sometimes women he'd never met call his hotel room from the lobby saying things like "'I don't want to disturb you, but I am coming up.' So you know what's going to happen" (44). Though Vilas mentions his steady girlfriend, it is only in passing and not by name. Discussion of tennis is relegated to the latter half of the article, which in its brief introductory paragraphs is described as being about "love, death, groupies, marriage, and—oh yes—tennis" (43).

The third and lengthiest story came out in December of 1979 in *Penthouse*, an article by Marjorie Rosen whose title designates Vilas a "renaissance tennis star," focusing its attention principally on his artistic creativity, introducing him in its opening paragraph as "soulful and sensitive" (161). This article includes no photographs at all, instead featuring only a cartoon with Vilas dressed up as an Italian renaissance scribe. Rosen follows Vilas to a tournament, but focuses much more ink on "his cerebral quality" and "poetic yearnings" (162). She recounts that he travels with books and notebooks, the latter filled with poetry and the draft of a novel, and that he has written lyrics for songs performed by his friend and Argentine rock star, "Arturo" Spinetta (*sic*). She also follows him to a recording studio in New York where he (not very successfully) rehearses for his own possible recording (238), and discusses the publication of his first collection of poems, of which the article prints three translations. Rosen is surprisingly critical of Vilas, aiming not so much to romanticize his artistic temperament as to assess it, noting how "ill at ease" he is in the recording studio (238) and that his self-published poetry book was "ravaged by the critics" (240), ultimately concluding that Vilas is "undermining his own spectacular tennis gifts" by "trading in a truly first-class singular talent in order to be a second-class Renaissance man" (247). Still, for Rosen, Vilas is a "prince" with a "glistening storybook smile [...] all charm" (247); she describes him from the start as "a heartthrob, a matinee idol," a sexualized popularity she finds inevitable given "the remarkable physical reality of the man. With large, soft-edged sensual features, languid and dreamy green eyes, and masses of curly Pre-Raphaelite hair that cascade about his face, Vilas [...] suggests the look of the rock star he occasionally fancies he'd like to be" (161–162). Her critique, in the end, does little to undermine his Latin lover mystique.

Interestingly, despite the often repeated datum of Vilas's early career penchant for POW bracelets, none of these later articles—including shorter profiles published in tennis magazines or newspaper sports pages—with the exception of the *Esquire* story, dares to broach the question of politics, most particularly Vilas's thoughts regarding what that journal called Argentina's "repressive military junta." Philip Taubman, who would later become chief of the Washington and Moscow bureaus of the *New York Times*, writes: "I wonder whether, with all his wealth and fame, he is concerned about human rights," asserting further that in his own experiences "people, with terror in their eyes, told me about friends arrested in the middle of the night and never heard from again. Just under the busy pace of Buenos Aires life, there is real fear" (45). Indeed at the time of the publication of the *Esquire* article, the Carter administration was publicly calling out the military government on human rights violations (*NYT* 4/3/77: 11). Vilas evaded the *Esquire* question: "I am not political. If I win a big tournament, the government may congratulate me, but I am not political." Other unnamed sources assure Taubman that Vilas remains silent out of necessity, as any negative comments about the regime might result in his "being banned from his homeland" (45). Meanwhile, as Vilas basked in his US Open win, it was being reported that crackdowns were already being carried out on the protests of the Mothers of the Plaza de Mayo (*NYT* 10/15/1977: 8), and soon thereafter Vilas himself had been threatened to either represent Argentina in the Davis Cup or face "automatic military service" (*NYT* 3/13/78: C1). Certainly Vilas, with his long hair and dabblings in rock music and poetry, looked more like a Montonero rebel than a model citizen of the military dictatorship.

Although Vilas is occasionally quoted as being devoted to his country, and intermittent references are made in these feature stories to the "pampa" or to Argentine beef, specific cultural references to Argentina are rare (tango, e.g., is never mentioned). Vilas is constructed for US audiences not as an Argentine, but as a passionate Latin. For example, his early nickname in the Argentine press, "the bull of the Pampas" (Rosen 236), is transformed by US journalists, as seen in an assertion from his *Playgirl* feature story that Vilas is "more temperamentally suited for the 'moment of truth' of the bullfight than the fierce dueling of his chosen sport" (Robbins 43), from a reference to the pastoral Argentine pampa, of little significance to most US fans, into a more familiar symbol, the bullfight, that has little to do with Argentine national traditions (bullfighting was banned in Argentina in 1899)—although it makes perfect sense in the United States, where the idea of "Latin" culture might conjure up any number of images (sexy dance styles, exotic tropical beaches, festive carnival parades, spicy cuisine), few of which are specific to any single national tradition. Vilas is thus constructed as a sensual Latin (in the Hollywood tradition), whose construction seems to avoid specific cultural or political references to his homeland.

Nor does Vilas ever bring up politics. Undoubtedly he had heard that just as his own extraordinary year of record setting victories was getting under way in the spring of 1977, a former opponent, an Argentine tennis pro named Daniel Schapira, was arrested, disappearing never to be heard from again (Lupo 435). By March of 1977, upon the first anniversary of the military coup, violence had increased dramatically. It was being reported that "bombings and assassinations by left-wing extremists are still an ominous reality," while "security forces and right-wing groups have killed about 1500 guerrillas and suspected subversives in the last year." This report continues: "From 5,000 to 10,000 persons are estimated to have been arrested. Some have been released after questioning, but others have disappeared" (*NYT* 3/25/77: 8). The press warned of worsening conditions, with extremist rightwing generals poised to gain greater power, which would enable them to better carry out their policy, articulated in chilling terms in a speech by General Ibérico Saint-Jean: "First we will kill all the subversives; then we will kill their collaborators; then [...] their sympathizers; then [...] those who remain indifferent; and finally we will kill those who are timid" (*NYT* 5/25/1977: 26). Recent debates in Washington on what to do about human rights abuses in Argentina (*NYT* 4/3/77: 11, 4/11/77: 25) led to an announcement from US Treasury Secretary W. Michael Blumenthal that "United States economic aid to Argentina would depend on whether the Argentine military regime improves its respect for human rights" (*NYT* 6/1/1977: 12).

It was also around this time that reports began appearing on possible anti-Semitism in the Argentine military regime. A Uruguayan who had been kidnapped while looking for his missing son in Argentina claimed he saw in the torture chamber where the latter was held—hung nearly naked by his wrists and interrogated while being submitted to beatings and electric shocks—a portrait of Adolf Hitler: "He said the guards spoke of their admiration for the Nazis—and asked every prisoner whether he was a Jew" (*NYT* 4/11/1977: 25). Less than two weeks after the Davis Cup victory, three prominent Jewish businessmen were arrested (*NYT* 5/15/1977: 17). Soon thereafter, the Argentine government reversed an announcement that they would extradite a German immigrant, Eduard Roschmann, accused of having commanded a Nazi death camp (*NYT* 7/6/1977: 8; 7/7/1977: 7). Roschmann, who had obtained Argentine citizenship under an alias, had been sought by German authorities for decades for atrocities committed under his command in Latvia. Nicknamed the "Butcher of Riga," he was the basis for a fictionalized portrayal in *The Odessa File*, a novel published in 1972 and made into a film in 1974. Argentina ultimately did not extradite him as he succeeded in escaping to Paraguay. Reports of arrests of Jews by the military regime became more frequent throughout the year (*NYT* 9/8/1977: 14; 11/20/1977: 13), and in the early fall the obituary of José Gebhard, a Jew who had emigrated from Poland in 1926 and had become Argentina's minister of the economy from 1973 to 1975, reported that he "had been a target of anti-Semitic attacks from inside the government," leading him to resign and ultimately flee the country, after which "the military rulers

[...] took away Mr. Gebhard's citizenship [...]. In what some pointed to as an example of rising anti-Semitism in Argentina, Mr. Gebhard was accused along with several other prominent Jews of helping left-wing guerrillas invest millions they had obtained from kidnapping ransoms" (*NYT* 10/7/1977: 42).

Late in the year, only a few weeks after Vilas's US Open victory it was reported that Argentine army chief of staff General Roberto Viola claimed: "of 10,000 guerrillas and collaborators who were enrolled in revolutionary groups in early 1976, only 1,200 remain alive and active in the underground," and that "3,000 extremists and suspected collaborators are believed to have been killed in the past year. Thousands have been arrested and interrogated, with family members reporting close to 1,000 persons missing" (*NYT* 10/2/1977: 20). The extent of the government-sponsored carnage of Argentina's dirty war was becoming clear, and protests in the United States began to mount (*NYT* 11/27/1977: 14).

Vilas remained silent on Argentine politics, the only clue to his thinking being the early remark, cited earlier, that Vilas was against "all wars," suggesting that he was in favor of neither the revolutionaries nor the military authorities, that he was ultimately a pacifist. However, tennis fans seemed to care little about terrorism or human rights abuses in Argentina, as is evident in the fact that the hundreds that did protest outside the gates of the 1977 US Open the very day of Vilas's final round victory there were not interested at all in Vilas's presence, but instead were enraged at the United States Tennis Association's refusal to take a stand on apartheid as the South African doubles team of Bob Hewitt and Frew McMillan had just taken the men's doubles crown (*NYT* 9/12/1977: 46).

Vilas in Argentina

What is clear is how important national success in sports was for the Argentine military junta for its power to distract Argentines from the politically motivated violence surrounding them and stimulate feelings of patriotism at a time when many doubted that the nation was on an ethically acceptable path (Alabarces 111–126). Thus the leader of the military junta, Jorge Videla, was present in the audience when Argentina defeated the United States in the Davis Cup competition in 1977, making it an event of national significance. The excitement generated by Vilas's many victories on the world stage was a prelude to the euphoria of the 1978 World Cup, which would be hosted by Argentina and, surprisingly, won by the home team for the first time ever (*NYT* 5/28/1978: S1; 6/19/1978: C5; 6/30/1978: A3).

If Vilas had little or no direct public contact with Videla, they had at least one extended meeting, in New York City in 1977, just prior to Vilas's US Open win, and after which Vilas was quoted in the Argentine press as follows:

> I had never spoken with the president. You can imagine that when I received the call I was surprised, and very pleasantly. I'm sure he's busy with many things and, while I know that tennis is now important in Argentina, I never expected that he would be able to spend a full half hour with me. It was a great honor, particularly when he told me that he would like to have attended my matches at Forest Hills, but that previous engagements made that impossible. (*Siete Días* 9/21/1977, quoted in and translated by Sheinin)

It is impossible to believe that literate Vilas was as ingenuous as his words might indicate. However, it should be noted that regardless of his views on the dictatorship, they were not communicated at all in the US sports press, which ignored this meeting, and generally exhibited no interest in promoting a major sports star in a way that would force readers to face the alarming news of disappearances, repression, torture, and genocide that regularly filled the international pages of news journals. The sports press seemed determined to maintain the entertaining world of tennis's radical separation from the unpleasantness of politics.

THE POLITICS OF THE US TENNIS PRESS

World Tennis magazine in a late 1975 editorial spoke out against what the journal saw as the attempts of some governments to inject politics into sports, most especially with regard to boycotts in the sport's annual international team competition, the Davis Cup. India, making it to the Cup's final round for only the second time in history in 1974, defaulted rather than play South Africa, which continued to maintain its apartheid system. The Davis Cup had already moved South Africa from the Europe-Africa zone to its Americas zone in order to avoid boycotts by African and Eastern bloc nations, but in 1975, Mexico and Colombia likewise boycotted the Davis Cup rather than play South Africa. Mexico later deported South Africa's top doubles team Hewitt and McMillan, effectively prohibiting their participation in a major competition that many had expected them to win. *World Tennis* argued:

> Despite arguments to the contrary, sport and politics are inextricably entangled on an international level [...] The truth is that tennis officials of many countries will do exactly what their governments order [...]

> The players, for the most part apolitical, a free and easy bunch with few prejudices and hangups over "sensitive" international issues, are never consulted. If they were, they would bitch about how heavy the balls were or how fast the court, but never, never the other guy's politics. (12/1975: 13)

This rejection of "sensitive" issues of international politics is particularly dubious coming as it is from *World Tennis*, a journal founded in the 1950s by Gladys Heldman, a key figure, along with Billie Jean King, in promoting the actively feminist agenda that made possible the foundation of the women's professional tennis tour in 1970. Although Heldman sold her interest in the journal in 1972, *World Tennis* was well known for frankly discussing at least those political causes of interest to its editors and palatable to the journal's US readers (Evans 101). Exclusion of and poor pay for women athletes was a worthy cause, apartheid much less so, and the violently repressive policies of military dictatorships were not even worth mentioning. It should be noted that a year later, the USSR would pull out of the Davis Cup semifinals against Chile in protest of the Pinochet dictatorship, an embarrassment never suffered by the Argentines (Cavalla 192).

Tennis in the 1970s United States, as media spectacle, was itself political in its own ways. Gender politics were of great importance at a time when it was only beginning to be made clear, thanks to the efforts of people like King and Heldman, that women's professional sports were at all viable. Renée Richards, a transsexual woman born as Richard Raskind, drew new attention to the game when she was prohibited from playing the US Open in 1976. She then sued and won a ruling in New York State Supreme Court to admit her to the women's tour, making the finals of the US Open in women's doubles in 1977. And while the tennis press may have complained about Davis Cup boycotts, the articulate Arthur Ashe's activism against apartheid was treated with respect and admiration (*SI* 12/10/1973; 9/7/1981). And international politics played out in sometimes melodramatic form through tennis as rising young Czech star Martina Navratilova defected to the United States in 1975, and soon after another up and comer, Soviet player Natasha Chmyreva, was prohibited from playing international events by Soviet authorities, likely due to her being seen as a defection risk. Soviet players were eventually removed en masse from international competition by their national tennis federation (*NYT* 4/20/1978: D15).

Vilas's background evoked neither gender politics, nor Cold War anxieties, nor the racial politics of apartheid, themes that were either the terrain of everyday debate in the United States (gender politics) or issues presented in facile terms of good versus evil (communism, apartheid); Argentine politics could not be described in terms that jibed effectively with the mainstream of the US political landscape. The state terrorism of the Argentine military dictatorship, an eminently antidemocratic enterprise, was being deployed to effectively wipe out a communist oriented political opposition, a situation that might have lent itself to a representation in the US press of one evil versus another, a context that would leave little room for a sports hero to signify in an appealing way. Vilas was therefore shaped not into an Argentine icon (a gaucho, a tango dancer, a *descamisado* remnant of Peron's 1950s populism), but into a much less nationally specific Latin lover.

He was always both tennis champion and poet—even though sources repeatedly turned to another world famous Argentine, the blind septuagenarian writer Jorge Luis Borges, who when asked to comment on Vilas's talent as a poet responded: "Just imagine me playing tennis" (Smilgis). Tennis journalists were not in a position to judge the esthetic quality of Vilas's poetry—although Marjorie Rosen, writing for *Penthouse*, did comment on "its greeting-card sentimentality" and its resemblance to "high-school haiku" (240)—particularly in its original Spanish form, but they loved to reference it and even quote it. On the other hand, although it could be said that they were equally unqualified to perform political analysis, the objective of boosting the entertainment value of the sport was not going to be met with references to concentration camps, torture chambers, kidnappings, or mass graves.

Sensually Foreign

Whether due to the difficulties the United States had in adjusting to the incorporation of African Americans into its mainstream in the aftermath of the civil rights movement of the 1960s, or because of the troublesome politics of Latin American nations, Latinness was still for the most part kept in the outer margins of the US national culture of the 1970s. Just as Hollywood's great Latin lovers were always foreign—even California-born Zorro was a Spanish subject—the 1970s Latin lover of tennis was presented as mysterious and always somewhat impenetrable for his US fans. He was Latin, but not Latino, as US sports, despite the success of a handful of US born Latino athletes—including tennis great Pancho González who had won the US Open in 1948 and 1949, and retired from the professional tour only in the early 1970s—was not ready to embrace US-born Latinos into its mainstream.

The 1970s US sports press notably never made anything of quarterback Jim Plunkett's Mexican roots. Plunkett, as Heisman trophy winner for best collegiate football player in 1970, number one draft pick, and then rookie of the year of the National Football League in 1971, was one of the biggest stars of what was fast overtaking baseball as the United States' most popular spectator sport, but unlike Mark Sánchez 40 years later, Plunkett was never promoted as a Latino icon; indeed it is unlikely that many of his fans had any idea of his humble family background: he was son of a Mexican American news vendor. When the *Los Angeles Times* remembered his stellar career (including a Comeback Player of the Year award and distinction as a Superbowl Most Valuable Player, as he led his teams to two late career Superbowl trophies in the early 1980s) in 2011, it took care to mention that he was "born to blind parents" and "worked odd jobs to help support his family as a teen" but did not note that he remains the most accomplished Latino quarterback in NFL history (1/24/2011: C2).

In tennis, Rosie Casals, a major star throughout the 1970s, was well known as a sometimes vocal supporting player in the early feminist theatrics of women's professional tennis, serving as a television commentator for the "Battle of the Sexes" and as one of the "ringleaders" in the founding of the original women's tour (Collins 557). However, very few of her fans knew that she was a Salvadoran American; indeed, tennis's most complete reference text refers to her only as "a born and bred San Franciscan" (557). It is only very recently that US Latino contributions to the sport are being recognized, for example, with the recent breaking ground of a Cal State-Los Angeles campus tennis center to be named after Pancho González and Rosie Casals (*Bob Larson's Tennis News* 4/17/2014).

Latinness, attractive as it might be portrayed, was clearly a foreign category in the 1970s US sports media. It might be argued that US sports journalists loved Vilas so much because he was foreign, and because he did not challenge the limits of mainstream US ethnic categories.

VILAS AFTER 1977

While Vilas would not duplicate his phenomenal success of 1977, he would win two more Grand Slam singles championships, the Australian Open in 1978 and 1979, maintaining a top ten ranking for five more years, and gaining admission to the International Tennis Hall of Fame in 1991. Not only did he "single handedly [trigger] the tennis boom in South America" (*WT* 5/1983: 41), but several Argentine players from later generations—Guillermo Coria and Guillermo Cañas, both of whom became world top tenners—were named after him. He came to be known in his home country as "a national hero, their campeón, a god"; there "people reach out to touch him as if he could somehow heal them" (*WT* 5/1983: 40). By the 1980s, it was estimated that over two million Argentines were playing tennis (Lupo 620).

Likewise, in the United States, he experienced a level of fame that would have been impossible for any tennis player, let alone a foreign one, only a decade earlier. Feature stories in nonspecialized magazines like *Esquire* reflected both the popularity and sex appeal of tennis, which had "grown from a backwater pastime into an industry that burst through the boundaries of a mere sport to become the fashion-leader of a life-style and a byword for excitement, fitness, and consumer spending" (Evans 107). Although he did not retire until 1989, his star had faded by 1983. Just as his rise to fame coincided with that of the brutal military repression of post-Perón Argentina, so was his decline simultaneous with Argentina's transition to democracy. The year 1983 marked not only the election of Raúl Alfonsín, but also the eclipsing of Vilas by a new Argentine tennis superstar and media darling, teenage prodigy Gabriela Sabatini.

Vilas and Nationalism

David Sheinin has argued persuasively that Vilas was a key instrument of the dictatorship in bolstering national morale: "Vilas came to represent ephemerally the dictatorship's 'new' Argentina [...] by 1980 Vilas was a key face of Argentina abroad and an idealized figure for Argentines, highlighting the military's promise of an Argentina able to transcend the chaos of the recent past" (35). While it would be a mistake to argue that the US sports press was complicit with the dictatorship's strategies of propaganda, US sports journalists' active blindness to the constant reports of guerrilla warfare, state-sponsored terrorism, and human rights abuses in favor of a focus on Vilas's sex appeal produced a similar effect. Any US fan that followed tennis through magazines and newspapers but did not bother to read the international news section of those same journals would never have had any idea of the atrocities committed by Argentina's military dictatorship. Indeed, the media made much of Vilas's reputation to not have "killer instinct" (Rosen 244), a buzz phrase of the sport in the 1970s, referring to a will to win at all costs, in contrast with less placid players such as Connors or fiercely stoic ones such as Borg. Argentina, understood through the image of its most celebrated citizen, was a civilized, modern, potentially powerful, and ultimately gentle nation.

However, rather than producing an image complicit with Argentine nationalist propaganda, the US sports press, by reducing its representation of Argentina to a handful of tropes associated not with Argentine national culture, but with the US promulgated Latin lover archetype, made any understanding of the kind of national character promoted through nationalist ideologies impossible. In fact, the only aspect of Argentine culture to obtain international attention through Vilas was the rock music of Vilas's friend and occasional collaborator, Luis Alberto Spinetta, a genre of cultural production that hardly presented the conservative image of the nation favored by the dictatorship, which routinely censored Argentina's rock stars, including the popular Spinetta. If the military dictators wished to disseminate an image of Argentines as Latin lovers, its rock musicians were not the model they would have chosen.

In the United States, however, even as activists had begun advocating for the incorporation of a Latino minority, still largely invisible in many parts of the nation, into the mainstream of national culture, the nation was not yet ready to face its own diversity. While Latino popular culture was beginning to make some limited headway into the mainstream—Latin music had been popular for decades, and a few actors made it big in movies and television in the 1970s (Freddie Prinze, Cheech Marín)—many US Latino sports stars were not identified as such, while Latin American sport stars were treated as exotically foreign.

CONCLUDING ANECDOTE

In October of 1977, barely a month after Vilas's greatest career triumph, his US Open win, *New York Times* correspondent Juan de Onís, a Chilean-born reporter who provided frequent and often incisive updates on violence in Argentina throughout the dictatorship years, published a travel article on Buenos Aires in which he reassured readers: "In recent years, security forces have been engaged in a bloody struggle with leftwing urban guerrillas, but few visitors ever see violence. The presence of security forces in the streets makes the city safer than New York" (10/30/77: 301). This article, in describing Argentine culture and suggesting activities for travelers, cites the popularity of tennis in Argentina, but its reference to the country's great national champion as "Ricardo Vilas" is emblematic of the utter disconnect between the international news and the sports pages of this and other journals of the era. US sports media preferred to turn a blind eye to Argentina's national politics and romanticize its most internationally celebrated export as, in the words of *Playgirl*, "the James Dean of the tennis courts" (Robbins 43).

BIBLIOGRAPHY

Alabarces, Pablo. *Fútbol y patria: el fútbol y las narrativas de la nación en la Argentina*. Buenos Aires: Prometeo, 2007.
Berg, Charles Ramírez. *Latino Images in Film: Stereotypes, Subversion, Resistance*. Austin: University of Texas Press, 2002.
Cavalla, Mario. *Historia del tenis en Chile 1882–2006*. Santiago: Ocho Libros, 2006.
Collins, Bud. *The Bud Collins History of Tennis: An Authoritative Encyclopedia and Record Book*. New York: New Chapter Press, 2010.
Evans, Richard. *Open Tennis: The First Twenty Years*. London: Bloomsbury, 1988.

Hansen, Miriam. *Babel and Babylon: Spectatorship in American Silent Film.* Cambridge, MA: Harvard University Press, 1991.

Herrerías, Antonio. "El lindo zorro y su diccionario de americanismos." *Fiérabras,* October 28, 2010. http://fierabrs.blogspot.com/2010/10/el-lindo-zorro-y-su-diccionario-de.html.

Kinkema, Kathleen, and Janet Harris. "MediaSport Studies: Key Research and Emerging Issues." *MediaSport.* Edited by Lawrence Wenner. London: Routledge, 1998. 27–54.

Leonardi, Paolo. "Guillermo Vilas, le bourreau des courts." *Le Soir,* April 16, 2008. http://archives.lesoir.be/guillermo-vilas-le-bourreau-des-courts_t-20080416-00FPHD.html.

Lupo, Víctor. *Historia política del deporte argentino (1610–2002).* Buenos Aires: Corregidor, 2004.

Puce435. "Guillermo Vilas." November 11, 2010. http://puce435.skyrock.com/1946873325-Guillermo-Vilas.html.

Robbins, Fred. "Guillermo Vilas." *Playgirl* VI:2 (December 1978): 42–44, 48, 94–96.

Rosen, Marjorie. "Guillermo Vilas: Renaissance Tennis Star." *Penthouse* 11:4 (December 1979): 160–162, 236–248.

Rowe, David. "Introduction: Mapping the Media Sports Cultural Complex." *Critical Readings: Sports, Culture and the Media.* Edited by David Rowe. London: Open University Press, 2009 [2004]. 1–22.

Sheinin, David. "Sport and the Nation in *Proceso Argentina*: Dictatorship Ideologies, Media Representations, and the Rise of Guillermo Vilas and Carlos Reutemann." *MACLAS* 22 (2008): 24–52.

Smilgis, Marta. "Tennis Gets a Classy Sex Symbol: Guillermo Vilas Seeks Muses, Not Groupies." *People* 9:4 (January 30, 1978): http://www.people.com/people/archive/article/0,,20070097,00.html.

Swanson, Philip. "Going Down on Good Neighbours: Imagining *América* in Hollywood Movies of the 1930s and 1940s (*Flying Down to Rio* and *Down Argentine Way*). *Bulletin of Latin American Research* 29:1 (2010): 71–84.

Taubman, Philip. "Vilas Tries Harder." *Esquire* 89:8 (May 9, 1978): 39–47.

Vilas, Acdel. "Tucumán, enero a diciembre de 1975." Unpublished manuscript. http://www.nuncamas.org/investig/vilas/acdel_00.htm.

JOURNALS CONSULTED

Boston Globe (*BG*)
Los Angeles Times (*LAT*)
New York Times (*NYT*)
Sports Illustrated (*SI*)
Tennis (*T*)
World Tennis (*WT*)

CHAPTER 12

The Meanings of Manu: Style, Race, and Globalization in the Culture of Basketball

Yago Colás

Can a basketball player be said to "mean" something? And, if so, in what sense or senses? A significant body of work in sports studies has persuasively argued that athletes can and do indeed "mean," at least in one sense. Thus, Professors Susan Birrell and Mary McDonald noted, already in 1999, that "our attention has been drawn to a new form of critical sport analysis: articles that conceptualize particular sporting events or celebrities as texts and offer readings of those texts" (283). Professors Birrell and McDonald elaborate on the features and value of such analyses:

> Critical analyses of the narratives surrounding events...and sport personalities...offer unique points of access to the constitutive meanings and power relations of the larger worlds we inhabit. We find this move to read non-literary cultural forms as texts significant because it ties sport scholars to other critical scholars in terms of the theoretical and methodological choices we make as cultural critics. And we find the analyses themselves compelling because they concern the popular yet deceptively innocent cultural form of sport. (283)

They go on to outline the key interdisciplinary theoretical and methodological components of what they call "reading sport critically," which include "cultural studies, critical studies (including feminism, Marxism, and racial-relations theories), quantitative methods, and poststructuralism" (284–285).

For Professors Birrell and McDonald and other critical sports scholars, an athlete like a basketball player, when viewed as a text,

> transcends the individual [athlete] and…is a site for reading broader social relations. What were once regarded as individuals, celebrities, or even heroes become repositories for political narratives, and our task as cultural critics is not to search for the facts of their lives but to search for the ways in which those 'facts' are constructed, framed, foregrounded, obscured, and forgotten. (292)

The upshot is that in the sense that he or she may be considered a text, as well as the subject of texts and narratives, a basketball player may certainly be said to mean something, probably many, even contradictory things, and therefore also read, interpreted, and read "against the grain," as it were. I take all this as salutary and enabling of my own work, and the first part of my essay will be a critical reading of the "social text" that is (and those that are about) the Argentine basketball player Emanuel "Manu" Ginobili.

However, there is another sense in which I believe a basketball player may be said to "mean," and, corresponding to this, another mode or genre of reading and interpreting that meaning. I am thinking of what I'd like to call "basketball criticism." Basketball criticism entails a close reading of individual plays, players, and a player's style of play in general. In this way, basketball criticism looks for—or generates, if one prefers—meaningful patterns amidst the apparently chaotic, kaleidoscopic flow of phenomena on a basketball floor. Basketball criticism would not present these patterns as definitive or conclusive, but rather as points of departure in a process of proliferating meanings and points of engagement between spectator and athlete. Such close readings can combine with the application of critical methodologies to sport discourses to further unsettle the assumptions of those discourses and the power relations they both depend upon and undergird.

THE GREATEST OF GREAT WHITE HOPES: THE MEANING OF MANU IN US BASKETBALL CULTURE

On September 4, 2002, during the FIBA (International Basketball Federation) World Championships in Indianapolis, Indiana, a watershed event occurred in the history of basketball. After 58 consecutive wins, dating back a decade to the Barcelona Olympics of 1992, a US team composed entirely of professional stars lost a game for the first time. The score was 87–80. Their victorious opponent was Argentina. The United States would go on to drop two more games (to Spain and Yugoslavia) and finish a disappointing sixth. Argentina, meanwhile, would take second place, losing the title game in overtime to Yugoslavia. More or less the same Argentine roster would defeat the United States again two years later in the semi-finals of the 2004 Athens Olympics en route to a gold medal finish, while the United States would settle for bronze—a more outrageous failure for the many American sports fans for whom the Olympic games rate much more highly than the FIBA World Championships.

Those few in the United States who were paying attention to the FIBA defeats in 2002 viewed them as the tipping point of a process in which the nation's basketball squad had in a decade declined from dominating to dismal. In Argentina, meanwhile, the 2002 team's defeat of the United States and runner-up finish was portrayed as a boost to a nation beset by the worst economic crisis in its history, and the 2004 Olympic gold medal squad were hailed as national heroes. The narratives practically generated themselves: hubris laid Goliath low at the hands of a plucky David. That "Goliath" in the case represented the late imperial power United States and "David" an economically and politically struggling Latin American nation only made this easy story more tempting (Buckley; Durkin; Feigen; Greco; Panno; and Rushin).

Standing at the center of this crossroads of national fortunes in a decidedly globalized basketball landscape was Emanuel "Manu" Ginobili, a slender 6' 6" shooting guard. Ginobili, already known to fans of Argentine and European basketball, was the brightest star of the 2002 Argentine squad. Just weeks after leading the team to victory over the United States, Ginobili would debut as a rookie with the National Basketball Association's (NBA) San Antonio Spurs. Though struggling with injury for much of his first NBA season, Ginobili shone in the playoffs as the Spurs won the 2003 NBA championship.

By now, of course, even casual fans of the NBA are likely to know Ginobili's name. After all, he has won three NBA championships and the NBA 6th Man of the Year award. He has made the NBA All-Star team twice, and he has made over US$100 million in salary. He is the only player in the history of basketball to have won an Olympic gold medal, a Euroleague Championship, and an NBA Championship. He has met the presidents of the United States and of Argentina, and is a national hero in Argentina, a local hero to Spanish speakers in San Antonio, and praised by such NBA peers as Shaquille O'Neal, Dwyane Wade, and Kobe Bryant as maddeningly effective and entertaining.

By 2007, Manu would make an appearance in an academic volume, *Basketball and Philosophy*, in which the noted philosopher of sport R. Scott Kretchmar would speculate that Manu represented a "a new style of superstar…one who, while flashy and entertaining, brings a diverse set of team-oriented skills" (43). On the face of it, Professor Kretchmar's invocation of Manu may seem unproblematic. After all, Manu *is* flashy and entertaining—his style is improvisational and athletic, and he frequently punctuates chaotic-seeming drives to the basket with acrobatic layups or powerful dunks—and he *does* possess a diverse set of team-oriented skills—he is an excellent ball-handler, passer, and shooter and effectively blends his own individual skills with the resources and needs of the rest of his team.

There is a problem, but it's not that Manu doesn't do these things. It is that there is nothing *new* in their being done. Even a casual fan of professional basketball in the United States over the past 25 years, if asked to think of players who "while flashy and entertaining" brought "a diverse set of team-oriented skills" might name such well-known figures as Lebron James, Kevin Durant, Chris Paul, Dwyane Wade, Michael Jordan, Scottie Pippen, Isaiah Thomas, and Magic Johnson. These players are among the most famous basketball players ever, and their ability to combine flash and entertainment with team-oriented fundamental skills was a frequently observed quality of their play. In view of this, Professor Kretchmar's assertion that in combining such elements Manu represents a new style of emerging superstar presents itself as not only problematic, but puzzling. It's highly unlikely that Professor Kretchmar, a respected scholar writing in a volume dedicated to basketball, is unfamiliar with the players I named or their abilities. So the question arises: why does he ignore them in hailing Manu for synthesizing in an unprecedented way these elements of the game? This puzzle, moreover, takes on a disturbing dimension when we consider that all of the players I named are African American and Manu Ginobili, of course, is not.

This disturbing puzzle emerges, I believe, as a result of the framework of presuppositions within which Professor Kretchmar offers his views of Manu. He introduces his essay as something analogous to moral philosophy, but applied to sport. What, Professor Kretchmar asks, is the best way to play basketball? This is certainly an interesting and valid question when posed in tactical and pragmatic terms in particular, concrete competitive situations. It might even be an interesting and valid question when posed (again, pragmatically) in a commercial context, say, when seeking to start a new league. Professor Kretchmar, however, renders the inquiry problematic first by narrowing the field of possibilities to two mutually exclusive styles of play—he calls them "purist" and "modernist" (see table 12.1)—and then by construing the purist style as the bearer of a putative essence of basketball, when it is in fact—to the degree that it exists at all—a contingent, historically, socially, and geographically specific version of the game.

Professor Kretchmar himself acknowledges the lists "may look like caricatures of basketball play" and that "most teams blend elements of the two styles," but he goes on to assert that they "show what is at stake in this debate and lay out unmistakable differences in how we play and

Table 12.1   Purist vs. modernist basketball (from Kretchmar)

Purist	Modernist
Centered on team capability	Centered on individual capability
Based on honing of skills, fundamentals	Based on exceptional athleticism
Emphasizes team-related skills and group achievement	Emphasizes individual skills and one-on-one matchups
Requires good team spacing/passing	Requires clearing out, beating a single opponent
Based on patience; more half-court play	Based on pressure; more full-court play
Grounded in help-defense	Grounded in man-to-man defense
Emphasizes quickness, deception, sound footwork, good positioning	Emphasizes raw speed, strength, brute force
Based on excellent shooting skills, often outside shots that come from half-court plays	Less emphasis on shooting skills; shots often come from transition play and feature inside opportunities, dunks, and put-backs
Emphasizes defense	Features offense over defense

value the game" and that they should clarify the "general tendencies of purist and modernist basketball."

It may be difficult to determine conclusively whether or not Professor Kretchmar believes that these categories actually refer to anything that actually exists, as such, on a basketball court. However, he does *associate* each style with certain actually existing basketball teams or phenomena. Among these associations perhaps the most illuminating emerges from his assertion that basketball "*retains* its distinctive charms if it emphasizes such qualities as quickness, touch, positioning, footwork, accuracy, and deception over brute force and blinding speed" (and that the purist style better fosters these qualities). In doing so, he explicitly invokes the game as devised by Doctor James Naismith in 1891 as an entertaining indoor sport designed to discourage roughhousing (Kretchmar 39–40). Considered together with Professor Kretchmar's nomenclature ("purist" vs. "modernist"), we may begin to surmise that "purist" basketball is played in some unsullied, idealized (hence "pure") past and modernist basketball in a degraded present. In other words, it appears that table 12.1 might be recast as a timeline: the left-hand column represents the "pure" beginnings and early history of the game, and the right-hand column represents the "modern" (and contaminated) version of the game.

I think this recasting better captures what Professor Kretchmar actually has in mind. Nonetheless, the facts of basketball history, from the time of its invention to the present day, simply do not support this narrative. Moreover, the modernist/contaminated version of the game is often associated with urban playgrounds ("streetball" is the word invoked by Professor Kretchmar to indicate this provenance) predominantly frequented—since around the time of World War II—by African American players. In this way, the misleading historical narrative becomes something worse than simply misleading. It carries a racializing and racist implication that once upon a time the game was pure and morally virtuous, and then it was taken over by black men from the ghetto who destroyed the game's uniqueness and the basis of its moral virtue by turning it into a serial exhibition of individual athleticism and—Professor Kretchmar's word—"attitude" (32). I would like, before coming back around to the role assigned to Manu Ginobili in this narrative, to briefly correct and historicize this disturbing narrative.

Professor Kretchmar is correct that James Naismith devised the rules of the game in part to minimize roughhousing and to reduce the advantages to be gained by superior height, strength, and speed (Naismith 42–56). However, it appears that this no-contact, high skill, and team-oriented version of the sport didn't survive for very long after making the trip from Naismith's mind to the actually existing gymnasiums, armories, dance halls, and playgrounds of the world. On the contrary, a point of consensus among historians of the early game at all levels is that it was brutal (Peterson; Isaacs; *FreeDarko*). Here is a description of the style of play predominating in the first regional professional leagues, between around 1910 and 1924: "games were dominated by one-on-one play, with the dribbler acting like a football running back and bowling over defenders by head-butting them" (*FreeDarko* 17). Or consider this account of the early years of the college game: "the play of the game was erratic, spasmodic, rough, and so totally unpatterned as to be called chaotic. Football, itself not yet having attained a modicum of discipline, was often the principal model for players and their actions" (Isaacs 39). Indeed, already by 1906, just 15 years after the game's invention, Harvard President Charles Eliot asserted that "basketball is very objectionable. It is too rough and there are too many chances for cheating. The rules have been stretched so that they spoil the game. It would be a good thing, especially, to have basketball discontinued" ("Eliot"). Merely 6 years after its invention, Luther Gulick, the very man who had charged Naismith with devising the new game, expressed his concern over the way the game was evolving, citing "discourteous and ungentlemanly treatment of guests," as well as "slugging and that which violates the elementary principles of morals" (qtd in Peterson 30).

So early basketball—contrary to Professor Kretchmar's idealized image of the highly distinctive, no-contact, complexly patterned, team-oriented purist style—was rough, difficult to distinguish from football, chaotic, and dominated by one-on-one play. Moreover, it appears from even this cursory historical glance that, almost from the time of the game's invention, "purists" were concerned about changes spoiling the game, though the idealized game that was being spoiled by change seems to have been just that: an ideal version of a game in the mind of its inventor James Naismith. In this respect, it may be best to understand Naismith's conception along the lines suggested by Bethlehem Shoals when he compares it to the US Constitution (*FreeDarko* 15). The comparison suggests that neither Naismith's original purpose and conception nor the original 13 rules ought to be given any final, essential, determining, or normative value. Rather than the ontological horizon distinguishing what is from what is not basketball, they might be seen as a set of combinatory elements that may be reconfigured inventively by subsequent generations; a point of departure from which, in very definite historical, geographical, and social situations, the game would evolve in different ways.

From this point of view, we may historicize the basketball elements comprising the supposedly contrasting, mutually exclusive "purist" and "modernist" styles that are the subject of Professor Kretchmar's essay and which Manu is supposed, for the first time in basketball history, to have synthesized. So, for example, in rural America, in the second quarter of the twentieth century, with its low population density, basketball became popular because it could be played and practiced by a solitary individual with equipment that could be found or easily fashioned from materials at hand. But those same conditions favored a certain kind of practice: the honing of fundamental individual skills like ball handling and, especially, shooting. Moreover, the familiarity of relatively stable social relationships in such rural communities probably lent themselves, in competitive team basketball, to the development of regularly patterned play. Far from representing some putative essence of the game of basketball, solid fundamental skills and team play were contingent emergent phenomena pertaining to a particular geographical and social configuration in American history (Lane).

Similarly, congested urban playgrounds, whether frequented by Irish Americans and Jews in the first half of the twentieth century or African Americans after World War II, present conditions that favor the emergence of the features attributed to the so-called modernist style. The sheer number of players on the court at one time and seeking to play, the volatility of informal team "rosters," the tradition that the winning team maintains access to the court—all of these put a premium on individual, improvisational, and creative skills and made it difficult, if not pragmatically undesirable in the context of a single contest, to attempt to devise and learn complex patterned plays. Moreover, the competition for court time and to be selected by whoever may be forming a team for the next game lends itself to attention grabbing plays. Again, this style of basketball is no more the essence of the game than the purist style of play. It simply informs us of a particular set of social, historical, and geographical factors that, combined with the rules of basketball, led to the cultivation of certain possible elements over others.

In view of this it appears that Professor Kretchmar's table should perhaps be recast once more, now as a Platonic ontological schema. Purist basketball seems to be the Platonic *noumenon* of basketball, while modernist basketball is the fallen, distorting phenomenal manifestation. Professor Kretchmar's mistake, then, lies in hypostasizing as essential and original a particular, contingent set of elements of the game, developed in one particular locale to meet particular needs. Through this error, basketball as played by one minority culture such as that of rural Indiana in 1951 comes to be raised as the pure, essential form of the game over and above basketball as played by another minority culture such as that in Coney Island, Brooklyn in 1987.

Of course, there is a little more to it than a simple logical error. For these particular locales, dates, and vernacular interpretations of basketball tend to be racialized as a result of the intersection of race, class, and patterns of migration in American history. A kind of unconscious pseudo-syllogism is thus formed and comes to be naturalized as fact. Thus, because the population of rural Indiana in 1951 was predominantly Caucasian, and given the hypostasis of their particular style of basketball as the pure essence of the game, then one comes to associate whiteness with pure, essential basketball. Conversely, because the inner ring of American urban centers came to be predominantly populated by African Americans after World War II, then the style of basketball played there comes to be associated with African Americans.

Professor Kretchmar's argument, despite its logical pitfalls, situates itself within the province of philosophy, not history. And Manu appears within it as an abstract philosophical—rather than historical—synthesis. In the work of respected *New York Times* sports columnist Harvey Araton, Manu appears again as a synthesis, but one that—while certainly bearing moral/philosophical implications—is plotted within a concrete historical narrative. Interpreting an acrobatic fast-break layup scored by Ginobili over a taller American player in the 2002 Argentina victory over the United States, Mr. Araton wrote: "from that moment on, the prototypical foreign player was no longer a mobility-challenged white boy in a crew cut. The story was no longer *Hoosiers* with subtitles" (146).

Hoosiers is a reference to what some consider the best, and most beloved, American sports film of all time. It tells the story of tiny Hickory High School in rural Indiana that, in the mid-1950s, defied the odds to defeat a much larger urban high school and capture the state championship. *Hoosiers* is based on the 1954 Milan, Indiana high school team that defeated Muncie Central for the State Championship. In the film, the rural team is composed entirely of Caucasians, whereas the urban team is primarily African Americans. In the final seven minutes of the film, which portray the state championship game, we see African American players from the big city high school leaping high for rebounds and using superior physical strength to power for easy layups and dunks, outrunning their opponents for fast break baskets, performing creative one-on-one spin moves for easy layups, and last, in the waning minutes of a close game, losing their composure and turning the ball over. Conversely, all-white Hickory High, the team that is, via the film's metonymic title, representative of the whole state of Indiana, is portrayed as moving in complex patterns without the ball, patiently passing in order to get the perfect uncontested jump shot (inevitably swishing through), obediently following their coach's instructions, and responding on defensive to his fiery motivation (Lane 158–166).

The point of Mr. Araton's comparison, of course, is that Ginobili's layup showed that international players could not only play "*Hoosiers*-style" basketball, but also a more athletic version of the game. But by making the reference to *Hoosiers*, Mr. Araton mobilizes the same dichotomous, racialized version of American basketball culture as Professor Kretchmar. In Mr. Araton's overall narrative, beginning in roughly the early 1990s, what Professor Kretchmar would call "modernist" basketball gradually took over and destroyed the culture of the game in the United States. Meanwhile, during the same period and partly inspired by the dominating success and celebrity of the 1992 US Olympic men's team, "Hoosiers with subtitles"—Araton's "mobility-challenged white boys" all over the world—would be learning and mastering the purist version of the game and gradually closing the competitive gap with the United States in international competition. Manu Ginobili, in this story, represents how—with a figurative and literal leap—international players surpassed American players at their own game by adding athleticism (Kretchmar's key "modernist" attribute) to their already fundamentally sound, team-oriented style.

As with Professor Kretchmar's "purist" style, it is difficult to glean from Mr. Araton's narrative exactly what he has in mind in recalling the "beautiful game of grace and skill." But it's clear that for him something essential to the professional game was lost in the 1990s. It may not be clear what Mr. Araton believes was lost, but it is clear to basketball historians what did appear as distinctive during the 1990s. A trickle of racial integration began in the early 1950s and by the early 1960s the top stars in the game were African American. By the early 1970s, the majority of NBA players were African American and, uncoincidentally, by the late 1970s, the mostly white fan base had lost interest in the NBA. The biracial and bicoastal duo of Earvin Johnson (African American, Los Angeles Lakers) and Larry Bird (Caucasian, Boston Celtics) entered the league in the fall of 1979 and began to revive its fortunes, a process that took off when new commissioner David Stern partnered with new superstar Michael Jordan (not to mention with Nike) in 1984 (Boyd; Rhoden; George; Thomas).

Professor Todd Boyd suggests that Jordan, born in 1963, was the last black NBA superstar to have been raised with a Civil Rights Era ethos of assimilation (16), which permitted him to project personal qualities appealing to white consumers as "race neutral" or universal (see also Rhoden 197–216; Andrews). By the mid-1990s, however, a generation of players raised in the urban disaster areas left in the wake of the unfulfilled promises of the 1960s (and aggravated by the 1980s policies of Ronald Reagan) were no longer interested in presenting images placating to whites. Boyd traces the lineage back to Kareem Abdul Jabbar's public conversion to Islam and refusal to play the gentle giant role in the early 1970s. But it's clear that the phenomenon he describes really takes hold in the 1990s when not only were the game's premier stars (and the vast majority of rosters) African Americans, but they—the face of this phenomena is Allen Iverson—unapologetically sported the symbols of poor, urban African American culture: hip hop music, tattoos, corn rows, baggy shorts, and trash talking (Boyd; Lane; Leonard).

Against this background, Mr. Araton's narrative begins to take on, like Professor Kretchmar's, a disturbing implication. In neither case do I mean to impute particular conscious attitudes to these writers. Rather, I wish to frame the implications I am drawing from their work as expressing a fantasy of the white basketball unconscious. Consider first that both narratives describe a tragedy: the purist game—though morally superior, and so through no fault or intrinsic deficiency of its own—cannot stand up to the easy thrills and crass showboating of the modernist game. Then recall that these putatively purely technical categories pertaining to style of play are moralized by these authors but also, within American basketball culture, saturated with racial associations. From that vantage point, what they appear to lament as the loss of "purity" (Professor Kretchmar) or "soul" (Mr. Araton) happens to coincide not only with the loss of white dominance at the highest levels of basketball culture, but with the carefree display of late-twentieth-century urban cultural signifiers by the game's premier players, African Americans raised in impoverished urban areas.

If already since the mid-1960s white America had craved and fashioned basketball Great White Hopes to compensate for the dominance of African American players in the game (Bill Bradley in the 1960s, Pete Maravich in the 1970s, Larry Bird in the 1980s), how much more desperately would such a figure be needed by the end of the 1990s, when Michael Jordan, with his racial "crossover" appeal, retired from the game? What is striking is that these historico-moral narratives of a contest between pure (white) basketball and contaminated (black) basketball culminate with the appearance of Manu Ginobili, who appears on the scene—in both cases—not to assert the superiority of one style of play over the other, but to obviate the debate by integrating the two styles of play in the body of one player. The problem, as I mentioned before, is that African American players had already successfully performed such an integration, and that this fact is obscured in these accounts by the light-skinned body of Manu Ginobili.

This fact slides Mr. Araton and Professor Kretchmar's interpretations unfortunately close to the grooves of a logic I doubt they intended. This logic first divides basketball into two styles, arranged hierarchically. One style is characterized as ontologically and historically prior and mor-ally superior, and associated culturally with whiteness. The other style is characterized as ontologically and historically secondary and morally dangerous and associated with blackness. As this first style is eclipsed in popularity in the United States by the second style, the white basketball unconscious looks abroad and finds there, first of all, light-skinned play-ers guarding the standard of the first style.

Both logics culminate with the discovery of Manu Ginobili, the light-skinned player, successful abroad and in the United States, who maintains the purity of the first style while garnering popularity by incorporating elements of the second. Now, to the degree that the figure of the Great White Hope has been the white body that—in the cultural fantasies of white Americans—stands for the entire nation, the fact that the white basketball unconscious had to import their latest Great White Hopes from abroad may say something about both the nation's diminishing centrality in the global order and about white Americans' willingness to adapt their unconscious fantasies to accommodate that diminishing cen-trality so long as it does not compromise the dominant position of white-ness. Simultaneously (and perhaps paradoxically), Manu—in the now globalized basketball culture of the United States—may be (secretly) the Greatest of the Great White Hopes for he is the Great White Hope who ends once and for all the need for a Great White Hope because he tran-scends the very antagonism—white game versus black game—that his-torically provoked white feelings of inferiority and the desire for a Great White Hope in the first place.

VIVEZA CRIOLLA, DECEPTION, AND THE ART OF THE GAME: THE MEANINGS OF MANU ON THE COURT

I've shown the disturbing racial implications of the way that Manu and his style have appeared as an international signifier in US basketball cul-ture. Among the problems attending this particular discursive version of Manu is what it obscures about his game on the floor, as well as all that a properly attentive close reading of his game on the floor might tell us about globalized basketball culture and its politics. As the beginning of a corrective to this and as a brief example of basketball criticism, I'd like now to offer a "close reading" of his game.

Watching Manu will likely leave you with the impression that, perhaps even more than his sound fundamental skills (purist), his raw athletic ability (modernist), or his integration of the two, what makes Manu remarkable and exciting is his improvisational creativity: his ability to make a successful play where there doesn't appear to be one. On first impression, Ginobili appears chaotic on the court. Almost constantly moving, he seems randomly to change speeds, with or without the ball. With the ball, he may throw himself headlong, seemingly out of control and against all sense, into a crowd of taller defenders near the basket. He seems to initiate particular moves or plays (e.g., a dribble between a defender's legs or a spin-move) without knowing how that beginning will resolve itself. Indeed, this chaotic unpredictability is what a number of his coaches, teammates, and opponents signal as Manu's standout characteristic: as what makes him next to impossible to defend, but also, sometimes, difficult to play with.

Without wishing to minimize the importance of this chaotic first impression or the genuinely improvisational character of Manu's style, I nonetheless want to point to several components of his style that appear with enough regularity as to suggest that they are practiced rather than devised on the spot. One might consider these as something like a partial catalogue of the "elements of Manu's style." It should perhaps not go without saying that all of these elements generate successful outcomes only because Ginobili also possesses excellent fundamental passing, shooting, and dribbling skills as well as physical abilities such as quickness, speed, leaping ability, and peripheral vision. That said, what makes Ginobili stand out, more than anything else, in my opinion, is the inventive way he combines the following elements (see table 12.2).

Ginobili combines these elements differently in response to the different situations that present themselves on the court and this, together with the fact that so many of the elements of his style involve change, helps to produce a kaleidoscopic impression of endless novelty. But, at a more elementary level, Ginobili's play actually consists of a rather limited repertoire that he employs with regularity. Overall, Manu's style involves deception through change and the appearance of vulnerability. In all the elements in table 12.2, Manu artfully generates a mistaken impression in his defender (that he is slowing down, that he is outnumbered, that he is out of control, that he is going right) and then exploits the inevitable erroneous reaction of the defender (however instantaneous) to create space in which to dribble, shoot, or pass to an open teammate. Manu seems almost to look for trouble only to always get out

Table 12.2 The elements of Manu Ginobili's style

Defender Sees:	Mutability			Vulnerability	
	Of speed	*Of direction*	*Of size*	*Bad judgment*	*Awkwardness*
What it is	With or without the ball, forward or laterally, rapid acceleration or deceleration	With or without the ball, of himself or of the ball, rapid alteration of the angle of attack	Rapid contraction or extension of his body	Attacking rather than avoiding a crowd of defenders	Presenting as off balance or out of control
How he does it	Some combination of lengthening or shortening his strides; speeding or slowing the pace of his strides, and if dribbling, pushing the ball to a spot further or closer to his own body	Multidirectional footwork, stepping one way with his right foot and then the opposite with his left; unorthodox ball handling techniques such as dribbling between his own legs or those of an opponent or moving or passing the ball around his back	Usually with the ball, shortens his steps, bends at the knees, hips, and waist, tucks his arms into his torso; or the reverse	With the ball, on the perimeter or near the basket, dribbles or leaps into a crowd	Through his left-handedness or through apparently arrythmic and mutlidirectional footwork or through unfamiliar contortions of his torso
What it does	Immobilizes defender by provoking hesitation	Immobilizes defender by provoking hesitation; forces defense to overplay one possible direction leaving another vulnerable to attack	Allows him to move through spaces defenders consider too cramped or closed entirely; may provoke defenders to diminish their own size or to extend their own size at the expense of mobility	Forces multiple defenders to guard him, leaving his teammates with a numerical advantage over the opponents; he also creates an appearance of vulnerability or futility, which can provoke a momentary relaxation on the part of defenders who consider the play completed	Presents unfamiliar physical shapes to defenders whose success depends partly on reacting reflexively to familiar situations, but he also, again, can generate instants of defensive relaxation

of it and transform what appears as inevitable constraint in the world around him—an opponent's dunk on a breakaway or a blocked path on offense—into the viral unstoppability of his own invention.

"We have," Gilles Deleuze once said, "to see creation as tracing a path between impossibilities...Creation takes place in bottlenecks" (133). To borrow a descriptive phrase from philosopher Nicholas Thoburn, Manu's game "operates in the 'cramped quarters' and 'impossible positions' of the 'small peoples' and 'minorities' who lack or refuse coherent identity" (44). Thoburn is actually paraphrasing Deleuze who was not, of course, talking about Manu. Deleuze was talking about what he called "minor politics," a term developed, in part, to recuperate what Marx disdained as the *lumpenproletariat*, referring to them as the "refuse of all classes," including "swindlers, confidence tricksters, brothel keepers, rag-and-bone merchants, and beggars" (83). Unlike the virtuous, hard-working, and productive members of the industrial working class, the cast-off trash of the *lumpenproletariat* were shifty and unproductive, lazy, trying to get something for nothing, politically unreliable, and deceitful. Perhaps rather than trying to think Manu's game in relation to the vexed American politics of race, it is more illuminating to think it in relation to class, specifically to the minor politics of the *lumpenproletariat*. I'm especially drawn to this when I consider the role of that class and its politics in Argentina around the time of Manu's debut.

Let me emphasize the where and when of Manu's debut: first, the FIBA championships in Indianapolis, Indiana—the symbolic heartland of so-called purist basketball, and second, the NBA, athletic emblem of untrammeled American corporate globalization at the dawn of the twenty-first century. And then, the when: 2002—just months after the most devastating economic crisis in Argentina's history and in the midst of the massive, subsequent political upheaval it provoked. That crisis, of course, was partly precipitated by the Argentine government's complicity with neoliberal economic policies originating in the United States, policies that, ironically, had facilitated the globalization of basketball and the NBA brand, leading, in turn, to the development of the game abroad, including in Manu's Argentina. In a very real way, the late 2001 crisis converted vast numbers of middle- and working-class Argentines into a contemporary *lumpenproletariat*.

At the same time, many of these individuals spontaneously organized themselves, not only to protest and not only to disrupt attempts to carry on business as usual, but also, as Marina Sitrin's beautiful volume *Horizontalism* documents, to form communities and networks of communities charged with providing education, health care, food, clothing, and social services. If Marx missed the political potential of the *lumpenproletariat*, Bakunin did not: he saw them as the "flower of the proletariat" (294) and believed, like Deleuze and Guattari after him, that those who were most alienated from the structures and values of power were in the best position to embody an alternative to the status quo—in much the same way that Manu relies upon the appearance of trouble to elude his defender, the way he uses the apparent inevitability of his own failure as a condition for his success.

There's a tradition of this in Argentina. A tradition, I mean, of radical, horizontal self-organizing that eludes wherever possible and by whatever means the apparatus of the state, and I mean the supposedly benevolent paternalist state as much as the nakedly repressive authoritarian state or the failed neoliberal state. But there's a tradition, also, I mean to point out, of crafty creativity in cramped spaces, of making something out of what seems like nothing. Hearing me talk about Manu's game, my wife connected it to "*viveza criolla.*" Jason Wilson speaks of viveza criolla in terms of "artful lying and cheating" and of the "*vivo,*" its practitioner, as "the improviser, the quick-fixer, the street-wise survivor" (34). Sometimes, these two traditions—the anarchist self-organizer and the crafty vivo—seem to wind together. Even what fans who don't like Manu don't like about his game—his "flopping," where he falls to the ground as if he's been fouled in order to deceive the referee into calling a foul on his opponent—expresses this quality.

In his 1974 *The Essence of the Game is Deception*, Leonard Koppett acknowledged that theoretically the goal of basketball is to throw the ball in the hoop, but adds that "on the real world, physical level," the game "boils down to getting good shots, and getting good shots boils down to deceiving the defense" (16). "So that," he concludes, "basketball is a game in which various types of fakes and feints, with head, hands, body, legs, eyes, are proportionately more important than in other games" (14). These are the kinds of physical actions Mr. Koppett has in mind when he says that the "essence of the game is deception." It's worth emphasizing that Mr. Koppett, by contrast with Professor Kretchmar and, to a lesser degree, Mr. Araton, eschews an idealizing Platonic scheme in identifying the distinguishing feature—"the essence"—of basketball. He seems to adopt instead—though without ever saying so—what I would characterize as an empiricist, materialist, and pragmatist approach.

He has clearly carefully observed what happens on the floor and he is trying to reverse engineer the game: to look at what *actually*—not what "ought" to happen, morally or otherwise—happens and imagine what sort of problems it solves, what sort of purpose it serves. In this sense, while deception is for him the essence of the game, it is a kind of immanent presence that expresses itself through myriad particular modes, subordinate aims, and complexly interrelated elements and forces that might play a much stronger role at any given moment than deception itself per se. The real essence of the game, for Mr. Koppett, can only to be found in an empirical, materialist, and pragmatist inquiry into what sorts of physical actions, in the course of real games, actually make it possible for one to succeed. Playing the game well, from this point of view, is not a matter of motive or morality, but rather of effectiveness in marrying actual physical play with the "theoretical goal" of throwing the ball into the hoop.

But if Mr. Koppett is pragmatic and materialist where other thinkers are idealist, this does not mean he is disinterested in moral—at least in the sense of "psychological"—or aesthetic questions. On the contrary, the first implication he draws from his assertion that deception is the essence of the game is a psychological one: that the game attracts individuals who enjoy deception; who are, as Koppett puts it, "poker" rather than "bridge minded" (19). Koppett does not claim that this sums up the totality of every basketball player's psyche; only that just as certain physical gifts draw on and are in turn reinforced by the particularities of a given sport, so that is also true of psychological propensities. In the case of basketball, it is a kind of delighted and delightful deception, a delight in deception—a viveza criolla—that basketball, what Pete Axthelm called "the city game"—whether in Bahia Blanca, in Brooklyn, or in Bloomington, Indiana—cultivates, attracts, and rewards. This is a tricky suggestion and probably indefensible if intended (or taken) to mean that all basketball players are intrinsically deceptive individuals. I believe it makes more sense to suggest that there is a mutually reinforcing feedback loop between the game of basketball and individual life experiences or cultural settings in which being on the wrong end of unequal relations of power make certain forms of deception inevitable for survival.

In addition to this psycho-moral implication, Mr. Koppett also derives an important aesthetic implication from the idea that deception is the essence of basketball: that "*style* attracts more attention in basketball than in other games" (19). Because a basket is always worth the same amount, and because there are so many in the course of a game, Koppett argues, "The peaks and valleys of spectator delight, therefore are reached as easily by awesome maneuver as by the mere fact of scoring: the dunk or 'stuff,' the high speed fast break, the blocked shot, a sequence of passes, fancy dribbling—all transcend sheer efficiency" (20). That is why, as he puts it, "any knowledgeable crowd will cheer louder for a fancy pass, behind the back, or through the legs, that *doesn't lead* to a score than it will for a *routine* basket. And an acrobatic shot that goes in is best of all" (20; emphasis added). Winning may still be what matters most, but it matters to a proportionally smaller degree than in other team sports. "In basketball," as Koppett puts it, "flair and style are less separable from result, and closer to the essence of the action, and the underlying logic of this attitude folds back over the subject of deception: style *is* deception, made visible" (20–21; emphasis added).

In asserting this implication, and not only in his empirically based, materialist, and pragmatically oriented method, Mr. Koppett distinguishes himself yet again from commentators such as Professor Kretchmar and Mr. Araton. Where both of these thinkers depend, even if only implicitly, on a hierarchized opposition between what is essence in basketball and what is mere appearance ("flashy and entertaining" in Professor Kretchmar's idiom), Mr. Koppett here refuses that opposition, declaring in effect that the essence of basketball is its appearance, and that this essence reaches its apex when it draws attention to itself in the form of style.

I would add one more implication to the two Mr. Koppett himself derives. If the essence of the game is deception, then I believe it is also the case that improvisation—I mean, experimentation on the fly (with its attendant risk of failure)—is likely to play a greater role in basketball. For, while certain deceptive moves can, should be, and are practiced by all successful basketball players, others are derived or developed through trial and error in the course of a single contest against a particular individual defender or team. A player who rigidly applied the same head fake, let us say, regardless of the observed tendencies of his opponent, would be unlikely to have much success and would, moreover, be guilty of a category mistake in substituting a particular manifestation of deception that has an indeterminate likelihood of success (that particular head fake) for a rigorously developed, finely tuned, and adaptable inclination toward deception that will generate whatever form circumstances require. Indeed, a large part of what is astonishing about basketball at its highest levels is the lightning speed at which players assess their rapidly changing circumstances and make successful perceptual, cognitive, and physical adjustments in response. Finally, this recognition of the importance to basketball of experimental improvisation allows us to appreciate the novel forms that appear in the game as well as the complex processes by which these forms are invented and transmitted before making their way into the "canon" of basketball lore.

It is not only that Mr. Koppett's framework for understanding basketball better accommodates Manu's style and those of other "poker-minded" players like him, be they from Argentina or Akron. It is also that from the vantage point of Mr. Koppett's framework—with pragmatic, experimental, stylistic deception at its core—we may offer a much more inclusive and accurate historical account of basketball culture, both in the United States and globally, than what is possible through the lenses offered by Professor Kretchmar or Mr. Araton. Of course, while such a perspective cannot by itself undo the material force of internalized ideologies like those unwittingly purveyed by Professor Kretchmar or Mr. Araton, to the degree that social history does shift in part through a shift in the stories we tell ourselves about that history, we would be foolish to underestimate and so deprive ourselves of the value of the histories of basketball that might be told from Mr. Koppett's point of view, as it were. In such a history, deception and style would not be degraded "supplements," wrongly associated with certain groups in order to exclude their members from some particular version of the game's history that is masquerading as universal, true, or morally superior. The manifold and ever-shifting shapes that deception as pragmatic means can take in myriad cultural settings and basketball situations would all be equally valid expressions of the sport.

Larry Bird's ball fake to lure a defender into the air before leaning in and under that airborne defender to get a shot off and draw a foul would be as much a part of the history of the game as Magic Johnson's looking to the left to freeze a defender before passing to the right on a fast break. Both players would thus be relieved of the limiting burdens of representing abstract, racialized pseudo-categories ("Indiana" or "white" or "playground" or "black"). Or, at the level of team play, four of Michael Jordan's 1986 Chicago Bulls' teammates clearing to one side of the floor to occupy their defenders with the (deceptive) threat that they may receive a pass for a shot, while Jordan utilizes his individual skills on the other side of the floor to beat his defender and get to the basket for a tomahawk dunk is as valid an expression of the essence of the game as a play by the 1970 New York Knicks in which all five players on the court are in constant motion and touch the ball before Bill Bradley swishes through a perfect 18-feet jump shot.

In such a history—and this is the case to the limited extent that Mr. Koppett actually offers such history in his volume—neither the race, nor the ethnicity, nor the nationality of players would be of primary importance by comparison with the means—especially the means of deception—they devise in order to put the ball through the hoop. At most, such a history would offer pragmatically oriented, materialist explanations for unusually preponderant correlations between certain means of deception and certain locales or cultural situations and the racial, ethnic, or national backgrounds of individual players executing those means of deception. Within a history like this, Manu takes his place, rightfully, as one of many superbly successful players—Caucasian, African American, Latino, Asian American, American, Argentine, Serbian, Spanish, rural, urban, and so on—who have understood and embodied the fact that in basketball, where the essence of the game is deception, there is no separating style from substance.

BIBLIOGRAPHY

Andrews, David L., ed. *Michael Jordan, Inc.: Corporate Sport, Media Culture, and Late Modern America*. Albany: SUNY Press, 2001.

Araton, Harvey. *Crashing the Borders: How Basketball Won the World and Lost Its Soul at Home*. New York: The Free Press, 2005.

Bakunin, Mikhail. *Bakunin on Anarchism*. Ed. Sam Dolgoff. New York: Black Rose, 1980.

Birrell, Susan, and Mary G. McDonald. "Reading Sport Critically: A Methodology for Interrogating Power." *Sociology of Sport Journal* 16 (1999): 283–300.

———, eds. *Reading Sport: Critical Essays on Power and Representation*. Lebanon, NH: Northeastern University Press, 2000.

Boyd, Todd. *Young, Black, Rich and Famous: The Rise of the NBA, the Hip Hop Invasion and the Transformation of American Culture*. New York: Doubleday, 2003.

Buckley, Tim. "Cry for U.S., Argentina." *Deseret News*. September 5, 2002. Sports, p. D01.

Deleuze, Gilles. "Mediators." *Negotiations: 1972–1990*. Trans. Martin Joughin. New York: Columbia University Press, 1995. 121–134.

Durkin, Duff. "Closing the Gap: American Losses at Worlds Were Simply Inevitable." *Washington Times*. September 6, 2002. Sports, p. C01.

"Eliot against Basket Ball." *New York Times*. November 28, 1906.

Feigen, Jonathan. "Head Scratcher: World Championships Fiasco Has U.S. Seeking Remedies." *Houston Chronicle*. September 9, 2002. Sports, p. 2.

FreeDarko Presents the Undisputed Guide to Pro Basketball History. New York: Bloomsbury, 2010.

George, Nelson. *Elevating the Game: Black Men and Basketball*. Lincoln: University of Nebraska Press, 1999.

Greco, Ariel. "Un triunfo memorable logrado con entrega y coraje." *Página12*. September 8, 2002.

Isaacs, Neil D. *All the Moves: A History of College Basketball*. New York: Harper, 1984.

Koppett, Leonard. *The Essence of the Game is Deception: Thinking about Basketball*. Boston: Little, Brown, and Company, 1974.

Kretchmar, R. Scott. "Basketball Purists: Blind Sentimentalists or Insightful Critics." *Basketball and Philosophy: Thinking Outside the Paint*. Edited by Jerry L. Walls and Gregory Bassham. Lexington: University of Kentucky Press, 2008. 31–43.

Lane, Jeffrey C. *Under the Boards: The Cultural Revolution in Basketball*. Lincoln: University of Nebraska Press, 2007.

Leonard, David J. *After Artest: The NBA and the Assault on Blackness*. Albany: SUNY Press, 2012.

Ludden, Johnny. "Street Savvy: Ginobili's Flashy Style of Play Belies Argentine Roots." *San Antonio Express-News*. February 2, 2005. Sports, p. 1C.

Marx, Karl. *The 18th Brumaire of Louis Bonaparte*. Trans. Daniel Deleon. Chicago: Kerr, 1913.

Naismith, James. *Basketball: Its Origins and Development*. Introduction by William J. Baker. Lincoln: University of Nebraska Press, 1996.

Panno, Juan José. "Nosotros ya lo dijimos." *Página12*. September 8, 2002.

Peterson, Robert W. *Cages to Jump Shots: Pro Basketball's Early Years*. Lincoln: University of Nebraska Press, 2002.

Pomerantz, Gary M. *Wilt, 1962: The Night of 100 Points and the Dawn of New Era*. New York: Three Rivers, 2005.

Rail, Geneviève, ed. *Sport and Postmodern Times*. Albany: SUNY Press, 1998.

Rhoden, William C. *Forty Million Dollar Slaves: The Rise, Fall, and Redemption of the Black Athlete*. New York: Three Rivers Press, 2006.

Rushin, Steve. "The Ecstasy of Defeat." *Sports Illustrated*. September 16, 2002.

Sitrin, Marina, ed. *Horizontalism: Voices of Popular Power in Argentina*. Oakland, CA: AK, 2006.

Thoburn, Nicholas. *Deleuze, Marx, and Politics*. New York: Routledge, 2003.

Thomas, Ron. *They Cleared the Lane: The NBA's Black Pioneers*. Lincoln: University of Nebraska Press, 2004.

Thomsen, Ian. "Man of the Worlds." *Sports Illustrated*. September 9, 2002.

Wilson, Jason. *Buenos Aires: A Cultural History*. Northampton, PA: Interlink, 2007.

CHAPTER 13

Latino Soccer, Nationalism, and Border Zones in the United States

Juan Poblete

This essay is part of a broader exploration of the internalization of what I call border zones, *inside* the United States and *beyond* the geographical borderlands. My general hypothesis is that some of the spatial and subjective dynamics that have dominated both the militarization of the physical border and the "maquilization" of the productive process, as well as the hybridization and contact among languages and cultures in the border regions, are reproduced in a postsocial context, in the daily lives of migrants and Americans well beyond the geographical borders. A new regime of sociality is thus in place, organizing and affecting the bodies and experiences of migrants and nonmigrants in the United States by differentially mobilizing their fears and insecurities. These border zones include the urban corner where day laborers seek work, the agricultural field where many immigrants find their mode of subsistence, and the backstage of restaurants where they perform the heavy tasks involved in food production.

In the United States, the soccer field is one special example of such internalized border zones. In it, the physical bodies of the Latino players—which in other internal border zones are both what is most visible and must be invisibilized in order to separate pure labor from the body that sustains it, and what is most productive but has to be disposed of when in excess—become central to a form of border zone encounter that is often Pan-Latino but as often interethnic and interracial. Using available ethnographies of nonprofessional Latino soccer playing in the United States I hope to illuminate the sociocultural dynamics of this form of internalized border zone (Poblete, "Productividad"; "Americanism/o"). In order to do that I will first explore the location of soccer in the American cartography connecting sports and the nation. Second, I will describe the practice of soccer by immigrants as an internalized border zone in the United States. Finally, I will examine the link between relative degrees of social incorporation and the practice of soccer at the high school level.

SOCCER, ALTERNATIVE SUBJECTS, AND US NATIONAL SPORTS

Any review of the literature on sports and nationalism makes clear that sports can be a way of creating a national community that is inclusive and accepting of others, that is, that others can be invited to play the game we play and to play in the way we play it. Sports can also be or perhaps are always simultaneously, as it is clear in the previous formulation, a way of imposing on others the obligation to play *our* games in *our* style, that is, the practice of the sport and the liking of the sport can become the mandatory test a foreigner other must pass in order to be considered properly assimilated: "The implicit expectation that immigrants can and should join in the sporting activities preferred by other Canadians may be held with an intensity that acts to blur the line between hospitality and expectations of assimilation" (Dyck 110).

Along these lines, the American preference for its national sports can be seen as strongly influenced by political and ideological claims to exceptionalism. American football and baseball can as a consequence become "games which are manifestly, proudly, even aggressively American" (Allison 344). As in the Canadian example earlier, the practice of these specific sports becomes, for natives and immigrants alike, a point of identification and/or a sign of having chosen or embraced assimilation into the nation. Conversely, how American could soccer playing be? What kind of American subject plays soccer instead of the national sports? Two of these subjects have historically been immigrants and, more recently, women.

When it comes to immigrants and soccer in the United States there are a number of paradoxes that are worth exploring. For instance, in the United States the national sports are more connected to cities and regions than to the nation itself via a national team competing in the international arena. So, while they have many of the nationalizing characteristics of modern sports, they do so more by looking inwardly than outwardly. American football and baseball, two of the three big sports, have not lent themselves easily to international competitions in which the whole country would rally behind a national team. So it has been through the Olympics and minor, mostly less-commercial and less popular sports such as track and field that national emotions have been historically connected to international sports contexts (Bairner 113). Moreover, soccer has been a sport that has suffered two denationalizing effects in the American context. While the past three decades have seen a significant and perhaps unparalleled expansion of the practice of soccer, this has come by way of two nontraditional means. First, the professional Major League Soccer and its antecedents have had significant and longlasting difficulties establishing themselves as viable corporate-style organizations, successfully attached to local or city-based franchises, but have been very successful at spreading the practice of the game itself among nonprofessional athletes through youth programs. Therefore, soccer in the United States has emerged historically as a heavily practiced amateur sport with serious difficulties turning itself into a professional commercial spectacle. Second, soccer has spread throughout the United States by way of two nontraditional actors in the American context: women and immigrants. Both of them highlight, from the viewpoint of the dominant national perspective on sports, the un-American nature of soccer. It has been seen in this light as a noncompetitive, commercially nonviable sport for women and for unassimilated immigrants. Those associations go against the city-based, corporate driven, highly competitive, and hypermasculine nature of American sports. However, it would be more accurate to say that due to its particular cultural association with white women and immigrants, soccer may be simultaneously the site of two contradictory processes. One highlights the degrees of racial and class separation of the suburbs, where soccer is king among youth. This process connects whiteness and soccer in the context of newly defined racialized and class-based nationalisms. The other underscores minor forms of emerging alternative cosmopolitanisms. Both processes meet and sometimes clash on the soccer field and in the stands. Soccer, then, has been simultaneously a form of relative inclusion (with regards to women and immigrants), a form of significant exclusion (with regards to African Americans, much more heavily represented in the traditional American sports), and a practice of self-segregation (as in white suburban flight from the urban centers).

Thus:

> Unquestionably, the racial signifiers contained within popular basketball [a fearful national fantasy involving both a fascination with the power of the black male body and its corresponding fear that it may be applied to crime and violence] (and, to a lesser extent American football) discourse have, in opposition, influenced soccer's symbolic location within the contemporary popular imaginary. In spatial (urban/suburban), racial (white/ black), and corporal (cerebral/physical) senses, soccer became the [white] antithesis of [black] basketball. (Andrews et al. 211)

The ascendancy of soccer in the suburbs was also due to its perceived capacity to foster the right to the practice of sports in a noncompetitive environment, incorporating millions of women into a healthy and self-forming activity. In the post-1960s, newly defined social ethos, manifested in the passing of Title IX and the multiple waves of feminism, soccer became an ideal sport: "Within this climate of increased gender awareness and activity in the realm of sport, and emerging as it was in the shadow of American football's physical and symbolic chauvinism, soccer assumed the mantle of the gender-inclusive American sport *par excellence*" (Andrews et al. 209).

Paradoxically, the degree of integration of women's sports attained via soccer in the suburbs came at the expense of urban blacks kids. Together, these two dynamics clearly mapped out, spatially, a new racializing and exclusionary process connected to the practice of sports: "Thus as with other manifestations of the middle-class suburban habitus, soccer is nonchalantly, if unwittingly, experienced and advanced as a compelling, popular euphemism for both class and race superiority" (Andrews et al. 215).

In correctly and convincingly pointing to the racialized spatial dynamics of suburban US soccer, Andrews et al.—following a long tradition of American sociology written in black and white—completely forget about the presence and significance of Latinos in and for the practice and meaning of soccer in the country (and for race relations, more generally). Soccer has been a racialized practice not just for white suburban youth but very significantly, and increasingly, for millions of Latinos, immigrants and US-born alike. The impact of their sport habits should not be underestimated when trying to understand the symbolic place of soccer in the national imaginary and the significance of the cultural practices of millions of Latinos and non-Latino US populations.

Soccer should also be seen as potentially developing forms of emerging alternative cosmopolitanisms. In their highly influential volume on soccer in the United States, Markovits and Hellerman, for example, state:

> While soccer fosters highly national sentiments and identities, it also offers an international language of communication and an international code that is truly binding and bonding. None of the hegemonic American sports offers either of these sentiments. American sports neither engender a deep sense of nationalism nor provide a genuine forum for internationalism. They remain confined to a world of their own. (43)

The supposed failure of soccer in the United States would have, for Markovits and Hellerman, an explanation in American exceptionalism, and the self-contained, inward-looking forms of sports nationalisms generated by its three main sports: American football, baseball, and basketball. Reflecting on their conclusion, Sandra Collins, in yet another example of the invisibility of Latinos for traditional American sociology, remarks: "America may be in the World, but the World is not in America. That is to say, the flows of global culture may emanate from the United States, but rarely do the flows from abroad make a deep impact on the psyche of American culture" (358).

"Rarely" only if you do not consider the presence and cultural practices of 50 million Latinos in the country. If, even in global times, American exceptionalism may explain the "failure" of soccer in the United States, it is other aspects of globalization—the massive migration of Latinos in the last four decades, their recreational practices here, and their technologically enabled cultural attachments to their countries of origin (including soccer leagues)—that help explain both its current ascendancy and built-in limitations. "The world that actually is in America" has thus struggled to make itself visible and viable as an actor without becoming hypervisible and liable as a target. In mostly Sunday ceremonies (since many players work six days a week), the ritual of soccer as a form of both intraethnic nationalism and pluriethnic cosmopolitan encounter has been unfolding for decades in the border zones of the soccer field and its surroundings, all across the country.

IMMIGRANT SOCCER AS BORDER ZONE

Anthropologist Keith Kleszynski credits soccer league participation in San Diego County by what he calls "Mexicano migrants" with maintaining social networks and producing a form of cultural visibility that furthers those networks and contacts. In his view, migrant-heavy soccer leagues are examples of community networks that "help both the new migrant and the existing citizenry of the United States by creating safe and secure places" and providing and concentrating resources. Such a soccer community "shortens the transitional period between being a new migrant and established community member" (42). In a cosmopolitan vision and wish, Kleszynski adds: "Perhaps the future of fully integrating disparate ethnic communities lies in the formation of inter-cultural fútbol leagues where the game brings disparate groups of people, such as US natives and Mexicano migrants into contact" (44).

This vision partially describes the self-imposed brokering task that Tim Wallace, another anthropologist, accepted for himself for more than a decade. Wallace helped create La Liga de Raleigh (LLR) in Raleigh, North Carolina, and solved this community's most difficult challenge: access to good and authorized soccer fields. Wallace describes one aspect of my own conceptualization of soccer as a border zone by using a similar category:

> The concept of the "borderzone" [here, borrowing from tourism studies] works for the soccer field because people from many different nations, cultures, and communities come together to participate in the international sport they love and then return to their (often) segregated living spaces. At the soccer field, congregants (including players, referees, and fans) are equal in their fervor and commitment and this forms the potentiality for learning about each other and understanding each other's differences. ("Soccer Wars" 65)

In what migration studies analysts have called "El Nuevo South," and more specifically in the so-called Triangle of Raleigh-Durham-Chapel Hill, there are, according to Wallace, 20 adult Hispanic soccer leagues, each with 15–40 teams, and around 90 Latino leagues operating in the state of North Carolina. While most of Wallace's article is devoted to a detailed ethnographic account—an account of the many players (government, media, nonprofit organizations, migrants) and dimensions involved and their frictions (a contrast between traditional American models of not-for-profit civil society sports organization striving to provide noncompetitive recreation and a Mexican model based on for-profit, cacique-style personalist administration, and highly competitive playing)—his conclusion is clearly within what I have called here the cosmopolitan vein: "The soccer borderzone is one in which the love for the game still enables long-term residents and newcomers alike to find common ground for building strong and lasting relationships" ("Soccer Wars" 76).

The soccer field can also be thought of as a special internalized border zone in at least two additional and distinctive regards. First, as a theater for the performance of a very special version of the nation as ritual in times of globalization. There are two kinds of such performances in the United States depending on whether the national US team plays a Latino or a non-Latino rival. If the rival is non-Latino often many if not most of the fans who cheer the United States from the stands are Latinos, and they wave both their own national flags and the American one. If the rival is Latino, and especially if the rival is Mexico, the American national team frequently finds itself playing in the United States, in Los Angeles or New York, as if it were the visiting team. This is another form of the soccer field as an internalized border zone. Here, the geographical coordinates give way to one of the most obvious manifestations of the actual shape of globalization in the country, "the world that actually is in America." The logic of business and the logic of patriotism clash as it becomes obvious that, often, the only or the surest way to fill a big stadium for a US soccer team is through the massive participation of Latinos (especially immigrants). Unsurprisingly, the turning of the tables that the collective muscle of the Latino multitude represents regularly ends up being, in the dominant public sphere, both another sign of the foreignness of soccer as a mass sport in the United States and a confirmation of the intractable so-called immigration problem.

Brian Straus provides a good example in 2011:

> Shortly after leaving Los Angeles International Airport, drivers headed northeast toward Pasadena's Rose Bowl pass a billboard promoting a beer to the left. It features the soccer team that is, by far, the most popular in Southern California—Mexico.
>
> On Saturday night, the championship of North America, Central America and the Caribbean will be determined on American soil. But that soil will offer no advantage to the U.S. national team, whose fans will be drowned out by the loud, passionate majority filling a sold-out Rose Bowl for the CONCACAF Gold Cup final.

This paradox was confirmed after the game in the words of a *Los Angeles Times* reporter: "It was imperfectly odd. It was strangely unsettling. It was uniquely American. On a balmy early Saturday summer evening, the U.S. soccer team played for a prestigious championship in a U.S. stadium [...] and was smothered in boos" (Plaschke).

A fan made explicit two of the contrasting affects that coexist in this sports ritual: "'I love this country, it has given me everything that I have, and I'm proud to be part of it,' said Victor Sanchez (*sic*), a 37-year-old Monrovia resident wearing a Mexico jersey. 'But yet, I didn't have a choice to come here, I was born in Mexico, and that is where my heart will always be'" (Plaschke).

So when it comes to Mexico playing the United States in a soccer match, Sánchez joins thousands of Latinos in cheering for the so-called visiting team. At the game mentioned earlier, while the official attendance was 93,420, it was estimated that some 80,000 fans rooted for Mexico.

Rubén Navarrete, a Mexican American journalist writing for CNN, expressed well the mainstream's and his own anger and confusion at what had happened at the Rose Bowl that evening when Mexico came back from 2–0 down to win 4–2: "Let's face it. Most Americans couldn't care less about soccer. Until, that is, a group of foreign nationals who presumably live in this country boo the U.S. team, disrespect the national anthem, and wave the flag of the nation they left behind. Then we care a whole lot."

Referring to Victor Sánchez, the fan quoted in the *LA Times* article, Navarrete concluded: "Most Americans hear a quote like that and they get confused. I'm confused—and a little angry. As someone who was born in the United States to parents who were born in the United States, I don't understand how you can 'love' one country if you've already given your heart to another."

First, then, the US national team's games, and professional soccer in general in the United States, are often a reminder of how deeply "the world [...] actually is in America," that is, the new global conditions of the American experience (including the experience of nationalism). Moreover, the commercial dependence of US soccer on immigrants as spectators and consumers highlights a paradox whereby the only way for soccer to become a viable American sport spectacle in the manner signaled by football, basketball, and baseball goes through the seemingly un-American immigrant population. This national discomfort is not new in a global postcolonial context: in 1990 a British Tory politician suggested in an interview that "Britain impose ' a cricket test' on migrants: 'Which side do they cheer for?' would sort out whether South Asians in England watching the local side play Pakistan or India had adequately assimilated" (Miller 24).

The second additional form in which the soccer field can be conceptualized as an internalized border zone in the United States has to do with the massive playing practice of millions of Latino immigrants and nonimmigrants and many US born non-Latinos. Contrary to most of the internalized border zones I consider elsewhere, the field as a space for the practice of soccer by nonprofessional athletes is defined by its ritualized nature, which separates it from the normal conventions organizing daily life. As Elias and Dunning remind us, the role of sports in society is to serve as socially regulated outlets for "instinctual, affective and emotional impulses. All societies provide some kind of emotional counterbalance for the constraints of everyday life" (Giulanotti 151). This is nowhere more true than in the case of pick-up and league games involving mixed populations of immigrants and nonimmigrants. Here the Latino worker enters a twilight zone in which his or her normal disposition, defined by what I have called the postsocial situation in the United States ("Productividad"; "Americanism/o"), can be joyously replaced by a much freer habitus.

While a postsocial dynamic of insecurity and fear in everyday life prevails in the regular working time of Latino day laborers at the city corner, fieldworkers in agriculture, and backstage restaurant cooks and dishwashers, in the soccer field the social game is redefined. Everybody, at least temporarily, belongs with equal rights within the borders of this social space, the rules apply equally to all players of the game. Even more so, the immigrant is often endowed with a form of accumulated skill or bodily capital that makes him or her a particularly endowed player. Here the worker, often used to being patronized or abused by exploitative bosses, regains a degree of control and can, sometimes, literally, call the shots. In this regard, it may be useful to remember that the body of the worker, not as a subject but as pure productive labor, is precisely the site in which the action of global capitalism is applied to and felt with the highest intensity. This body is routinely racialized and discriminated against and thus, because of that social mark, it becomes a highly productive and efficient (i.e., highly exploitable) machine for postsocial capitalism. It is that same body, but now as free bodily capital (soccer skills) along with the playful subject it partially constitutes, that engages in soccer as ritual in a new social scenario. Here, like in many ritualized performances, the rules of the world are, at least for the duration of the ritual, bracketed and replaced by clearer, more fair, or understandable ones. The world is reenchanted, and a symbolic renegotiation of the status of the subject-body seems and feels possible.

This does not mean that the soccer field becomes a completely liberated or utopian space. In fact, oftentimes, the space itself, the soccer field, is the first contentious issue: who has access, who has rights to its use, and what are its legitimate (or traditional) uses? What it does mean, however, is that, once access to it is acquired, the field has been significantly leveled for all playing.

Most of my analysis has, up to this point, occurred along predictable masculine gender lines. Nevertheless, the practice of soccer, as mentioned earlier, has been greatly developed by women's involvement in the sport and by the world leading position of the US women's team. In fact, a significant paradox of the relative feminization of the practice of soccer in the United States is that, while its originating ethos was noncompetitive, it generated the only US national soccer squad that was not just competitive but actually dominant in the international context (including the FIFA and Olympic levels). However, it is clear that when it comes to Latino immigrants the soccer field as a playing space has been mostly a masculine affair. In fact, in an analysis of social networks and relative degrees of incorporation by gender within a Maya community in Houston, Jacqueline Maria Hagan highlights how the concentration of women in domestic in-house labor, but also their lack of access to the possibilities of contact and exchange with others in voluntary associations, including soccer leagues, common for their male counterparts, limits their ability to find crucial information for legalization and jobs and their chances of accessing available resources. According to Hagan, the Maya men often enjoy the networking benefits of a male-centered leisure sociability through soccer. The latter, for example, regularly functioned for these men as a space to learn how to fill out legalization and employment paperwork.

Juan Acevedo, in a cross-cultural and comparative analysis of the lei-sure activities among Mexicans in Guerrero and Guerrero immigrants in the United States, also mentions how participation in soccer breaks allowed some overexploited Chicago-based workers, especially younger ones, a form of relief from working schedules of ten or more hours a day. This was also often an affirmation of their Mexican masculinity, as leisure activities were the almost exclusive preserve of men. However, Acevedo also mentions in passing how family outings and picnics often included a soccer pick-up and some shared drinking across genders. He concludes proposing that policy developments targeting the leisure needs of these immigrants should consider the family oriented nature of many of their recreational practices. While recognizing the gendered nature of the practice of soccer, Keith Kleszynski was quick to point out that "this did not mean that women were not socially networking on the sidelines" and that "some women were also food vendors" (44). If soccer as weekly ritual takes place on Sunday, because it is the only free day for the male soccer players and workers, this weekend ceremony also includes the par-ticipation of many other actors:

> [Sunday] is also a time when families can get together and eat traditional foods sold by Hispanic vendors, eating lunch or snacking. Some of the vendors bring a tent and put tables under the tent so that the fans can eat there out of the sun. Some of the vendors drive *loncheras* (lunch trucks). There are also *paleteros*, popsicle and ice cream vendors, selling from a push cart. (Wallace, "Soccer Wars" 73)

Significant ethnographic work remains to be done to understand the complex cultural dynamics involving what one could call "the other soc-cer moms," not the upper-middle class, suburban, white women shut-tling their kids to weekend meets, but the poor Latina working moms, hoping to spend some time with their families on their only day off.

High School-based Soccer and American Socialization

There is one more site of interest here, perhaps the most important for the future of the sport in the country and for its potential capacity to function as adaptive mechanism in the contact-zones, where traditional American practices meet the needs and aspirations of new and old Latino popula-tions. I am referring to the high school level. This scenario is particularly relevant because the Latino population in the United States is overwhelm-ingly young. Of the close to 50 million Hispanic residents in the country in 2009, 18 million were under 19 years of age, that is, 36 percent of them (by comparison, of the 200 million whites (non-Hispanic), 47 million or

23.5 percent were under 19 years old) (US Census). In California, 2010 Census figures indicate that there were as many Latinos as whites overall in the state—51 percent of California Latinos are under 18 years of age (by comparison, 27 percent of whites are under 18) (Morello and Balz).

Another factor that makes the high school context particularly important are academic regulations. In order to play at this level a player-student must comply with certain minimal academic and social standards. Given Latino students' high dropout and low national graduation rates, high school soccer can become an incentive to remain in school and a point of entry into the American social system.

The final section of this chapter will then refer to three books that will allow a more detailed exploration of US soccer practice as a border zone in the high school context. They are Paul Cuadros's *A Home in the Field: How One Championship Team Inspires Hope for the Revival of Small Town America* (2006), Sam Quinones's *Antonio's Gun and Delfino's Dream: True Tales of Mexican Migration* (2007), and Steve Wilson's *The Boys from Little Mexico: A Season Chasing the American Dream* (2010).

Paul Cuadros—a Peruvian American journalist, now a professor at UNC-Chapel Hill—devoted more than three years to coaching the Jordan Matthews High soccer team in Siler City, North Carolina. Like the rest of the state in the past 15 years, the town, which is in the middle of an industrial zone for poultry processing, has seen a very significant influx of Latino workers many of them undocumented. This massive population displacement and labor force change have been described as configuring the New Latino South or Nuevo South. This transnationalization of rural spaces involves a demographic change that went from 580,000 Latinos in the South in 1990 to a fourfold increase to 2.6 million by 2006 (Popke 244). Some of these workers or their sons played on Cuadros's team.

Originally Cuadros had come to Siler City to write a book about migrant workers in the poultry industry in what he calls "emerging Latino communities in the rural South" (12). The meat-packing and poultry industries are two of the engines pulling migrants into new rural territories. They have high turnover ("as high as 100% a year. These plants literally chewed up and spat workers out" [11]) and most of those workers were documented and undocumented Latinos ("a highly pliable labor force" [11]) But out of Sunday boredom, Cuadros started coaching, first, a team of white ten year olds, and then, realizing that those kids had no contact with the Latino kids in the area and the latter had no chance of playing the sport competitively, he decided to create a relatively competitive and integrated team for a tournament. In Cuadros's words: "I decided to bring these two worlds together on a special 'challenge' team [...] I wanted the parents from both groups to get to know one another [...] I had come to realize how segregated the communities were" (20).

When the tournament was over, given that the Latino kids would not have the option their white peers would of continuing on to expensive club leagues, Cuadros decided to create an unheard of soccer team at Jordan Matthews (JM) High School in Siler City, which most of the Latino kids attended.

The obstacles to be overcome were multiple. They included the racial tensions already affecting the town and the fact that nobody other than the Latino workers on their day off had ever played the sport in the town. Important too was the absence of a soccer field. The space, literally and metaphorically, would have to be argued and struggled for, mixing courage and persuasion:

> Siler City was a football town, it was not a soccer town, and many wanted to keep it that way. Soccer was seen by the longtime residents as yet another imposition on the traditional Southern way of life. Latinos had already "taken over" parts of the local park with their game. For some a line had to be drawn around the football field at JM. There would be no soccer there. (27)

These literal turf wars are part of the broader territorial wars and negotiations over parks and spaces that Latinos are engaged in across the country. In describing the difference between the highly extended informal practice of soccer in Latin American parks compared to the much higher regulation of sports spaces in the United States, Santamaría reports that in many parks in California there are signs that say "No Soccer" and sometimes, more explicitly, "This game is not American" (294). Such turf wars are also a reminder of why it is important to consider space and spatialized dynamics as a crucial component of sociocultural analysis. Internalized border zones are characterized by these spatial tensions and defined by the same basic impossibility of the neoliberal capitalist dream: labor does not exist in a pure state, as sheer labor power in a vacuum. Instead, it always depends on the physical bodies and lives of real life workers: "The white power structure in the town was being challenged by fast migration. Its members didn't know how to handle it. They needed the Latino workers to man the chicken plants and keep their economy going, but they didn't necessarily want the people or their children to live with them and share resources" (41).

One of their answers was to invite former Ku Klux Klan leader David Duke to visit the town. Duke's complaints that "this massive migration is changing [...] the face of America, and it will transform America into something alien to the principles and the values of the founding fathers" (quoted in Cuadros 52) was nothing new to his supporters or detractors. The broader reaction of Latinos in Siler City and their community allies is best captured in the riveting PBS documentary *Matters of Race*.

In that context, and having won his discussion with JM's principal about potential interest among students in the practice of soccer in a football town, Cuadros set out to first recruit, then keep, and finally train his players. As expected: "There were more than thirty boys— all Latino except for two—on that first day" (69). Selecting, keeping, and training the students were not easy. The main hurdles were three: eligibility requirements, labor demands, and family and financial instability. The academic performance requirements to participate in high school soccer (passing 75 percent of the previous year's classes, attending 85 percent of class meetings, missing no more than 14 school days without an excuse) are relatively simple to comply with for white middle-class students but much more complicated for working-class Latinos, as Cuadros's book shows. The next challenges were the demands of work: "Work was very important to these kids. Most had jobs or were looking for them. Work defined who they were" (76). Finally, many faced uncertainties in their family situations. During the course of their three seasons together, some of Cuadros's players had to leave for Mexico and cross back through the desert illegally, and some tore their knee ligaments while having no health insurance. An additional obstacle was the kids' disciplinary and sports behavior: "So much of their lives had already been spent getting around rules [...] Many of them owed their presence in North Carolina to deceit. Their parents worked with *chuecos*, fake documents [...] They lived in two different worlds with two different identities" (84).

The biggest obstacle was, however, racism and the general resistance at JM and the other schools to having a soccer team composed mostly of poor, immigrant Latino kids. During their very first official game visiting the neighboring South Stanly High School, Cuadros's players complained that "white players had been taunting them, saying things like 'Stupid Mexicans,' or 'Go back to Mexico,' and the usual 'Bunch of wetbacks'" (86). The parents and fans did not fare much better: "They yelled terrible things from the stands to the players on the field. 'Go back to Mexico!' and 'We're going to call the INS' and my personal favorite, 'Hey, give that kid a green card, not a yellow card'" (87).

At their third annual try, Cuadros's JM Jets won the state championship. In the process, they helped changed the culture of the town and, more importantly for future players, the institutional culture at their school. Right before their last game for the championship, Cuadros took these kids—many of whom had internalized racist prejudices about

Latinos not belonging in a school—to the school gymnasium's Hall of Champions. He wanted to show them that

> nowhere on the wall of champions were there any students who looked like my team. [...] I had started the team for a number of reasons—to give these kids a chance to play, to keep them in school, to give them a shot at college, but there was one motivating factor that burned in my mind more than any other: the wall. (243)

From that moment on, as one of the student-players put it, they all understood "that our people can be champions. That we can be great. This was history for us. We were making our mark in Siler City for the first time" (244).

A similarly encouraging and sobering high school soccer story is told by Sam Quinones in *Antonio's Gun and Delfino's Dream. True Tales of Mexican Migration* (2007). The book includes an extended piece titled "A Soccer Season in Southwest Kansas." It chronicles the 2003 campaign of an all-male, almost exclusively immigrant varsity soccer team at Garden City High School. Garden City, population 29,000, is a western Kansas town whose demographics have been radically altered in the past few decades. Like the poultry operations in Siler City, and for similar social and labor reasons, the engine behind this transformation, which has brought in a significant number of Mexican and Central American workers, has been the industrialization of meat processing.

Like Cuadros, Joaquin Padilla, the Mexican American coach of the Garden City Buffaloes, initially spent significant time trying to convince the school's administration that soccer was worth supporting as a way of retaining and helping immigrant students. Here both Quinones and Padilla see two strong connections between soccer and the nation. First, as a sport practice, soccer could develop personality traits that were historically important in the moral constitution of the United States. Second, soccer reveals some of the contradictions and tensions embedded in the new American landscape:

> In the Unites States, soccer fulfilled the mission of student athletics in a way that football and basketball often didn't anymore. Those sports, in fact, tended to teach Old World lessons: that your behavior has fewer consequences if you belong to a privileged elite. In the United States soccer was assiduously ignored and was, therefore, more egalitarian. [...] A high-school soccer season in the High Plains heartland where football was king would afford glimpses of America, of the Mexico within it, and of what had become of the country's melting pot. (227)

Some of the most crucial of these transformations have to do with the impact of economic restructuring and the subsequent globalization of labor affecting Mexico, Central America, and the United States. In revolutionizing meat processing, the Iowa Beef Processors—one of the United States' largest beef processors and packers, now IBP and a Tyson Food company—had not simply transformed the supply chain for meat in the United States, but also radically altered working and social relations: "They'd also ended butcher unions and brought millions of Mexican immigrants to the heartland" (Quinones 232). The new meat plant workers and their families, constituting now more than half the population of Garden City, had brought with them their love for soccer. These new working-class Latino high school kids confronted the same challenges their peers in North Carolina had to overcome: "Some students' poor English held them back; others were academically ineligible. Just as often, though, Latino students suffered from feelings of inferiority" (226).

In a school of two thousand students, more than half of them Latinos, soccer was a poor relative to football. The latter enjoyed official school and parental support, played in its own stadium, and granted popularity to its players, while "on campus soccer was considered low class" (239), "played on a nondescript field [...] a mile away" (240), without lights, scoreboard, or dressing rooms. The stage was, then, set for what has emerged as one of the defining rhetorical tropes of high-school soccer literature: a highly spatialized social struggle showing how America changes under the twin pressures of global economic restructuring and immigration. Soccer as practice and the soccer field as a space become the overdetermined arena of a national drama involving football versus soccer, white middle-class parents and administrators versus Latino immigrant parents and coaches, white students versus Latino students, and socially and racially segregated places versus spaces that are more representative of the community's actual diverse composition: "at Garden City the inequality in the two sports simply magnified the town's class and racial differences. The recognition of football reflected the class of the kids who played it. [...] As Rey Ramirez put it, 'Their parents own farms and cattle feed yards. Our parents work for their parents'" (241).

But as drama, this narrative always involves a second act in which things begin to change and soccer emerges, quite literally, as one of the social spaces that can provide social and school recognition, and positive visibility to both the Latino soccer player-students engaged in the practice of the sport and their immigrant parents. Eventually, the school paid for a new artificial turf that could accommodate both football and soccer in one stadium. Quinones fully understood the important social transformation inscribed in this new space:

> White and yellow lines now traced the limits of both sports, creating a chaotic geometry across the emerald field. Football had made way for

soccer in the cattle country of southwest Kansas. At Garden City High School [...] the field seemed a lot like the heartland nowadays: a place that had once been simple and homogenous was now a bit more complicated, maybe a bit more interesting. (275–276)

In closing, Quinones highlights two challenges high school soccer in Garden City faces. They both connect the practice of the sport with the history and future of the nation as a whole. While the academic results of coach Padilla's soccer-based retention and graduation effort are impressive ("Most of the players on the 2003 squad would go on to at least junior college. Several would go on to four-year colleges" [279]), Quinones insists on the partially self-inflicted nature of some of the obstacles his student-players must overcome. In addition to class differences, and with outright racism mostly absent from his account, he attributes a significant weight in the overall academic performance of the player-students to the burdens of their cultural traditions unfolding now in a more socially developed context. Here, their Mexican reluctance to leave their families or acquire student loans to go to college, and their refusal to postpone the immediate satisfaction and access to consumption offered by a meat processing plant job, conspired against their social mobility and their chances of truly embodying the American dream: "Out in the High Plains of southwest Kansas, these enduring Mexican attitudes combined with the beef plants [and the dangerous but available jobs they offer] to create a mixture as hazardous as heroin" (259).

The second challenge for Garden City High School soccer is that of integration. Capturing the dual track nature of the historical development of soccer in the United States—the white middle-class suburbs on the one hand, and the immigrant ghettos on the other—and its social limitations and potential, Quinones declares: "Padilla, the team, and the school will have to decide if they want soccer to be a racially diverse and consistently winning program or a segregated program designed to keep Latino kids in school. Doing both probably won't be possible" (278).

Finally, I turn to Steve Wilson's *The Boys from Little Mexico: A Season Chasing the American Dream* (2010). The book depicts the 2005 sports struggle of an all-Hispanic soccer team, the Bulldogs, or Los Perros as they are known locally, from Woodburn High School in Woodburn, Oregon. The town's Latino population had grown "from about 10 percent of the town's 11,000 people in 1980 to just over 50 percent of the 20,000-person population in 2000" (49). According to the 2010 US Census, today 58.9 percent of the 24,080 population of Woodburn is Latino. Wilson writes: "About half the Bulldogs had been born in Mexico, although many came to Woodburn at such a young age that they had no memory of their homeland. One kid, Jovanny, was from El Salvador. Nearly all the others, born in the United States, had immigrant parents" (19).

Eight of the students were undocumented, three spoke almost no English, one of them, Octavio (a Mexican semi-pro midfielder), was the star of the team, while Carlos, the goalie, was in his third foster home. Somehow, however, as they prepared for the 2005 season (which they would finally not win) the Bulldogs had made the state playoffs for 24 straight years but had never won the tournament. One of their archrivals was a team, the Lakeridge Pacers, from suburban Portland. An almost all upper-middle class school, Lakeridge showcases an 80 percent four-year college attendance rate and a 10 percent community college rate. Woodburn, on the other hand, is 50 percent working-class Latino, their graduation rate is very low, and 75 percent "of the students are eligible for a free or reduced-price lunch" (xii). This is a tale of two Americas coexisting in near but parallel universes and sometimes meeting on the border zones of the soccer field.

Even in that context, the Bulldogs were under significant pressure to perform:

> They were afraid to fail. They were the first generation, or immigrants themselves, and they were supposed to make everything better. By winning the championship. By learning English. By graduating from high school. By going to college. By making a good living. His guys were supposed to break the pattern, and they knew it and it weighed on them. (58)

What makes Wilson's book both illuminating and sobering is his clarity about the possibilities and limitations of soccer as a space for social mobility and social validation. Even though in a postscript, he describes how, almost by a miracle, a number of the Bulldogs have ended up attending a community college that started a soccer team (as part of its effort to reach out to working class Latinos), but the truth is the deck is stacked against them. No matter how talented, for example, college soccer coaches will not recruit them, instead looking only in wealthier and whiter private leagues.

The Bulldogs' own Irish teacher-coach oscillates between limited enthusiasm: "for a lot of these guys, soccer really gives them their first taste of success" (29), and sobering realism: "His students had no history of success. They had few positive role models. They grew up in homes with poorly educated parents who spoke little English; some of them did not have permission to be in the country. Most were poor [. . .] In the classroom they stopped trying" (25).

Two of the players' stories encapsulate this dual outlook. One of them, Cheo, who came from Mexico, is finally reunited with his longtime field-worker immigrant father (and now legal resident) who decides to teach him a lesson about the value of education by making him work for a few weeks in the fields: "Cheo Sr. wanted his son to experience the low-back pain, the long hours, the poor wages, the shirt sticking to his back in the sun [...] This is your opportunity to get a good life, he told Cheo. You have to do work hard at school" (116).

What Cheo learns in his low-graduation rate school and at Woodburn in general is, however, slightly different: "'It is both good and bad,' Cheo said about Woodburn. 'It is so easy to get by here with just Spanish. That makes it easy to move here. But it also means that you don't have to use English, which makes it hard to leave'" (122).

Octavio, an undocumented student, on the other hand, is the rare Latino role-model—successful in school, career oriented, and very talented on the field—that many books like Wilson's are always looking for. It is one of Wilson's merits to give him a full profile while warning against easy generalizations:

> Like teachers and administrators at Woodburn High School, [Octavio's new coach in college] seemed to need some of his players to succeed, as if he was looking for proof that the world is the way he hopes it can be, a place where all one needs to do is work hard and walk straight, a place where the American dream really can come true. For all the well-meaning Anglos around him, Octavio provides a concrete home for those earnest fantasies while his teammates bring teachers and coaches back down to reality. (223)

At the end of the book, best friends Cheo and Octavio make the team for Chemeketa Community College in nearby Salem.

CONCLUSION

Soccer can be used to explore some of the tensions, contradictions, and possibilities involved in new ways of being American in the postsocial era. This means at least two different things for two different groups. For many middle- and upper-middle-class white Americans, the immigrant soccer players found in "their" parks and streets represent both the possibility of adjusting to the economic restructuring of the American economy and, simultaneously and contradictorily, a threat to their investment in white social hegemony and a society of (white) equals based on cultural homogeneity. Those same workers that allow for the state-subsidized continuation of farming in Kansas, the low-wage dependence of the meat and poultry industries throughout the Midwest and the South, and the very existence of California's agribusiness are the racialized others, seen in their streets and often perceived as a menacing alterity. Those immigrants' children are the low-performing, discriminated-against students populating many of their high schools. For the immigrants and their progeny, on the other hand, soccer as a social practice and the soccer field as a physical space offer an alternative point of contact and interaction both with white America and with many other immigrants. As a practice and space, soccer emerges as a more egalitarian platform, a scenario in which claims of cultural citizenship, relative belonging, and empowerment can be performed. As such, soccer appears as one of the windows into a newly defined American social and political cartography. What I have called a postsocial condition is a landscape defined by its internalization of border zones and the social, economic, and cultural contradictions and possibilities defining them:

> As the twenty-first century began, the sparse prairie of southwest Kansas again offered a clear view of an America under construction. It was different from that which earlier pioneers had created. Its values included not gratification postponed, but excess consumption; not self-reliance, but dependence on others' labor; a class, not a classless society.
>
> What seemed closest to the American spirit that southwest Kansas had forged was the attitude of the Latino immigrants who'd come to work as hard as it took to get ahead. (Quinones 236)

BIBLIOGRAPHY

Acevedo, Juan C. "A Cross-Cultural Study of Leisure among Mexicans in the State of Guerrero, Mexico and Mexican Immigrants from Guerrero in the United States." Master's thesis in Recreation, Sport & Tourism University of Illinois at Urbana-Champaign, 2009.

Allison, Lincoln. "Sports and Nationalism." *Handbook of Sports Studies.* Edited by Jay Coakley and Eric Dunning. London: Sage, 2000. 344–355.

Andrews, David L. et al. "Soccer, Race and Suburban Space." *Sporting Dystopias: The Making and Meanings of Urban Sport Culture.* Edited by Ralph C. Wilcox et al. Albany: SUNY Press, 2003. 197–220.

Bairner, Alan. *Sport, Nationalism, and Globalization: European and North American Perspectives.* Albany: SUNY Press, 2001.

Collins, Sandra. "National Sports and Other Myths: The Failure of US Soccer." *Soccer and Society* 7:2–3 (2006): 353–363.

Cuadros, Paul. *A Home in the Field: How One Championship Team Inspires Hope for the Revival of Small Town America.* New York: Rayo, 2006.

Dyck, Noel. "Playing Like Canadians: Improvising Nation and Identity through Sport." *The Discipline of Leisure: Embodying Cultures of "Recreation."* Edited by Simon Coleman and Tamara Kohn. New York: Berghahn Books, 2007. 109–125.

Giulanotti, Richard. "Civilizing Games: Norbert Elias and the Sociology of Sports." *Sports and Modern Social Theories.* Edited by Richard Giulanotti. Palgrave Macmillan: New York, 2004. 145–160.

Hagan, Jacqueline Maria. "Social Networks, Gender, and Immigrant Incorporation: Resources and Constraints." *American Sociological Review* 63:1 (February 1998): 55–67.

Kleszynski, Keith. "Fútbol and Community: Mexicano Immigrants in San Diego County, California." *Practicing Anthropology* 30:2 (2008): 42–44.

Markovits, Andrei S., and Steven L. Hellerman. *Offside: Soccer and American Exceptionalism.* Princeton, NJ: Princeton University Press, 2001.

Miller, Toby. "Competing Allegories." *Sportcult*. Edited by Randy Martin and Toby Miller. Minneapolis: University of Minnesota Press, 1999. 14–38.

Morello, Carol, and Dan Balz. "More than Half of California Children Latino, Census Shows." *Washington Post*, March 9, 2011. Available at http://www.washingtonpost.com/wp-dyn/content/article/2011/03/08/AR2011030805866.html.

Navarrete, Rubén. "U.S. played Mexico at Rose Bowl soccer game; Mexican-Americans booed U.S." http://articles.cnn.com/2011-07 21/opinion/navarrette.soccer_1_national-anthem-soccer-team-mexico-jersey?_s=PM:OPINION.

Quinones, Sam. *Antonio's Gun and Delfino's Dream: True Tales of Mexican Migration*, Albuquerque: University of New Mexico Press, 2007.

PBS. *Matters of Race. I The Divide*, an unreleased four-part PBS documentary. Roja Productions, 2003.

Plaschke, Bill. "Again It's Red, White and Boo." *Los Angeles Times*, June 26, 2011. Available at http://articles.latimes.com/2011/jun/26/sports/la-sp-0626-plaschke-gold-cup-20110626.

Poblete, Juan. "Americanism/o: Intercultural Border Zones in Post-social Times." *Keywords in Caribbean and Latin American Thought*. Edited by Ben Sifuentes Jáuregui and Yolanda Martínez-San Miguel. New York: Palgrave Macmillan, 2015.

———. "La Productividad del afecto en un contexto post-social." *El Lenguaje de las emociones. Afecto y cultura en América Latina*. Edited by Mabel Moraña and Ignacio Sánchez Prado. Madrid: Iberoamericana, 2012. 55–72.

Popke, Jeff. "Latino Migration and Neoliberalism in the US South: Notes toward a Rural Cosmopolitanism." *Southeastern Geographer* 51:2 (2011): 242–259.

Santamaría Gómez, Arturo. *Futbol, Emigrantes y Nacionalismo*. Culiacán, Mexico: Universidad Autónoma de Sinaloa, 2010.

Straus, Brian. "Americans are visitors in their own home versus Mexico." *Sporting News.com*, June 24, 2011. Available at http://aol.sportingnews.com/soccer/story/2011-06-24/americans-are-visitors-in-their-own-home-vs-mexico-landon-donovan-clint-dempsey-.

US Census Bureau, Statistical Abstract of the United States: 2012 Table 11. Resident Population by Race, Hispanic Origin, and Single Years of Age: 2009. Available at http://www.census.gov/compendia/statab/cats/population/estimates_and_projections_by_age_sex_raceethnicity.html.

Wallace, Tim. "Brokering Playing Fields: Latinos and La Liga de Fútbol in Raleigh, NC." *Practicing Anthropology* 25:1 (2003): 34–37.

———. "The Soccer Wars: Hispanic Immigrants in Conflict and Adaptation at the Soccer Borderzone." *NAPA Bulletin* 31 (2009): 64–77.

Wilson, Steve. *The Boys from Little Mexico: A Season Chasing the American Dream*. Boston: Beacon Press, 2010.

Contributors

Pablo Alabarces, professor, Seminar in Popular Culture, Department of Communication Sciences, University of Buenos Aires

Maria Tarcisa Silva Bega, chair, Division of Humanities Arts and Letters, and associate professor, Federal University of Paraná

Vander Casaqui, professor, Graduate Program in Communication and Consumption Practices, Escola Superior de Propaganda e Marketing

Yago Colás, associate professor, Department of Comparative Literature and Arts and Ideas in the Humanities, University of Michigan

Héctor Fernández L'Hoeste, professor, Department of World Languages and Cultures, Georgia State University

Dexter Zavalza Hough-Snee, graduate student, Department of Spanish and Portuguese, University of California, Berkeley

Robert McKee Irwin, chair, Graduate Group in Cultural Studies, and professor, Department of Spanish and Portuguese, University of California, Davis

Hortensia Moreno, chair, Program in Semiotics of Gender, University Program in Gender Studies, National Autonomous University of Mexico

Joshua Nadel, assistant professor, Department of History, North Carolina Central University

Juan Poblete, professor, Department of Literature, University of California, Santa Cruz

Juan Carlos Rodríguez, assistant professor, Department of Spanish, Georgia Institute of Technology

Chloe Rutter-Jensen, associate professor, Department of Languages and Sociocultural Studies, University of the Andes

Renata Maria Toledo, graduate student, Sociology Department, Federal University of Paraná

Sergio Villena Fiengo, associate professor, School of Sociology, University of Costa Rica

INDEX

Note about tables: page numbers in bold refer to tables

Note about terms: "football" and "football (association)" refer to soccer, "football (American)" refers to American football, and "rugby" refers to Australian/British rugby

Lightning Source UK Ltd.
Milton Keynes UK
UKOW06n0942120515

251268UK00006B/65/P